Music and Cultural Rights

Music and Cultural Rights

Edited by

ANDREW N. WEINTRAUB
AND BELL YUNG

University of Illinois Press
CHICAGO AND URBANA

Supported by the Human Rights Division under the
Peace and Social Justice Program of the Ford Foundation.

Manufactured in the United States of America
1 2 3 4 5 C P 5 4 3 2 1
∞ This book is printed on acid-free paper.

Library of Congress Cataloging-in-Publication Data
Music and cultural rights / edited by Andrew N. Weintraub
and Bell Yung.
p. cm.
Includes bibliographical references (p.) and index.
ISBN 978-0-252-03473-2 (cloth : alk. paper)
ISBN 978-0-252-07662-6 (pbk. : alk. paper)
1. Music—Social aspects.
2. Cultural property.
3. Human rights.
I. Weintraub, Andrew N. (Andrew Noah)
II. Yung, Bell.
ML3799.M75 2009
306.4'842—dc22 2009026689

Contents

Preface

BELL YUNG

The seed of this book can be traced to a 1946 article by Charles Seeger that I first read as a graduate student. Seeger wrote that musicologists, aside from their academic activities, "need to research on existing and potential controls of music, both from within and from without the art." He elaborated:

> Like our industrial life, our music life is passing gradually from control by private enterprise, under terms of "free competition," to other kinds of control. Government is mixing in, and large power groups are emerging. Whether these may act as checks and balances to government, or become allied with it, is a question. I am not here concerned with the morals or wishful thinking of the situation. I want only to say that it is my considered opinion that the type of knowledge and experience, and the type of aims and purposes represented in our [musicological] societies, are types necessary to keep the situation I have alluded to on an even keel and oriented toward the best interests and aspirations not only of music but of cultural democracy. Unless we give expression to this knowledge and experience and these aims and purposes on a sufficiently high level of discussion, we stand not only to lose a considerable portion of our present autonomy as artists, scholars, and teachers, but also to come increasingly under controls most unpleasant to us as individuals and unsuited to the fields we serve.[1]

Decades before many scholars became aware of the social responsibility of the musicological profession, and nearly half a century before the term "applied ethnomusicology" was in wide usage, Seeger challenged musical scholars to step down from the ivory tower of academic research and examine the issue of "control": the political foundations of both music and musicology. The article left an indelible impression on me.

Years later, when teaching at the University of Hong Kong from 1996 to 2002, I was involved with various non-governmental organizations and non-profit organizations, most notably Zuni Icosahedron, an avant garde theater company-cum-research group on creativity and cultural policy, and the Hong Kong Institute of Contemporary Culture, whose mission is to promote cultural development at the local, regional, and international levels. In 2001, in collaboration with colleagues in these organizations, I founded the Center for Cultural Policy Research at the University of Hong Kong, the goal of which was to understand cultural dynamics in the society and to mobilize culture workers to become involved in policy matters.[2]

After returning to teach full time at the University of Pittsburgh in 2002, I formulated the idea of a conference on cultural policy and cultural rights. With advice from alumnus Damien Pwono, who at the time was a program officer in the Media, Arts and Culture Program of the Ford Foundation, I submitted to that program in March 2003 a proposal entitled "Cultural Rights and Academic Responsibility: Politics and Economics in the Globalization of Music." The officers in that program saw its potential elsewhere in the foundation and forwarded the proposal to the Human Rights Division under the Peace and Social Justice Program. The proposal was enthusiastically embraced by Natalia Kamen, the division head at the time, and was quickly approved in September with full funding. Upon notification of the grant, I invited my colleague Andrew Weintraub to be a collaborator on the project. Since then, he and I have worked closely on all aspects of the project.

The project consisted of three stages. The first was the formation of a planning committee, which conducted a one-day planning workshop on February 21, 2004, at the University of Pittsburgh.[3] After extensive discussion, the committee changed the project and conference title to "Music and Cultural Rights: Trends and Prospects," redirected the theoretical focus of the conference, assembled a roster of invited speakers, and settled logistical details of the conference.

The second stage was the conference itself, held at the University of Pittsburgh April 7–10, 2005. The international and interdisciplinary event aimed to create alliances and partnerships among scholars, musicians, producers, policy makers, and cultural activists. Sessions were structured around four paper panels, four roundtables, two special reports, and two sessions entitled "Performer's Voice." The conference also included a special concert related to cultural rights performed by musicians from Colombia, Hawai'i, and the Philippines. The twenty-six participants were from ten nations on five continents. The diverse voices also included three African/African Americans, four

Latin American/Hispanic North Americans, and six Asian-Pacific-Islander/API-Americans. The conference themes were:

- What Do We Mean by Cultural Rights?
- Culture as Intellectual Property and Community Rights
- Individual and Community Entitlement
- Authority, Ownership, and Representation
- Alliances and Partnerships
- Promoting Awareness of Cultural Rights
- Cultural Policy and Economic Development
- Music and Cultural Rights Violations
- Indigenous Musics in the Global Marketplace
- Music, Youth, and the Police in Brazil

The third and final stage of the project was the planning and publication of a volume consisting mainly of papers from the conference. As the book comes to fruition, I look back to note that, when the idea of the conference was first formed and proposed to the Ford Foundation in 2003, the term and concept of "cultural rights," though already appearing in the literature, was limited mainly to intellectual property rights on the one hand and to individual human rights in the realm of culture on the other. To the extent that the term embraced community rights, it addressed only cases involving "indigenous peoples." Our project was the first to focus on music and community rights with a global scope, including both intracultural and intercultural concerns. Because of the unique nature of music in terms of its intrinsic properties and extrinsic social functions, I hope that this volume will help define and refine the understanding of the general concept of cultural rights and how these rights pertain specifically to music.

Notes

1. Charles Seeger, "Music and Musicology in the New World 1946," in *Studies in Musicology 1935–1975*, by Charles Seeger (Berkeley: University of California Press, 1977), 219. Originally published as "Music and Musicology in the New World," *Proceedings of the Music Teachers National Association*, ser. 40 (1946): 35–47.

2. After I left the university in 2002, the directorship was assumed by Professor Desmond Hui in the Department of Architecture.

3. Committee members were Franz Patay, Damien Pwono, Dan Sheehy, Ricardo Trimillos, Andrew Weintraub, and Bell Yung. Lei Bryant was secretary.

Acknowledgments

We wish to thank Judith McCulloh and Laurie Matheson at the University of Illinois Press for their belief in this project, and Laurie Matheson for her support and advice in the preparation of the manuscript. Beverly Diamond and a second anonymous reader provided valuable and constructive criticism of the entire manuscript. Three graduate students at the University of Pittsburgh served as assistants during the three stages of the project: Lei Ouyang Bryant for the planning workshop, Chris White for the conference, and Lisa Bona for the preparation of the book manuscript. The Asian Studies Center at the University of Pittsburgh provided assistance for the planning workshop and the conference. We would particularly like to thank staff members Dianne Dakis, Debee Werntz, and Elizabeth Greene.

The project was generously supported by a grant from the Human Rights Division under the Peace and Social Justice Program of the Ford Foundation. We thank Natalia Kamen, former director of the division, who strongly encouraged and supported the grant proposal, and Damien Pwono, an alumnus of the University of Pittsburgh Music Department and former Ford Foundation program officer, who advised on the writing of the proposal. We would also like to thank the following units at the University of Pittsburgh for their support of the Conference on Music and Cultural Rights in 2005: Graduate School of Arts and Sciences; Department of Anthropology; Cultural Studies Program; School of Law; Centre for Latin American Studies; Centre for Russian and East European Studies; Center for International Legal Education; and the Indo-Pacific Council.

Music and Cultural Rights

Introduction

ANDREW N. WEINTRAUB

This collection of nine essays lays the groundwork for the comparative study of music and cultural rights. Cultural rights refer to both proprietary and proprietary-related assertions based on cultural grounds. Cultural rights claims have become increasingly prominent in discourses of human rights, international law, and struggles for social justice throughout the world. Culture as an object of rights discourses has received growing attention in anthropology since the 1980s, especially in advocating rights of indigenous peoples to political self-determination, economic development, land, and education.[1]

What constitutes rights in music? The essays in this volume address the historical and social conditions that structure ways of thinking about music as an object of rights discourses in different societies and historical periods. In this comparative analysis of music and rights, we take into account a vast range of meanings about the nature and practice of music. The essays link the cultural practices and social activities surrounding the human act of music-making with notions about music as a sonic entity, an aesthetic object, a recording, or a form of cultural property that can be controlled or owned (including rights enshrined in United Nations documents or rights allegedly protected by legal mechanisms such as copyright laws). We emphasize the social institutions and actors that have enabled music to be situated within cultures of music and rights. In this discursive terrain, music serves as a point of negotiation concerning the rights of representation—why do certain people have them and others don't? What are the rules that govern their use? How might those rules be changed?—as well as a vehicle for building new forms of political community around rights agendas and discourses.

Based on case studies from six countries—Brazil, China, Peru, the Philippines, Ukraine, and the United States—the essays in this volume illustrate the ways in which music has become entwined with debates about rights. The authors address the topic of music and rights from multiple theoretical perspectives in order to understand the complexities of these contemporary debates surrounding access, use, representation, and ownership of music.

Music has a cultural specificity that sets it apart from other cultural expressive forms. Case studies based on ethnographic field research, such as those herein, illustrate the special role of music in rights discourses. For example, ways of thinking about the use of music have been recast in light of cultural rights and notions of ownership (Rees). Musical performance as a form of cultural representation provides unique ways to assert and negotiate power among groups with competing ideological interests (Trimillos). Access to a group's tangible historical sources of music (including printed songbooks and recordings) has an important intangible connection to a group's history and sense of shared identity (Stillman). Music embodies social relationships that can reinforce or change ideas about what constitutes community (Ramos and Ochoa). In globalized exchange, music signifies a whole range of social relations within complex economic and political arrangements that challenge simplistic views of rights based on essentialized understandings of cultural identity (Baranovitch). In rights legislation, music is treated differently from other artistic and cultural activities (Sandler). Music as a privileged marker of social identity can perpetuate regressive cultural stereotypes, but it can also raise awareness of cultural rights issues (Helbig). Discourses about rights introduce new forms of power into societies where ideological struggles over the representation and meaning of musical practices have long histories (Yung). In these examples, and others throughout the book, the analysis of music casts new light on cultural rights.

Cultural Rights: Definitions and Concepts

The concept of "cultural rights" comes from Article 27 of the United Nations Universal Declaration of Human Rights (UDHR), adopted in December 1948, which states that "everyone has the right to freely participate in the cultural life of the community [and] to enjoy the arts."[2] Rights carry with them a connotation of universality, issuing from a higher authority and representing a moral claim. The universalist and moralistic tone of the UDHR, which established the basic framework for human rights, has been criticized for being Western-centric, prescriptive, imperialistic, and antithetical to the aims and practices of cultural relativism and pluralism. For example, in 1947, the American Anthropological Association rejected the idea of a declaration of universal rights on empirical, epistemological, and ethical grounds.[3] In a recent example from the 1990s, some governments in Asia (including those of India, Indonesia, Malaysia, and Singapore) rejected the notion of universal human rights, claiming that they do not represent "Asian values."[4] Yet the considerable problems in circumscribing and implementing frameworks of mutually agreed-upon rights for all human beings in every human society does not condone basic human rights violations by nation-states, especially when they breach the rights and interests of minorities and indigenous peoples. In an age when cultural processes of production, exchange, and consumption have become increasingly globalized, it is crucial to understand the relationship between universal rights and cultural specificities as dialogic rather than oppositional. Therefore, the essays in this volume emphasize a position in which concepts of "culture" and "rights" are tied together and constantly evolving in a dialectical relationship. At the base of *Music and Cultural Rights* is a focused effort to present deeply contextual ethnographic and historical case studies of the various ways in which music and rights are engaged by individuals, groups, and communities in particular times and places.

The concept of cultural rights has been articulated within the larger international framework of human rights as an individual's right to claim and practice what is considered "culture"; this is in addition to the fundamental human rights of life, liberty, and economic security. The UDHR asserts that full recognition of personhood includes cultural rights, and these rights are considered indispensable for the maintenance of dignity and development of one's personality (Article 22). The UDHR protects a person's individual right to practice a certain religion, prepare certain kinds of food, wear certain clothing, sing certain songs, and play certain musical instruments—all in order to define and assert one's cultural identity and heritage.

However, there has been an increasing awareness that the protection of "the cultural life of the community" is as important as an individual's right to be part of that community.[5] If what identifies and distinguishes such a community through its cultural practices is drastically altered by forces beyond the control of its membership, then it becomes meaningless to protect an individual's right to be part of that community. Such awareness marks a move from individual rights to collective or group rights, in particular because of the struggles of indigenous peoples and minority groups. As Robert Albro and Joanne Bauer write: "Indigenous peoples pose the issue of collective cultural rights in a uniquely compelling way. Historically they have been the most dramatic casualties of the global consolidation of the nation-state, the groups most clearly set apart by their distinctiveness, and the first groups to begin to advance cultural claims in human rights terms, a process underway in earnest by the late 1980s."[6] The emphasis on group rights does not mean that certain groups of people are inherently more collective than others. Nor does it mean that collectivities are devoid of their own internal power dynamics. Rather, these struggles over collective rights demonstrate critical and creative ways that rights have been framed within the cultural norms of particular communities.

Cultural rights embrace group rights and "include a group's ability to preserve its culture, to raise its children in the ways of its forebears, to continue its language, and not to be deprived of its economic base by the nation-state in which it is located" or by the transnational and globalized environment within which it is located.[7] The question of group rights arises when a group's access or ownership of culture has been threatened, limited, or appropriated by other people, groups, or institutions through conquest, occupation, settlement, or other means. In many cases, there are no legal mechanisms for protection, with often damaging and irreversible consequences.

The globalization of music brings these issues into sharp relief. In the global production and circulation of commercial recorded music, multiple actors are involved in different geographical locations and with complex economic and marketing arrangements. For example, the genre labeled "world music" signifies a commodity of sounds, genres, and forms that participates in rapidly changing global processes of cultural production, distribution, and consumption.[8] World music draws from the great variety of musical genres, sounds, instruments, and artists from around the world but represents new constellations of actors, new modes of circulation, and new aesthetic forms to satisfy global markets.

Globalization is understood today as a paradox, both celebrated and vilified.[9] On the one hand, global markets and new forms of distribution enable musicians to have unprecedented access to consumers. Globalization has generated new musical styles, new musical technologies, and new hybrid genres and has created new possibilities for musicians to earn a living from their art. A new global aesthetic has introduced new ways of expressing identity. On the other hand, the globalization of music has resulted in the redefinition of aesthetic criteria, the potential loss of traditional knowledge, and the commoditization of music at a greater scale than ever before. For musicians, the globalization of music has meant opportunities for some and hardship for others as some forms of music are valorized while others are devalued and excluded from representation (see Baranovitch in this volume).

Several recent cases show that world music producers have paid very little attention to the cultural rights of groups whose music they have used. For example, ethnomusicologist Hugo Zemp describes a case in the mid-1990s where his field recordings of music made in the Solomon Islands and in West Africa were sampled by the French duo Michael Sanchez and Eric Mouquet known as Deep Forest.[10] The musicians on the recording were not adequately credited or compensated for their work on an album that went on to sell millions of copies. Importantly, the Deep Forest production team did not consider the cultural interests or moral rights of the people of the Solomon Islands and West Africa, whose ideas about music differed from those of the producers. In a case described by Nancy Guy, Ami musicians in Taiwan were not consulted for their contribution to the album *Return to Innocence* by the group Enigma.[11] Two of the musicians won a settlement against the artist Michael Cretu and his record company (EMI). In these cases—and there are many more—there was no legal mechanism to protect the cultural rights of the groups represented on the recording.

Cultural Rights Legislation

Who has the right to make public policy that privileges certain kinds of music over others? What gives social institutions the right to make decisions regarding access, use, representation, and ownership of music? Central to these concerns is the role of international regulatory agencies such as the United Nations, the United Nations Educational, Scientific, and Cultural Organization (UNESCO), the World Intellectual Property Organization (WIPO), and the World Trade Organization (WTO). It is beyond the scope of this book to provide a complete historical overview of the many treaties, agreements, covenants, and declarations related to cultural rights. There are, however, a few key international legal institutions and documents that form the backbone of cultural rights legislation that aim to protect traditional forms of knowledge and expressions of culture.

The UDHR established the basis for a universal definition of cultural rights that focused on the rights of individuals (not groups). This new set of rights introduced "culture" into the concept of human rights, although the term "cultural rights" was not used. It also cited "moral and material interests" resulting from artistic production, which laid the groundwork for notions of cultural entitlement (including intellectual property). Two subsequent covenants strengthened the UDHR by providing legally binding protection of cultural rights and by focusing on collective rights rather than on individuals only. The International Covenant on Civil and Political Rights and the International Covenant on Economic, Social, and Cultural Rights (both adopted in 1966 and entered into force in 1976) are binding agreements under international law that commit states to work toward the granting of economic, social, and cultural rights for all human beings.

However, the rights outlined in these two covenants did not extend fully to indigenous peoples, who in 2007 numbered more than 370 million people in some seventy countries worldwide.[12] Indigenous peoples are defined as descendants of people who inhabited a geographic region before its colonization or annexation. Indigenous peoples have "retained unique social, cultural, economic and political characteristics that are distinct from those of the dominant societies in which they live. Despite their cultural differences, the various groups of indigenous peoples around the world share common problems related to the protection of their rights as distinct peoples."[13] They "have suffered from historic injustices as a result of, inter alia, their colonization and dispossession of their lands, territories and resources, thus preventing them from exercising, in particular, their right to development in accordance with their own needs and interests."[14]

In 1982, intensified discussions about the rights of indigenous peoples within the framework of the United Nations resulted in the creation of the Working Group on Indigenous Populations. These discussions also led to the establishment of the Permanent Forum on Indigenous Issues in 2000, an advisory body to the UN Economic and Social Council with a mandate to "discuss indigenous issues related to economic and social development, culture, the environment, education, health and human rights."[15] On September 13, 2007, the UN General Assembly adopted a resolution on the Declaration on the Rights of Indigenous Peoples. The result of over two decades of debate, the document recognized indigenous peoples' rights to political self-determination, to control over land and resources, and to maintain and strengthen cultural expressions. Felicia Sandler's essay in this volume describes in detail the kinds of rights covered by the declaration.

UNESCO conventions have focused attention upon intangible cultural heritage and cultural diversity. The Culture Sector of UNESCO operates according to three "pillars of the preservation and promotion of creative diversity": (1) the 1972 Convention Concerning the Protection of the World Cultural and Natural Heritage; (2) the 2003 Convention for the Safeguarding of the Intangible Cultural Heritage; and (3) the 2005 Convention on the Protection and Promotion of the Diversity of Cultural Expressions.[16] These international conventions define rules with which the member states undertake to comply.[17]

In 2003, UNESCO established the Convention for the Safeguarding of the Intangible Cultural Heritage as manifested in the following "intangible" domains: (1) oral traditions and expressions, including language, as a vehicle of the intangible cultural heritage; (2) performing arts (such as traditional music, dance, and theater); (3) social practices, rituals, and festive events; (4) knowledge and practices concerning nature and the universe; and (5) traditional craftsmanship.[18] The 2005 convention aimed to (1) reaffirm the sovereign right of states to draw up cultural policies; (2) recognize the specific nature of cultural goods and services as vehicles of identity, values, and meaning; and (3) strengthen international cooperation and solidarity so as to favor the cultural expressions of all countries. These policies have had mixed results, leading in some cases to increased state monitoring of cultural heritage and the reification of cultural traditions. In this volume, Bell Yung demonstrates how UN mechanisms for safeguarding culture often run counter to the interests of the very musicians those mechanisms are intended to benefit. The people or communities whose cultural heritage has been designated for protection do not necessarily enjoy more rights or privileges to music (see León in this volume).

Copyright laws, both domestic and international, are legal instruments for determining and enforcing individual ownership and control to access of music. The Berne Convention for the Protection of Literary and Artistic Works (concluded in 1886 and later revised) standardized international copyright conventions for signatory countries. Intellectual property rights have been framed as "rights to protection" of the moral and material interests resulting from artistic production, specifically pertaining to works of which one is an author.[19]

The World Intellectual Property Organization, created in 1967, is one of sixteen specialized agencies of the United Nations. Its function is to promote the protection of intellectual property throughout the world. The member states of WIPO (numbering 184 in 2007) adopted the WIPO Copyright Treaty in 1996 to cover information technology (software, Internet) that was not covered in previous treaties. The World Trade Organization administers the Agreement on Trade-Related Aspects of Intellectual Property Rights (TRIPS). TRIPS, negotiated in 1994, is an international agreement that establishes basic terms relating to copyright, including the rights of performers and producers of sound recordings and other media (film, photographs, computer software). The TRIPS agreement is the most comprehensive and powerful mechanism in international intellectual property law.

Numerous problems arise when music is treated as intellectual property. Intellectual property rights laws were created for Western music made for (potential) profit, with specific characteristics (namely, an original work by an author that is fixed in a tangible form of expression).[20] These conditions are antithetical to the collective nature of traditional music.[21] In Ghana, for example, where folk and popular music blend freely within one composition, determining the author is not a simple task.[22] In this volume, Felicia Sandler shows that the framework described in the WIPO Copyright Treaty does not adequately encompass indigenous rights to heritage, which is conceptualized as a "bundle of relationships, rather than a bundle of economic rights."[23] As Anthony Seeger's research demonstrates: "In the case of the Suya Indians of Brazil, how does one register a song composed by a jaguar, learned from a captive over 200 years ago, and controlled not by an individual but by a ceremonial moiety?"[24]

This volume aims to extend the discourse of cultural rights beyond issues of intellectual property rights, because music is both an individual and a communal activity. The consideration of individual rights inevitably points to group rights, particularly since creative activities and processes of music-making are collaborative activities in most, if not all, societies. Music provides an important means for the transmission of knowledge and ideas across regions and generations. Therefore, the loss of access to music can mean the loss of a group's sense of shared identity and, ultimately, group members' sense of self. The recent focus on collective cultural rights draws attention to the important role music can play in challenging the concepts and laws governing such collective rights.

Ethnomusicology, the Public Sector, and Rights

The essays in this volume reveal the highly politicized nature of protection and preservation that often accompanies the discussion of rights and music. The birth of ethnomusicology goes hand in hand with the documentation and preservation of music, a key component of nationalism in nineteenth-century Europe.[25] The invention of Edison's phonograph in 1877 enabled scholars to record music from around the world. Collections or archives of these recordings were established in the United States and Europe for the purpose of scientific study and preservation of musical sounds.[26] Bruno Nettl states that "collecting and preserving have sometimes become ends in themselves. In the nineteenth century particularly, but also later, many devoted themselves more or less exclusively to preservation."[27] The goal of the institutions that governed archives was not to preserve the music for the benefit of future generations of people descended from the groups who had been recorded but to preserve it on recordings for study and analysis. Scholars were also afraid that the music would become extinct and unavailable for future study, and so these recording efforts could help to salvage traditions that were dying out ("salvage ethnomusicology").[28]

Discourses of preservation and protection have been criticized for standing in for colonial relations of power and representing outsider modes of authority.[29] Discourses of protection tend to reinforce the trope of the noble savage living in a traditional bounded world, for whom all knowledge, objects, and values originating elsewhere "pollute" some reified notion of culture and innocence.[30] An emphasis on protection has led some to ask, "Protection from what?" In his address to participants at the 2005 Conference on Music and Cultural Rights: Trends and Prospects, Filipino musician and activist Joey Ayala asked, "What do you want to protect in music? Is it the 'work of art'? Or is it the processes and practices of musical creativity? These are different issues."[31] Cultural preservation and protection can perpetuate unequal relations of power, especially in societies with long colonial histories. As Hawaiian musician and scholar Jon Kamakawiwoʻole Osorio reminded the participants at the 2005 conference, "Sometimes culture has to be protected from the protectors."[32]

Amy Kuʻuleialoha Stillman's article in this volume shows that archives of musical recordings and sheet music clearly have an important function, but they need to be more responsive to people whose access and control of their ancestors' music has been central to group identification.[33] Recent projects to repatriate materials to indigenous groups are making headway in this regard. For example, the U.S. Library of Congress houses the country's largest collection of early recordings of American Indian music, numbering over 10,000 wax cylinders. The Federal Cylinder Project, completed in 1985, has copied and cataloged these recordings and made them available directly to their communities of origin.[34] In Australia, Aboriginal songs, myths, and rituals provide evidence for historic land claims. In 1992, in a land rights struggle waged on Murray Island in the Torres Strait, the Meryam people used archival materials created by the Cambridge Expedition to the Torres Strait in 1898 to prove their ownership of the land.[35] In India, the Archive and Research Center for Ethnomusicology has repatriated thousands of recordings of Indian music made abroad and made them available to people in India.

Ethnomusicologist Alan Lomax argued forcefully for the grouping together of music, culture, and rights. Lomax believed that the world's musical and cultural diversity was being threatened by an ever-expanding, "over-centralized electronic communication system" that encouraged "standardized, mass-produced, and cheapened cultures everywhere." This process would eventually lead to destruction of local cultures, or cultural "grey-out."[36] It was Lomax's belief that all musics were equally expressive, equally communicative, and equally valuable. Lomax argued that scholars and institutions have a social responsibility to commit time and resources to cultural equality, just "as we have committed ourselves to the principles of political, social, and economic justice." Lomax advocated what he called "cultural equity": the right of every musical community to have "their fair share of the air time" as well as "equal local weight in the education systems."[37]

In a similar vein, applied ethnomusicologists use knowledge about music to promote the public cultural expressions of people through festivals, recordings, and exhibits, among other media. Although not explicitly formulated in terms of rights, the goals of applied ethnomusicology are to influence public policy and to empower communities.[38] For example, the Smithsonian Center for Folklife and Cultural Heritage sponsors an annual Folklife Festival in Washington, D.C., that includes music and dance traditions as well as other cultural expressions by visiting troupes. The festival, described in Ricardo D. Trimillos's chapter in this volume, is "an exercise in cultural democracy, in which cultural practitioners speak for themselves, with each other, and to the public."[39] These exercises have had an impact on government policies abroad as "many states and several nations have remounted Festival programs locally and used them to generate laws."[40]

The activism of applied ethnomusicology is cogently formulated in the 2007 mission statement of the International Council for Traditional Music Study Group on Applied Ethnomusicology: "Applied Ethnomusicology is the approach guided by principles of social responsibility, which extends the usual academic goal of broadening and deepening knowledge and understanding toward solving concrete problems and toward working both inside and beyond typical academic contexts. The ICTM Study Group on Applied Ethnomusicology advocates the use of ethnomusicological knowledge in influencing social interaction and course of cultural change."[41]

This volume is intended to help scholars clarify their roles in mediating rights claims based on cultural grounds. Several chapters engage reflexively with rights discourses and practices. Adriana Helbig's tales from fieldwork expose the intracultural dynamics that are integral to understanding the larger culture of rights as a system of exclusionary social practices carried out by non-governmental organizations in Ukraine. Amy Kuʻuleialoha Stillman's privileged status as a scholar allowed her to access historical records pertaining to Hawaiian music housed in archives, museums, and libraries, but access to those same records was denied to Native Hawaiian practitioners. Based on these research experiences, Stillman argues that access to such resources is a fundamental cultural right for Native Hawaiians. From the perspectives of planner, presenter, board member, and volunteer for the Folklife Festival in Washington, D.C., Ricardo Trimillos reflects on access, stewardship, and control of music and representation at cultural festivals. Case studies such as these can help to stimulate academics to ensure a more active, enduring, and engaged role in the lives of the people and communities they study.

Overview of Chapters

Claims surrounding music as a right have given rise to a new vocabulary about music aesthetics, discourses, and practices. The essays in this volume illustrate how cultural rights vary across societies, how definitions of rights have evolved, and how rights have been invoked in relation to social struggles over cultural access, use, representation, and ownership. In particular cultural and historical circumstances, who is claiming rights surrounding music, when are they being claimed, and why? Through localized case studies, many of them based on ethnographic research, the authors in this volume situate rights surrounding music within broad historical, material, and cultural contexts. This volume documents and analyzes the social and ideological stakes involved in a group's right to access, perpetuate, and control music. The contributors examine these issues from various theoretical perspectives.

Trimillos reports on the 1998 Smithsonian Folklife Festival in Washington that featured the Philippines. As a member of the planning group, Trimillos was privy to details surrounding the deliberations and solutions to the myriad concerns about representing culture among the various parties responsible for the event. Using this event as a case study, Trimillos introduces three broad categories of rights—access, stewardship, and control—and articulates these categories through five "voices," including the state (the Philippines), the cultural community, the practitioner group, the individual artists, and the scholar/researcher. Based on an analysis of these voices, Trimillos proposes an analytical framework for understanding cultural rights that is both theoretically innovative and practically useful for a variety of settings.

Helen Rees addresses individual property rights of folk musicians in China and looks at the larger issue of cultural rights in a country that is developing an increasing awareness of human rights. Citing four recent court cases, Rees shows that in China, "folk music" has a different valence for politicians, musicians, scholars, and world music producers. She offers a thick description of the debates surrounding the ownership and use of music in various cultural spheres, particularly the controversial roles of large numbers of ethnic minorities in the country. The chapter also documents the stakes involved for the various actors who have participated in these struggles over ownership.

Stillman addresses a topic of great historical and cultural significance: the writing of history as a cultural right. Stillman asks how it is possible for people to fully understand a group's cultural history when important fragments of that history have been taken away. In the case of Hawaiʻi, this problem is especially acute as Native Hawaiians have been excluded from access to archives, which house materials related to understanding their own cultural history. Stillman outlines steps in reclaiming Native Hawaiian history through repatriation of historical musical resources. As a Native Hawaiian, Stillman brings firsthand experience and knowledge of the political and social obstacles of access and representation.

Javier León documents the circumstances that led to the naming of an Afroperuvian instrument (the *cajón*) as cultural patrimony of the Peruvian nation-state. The resolution to declare the cajón a national instrument, issued by the Peruvian National Institute of Culture in 2001, occurred during a time when the instrument's origins were being challenged by non-Peruvian interests. The resolution ensured that the cajón would be rescued from foreign claims and enshrined as a Peruvian national symbol. However, it also raised concerns that the instrument's identity as a cultural marker of Afroperuvian culture would be displaced or obscured. These claims have important stakes for Afroperuvians, a marginalized community characterized by "social invisibility." León notes that symbolic markers, including music, dance, and the cajón in particular, distinguish the Afroperuvian community from other groups and allow the community to make claims for collective rights. Therefore, the subsequent integration of the cajón into the national imaginary has the potential to weaken Afroperuvian claims for rights in the name of culture. On the other hand, recognition within the national cultural sphere signifies a growing awareness of the contribution of Afroperuvian culture within the dominant culture. Although this case is still playing out, the essay shows that national efforts to safeguard cultural symbols rooted in traditions of marginalized groups may have unintended effects for the cultural rights of those groups in the future.

Bell Yung reports on the changes of the musical tradition of the *qin* instrument in the twenty-first century, a tradition that has been for two millennia associated almost exclusively with a small and elite class of scholar-officials. Its distinctive musical features developed within this social environment. When in 2003 UNESCO proclaimed the qin as one of the "Masterpieces of the Oral and Intangible Heritage of Humanity" with the noble intention to safeguard the tradition, the consequence of the honor could hardly be foreseen. Describing the political and economic ramifications that directly affected the musical tradition, Yung examines the paradox of intention and consequence by tracing the drastic changes of qin music in the last few years and challenges the simplistic notion of "safeguarding" by an august international body.

Adriana Helbig introduces the key concept of intracultural dynamics into the discourse about cultural rights in Ukraine. Intracultural dynamics have important implications for determining which communities within a group have access to economic and political resources, cultural rights, and social representation. The Roma community in Ukraine is historically differentiated along axes of gender, class, occupation, and education level. Yet, ethnic homogeneity is a key trope in Romani representation, for both Roma and non-Roma alike. For example, the stereotype of Roma as musicians gets used in all sorts of ways, and yet there are important distinctions that exist among classes of musicians. Helbig examines the implementation of cultural rights policies and projects funded by international philanthropic organizations and government agencies. She discusses a complex intersection of socialist and post-socialist concepts of culture, the dynamics between minority and majority, and the agenda of philanthropic aid projects that tend to define all Roma in terms of ethnicity, obscuring important social distinctions within the minority group. In the name of culture, projects funded by international philanthropic foundations and realized by Romani non-governmental organizations privilege certain segments of Romani society over others, often to the detriment of those most in need. Using examples from her fieldwork, Helbig shows how divisions within Romani communities have been reinforced and reshaped in post-socialist Ukraine, often in harmful ways. Moreover, she argues that a Western-based framework of cultural rights discourse, as promoted by Western philanthropic organizations in this case study, should not be applied uncritically worldwide.

Nimrod Baranovitch addresses how a half-Han, half-Tibetan singer confronts and negotiates her role as a Tibetan minority in the mainstream Han society and how she has exploited her ambiguous cultural identity and unique musical heritage to carve out a place in the Chinese popular music scene. This case study shows how external perceptions of cultural practice shape its market identity, for better or worse. Baranovitch challenges the usual political position of advocates of cultural rights that a minority culture tends to suffer from the dominant majority, writing that "while fully recognizing the validity and importance of the concern to protect minority cultures, and while acknowledging the severe cultural loss that some ethnic minorities in China have experienced in recent decades, this essay aims to shift the focus to the gray area that lies in between cultures." Baranovitch takes an original position that forces us to rethink majority-minority relationships pertaining to issues of cultural rights.

Silvia Ramos and Ana María Ochoa describe the work of the activist Afro-Reggae Cultural Group in Brazil that uses music as a powerful agent in struggles for human rights. The report details the tragic social problem of violent deaths among poor urban black youths in Rio de Janeiro who have been the subjects of police brutality. This essay stands apart from other essays in this volume that place music at the center of cultural rights in order to examine issues of access, representation, and ownership. Instead, this chapter reverses the relationship between "music" and "cultural rights" to demonstrate the ways in which music can be exploited as a weapon to fight social injustice. In this case, music contributes to the harmony of a society and the protection of life, the ultimate objectives of human rights. The authors show how effectively the use of music draws people together, reduces violence and conflict, and helps to construct new forms of community.

Felicia Sandler raises crucial questions about defining what counts as a right. Sandler uses the example of David Fanshawe, a composer whose *African Sanctus* work is based on sounds he recorded in North Africa. Copyright law outlines a set of regulations that govern what is permissible within particular communities. Although the Berne-WIPO international treaties suggest an extended treatment of copyright law, indigenous rights have not been fully recognized within the legal frameworks that have been developed thus far. In the case of indigenous peoples, whose music was not governed by the question of rights, there does not yet exist a rights language that can fully frame questions about culture. When cultural products are separated from the people who use them and the spirits that attach to them through rituals, what are the implications for the society? Sandler argues that legal frameworks have not been adequate to address this issue. As a composer who is keenly sensitive to intellectual property rights pertaining to her own work, Sandler addresses issues of rights of indigenous communities from a unique perspective.

Rethinking Music and Cultural Rights

Cultural rights frame issues of indigenous media, the preservation and development of traditional musical practices, and the rapid transformation of local music traditions throughout the world. Questions about music as a right bring into focus emergent social relationships among a variety of social actors, including musicians, cultural policy makers, commercial music producers, academics, and activists, among others.

The nature and definitions of music described in this book vary greatly across geocultural regions and encompass a range of diverse social groups. The authors describe widely divergent practices of musical production, circulation, and consumption. Music can be a form of creative activity carried out by individual composers (Sandler), and it can be a commodity for sale (Baranovitch). Music can be a key component in a group's sense of its past (Stillman; Yung) as well as a site for mediating new forms of community (Ramos and Ochoa). Music plays an important symbolic role in mapping out the boundaries of belonging in terms of ethnicity (Helbig; Trimillos) and nationality (León). Music mediates changing relationships between "tradition" and "modernity" (Rees). Despite the wide diversity of musical uses and functions described in these pages, each essay demonstrates the important ideological stakes involved in struggles over the representation, meaning, and value of music. Further, whatever and wherever music may be in the contemporary world, it seems that rights are not far behind.

Rights can be extended only to those who are acknowledged as proper subjects "before the law." But rights surrounding music fall short, as demonstrated by this volume, by either not accounting for music in all of its complexity or by fixing and reducing music to a category that fits current legal frameworks. These shortcomings have serious consequences for societies that must be sensitive to the cultural needs of everyone. Although cultural notions of entitlement and legal notions of entitlement (including property) are not the same, there is an important relationship between them. Case studies in which de facto laws have been inadequate to deal with music and rights can help cultural policy makers to understand the issues involved more clearly.

Laws are not universal or atemporal: they do not simply recognize "what's out there" but are productive and creative. Laws call into being new subject positions as people are forced to adjust to laws.[42] They also call into being new forms of commitment to change. The essays in this volume show the evolving nature of concepts, practices, and institutions pertaining to music and cultural rights. These changes represent new possibilities for thinking through the issues involved and for developing better policies and practices in the future.

As Ana María Ochoa noted in her address at the 2005 Conference on Music and Cultural Rights, how do desires and hopes for a more just society get translated into social codes of behavior (specifically rights)?[43] Music as a creative social force helps to mediate those desires. Music calls attention to social relationships that are crucial for maintaining as well as for changing forms of community. But we still need more effective mechanisms and new forms and practices of mediation for linking culture with rights.

Through an understanding of the cultural, historical, and material conditions that underpin rights discourses in relation to musical aesthetics and practices, this volume intends to increase the level of awareness and sensitivity to cultural rights and music in the contemporary world. But ultimately, the creation of equitable rights surrounding music will depend on developing alliances and partnerships among cultural actors, political communities, public and private sector interests, educational institutions, and legal mechanisms.

Notes

I would like to thank Bell Yung, Beverly Diamond, and one anonymous reader for their constructive commentaries on previous versions of this essay.

1. Ellen Messer, "Anthropology and Human Rights," *Annual Review of Anthropology* 22 (1993): 221–49; Mark Goodale, "Introduction to Anthropology and Human Rights in a New Key," *American Anthropologist* 108, no. 1 (2006): 1; Jane K. Cowan, Marie-Bénédicte Dembour, and Richard A. Wilson, eds., *Culture and Rights: Anthropological Perspectives* (Cambridge: Cambridge University Press, 2001), 3–13. The last source identifies the relationship between rights and culture as having three trajectories: (a) *rights versus culture* presents an either/or choice between universalism and cultural relativism, which reinforces a false binary opposition between rights and culture; (b) *a right to culture* is the formulation enshrined in UN documents, in which culture becomes an *object* of rights claims, as opposed to culture as "a field of creative interchange and contestation, often around certain shared symbols, propositions or practices, and continuous transformation" (5); and (c) *rights as culture* treats rights as a kind of culture in itself (rights talk, rights thinking, rights practices). This has been the most productive formulation, although it can tend to essentialize the notion of culture as a structural matrix of bounded rules, conventions, and rhetoric.

2. Universal Declaration of Human Rights, Article 27, at http://www.un.org/Overview/rights.html (accessed June 1, 2008).

3. Goodale, "Introduction."

4. Lynda S. Bell, Andrew J. Nathan, and Ilan Peleg, "Introduction: Culture and Human Rights," in *Negotiating Culture and Human Rights,* ed. Lynda S. Bell, Andrew J. Nathan, and Ilan Peleg (New York: Columbia University Press, 2001), 3–20.

5. In Krister Malm's formulation, "human rights" is focused on individual rights, whereas "cultural rights" call attention to group rights. This framework forms the basis of modern cultural policy, where "cultural diversity" tends to focus on individuals and "multiculturalism" tends to focus on groups. Music plays an important role in both paradigms, creating tension between notions of "human rights" and "cultural rights." Krister Malm, "Music in the Field of Tension between Human Rights and Cultural Rights," in *Music and Minorities: Proceedings of the 1st International Meeting of the International Council for Traditional Music (ICTM) Study Group on Music and Minorities* (Ljubljana, Slovenia: ICTM, 2001), 31–36.

6. Robert Albro and Joanne Bauer, "Introduction," in "Cultural Rights," special issue, *Human Rights Dialogue,* ser. 2, no. 12 (Spring 2005), Carnegie Council, http://www.cceia.org/resources/publications/dialogue/index.html (accessed February 26, 2007).

7. Conrad P. Kottack, "Cultural Anthropology," 2002, McGraw-Hill Online Learning Center, http://highered.mcgraw-hill.com/sites/0072500506/student_view0/chapter3/key_terms.html (accessed June 1, 2008).

8. I have put "world music" in quotes to indicate the multiple meanings of the term. I am referring to popular musics that are mass-distributed worldwide and yet associated with minority groups and small or industrially developing countries. These musical genres combine local musical characteristics with those of mainstream genres mass-circulated by today's transnational music-related industries. Often collaborative, the recording, mixing, and distribution of products are done in different countries and involve a wide variety of people and institutions.

9. Philip V. Bohlman, *World Music: A Very Short Introduction* (New York: Oxford University Press, 2002), xi.

10. Their first album was the self-titled *Deep Forest.* Hugo Zemp, "The/An Ethnomusicologist and the Record Business," *Yearbook for Traditional Music* 28 (1996): 36–56.

11. Nancy Guy, "Trafficking in Taiwan Aboriginal Voices," in *Handle with Care: Ownership and Control of Ethnographic Materials,* ed. Sjoerd R. Jaarsma (Pittsburgh: University of Pittsburgh Press, 2002), 195–209.

12. "Who Are Indigenous Peoples?," World Health Organization, http://www.who.int/mediacentre/factsheets/fs326/en/index.html (accessed June 1, 2008).

13. "UN Permanent Forum on Indigenous Issues: History," UN Permanent Forum on Indigenous Issues, http://www.un.org/esa/socdev/unpfii/en/history.html (accessed June 1, 2008).

14. "United Nations Declaration on the Rights of Indigenous Peoples," UN Permanent Forum on Indigenous Issues, http://www.un.org/esa/socdev/unpfii/en/drip.html (accessed June 23, 2008).

15. "UN Permanent Forum on Indigenous Issues: Structure," UN Permanent Forum on Indigenous Issues, http://www.un.org/esa/socdev/unpfii/en/structure.html (accessed June 23, 2008).

16. "UNESCO: Culture," UNESCO.org, http://portal.unesco.org/culture/en/ev.php-URL_ID=34603&URL_DO=DO_TOPIC&URL_SECTION=201.html (accessed June 1, 2008).

17. The 1972 Convention Concerning the Protection of the World Cultural and Natural Heritage covers tangible heritage: monuments, groups of buildings, and "sites [which are] of outstanding universal value from the historical, aesthetic, ethnological or anthropological point of view" ("Convention Concerning the Protection of the World Cultural and Natural Heritage," UNESCO.org, http://whc.unesco.org/archive/convention-en.pdf). Natural heritage covers outstanding physical and biological formations, habitats of threatened species of animals and plants, and natural sites.

18. "What Is Intangible Cultural Heritage?," UNESCO.org, http://www.unesco.org/culture/ich/index.php?pg=00002 (accessed June 1, 2008).

19. Universal Declaration of Human Rights, Article 27. See note 2 above.

20. Sherylle Mills, "Indigenous Music and the Law: An Analysis of National and International Legislation," *Yearbook for Traditional Music* 28 (1996): 57–86.

21. Anthony McCann, "All That Is Not Given Is Lost: Irish Traditional Music, Copyright, and Common Property," *Ethnomusicology* 45, no. 1 (2001): 89–106.

22. John Collins, "Copyright, Folklore, and Music Piracy in Ghana," *Critical Arts* 20, no. 1 (2006): 158–70.

23. Erica-Irene Daes, *Protection of the Heritage of Indigenous People,* Publication E.97. XIV.3 (New York: UNOHCHR, 1997), 3, cited in Sandler's chapter in this volume.

24. Anthony Seeger, "Ethnomusicologists, Archives, Professional Organizations, and the Shifting Ethics of Intellectual Property," *Yearbook for Traditional Music* 28 (1996): 90.

25. Bruno Nettl, *The Study of Ethnomusicology: Twenty-nine Issues and Concepts* (Urbana: University of Illinois Press, 1983), 273. Documentation of North American Indian culture began in 1846 and developed into the Bureau of American Ethnology (1879–1964). See National Anthropological Archives, http://www.nmnh.si.edu/naa/about.htm (accessed June 1, 2008).

26. James Porter, "Documentary Recordings in Ethnomusicology: Theoretical and Methodological Problems," *Association for Recorded Sound Collections Journal* 6, no. 2 (1974): 3–16.

27. Nettl, *Study of Ethnomusicology,* 270. The scholars Béla Bartók (Eastern Europe) and Frances Densmore (Chippewa and Sioux) are exemplary in this regard.

28. Shubha Chaudhuri, "Preservation of the World's Music," in *Introduction to Ethnomusicology,* ed. Helen Myers (London: Macmillan, 1992), 365.

29. David Whisnant, *All That Is Native and Fine* (Chapel Hill: University of North Carolina Press, 1983).

30. Faye Ginsberg, "Indigenous Media: Faustian Contract or Global Village?" *Cultural Anthropology* 6, no. 1 (1991): 92–112.

31. Joey Ayala, "What Do We Mean by Cultural Rights?," Conference on Music and Cultural Rights: Trends and Prospects, Pittsburg, Penn., April 8, 2005.

32. Jon Kamakawiwo'ole Osorio, "Music and Cultural Rights Violations," Conference on Music and Cultural Rights: Trends and Prospects, Pittsburg, Penn., April 9, 2005.

33. See Anthony Seeger, "The Role of Sound Archives in Ethnomusicology Today," *Ethnomusicology* 30, no. 2 (1986): 261–76.

34. Judith Gray, "Returning Music to the Makers: The Library of Congress, American Indians, and the Federal Cylinder Project," *Cultural Survival Quarterly* 20, no. 4 (1997): 42.

35. Grace Koch, "Songs, Land Rights, and Archives in Australia," *Cultural Survival Quarterly* 20, no. 4 (1997): 38–41.

36. Alan Lomax, "Appeal for Cultural Equity," *World of Music* 14, no. 2 (1972): 3–17.

37. Ibid.

38. Daniel Sheehy, "A Few Notions about Philosophy and Strategy in Applied Ethnomusicology," *Ethnomusicology* 36, no. 3 (1992): 323–36.

39. "Smithsonian Folklife Festival," Smithsonian Center for Folklife and Cultural Heritage, 2005, http://www.folklife.si.edu/center/festival.html (accessed June 12, 2008).

40. Ibid.

41. Svanibor Pettan, Klisala Harrison, and Eric Usner, "New ICTM Study Group on Applied Ethnomusicology First Meeting," Appliedethnomusicology.org, http://appliedethnomusicology.org/index2.php?option=com_content&do_pdf=1&id=159 (accessed June 1, 2008).

42. Rosemary Coombe, personal communication, 2005.

43. Ana María Ochoa, "Music and Cultural Rights Violations," Conference on Music and Cultural Rights: Trends and Prospects, Pittsburg, Penn., April 9, 2005.

1 Agency and Voice

The Philippines at the 1998 Smithsonian Folklife Festival

RICARDO D. TRIMILLOS

In the environment of modern nation-states, expressive culture has often been appropriated for the purposes of constructing national identity or conflated with it, be it a physical object, such as the sprawling complex of the Cultural Center of the Philippines, or a song, such as the late George Canseco's "Ako ay Pilipino" (I am Filipino), composed in 1982 on commission from then First Lady Imelda Marcos. The contemporary nation with its bureaucratic apparatus often claims itself as principal steward of expressive culture within its borders, including concomitant rights. Thus, ministries of culture in Asia, arts councils in Commonwealth countries, and the National Endowment for the Arts in the United States assume similar responsibilities for the arts as part of the national project.[1]

In the Philippines, the National Commission on Culture and the Arts (NCCA) and the Cultural Center of the Philippines (CCP) constitute this apparatus. The NCCA stewardship of minority cultural communities, including Lumad and Muslim populations, is notable in this regard.[2] The term "cultural communities" is the current Philippine bureaucratic term for linguistic, tribal, or ethnic groups.

In a time when "ethnic" is very much the mode, the question can arise as to the locus of ownership and stewardship of cultural expressions: the nation, a region, a community, a specific family, or an individual.[3] Differing notions of ownership and cultural property offer sites for confrontation or negotiation, especially when a cultural expression enters a globalized or transnational sphere.

In the first part of this essay, I present working definitions and descriptions for some of these rights as a general framework for further studies and discussions. In the second part, I discuss rights of display in one specific transnational sphere: the Philippines cultural delegation to the 1998 Smithsonian Folklife Festival in Washington, D.C. In the third part, I briefly explore the complex interactions of agency and cultural rights. I present a wider view of cultural rights, a prolegomenon to a general schema. Principal illustrations are drawn from the Philippines.

One View of Cultural Rights

A Working Description of Cultural Rights

The nature of cultural rights is collective, in contrast to human rights, which are individual. Therefore, at a basic level, cultural rights require consensus. Useful for this discussion are working definitions for rights and related entitlements formulated by the Scottish Museum Council.[4] The council argues that rights constitute an ethical position at a broad level of generality. Entitlements are specific benefits that accrue to that ethical position. I apply these concepts of rights and related entitlements to three broad categories: the right to access, the right to stewardship, and the right to control.

Right to Access

Among the Siasi Tausug of the southern Philippines, only males may learn and perform the repertory of *tarasul,* sung homilies describing behavior for an observant Muslim. However, females are expected to listen to these performances, presumably taking the admonishments for a religious life to heart. Thus, both genders possess a right to access, however different in type. Only the male has access to learning and performing the tarasul; the female has access to its performance and listens to the texts. In terms of gendered function, males are accorded an active role in maintaining the tradition; females are not. Both males and females may be listeners and audience members, a passive role. The Tausug case, in which rights of access are differentiated by gender, contrasts with cases in other cultures in which the right to access is available only to one gender segment. For example, females are forbidden to hear certain genres of male songs in Australian Aboriginal and New Guinea cultures.[5] Thus, a categorization of rights might include rights to access that are the same for the entire society, rights differentiated for different segments of a society, and rights exclusively available to only one segment of a society and explicitly denied to others.

What are the entitlements that follow on the right to access? In the Tausug example, specific entitlements accompany the male's right to access as practitioner and performer. One entitlement is community recognition, evidenced by invitations to private and public rituals, ceremonies, and observances. The performance of tarasul is desirable at auspicious occasions; males who can perform well are known within the community. A second entitlement is the accumulation of social and religious capital. As folk homilies, tarasul constitute nuggets of advice, presumably reflecting the wisdom and religious depth of the performer. This capital can be actualized as influence and power in the community. A third entitlement is the performance of a religious text in the Tausug language, a text that can be universally understood in the community. This contrasts with the recitation of the Koran and the performance of the Maulid, which is available equally to men and women.[6] However, those texts are in Arabic, a language not understood by most Tausug. The performance with texts in a language minimally understood by its listeners shifts the communication value from the logocentric to the culturally symbolic. The tarasul texts in Tausug are immediately understandable; thus, the genre holds major logocentric value, its symbolic and ritual associations notwithstanding.

The entitlements described above are denied the Siasi Tausug female, no matter how religious or knowledgeable she may be. Here, rights to access based upon gender are constructed through community tradition and practice. They are ascribed.

Rights of access rest not only within the subject community. Entities outside the community may assume rights of access. In addition to United Nations Educational, Scientific, and Cultural Organization representatives, national culture commissions, and world music collectors, we ethnomusicologists assume a right of access.[7] We go into a new field site, ask for performances, and characterize ourselves as answering to a higher calling than other Others: our work is for scholarly and intellectual purposes. Whether the target community understands or valorizes our rationale is certainly an open question. Our expectation from the outset is that we should have the right of access. We regard it as more the exception than the rule when we encounter a community that denies us access. Unlike the first example in which the right is ascribed, here the right is assumed as possibility.

Right to Stewardship

By stewardship, I mean conserving and advocating for a musical practice or tradition. In an era of internationalism and globalization, stewardship becomes complex and multifaceted. Like rights of access, rights of stewardship devolve upon members of the community and may be claimed by those outside the community. Those who control are not necessarily those who steward or "care" for the tradition.

As an example of stewardship within the community, the performance of the Subli-an is instructive. The observance, ritual music, and dance to venerate the Holy Cross is maintained in the southern Tagalog province of Batangas.[8] In the town of Bauan, the Subli-an is regarded as the purview of specific families, including the Cruzats, the Maquimots, and the Manalos. Although there may be others who participate and may claim their own authority over the practice, these families continue to be recognized as major keepers of tradition.[9] In recent times, stewardship includes designing workshops for public school children and consulting for regional cultural tourism, for which Subli-an festivals or gatherings have been featured.[10]

Although examples of entitlements of stewardship are many, I present only two here. First, within the performance itself, particular statuses devolve from stewardship. A female may be named *matremayo* (leader), which entitles her to occupy the lead position in the line of female dancers. The matremayo is assumed to be knowledgeable about all aspects of the tradition. First, during performance, she makes appropriate decisions for the female line. Second, post-performance, she is entitled to critique details of the performance, although direct criticism is a delicate matter. In one such instance at the festival, the matremayo told all the women that they were not being serious enough during the presentation rather than address the single "guilty" performer.

Individuals outside the community may also claim the right of stewardship. A contentious and recent instance involves the criticism of an acknowledged traditional practitioner of *kulintang* gong chime ensemble by a Caucasian American.[11] The gong chime ensemble is indigenous to Muslim Filipinos in the southern regions, Mindanao, and the Sulu Archipelago. The practitioner is a master teacher living in the United States. He constitutes one of the important resources for the Filipino-American kulintang movement and has served as mentor for kulintang groups throughout the nation. Some five years ago, criticism of him as carrier of tradition and purveyor of authentic performance was disseminated via the Internet. The critic was a Caucasian American who had been active and very committed to the U.S. kulintang movement.

The critic characterized himself as concerned with maintaining the integrity and authenticity of the form. It is understandable that someone who has supported and championed a music in the United States feels an investment in the tradition as he learned it. In his view, stewardship may be not only a right but also a responsibility. Although the source of the criticism was questioned by some Filipinos and Filipino Americans, the readiness of a music practitioner from outside the culture to criticize in a strong and public way presumes a right of stewardship and an entitlement to criticize, whether defensible or not. Clearly from the point of view of one American kulintang practitioner, both the right and the entitlement were his.

Right to Control

The right to control may be invested in leaders within the community. Although only tangentially related to music, this case concerns the right to control participants in Good Friday crucifixions in Pampanga. Individuals elect to have themselves crucified by nailing as an act of faith or to fulfill a vow to God for a favor granted, reenacting the sufferings of Christ. This practice of self-mortification attracts annual worldwide media attention. The need for control was underscored in 1996 at Barrio San Pedro Cutud, San Fernando, following a scandal involving a Japanese national.[12] Since 1997, the barrio council allows only Filipino nationals from the region to participate.

Right to control can include limiting or sanctioning physical locale. For example, the *pasyon* or *pabasa* is a folk practice of reciting and singing a vernacular account of the Passion of Christ in the Catholic Lowland Philippines.[13] In Guagua, Pampanga, participants set up a temporary altar outside the main entrance to the church. The church clerics allow the pasyon to be performed in front of the church but not inside it, citing the presence of the Host or the Holy Sacraments as reason. The priests supervise the church as an orthodox space. The pasyon is not an orthodox Holy Week practice, although the church leadership tolerates it.

Entitlements relative to the right to control include the public construction of performance. It entitles community leaders to define the model or ideal performance, which for the crucifixions means the regularizing of the participant group to Filipino nationals.[14] For the pasyon in Guagua, the priests, exercising rights to control, determine the location of performance, or more precisely, determine the location of non-performance—that is, within the church.

Issues Emerging from Cultural Rights

I argue here that the most challenging issue is no longer the justification of cultural rights per se but determining the locus of agency. That is, upon which individual, individuals, or groups do these rights devolve and by what mechanisms? There are competing or conflicting claims for agency and authority that complicate questions of cultural ownership.[15] Two recent instances involved the world music groups Deep Forest and Enigma and two ethnomusicology colleagues.[16] Advocacy or activist positionalities may be forced upon or claimed by researchers and scholars. For example, Hugo Zemp was unwittingly pulled into an advocacy position against Deep Forest through ethnographic recordings he collected some two decades earlier. In contrast, Nancy Guy assumed an activist stance, championing the rights of the two Ami singers whose performance was sampled by Enigma.[17] Agency of the scholar/researcher is certainly one issue. The American kulintang performer, another cultural outsider, also assumed an activist stance and therefore cultural ownership.

A second issue queries, "Who is entitled to speak for such rights and in which contexts?" The instances in which the issues of cultural rights are most problematic involve minority or disempowered populations exploited or—even worse—victimized by the more empowered. When this occurs, who most effectively speaks for a group's rights? Is Gayatri Spivak's pronouncement on the subaltern absolute?[18] Or perhaps more to the point, when the subaltern speaks, who listens?

Implicit in this discussion is an even thornier issue: the control of cultural rights, often articulated in the Philippines as "ownership." The issue can also generate contestations of entitlement. For example, does a foreign individual who has practiced and maintained an indigenous art form have more claim to this notion of ownership than an individual of the relevant ethnicity who no longer practices or maintains the art form? In questions about control and ownership of cultural rights, the stewardship versus lineage dichotomy becomes a complicating element.

The agency of the ethnomusicologist regarding these three rights is inevitable. Certainly all of us subscribe to a right of access. Many of us are involved with issues of stewardship. And some of us, particularly those in government service, exercise the right of control. I explore the complexity of multiple agencies by examining the 1998 Philippine participation in the Smithsonian Folklife Festival.

Case Study: The 1998 Smithsonian Folklife Festival in Five Voices[19]

"I Know the Festival": The Author's Voice(s)

The Smithsonian Folklife Festival is an annual two-week celebration of folklife on the Washington Mall during the last week of June and the first week of July. It has been variously critiqued, deconstructed, and championed.[20] "Folklife" originally celebrated U.S. cultures and practices outside the elitist and hegemonic spheres. The term in current festival usage includes "folk" expressions of foreign nations and occasionally their elitist traditions as well.

My first encounter with the festival was in 1979, when the late Ralph Rinzler invited me to visit the Festival of American Folklife on the Mall. I was an out-of-town visitor, rushing to the Mall in order to do a colleague a favor between other appointments in Washington. My second significant experience was as member of the planning group and as presenter for the 1989 Hawai'i State participation. The 1998 festival was my third involvement; it was the most intense and committed experience to date. In 2000 and 2004, I participated in two capacities, as member of the Advisory Board for the Center for Folklife and Cultural Heritage and as an "anonymous and on the ground" volunteer. Thus, I know the festival from a number of perspectives. For this discussion, I focus upon the right of display, a subcategory of the right to control.[21]

For the Republic of the Philippines, the 1998 festival provided a globalized site and an international opportunity for cultural display, ostensibly to celebrate the centennial of its independence from Spanish colonial rule. A magnificent open space facing the U.S. Capitol, the Mall carries its own set of ironies for Filipinos, of which cultural rights is but one.[22] Filipinos have an ambivalent attitude toward Americans—friend, arbiter of modernity, and liberator after World War II on the one hand; colonizer, "big brother," and economic taipan on the other. This ambivalence played itself out in various aspects of planning, festival presentation, and post-event activities, but the general sentiment for the Filipino planners and participants was positive.

Each year, the Smithsonian Center for Folklife and Cultural Heritage transforms the Mall into a series of performance stages and cultural exhibit areas. Its curatorial philosophy comes out of a liberal multiculturalism that is further informed by American notions of authenticity, rootedness, and the nostalgia of community. It is committed to principles of diversity, enfranchisement of the disfranchised and unenfranchised, and a positivistic social stance. Its nature has been formed by (among others) Ralph Rinzler and articulated by the present director, Richard Kurin, who has often characterized the festival and the Center for Folklife and Cultural Heritage as part of a guerrilla movement to decenter the conservative hegemony of the Smithsonian as institution.

The strategy (and in large part, the success) of the festival is to present all aspects of culture as performance, including craft, foodways, music, dance, and reflexivity. The festival privileges process; for example, the act of weaving is foregrounded by the presence of weavers throughout the day. The woven object assumes a secondary role as static display. It becomes the main focus only when a weaver is not present, which changes the nature of the visitor experience. A performative emphasis speaks to agency and the right of display: the visitor encounters the weaver, an individual who holds that right.

Even more notable is the success of the Narrative Stage, which "performs" reflexivity and analysis. The Narrative Stage for the Philippine event was constructed as a *sari-sari* store, the ubiquitous neighborhood retail stall found throughout the Philippines, from urban neighborhoods to isolated hamlets. It is the local gathering place for discussion, news, and gossip, often extending late into the night. The Narrative Stage aka sari-sari store hosted discussions over a wide range of social and cultural topics, including traditional craft ("Talaandig Beadwork"), Muslim minorities ("The Cross and the Crescent"), family ("Concepts of Home"), and history ("Surviving Modernity").

The Philippines participation was entitled "Pahiyas: A Philippine Harvest," which conflated two features of Filipino identity—generosity through gift-giving (*pahiyas*) and a cultural base in agriculture.[23] Pahiyas on the Mall was part of a yearlong centennial celebration of Philippine independence from Spain, cited earlier. The delegation consisted of one hundred persons. Eighty were cultural practitioners from Lowland, Upland, Muslim, and Lumad groups (see table 1.1).[24] In addition, there were twenty curatorial and support staff members, primarily from the Cultural Center of the Philippines as lead Philippine agency. Other staff came from the Intramuros Adminis-

Table 1.1. The Philippine delegation to the 1998 Folklife Festival

Geographic and language distribution			
Group	Genre	Number of participants	
Luzon and Tagalog-centric	(11 genres)	45	
Tagalog:	Subli-an—folk Catholic ritual group	10	
	Musikong bungbung—bamboo band	14	
	Rondalla—plucked string band	06	
	Foodways	02	
	Santo carver	01	
	Pahiyas—rice wafer decoration	01	(34)
Other Lowland:	Altar carver	01	
	Goldsmith	01	
	Silversmith	01	(3)
Upland:	Kalinga music/dance group	07	
	Wood-carver	01	(8)
Visayas	(4 genres)	14	
Cebuano:	Arnis—stick fighting	02	
	Cantoras—church singers, celebrations	08	(10)
Aklanon:	Boatmaker	02	
	Piña pineapple fiber weavers	02	(4)
Mindanao	(8 genres)	21	
Bagobo (Lumad):	Double *ikat* weaver[a]	01	
	Musician-photographer	01	(2)
Talaandig (Lumad):	Dance-music-foodways group	08	(8)
T'boli (Lumad):	Double *ikat* weaver[a]	01	
	Dancer-storyteller	01	(2)
Magindanao (Muslim):	*Kulintang* gong ensemble	06	
	Boat maker	01	
	Kudyapi lute virtuoso[a]	01	
	Kulintang gong maker	01	(9)
Total		80	

[a] *Gawad sa Manlilikha ng Bayan* holder

tration, the Office of Muslim Affairs, and the University of the Philippines. I served as ex-officio liaison between the CCP and the Center for Folklife curatorial staffs.

To advance the discussion, I resort here to a traditional expository practice, *kuwento-kuwentuhan,* or conversational storytelling.[25] Each story presents an environment for cultural rights. For the analysis, I focus upon one subcategory of the right to control—the right to display. As stated earlier, my emphasis is upon agency. Each story asks, "Who exercises a right to display and how?"

"No Killing of Animals on the Grounds": U.S.-Smithsonian Voice

A popular feature of every Folklife Festival is foodways, where traditional foods and ways of cooking are demonstrated. Cuisine from Lumad, Muslim, and various Lowland groups of the Philippines were presented throughout the day.

Early in the planning process, the Smithsonian Folklife staff advised the CCP that there was to be no killing of animals on the grounds. The Washington planners were particularly sensitive to the highly political and vocal antivivisection organizations that had actually surveilled previous festivals. These organizations had made complaints about possible cruelty to animals; slaughtering on the premises was completely out of the question. This proscription affected the foodways presenters.

One of the highlights of the cooking demonstrations is the preparation of *lechon,* a whole pig roasted on a spit. Folkways associated with this preparation include ritual prayers, speeches, or songs delivered before and during the killing of the animal, which is bled to death. The blood must be collected in a prescribed way; it is used in the preparation of another dish, *dinuguan,* trotters in blood sauce. Although a bit disappointed that the slaughtering process could not be shown, the men preparing the lechon were content to accept a pre-slaughtered carcass, mount it on a spit, and demonstrate the cooking phase. They did not insist upon the right to display the slaughtering process as cultural experience.

However, another practice involving the killing of animals was insisted upon. The Talaandig is a Lumad group from Mindanao. Members of this group felt very strongly that for their own protection and that of the entire delegation, a consecration of the site was necessary. The ritual involves bloodletting of chickens, which are then buried while dying in ritually significant locations of a site. Coins smeared with chicken blood are placed around the perimeter of the area as a further means of protection. The concern for protection increased when the entire delegation assembled in Manila for three days of orientation prior to departure for Washington.

These two kuwento concern the right to control. For the prohibition of killing animals on the Mall, the Smithsonian right to control superseded the Filipino right to display the complete lechon process (humorously referred to as "from squeal to meal"). This instance of U.S.-invoked control made cultural sense to Filipinos—one should, as much as possible, be the good guest in another's land. The right to control invoked by the United States regarding blood consecration on its own land was equally understandable.

However, in the case of the Talaandig ritual, this right to display was more urgent. Agreeing that the ritual was necessary, the entire hundred-person delegation participated in a Talaandig-led consecration ritual in a Filipino national cultural space—the grounds of the Cultural Center of the Philippines. The ritual constituted a Filipino right to display in the face of a U.S. sanction against it. The display was both for the delegation and for the spirits to be propitiated. Displacing the ritual in both time and place was acceptable to the Talaandig, the other Filipino celebrants, and apparently the spirits. Travel was safe and uneventful, there were no untoward experiences during the two weeks on the Mall, and all one hundred participants returned home after the festival. There had been attempted defections by foreign delegations at previous festivals, and Filipino nationals have been notorious as illegal aliens.[26] Given this background, the 100 percent return was a particular point of pride for the delegation.[27]

"CCP Cannot Be Responsible for Children": Republic of the Philippines Voice

The *musikong bungbung* is a bamboo ensemble that imitates the European wind band. The ensemble is remarkable as visual mimesis: although the instruments are faithful copies in bamboo of wind instruments, the sound for most of them is produced by humming or singing into a kazoo-like mouthpiece. The trombonist manipulates the movable slide and the trumpet player works the three valves, but each sings rather than blows into his instrument. The musikong bungbung ensemble continues to be a popular novelty throughout the Lowland region.

The CCP curatorial staff had a choice of three different bamboo bands to invite. Although the two finalists were of fairly equal musical quality, the staff decided upon the Banda Bulacan, in part because all its members were adults. The other group, Banda Malabon, is notable for its inclusion of three generations of musicians—children, parents, and grandparents. The CCP felt it could not be responsible for children and decided upon the all-adult Bulacan ensemble, which proved to be a popular attraction on the Mall.

However, the Malabon group was upset. Members had performed countless times for CCP events, which they continually referred to as "service." They felt that traveling to the Smithsonian should have been their reward. The Filipino social mechanism of *utang na loob,* a debt of gratitude, was invoked; the Malabon musicians believed the CCP was in their debt.[28]

However, the operational right to display rested with the CCP as governmental entity. It invoked the right to display not itself but traditions of cultural communities over which it claimed stewardship. Co-optation by a national government of a regional and cultural expression complicates relationships of a modern nation-state to its cultural communities. At present, the nation-state seems to be primarily a political entity, particularly if one accepts the efficacy of globalized economies. It could be argued that like the economic domain, the cultural domain may no longer be exclusively owned or stewarded by the state. Following this line of reasoning, cultural rights should rest primarily with the community that maintains the form. For the musikong bungbung at the festival, however, the right to display was claimed by the Philippine state through the CCP.

"That Is the Way It Should Be": Community Practitioners' Voices

Choral singing in the Lowland Philippines, introduced by the Catholic Church during the seventeenth century as part of Spain's colonial project, is universally popular and strongly supported. Choral music flourishes at a surprisingly high level of artistry throughout the country, evidenced by the number of international choral competitions won by Filipino groups.[29] Every provincial town and village is home to a choral ensemble, generally associated with the Catholic Church.

For the festival, the CCP identified an extraordinary group of *cantoras,* church singers at St. Augustine de Hippo in Bacong, Negros Oriental. Bacong is a rural *poblacion* (municipality), some twenty kilometers from Dumaguete town, the provincial capital and major seaport. For most masses and observances at St. Augustine, the cantoras sing a cappella. Although there is a pipe organ in the large church, it has fallen into disrepair and has remained unused for over two decades. The group's repertory is quite varied. In addition to Marian hymns, parts of the Mass, and Stations of the Cross in at least four languages (the regional language of Cebuano, the national language of Tagalog, English, and Latin) the group possesses an active repertory of Cebuano folksongs and of Western pop hits popular throughout the country. Even more remarkable, the extensive repertory and vocal arrangements are rehearsed and performed from memory. The cantoras as music practitioners possess extensive knowledge of and about their tradition; in Negros Oriental they are accorded both the authority and the right to display.

As an ethnomusicologist, I find the a cappella singing in two or three parts by this Cebuano group particularly interesting and arresting. Clearly based upon common practice harmony and major-minor modalities, the cantoras' performance tends to use neutral thirds, especially when unaccompanied. The neutral thirds produce a rich and resonant texture from among the two or three parts. Both the distinctive multiphonic texture and the innate musicality of their a cappella singing make the Bacong cantoras fine representatives of this folk genre.

For special occasions, such as Christmas Eve and Good Friday, an electronic keyboard accompanies the cantoras, an apparent substitution for the now unplayable pipe organ. Although the keyboard is in tempered tuning, the vocalists maintain the distinctive texture produced by neutral thirds.[30] The two streams of intonation are remarkable, both for the singers who maintain this dual intonation and for a listener accustomed to a single intonation system. It was my personal concern that a Washington audience would consider the singers simply "out of tune" and even presume they were lacking in musical skill.

As part of the curatorial group, I suggested to the Bacong singers that the unaccompanied performance was the more effective setting. Although true, it was also my failed strategy to avoid "out of tune" vocal-with-keyboard performances on the Mall. However, the cantoras insisted upon the keyboard. One rationale articulated was "to show the Americans we can afford it [the electronic keyboard]." Embedded in this statement are subtexts of modernity, status, and economic capability. In their view, the festival was a special occasion; as such, inclusion of the keyboard was appropriate. Their rejoinder to my final attempt to sideline the keyboard was, "No, that is the way it should be."[31]

A practitioner can invoke multiple kinds of authority. The Philippines sent some of its most outstanding traditional artists with the delegation, including three designated by the national government as National Living Treasure (Gawad sa Manlilikha ng Bayan). Samoan Solaiman was one of these. He is a virtuoso master of the *kudyapi,* the two-stringed long lute from Magindanao Province in Mindanao.[32] Kudyapi music consists of a single, highly ornamented melodic line and a simultaneously sounded drone supplied by the second string. The melody-drone texture suggests comparisons with Indian music. A charismatic personality, Solaiman can win over an audience by his presence alone—even before playing a note. He was a deeply philosophical and thoughtful Muslim who became one of the iconic figures for the festival.

In the Smithsonian Folklife Festival format, the craft areas are deliberately separated from performance stages, so that a minimum of sound leak from a performance will disturb the craft presentations. Solaiman was assigned to the Narrative Stage, the sari-sari store described earlier. The Narrative Stage is located within the craft area but is separated from the various craft stations for sound considerations—that is, the Narrative Stage is the site of ongoing amplified conversation. The overall volume of the kudyapi (even when amplified) is soft and delicate, so that the Narrative Stage was more appropriate than the two large performance stages. Nevertheless, as music performance, the kudyapi produces an environment of continuous sound.

In contrast, the craft stations feature a sound environment that is low-level and intermittent. Short periods of time without programmed sound encourage contemplation and observation of the demonstrator and the objects. They alternate with narration by the presenter or with question-answer exchanges. Thus, the planners had designed three areas for different soundscapes: the high-volume, amplified, and continuous sound of the performance stages; the low-volume and continuous sound of the Narrative Stage (where Solaiman was to perform); and the low-volume, unamplified, and intermittent soundscape of the craft spaces.

Upon arrival at the Mall, Solaiman spent two of the three preparation days studying the site and the location of the various presentations. He then announced that he would not play at the Narrative Stage, but his performance space would be in the craft area. In that space were a Magindanaon weaver and Talaandig and Bagobo artisans, all people from Mindanao. As a National Artist and as a Magindanaon of the elevated *dumatu* class, he had two authoritative claims for control—national recognition and his indigenous privileged status. Respecting the former, the CCP staff accommodated his wishes; acknowledging the latter, the artists and artisans from Mindanao found his decision appropriate.

After hurried consultation and some masterful three-way negotiations, the festival staff created a performance space with seating immediately adjacent to the weavers and the instrument makers. For Solaiman, one of his entitlements was to determine the optimal environment for his performance. His reason for selecting his location: "I want to create where other people are creating [at the same time]."[33] The juxtaposition of music performance with craft, not a usual festival format, made a statement important for the Filipino delegation. It was probably less apparent to the many visitors who crowded about (and through) the craft displays to see and hear Solaiman's virtuosity.

In both cases, the carriers of the tradition had clear ideas about how to frame their performances and claimed the entitlement to determine that frame. Curatorial pressures notwithstanding, the cantoras and the kudyapi virtuoso asserted their respective right to display—and they persevered.

"He Is Only Making Kuwento": Hegemonic Voice versus Community Voice

The final story describes the tension between a Manila-based presenter and the Kalinga performing group from the highlands of Luzon. In the festival format, each performance or exhibit unit has a presenter who introduces the artists, explains the traditions, and fields any questions. This function is particularly useful when the artist has limited English abilities or cannot answer queries without interrupting the production of his art. The presenter for the Kalinga group was a highly respected dance researcher and culture consultant from Manila. He is valued for his extensive field collecting in all parts of the Philippines and for the dance theater he has created. During his introduction of the Kalingas, he spoke with authority using the perspective and descriptions familiar to Manila presentations of national folkloric troupes, such as Bayanihan or Filipinescas. However, the Kalinga artists, who all spoke English, were not happy with the presenter's rhetoric. He used such phrases as "these people," "savage practices," "tribes," and "in contrast to Filipinos" (meaning Lowland Christians). At the outset, he occasionally "corrected" their performance in a public way. It was a problematic case of a national hegemony casting its gaze on one of its own minority groups and disfranchising it in the presence of an overseas and foreign public.

Following the first day of presentations, the Kalinga participants expressed their dissatisfaction to me and others. Rather than provoke a confrontation, the group began introducing themselves to the audience before the presenter arrived. By the third day of performances, the Kalingas had de facto usurped the presenter function; the official presenter was reduced to making an occasional comment. The Kalinga artists, presenting themselves, contextualized their rituals and performing arts in the realities of a contemporary Philippines rather than in the utopia of a pristine and uncolonized historical past. They dismissed the designated presenter's commentary as "only making *kuwento*," an idiom that suggests surface commentary rather than serious, substantive communication. One group member commented, "Why should we have a Manileño speak for us? The Americans will think we are uneducated."[34] The appellation "Manileño" denotes a person from the urban metropolis of Manila; in this context it marked the outsider (in Tagalog, *ibang tao*). The right to display and its entitlements became flashpoints between national voice and community voice.

In this case, the Kalingas asserted their right to display themselves and to use voices from their own community—the subaltern spoke. Many Kalingas regard themselves as a distinctive culture operating within a framework of the modern nation-state. They express a willingness to engage with—but not necessarily assimilate to—a Lowland and "Westernized" national hegemony, perhaps more readily in political than cultural domains. For the Kalingas at the festival, the right to display meant to appear simultaneously as contemporary Kalingas and Filipinos, not as a living "Smithsonian Natural History diorama" constructed from the gaze of a national, non-community Other.

This narrative problematizes the locus of cultural rights in very concrete terms. From a "Western" academic or public policy perspective, cultural rights in so-called third world areas are often regarded as the purview and the responsibility of the nation-state.[35] Indeed, Philippine governmental agencies such as the NCCA and the CCP claim that function. The NCCA in its founding legislation is directed to "promote the interest and welfare of artists and culture workers by protecting their rights to intellectual and artistic properties as well as by associations which shall promote and protect the economic and moral rights of artists all over the country."[36]

The national government also serves as arbiter of excellence for traditional culture, bestowing the prestigious title of National Living Treasure on practitioners selected through NCCA mechanisms. The title is one of a series of national awards made by the NCCA and the CCP.[37]

The equivalence of national patrimony and indigenous cultural property certainly extends beyond the Philippines, as the Enigma and Deep Forest examples show. These cases and their resolution are cautionary; the rights of ownership and display cannot be presumed to rest at the most obvious or most accessible level, here that of a national entity.[38] The institution of nation as state may not satisfactorily accommodate the ethos and sensibility of specific communities or their cultural expressions.[39]

The Intersection of Agency and Cultural Rights

Agency

The Smithsonian Folklife Festival provided a provocative laboratory setting for playing out agency and cultural rights, problematizing both. Further, it interrogated the validity of agency, whether bestowed or claimed.

In brief, cultural rights and locus of agency at the Smithsonian Folklife Festival were distributed and contested among various interested—and invested—parties:

1. The state (here, the Philippines) and its claims of culture as part of its heritage and patrimony
2. The cultural community (term used by the NCCA) and its claims of culture as part of its community expression
3. The practitioner group and its claims as the producers and the stewards of the specific cultural expression
4. The individual practitioner and his or her claims as the repository of cultural knowledge
5. The scholar/researcher (sometimes a non-national and often a non-community member) and his or her claims for investment, stewardship, and special expertise concerning a cultural expression

This taxonomy has been the basis for the examination of agency at the festival. I suggest that it has wider application for discussions of cultural rights worldwide, principally because it identifies and recognizes multiple agencies. The analysis of agency points up domains in which claims or assumptions of rights overlap or are in conflict. Perhaps more important for disfranchised and marginalized groups, it also reveals areas in which there is no articulation of rights and in which agency is not identified. In both cases, there is a reasonable expectation of action or establishment of practice based upon these findings. An actualization phase brings ethical and moral considerations into play, which will inevitably generate similar negotiations, mutatis mutandis, concerning agency and authority.

Cultural Property Rights

The complexity of the issue is undeniable. As further contextualization of the foregoing discussions, I provide a fuller explication of the schema used in this discussion in table 1.2. Viewed as a whole, the schema points up the intersection of rights with various kinds of agency. It presents two levels of rights. The first level, the three items discussed in the first section, are arranged in an order of increasing degree of agency. Thus, rights of access are not as intrusive as rights of control. Additionally, the former is less potentially damaging to the tradition. In this section, I focus upon the second level of rights. The complicity of academe as one locale of agency is part of the discussion.

Table 1.2. Cultural property rights: A schema

Right to access	Right to steward	Right to control
Right to perform	Right to critique	Right to display
Right to observe	Right to advocate	Right to create
Right to research	Right to transmit	Right to change
	Right to inform	Right to suppress
		Right to own

Right to access: the right to perform has been described previously. The Siasi Tausug tarasul example above posited that all males potentially have the right to perform, although not all males do. In theory, a male can perform, even though badly; he may not be invited to perform again in a public venue, but he cannot be enjoined from performing, for example, in the privacy of his own home or in the rice fields. In numerous folk music and dance traditions, including the *pangalay* dance of the Tausug and the *palook* gong and dance genre of the Kalinga, individuals often jump into the performance from the audience. Such "volunteer" performers reenact this right to perform. The *right to observe* has also been described: for the Tausug tarasul, the female segment is enfranchised to observe but not to perform. The right to observe carries a number of entitlements. For example, in the Lowland pasyon performances during Holy Week, anyone may attend and observe. However, observers of high status or rank in the community are entitled to come into the house and receive the highest level of hospitality from the sponsors of the event. Ordinary folk, those with no social relationship to the sponsors, may enter the yard or the compound to listen, but they are not entitled to enter the house or to receive hospitality.

The *right to research* reflects the volatility of our field. Although agency historically has resided with an outsider, for example a European or American researcher, the increase in national and native scholarship has expanded agency to include individuals within the country or within the specific community. For example, the University of the Philippines Center for Ethnomusicology assumes the right to research throughout the Philippines, even though the scholar may come from a region or linguistic group different from that of the site for study. The right to research at the community level has long been the purview of the Philippine Department of Education. It regularly directs public school teachers to collect and publish songs and dances from their regions. The first major compendium of Filipino dance was collected by Philippine Normal College (now University), the major teachers' college in Manila, where students from the various regions came to train as public school teachers.[40]

Right to steward: the right to critique and its agency were problematized in the first part of this discussion concerning the incident with the American kulintang player. Particularly when the individual comes from outside the community, this question is a troublesome one. Regarding the foreign ethnomusicologist or foreign performer (who may often be more knowledgeable in the musical genre than the average indigene), the right to critique may be claimed by the foreigner but subsequently contested by the native. A potential conflict arises between the foreigner's claim of "I know the tradition" and the native's equally valid claim of "I am from the tradition." The *right to advocate*, particularly in a transnational or globalized context, appears to be an appropriate and relatively uncontested field for the outsider or foreigner. Advocacy for minority traditions, especially in a globalized context, often falls to the outsider, as was the case for the Ami singers in their suit against the group Enigma. However, we saw that agency can reside with the group itself, such as the Talaandig ritual, as well as with the national government, such as the National Living Treasure award. The general sentiment in the Philippines is that outside advocacy for cultural rights is welcome at the moment. External advocates in this era of decolonization have not always been as welcome in other struggles for cultural rights.

By the *right to transmit,* I intend the active teaching and the active learning of a tradition, that is, passing on of skills, techniques, rituals, and repertory. In various communities, this right has to be formally granted by the teacher to the student; in others, it is ideally transmitted only within the family line. Thus, it affects not only the individual who teaches but the individual who is allowed to learn. Most societies have a clear set of protocols for this right, be it the *iemoto* system of Japan, the Associated Board of the Royal Schools of Music examinations throughout the Commonwealth, or the *'uniki* ceremony for Hawaiian hula and chant. There may be contestation of this right within the community itself, usually having to do with secret knowledge and the ascendancy or authority of one school or substyle over another. This right becomes more problematic when the tradition is transmitted outside its primary venue, for example through ethnomusicology programs or international music centers. While no one would question the right of the Ali Akbar College of Music to transmit Indian music in California, that right and related entitlements for ethnomusicology programs may not be so clear-cut. What are the rights, entitlements, and responsibilities of an American institution of higher learning vis-à-vis Maranao dance or Lowland *rondalla?* These and other questions concerning an institutional right to transmit are in active discussion in the field.[41]

The *right to inform* concerns the messenger. At the community level, it includes office—that is, who has the right to speak for the tradition? Is it the master teacher, the village headman (or in the Philippines, the *barangay* captain), or the provincial officer for tourism or for culture and sport? The right to inform is closely intertwined with the right to advocate, which again foregrounds the issue of cultural insider and outsider. Hypothetically, what are the rights, entitlements, and responsibilities of ethnomusicologists when they present Kalinga music in their classes? The Kalingas at the festival not only contested the right of a Manila researcher to inform the general public, they claimed that right for themselves.

Right to control: the right to display was the major focus for the discussion of the festival. I only add here that various parties feel justified in exercising this right. The *right to create,* as illustrated in the kulintang incident, often comes under scrutiny. The current discourse concerning cultural rights assumes that this right lies solely with carriers of the culture. In the practice of musical creativity, this is not true. One historical example concerns the Subli-an of Batangas. When dance researcher Francisca Reyes Aquino collected and arranged the Subli dance for her published collection, she asked well-known film and popular song composer Juan Silos Jr. to create musical accompaniment that was more tuneful.[42] The original music consisted of percussion and occasional song, which she felt was not "Lowland" enough. Thus, the music most associated with Subli-an, disseminated primarily by the Bayanihan folkloric dance company through their world tours, was created outside the province of Batangas and outside the authority of tradition bearers. Agency was at the national level and in the service of creating a national canon of Philippine dance.

Closely related to creativity is the *right to change* a tradition or its practices. A very evident and dramatic change for the pasyon tradition throughout the Philippines is amplification. Almost every rural barrio and urban neighborhood broadcast their observances over loudspeakers, so that there may be a dozen or more different performances assaulting the soundscape simultaneously. While electronic mediation may not be pleasing to the researcher or to the cultural purist, it is a choice that the community and its practitioners have a right to make. Asserting agency, local governments reframe folk traditions for tourist attractions. City officials in Batangas City established a Subli-an festival with competitions among groups and with workshops to teach youth. Change is instigated at the governmental level but with cooperation from the practitioner group.

The *right to suppress* is often assumed to be the purview of a central government, for example, the ban on the patriotic song "Bayan Ko" (My Country) during Martial Law (1972–86). The festival experienced an attempt at suppression coming from a high national government official: he sent a directive that there were to be no Cordillera participants dressed in *bahag* (the colorful traditional loincloth worn by males that leaves the buttocks and the upper body exposed). The official was concerned about an image of Filipinos as uncivilized. However, the directive was immediately contested and rejected by the CCP curatorial staff. At the official opening of the festival on the Mall, the Philippines was represented by a Kalinga noseflute artist dressed in bahag.

The *right to own* is potentially the most troublesome, given the globalization of music as mediated entertainment and the pervasiveness of commodification through tourism. Contentious in Philippine land rights are the conflicting concepts of stewardship and ownership. Most traditional societies regard their land rights as stewardship; a similar attitude often obtains about music. No single individual owns Salidommay, a song genre shared among the mountain peoples of Luzon; no one owns the Tausug tune "Sua ko sua" (My dear orange tree), although it is most closely associated with the musician Albani. Hypothetically, if a world music group chooses to sample an Itneg Salidommay, to whom does it direct royalties for performer rights and mechanical rights? More important, who pursues the record producer if he or she does not agree to pay these royalties?

In this final section, I have argued that agency is a major factor in the exercise of cultural rights. At this point, I wish to be self-reflexive and suggest the positionality of the ethnomusicologist and researcher within the taxonomy and the schema. The rights to observe, research, and advocate may appear to be safe spaces for the researcher; for other rights, we researchers probably have no place—for example, rights to perform, to create, or to own.[43] Other rights fall into a gray area of those variously claimed, ascribed, or appropriated. The positionality for government workers, cultural activists, and media specialists form different and separate configurations among elements of the schema. Whether each of these groups is self-reflexive about its positionality is an open question.

Conclusion

At the outset, I problematized two forms of agency: national governments and academic researchers. Regarding the former, I realistically offer only descriptive reportage and analysis. Regarding the latter, I choose to be more prescriptive. I find the most challenging and problematic domain to be advocacy; it is critical for agency. What are the levels of advocacy within our purview, and are they appropriate or desirable? At this juncture, the ethnomusicologists as well as the field collectors should reflect upon and assess their role, which is very much about entitlement and responsibility rather than rights per se. It is at the nexus of the ethics of advocacy, the social conditions of entitlement, and the moral implications of responsibility that we should engage ourselves.

We should weigh our notions of agency against those of the relevant cultural community. I close with the admonition from Lyndel V. Prott: "For community-based systems, the intrusion of individualism from an encroaching culture may make decisions about preservation and development of traditional cultures particularly acute and prone to gender or age conflicts."[44] This caveat resonates with the Smithsonian Folklife Festival project and with our own lifework.

Notes

This essay is an expanded version of the paper read at the Conference on Music and Cultural Rights held at the University of Pittsburgh on April 7–10, 2005. I wish to thank Patrick Alcedo, Barbara B. Smith, Andrew Weintraub, and Bell Yung for their close reading and constructive comments during its revision.

1. Ministries of culture in Asia are often combined with sports and, less frequently, with education.

2. "Lumad" is the current national designation for an array of tribal or aboriginal groups that are not considered either Muslim or Christian. Many of them are in fact nominally Christianized, e.g., the T'boli of Mindanao (Catholic) and the Benguet of Luzon (Protestant).

3. Vincent J. Cheng, *Inauthentic: The Anxiety over Culture and Identity* (New Brunswick, N.J.: Rutgers University Press, 2004).

4. Scottish Museums Council, "Cultural Rights and Entitlements in the Scottish Museums Context," 2004, http://www.scottishmuseums.org.uk/pdfs/Cultural_Rights_and_Entitlements.pdf, 7-13 (accessed September 1, 2004).

5. Linda Barwick, Allan Marret, and Guy Tunstill, *The Essence of Singing and the Substance of Song: Recent Responses to the Aboriginal Performing Arts and Other Essays in Honour of Catherine Ellis* (Sydney: University of Sydney, 1995).

6. Ricardo D. Trimillos, "Vocal Music among the Tausug of Sulu, Philippines," in *Traditional Drama and Music of Southeast Asia,* ed. Mohd. Taib Osman (Kuala Lumpur: Kementerian Pelajaran Malaysia, 1974), 274–89. The Maulid is an account of the birth of the prophet Mohammed.

7. I use the first person, so that we as researchers continually acknowledge our own subject position.

8. [Elena R. Mirano,] *Subli: One Dance in Four Voices* (Manila: Cultural Center of the Philippines, 1989).

9. Other towns noted for Subli-an include Agoncillo and Lobos in Batangas province.

10. Discount Hotel Resort, "Batangas City Travel Tips & General Informations [*sic*]," Philippines Hotels and Travel Guide, http://www.philtravelcenter.com/philippines/travelinfo/batangas-festivals (accessed September 5, 2005).

11. The ensemble features a single row of melodic bossed gongs in a ladder frame supported by a single membrane drum and a battery of larger gongs with colotomic and rhythmic functions. It is iconic of the Muslim groups of the southern Philippines. It is often characterized as the most Asian of Filipino musics, representing a Filipino population that was never fully subjugated by either the Spanish or American colonials.

12. Nicholas Barker, "Revival of Religious Self-flagellation in Lowland Christian Philippines," in *Religious Revival in Contemporary Southeast Asia,* ed. Naimah Talib and Bernhard Dahm (Singapore: Institute of Southeast Asian Studies, 1997), 13–26.

13. Ricardo D. Trimillos, "More Than Art: The Politics of Performance," in *Looking Out,* ed. David Gere (New York: Schirmer, 1994), 23–39.

14. Minerva Zamora-Arceo, "Thousands to Witness Crucifixion of 13 Faithfuls in San Pedro Cutud," *Sun Star Pampanga,* http://www.sunstar.com.ph/static/pam/2004/04/10/news/thousands.to.witness.crucifixion.of.13.faithfuls.in.san.pedro.cutud.html (accessed September 3, 2005).

15. Michael A. Bengwayan, *Intellectual and Cultural Property Rights of Indigenous and Tribal Peoples in Asia* (London: Minority Rights Group International, 2003).

16. Hugo Zemp, "The/An Ethnomusicologist and the Recording Business," *Yearbook for Traditional Music* 28 (1996): 36–56; Nancy Guy, "Trafficking in Taiwan Aboriginal Voices," in *Handle with Care: Ownership and Control of Ethnographic Materials,* ed. Sjoerd R. Jaarsma (Pittsburgh: University of Pittsburgh Press, 2002), 195–210.

17. The two singers were unfortunately deceased in 2003.

18. Gayatri Spivak, "Can the Subaltern Speak? Speculations on Widow Sacrifice," *Wedge* 7/8 (Winter/Spring 1985): 120–30.

19. I wish to acknowledge friend and colleague Elena Mirano, whose Subli-an title *Subli: One Dance in Four Voices* is clearly the inspiration for the heading to this section.

20. Richard Price, *On the Mall: Presenting Maroon Tradition-Bearers at the 1992 FAF* (Bloomington: Folklore Institute, Indiana University, 1994); Richard Bauman, *Reflections on the Folklife Festival: An Ethnography of Participant Experience* (Bloomington: Folklore Institute, Indiana University, 1992); Richard Kurin, *Reflections of a Culture Broker: A View from the Smithsonian* (Washington, D.C.: Smithsonian Institution Press, 1997).

21. Part 3, following, presents an overview of my schema of cultural rights.

22. Independence from Spain was declared at Biak-na-Bato on June 12, 1898. American occupation of the Archipelago began on December 10, 1898. The Philippine-American War began on February 4, 1899. American civilian colonial rule of the Philippines was established on July 4, 1902, and continued until the outbreak of World War II. At the close of the war, a sovereign Republic of the Philippines was declared on July 4, 1946. In another historical confluence, the architect Daniel Burnham, major planner for the Washington capitol district, was also the major architect for the capitol district in Manila, located near the Luneta and Manila Bay. Charles Moore, *Daniel H. Burnham Architect: Planner of Cities* (Boston: Houghton Mifflin, 1921).

23. [Smithsonian Institution], *1998 Smithsonian Folklife Festival* booklet (Washington, D.C.: Smithsonian Institution, 1998).

24. "Cordillera" is a collective term for tribal peoples located in the Gran Cordillera mountain chain on the island of Luzon. Another term is "Igorot," which sometimes carries negative associations.

25. I wish to acknowledge my colleague Jon Osorio, whose effective use of the Hawaiian *mo'olelo* story as an expository strategy in scholarly writing impressed me (Jonathan K. Osorio, "'What Kine Hawaiian Are You?' A *Mo'olelo* about Nationhood, Race, History, and the Contemporary Sovereignty Movement in Hawai'i," *Contemporary Pacific* 13, no. 2 [Fall 2001]: 359–79). The festival section draws primarily upon field observation and personal experience.

26. Defection is so widespread it has its own Tagalog acronym, TNT, which stands for *tago na tago,* or concealing oneself from place to place.

27. Cultural Center of the Philippines, *Pahiyas sa Mundo,* VHS (Manila: Cultural Center of the Philippines, 1999).

28. Frank S. J. Lynch, *Four Readings on Philippine Values* (Quezon City: Institute of Philippine Culture, Ateneo de Manila, 1968).

29. The concert choirs of the University of the Philippines, the University of Santo Tomás, Mindanao State University at Iligan, and the Ateneo de Manila are examples.

30. During the oral presentation, two field recordings of the Bacong cantoras performing in Washington, D.C., were played. The first was a cappella and the second with keyboard accompaniment. In both instances, the singers continued to use neutral thirds, even when sung pitches conflicted with the tempered pitches of the keyboard.

31. Informal conversation between author and Simplicia Baro, June 24, 1998.

32. Two other awardees at the festival were traditional abaca *ikat* weavers: Lang Dulay of the T'boli group and Salinta Monon of the Bagobo group. All three awardees at the 1998 festival were from Mindanao.

33. Informal conversation between author and Samaon Solaiman, June 22, 1998.

34. The speaker asked to remain anonymous.

35. This is frequently the position of UNESCO in issues of cultural and property rights.

36. Republic of the Philippines, Republic Act No. 7356, National Commission for Culture and the Arts [English and Tagalog versions] (Manila: National Commission for Culture and the Arts, 1992).

37. The highest national award for the arts is National Artist of the Philippines (Gawad Pambansang Alagad ng Sining), which recognizes artists of mainstream genres in the categories of architecture, dance, cinema, historical literature, visual arts, music, literature, and theater and film. Additional national awards include Outstanding Service Award (Gawad Alab ng Haraya) for culture workers and Lifetime Achievement Award (Dangal ng Haraya) for other kinds of performers.

38. Victor Wong, "Deep in the Jungle; Taiwan Aboriginal Singers Settle Copyright Lawsuit," *Billboard Magazine* (1999), http://www.deepforestmusic.com/dfpress_99-31-07difanglawsuit.htm (accessed September 12, 2005).

39. Andrew N. Weintraub, *Power Plays: Wayang Golek Puppet Theater of West Java* (Athens: Ohio University, Center for International Studies, 2004).

40. Francisca Reyes [Aquino] Tolentino, *Philippine National Dances* (New York: Silver Burdett, 1946).

41. Ted Solís, *Performing Ethnomusicology: Teaching and Representation in World Music Ensembles* (Berkeley: University of California Press, 2004).

42. Francisca Reyes [Tolentino] Aquino, *Philippine Folk Dances,* vol. 2 (Manila: Francisca Reyes Aquino, 1953), 122–27.

43. My statement here concerns only the researcher. The practitioner/performer from outside the culture is a separate consideration (Solís, *Performing Ethnomusicology*).

44. Lyndel V. Prott, "Some Consideration on the Protection of the Intangible Heritage: Claims and Remedies," in *Safeguarding Traditional Cultures: A Global Assessment,* ed. Peter Seitel (Washington, D.C.: Center for Folklife and Cultural Heritage, Smithsonian Institution, 2001), 108.

2 Use and Ownership

Folk Music in the People's Republic of China

HELEN REES

In this essay, I examine the extraordinary changes that have taken place since the late 1980s in the ways that folk music is used and thought about in the People's Republic of China and how these changes inform and address the issue of cultural rights. I am using the notoriously slippery term "folk music" in the general sense implied by the common Chinese phrase *minjian yinyue* (music [from] among the people). A helpful definition and explanation of this concept is offered by senior ethnomusicologist Qiao Jianzhong of the Music Research Institute in Beijing: it refers to all kinds of traditional music "disseminated in the everyday lives of the ordinary people." He lists as examples the many different kinds of folksong: vocal and instrumental music associated with calendrical and life cycle events; playing for secular pleasure by local music societies; and genres combining music with drama or dance, such as local opera, narrative song, and folk dance. Qiao contrasts such genres with three other main categories of traditional music: that of the former royal court; that of the literati (for example, the elegant and highly literate tradition of the seven-string zither *qin*); and that associated with religious activities and institutions, such as the Confucian, Taoist, and Buddhist temples and lay religious groups.[1] For the purposes of this essay, however, I am including under the "folk music" rubric these traditional religious musics, since in practice so much music performed by lay and professional religious personnel is inextricably intertwined with *minjian* (among the people) events, contexts, and aesthetics and occupies a similar discursive space in any discussion inspired by the concept of cultural rights. Specifically excluded here from definition as "folk music" (in addition to Qiao's categories of court and literatus music) are products of the commercial, mediated popular music industry, along with recently developed genres—such as the modern Chinese orchestra—that borrow heavily from European art music and self-consciously seek to create a modern, urban, internationally oriented aesthetic.[2]

The significance of the People's Republic of China in any discussion related to cultural rights obtains at multiple levels, beyond the simple fact that Chinese citizens now number over 1.3 billion, constituting approximately one-fifth of the world's population.[3] First, and perhaps most obvious to the outside world, is the country's engagement with global initiatives in the cultural arena. For example, China ratified the International Covenant on Economic, Social and Cultural Rights on June 27, 2001, and in the early twenty-first century has become an enthusiastic participant in many United Nations Educational, Scientific and Cultural Organization (UNESCO) initiatives, as discussed in detail below.[4] China, in other words, is a prominent global player in this field in very visible ways. Second, as a multi-ethnic socialist country rapidly opening up to the market economy and the rest of the world, China brings a distinctive history of cultural policy and practice to the global discussion of cultural rights.[5]

Especially instructive, as this essay will show, are two particular characteristics of China's situation: first, the constant interactions between the concept of group rights/ownership on the one hand and individual initiative on the other; and, second, the prominent presence of ethnic minorities in the country. New Zealand legal scholar Paul Hunt argues in a recent paper that one of many reasons for the relative neglect of cultural rights at the international level is that the United Nations' human rights system, of which cultural rights is a part, has generally emphasized the rights of individuals rather than of groups. In addition, he points out that since dominant cultures in the member nations are inevitably more actively represented at the United Nations than are subordinate groups, collective rights of minorities have tended until recently to be overlooked.[6] Of late, however, high-profile initiatives such as the UN Declaration on the Rights of Minorities (1992) and the UN Declaration on the Rights of Indigenous Peoples (2007) have focused attention on groups and their entitlement to preserve and develop their language and culture.[7] This is in addition, of course, to similar developments in individual nation-states.

The People's Republic offers a valuable case study of a country that has since its inception in 1949 provided a legal framework for recognition of collective minority rights. That year, the seminal Common Program of the Chinese People's Political Consultative Conference declared that "all national minorities shall have freedom to develop their dialects and languages, to preserve or reform their traditions, customs and religious beliefs."[8] All four of China's constitutions enacted since then (in 1954, 1975, 1978, and 1982) have included similar wording, even if this admirable goal was honored more in the breach than the observance during the extremist political movements of the 1950s, 1960s, and 1970s.[9] Since the end of the destructive convulsions of the Cultural Revolution (1966–76), political rhetoric and much of the practice on the ground have once again enshrined this principle, albeit not without controversy.[10]

Perhaps not surprisingly, a recent paper by a senior Chinese social scientist defines "cultural rights" (*wenhuaquan*) in terms that not only explicitly conceptualize the idea in terms of an ethnic collective but also tie it both to China's longstanding minorities policy and to UN rhetoric: "Cultural rights are the rights of an ethnic group [*minzu*] to have their own ethnic culture achieve preservation, protection, and development. This has great significance for measuring ethnic equality and the existence and development of an ethnic group, and for inter-ethnic respect and cohesion. [Cultural rights] are an important component of human rights."[11]

This essay will demonstrate that in terms of the use of and context for folk music in China today, collective and ethnic minority rights are still very much on the agenda, albeit often in very contemporary transformations. Moreover, they are joined by a new sense of individual enterprise and entitlement growing out of the seismic economic, legal, and conceptual upheavals in progress since the 1980s. The potential for conceptual and actual conflict between group and individual rights is well recognized in cultural rights scholarship, as are concomitant issues of cultural change and the fuzziness of cultural boundaries.[12] These issues are certainly illustrated in China as both individuals and certain subaltern groups become ever more able to speak out and as improved infrastructure and the forces of globalization connect communities as never before.

Below, after reviewing pre-1990s thinking on folk music in China, I identify the principal transformative forces of that crucial decade. I then present four major controversies that highlight the unanticipated collisions of values, assumptions, and rights arising as folk music finds new roles in China's breakneck rush toward modernization and globalization. Finally, I suggest lessons we can learn from the Chinese experience and ways in which that experience intersects with lines of thought in the broader international discourse on cultural rights.

Conceptual Environment of the 1950s–80s

China's folk music traditions have seldom existed in immutable isolation. The country has a long history of the literatus collection of folksongs and of the creative adaptation of traditional music materials—be it villagers improvising new words to preexisting folksong melodies, regional opera forms developing out of folksong predecessors, or European-influenced art music composers of the early twentieth century incorporating local influences into their works.[13] Such processes continued apace on the mainland after the establishment of the People's Republic in 1949: state-employed musicologists went out to record traditional music from 1950 on, with many of their recordings now held in the Music Research Institute in Beijing;[14] local cultural cadres collected folk music of their regions, to be transformed into professionalized stage and propaganda performances by the dozens of song and dance troupes that sprang up throughout the country during the 1950s;[15] professional Western-influenced composers continued to draw on folk materials for inspiration; and many of the propaganda songs that became nationally popular during the 1950s and 1960s took their origins from folksongs.[16] As discussed in detail below, such uses of traditional musics were underpinned by a socialist ideology that privileged communal creation, discouraged individual ownership and profit-making, favored production of catchy propaganda ditties, and tended to view folk music as raw material waiting to be improved by conservatory-trained composers. Consequently, before the 1990s, these practices were generally taken for granted and seldom problematized—at least in published utterances.

To give some sense of the general atmosphere regarding the origination and use of folk music that obtained from 1949 through much of the 1980s, I provide several representative comments by people involved in its study and adaptation. First, from the standard dictionary of Chinese music published in Beijing in 1985 comes a definition of folksong: "Folksongs . . . are an art form communally created by the laboring people in order to express their thoughts and feelings. . . . They have been elaborated through oral transmission down the generations of the masses."[17] To underline an obvious but important point here, the presence of named individual creativity within this quintessential genre of the people is downplayed, despite the well-documented role of individual style, adaptation, idiosyncrasy, and sometimes outright invention in many regional traditions.[18] A number of major reference works of the 1960s and 1980s present folksong transcriptions without naming the singers from whom they were presumably collected.[19] Such anonymizing of folk performers is far from universal, but its prevalence in some influential tomes of this era accords with the tone of the dictionary entry above and with the more general socialist emphasis on the collective rather than on the individual.

Second, there is an intriguing request for advice in a letter mailed to the national journal *Renmin yinyue* [People's music] in 1953 by Liu Tieshan, later leader of the Central Nationalities Song and Dance Troupe. Sent to the southwest to collect folk music of local ethnic minorities for use in compositions praising Communist Party leaders and the new socialist life of the minorities, Liu and his colleagues encountered some practical difficulties: Should they stick to the style of a single ethnic group in this multi-ethnic region? How should they resolve use of Han Chinese language with minority musical style? Which language should they use when performing the songs of one ethnic group to members of another?[20] To state the obvious again, broader questions as to what members of those minorities would consider culturally appropriate uses of the music collected are not raised—quite understandably, given the historical context.

Third is a brief comment by ethnomusicologist Du Yaxiong, speaking in 1992 on the limitations he saw in mainland Chinese music research before that date: "[M]usicologist[s'] main aim is to [serve] composers. . . . They . . . fail to record the cultural background of the musical pieces." [21] Along these lines, the introduction to a standard textbook on folksong published in 1982 offers fascinating insights under the heading "The Purpose, Meaning, and Method of Studying and Researching Folksong." The very first point made is that "studying and researching folksongs is very important, both with regard to *professional composition* and with regard to vocal and instrumental performance work," although "professional music workers should not limit their studying and research on folksong just to *their own composition* and performance activities" [my emphasis]. Such research, the author adds, can also make a contribution to Marxist culture and arts theory.[22]

This final comment segues neatly into the general thrust of the last musicological source I wish to quote here. A landmark textbook on Chinese folk and traditional music, first published in 1964, summarizes the officially endorsed philosophy of the era:

> Carrying forward the heritage of Chinese music [*minzu yinyue*] with a discriminating eye will not only result in many fine traditional works being arranged in order to serve the people today; even more important is innovation and creativity, so as to develop a socialist new Chinese music. . . . If we want to use [Chinese music] to express the new life of socialism, the new ideology and new feelings . . ., then we must boldly instigate innovation and creativity, while at the same time paying attention to preserving its characteristics. This will cause the form of traditional Chinese music to achieve continuous development, enrichment, and improvement; it will always be vigorously striding forward, keeping pace with the times.[23]

The implication here, that unvarnished folk music as created by the masses needs improvement in order to serve socialist ends, springs directly from the thoughts of the most influential theorist of them all, Mao Zedong. Mao's famous "Talks at the Yan'an Forum on Literature and Art," given in 1942, were reprinted numerous times between 1943 and 1966 and provided a strong ideological referent for national arts developments after 1949.[24] In the "Talks," Mao underlines the need for "a cultural as well as an armed front" in the Communist forces and for the subordination of literature and art to politics, thus strongly endorsing the use of the arts in propaganda, as we might expect.[25] Perhaps more surprising to Western readers, he also characterizes the workers, peasants, and soldiers privileged by his ideology as "illiterate, ignorant, and uncultured" and professional cultural cadres as "on a higher level," "helping and guiding" the uncultured masses.[26] This explicit disparagement of folk arts as found in their "unimproved" form among the people and the concomitant urge to "raise standards" have exerted a powerful influence ever since in public rhetoric, state institutions, and urban middle class culture.[27]

Given this background, it is perhaps not surprising that when I arrived at the Shanghai Conservatory of Music in 1987 as a graduate student, variants on these themes appeared to be standard thinking among many students, faculty, and ordinary people I encountered. Most people, other than the aficionados themselves, appeared to view local Chinese folk music as "backward" (*luohou*), "unscientific" (*bu kexue*), and aesthetically inferior to Western art music or Westernized modern Chinese genres that use the equal-tempered scale and simple functional harmony.[28] There were no commercially available recordings of village performers, and teachers rarely played their own field recordings in class, in part because of apprehension about student response (as one professor freely admitted to my Dutch classmates and myself). Even students majoring in Chinese instruments almost never attended or observed local folk music events, which could be found any day of the week in and around the city. Indeed, as an American observer noted earlier in the 1980s of a famous local folk genre, "Many performers and scholars in professional circles feel that the amateur [Shanghai] *sizhu* musicians are hopelessly conservative, unable to appreciate anything new, and unwilling to see their music develop."[29] Nor do I remember a single discussion in or after class of culturally appropriate use of folk materials or of folk originators' moral rights in what they and their neighbors and ancestors had created.

By contrast, questions of ownership, copyright, and ethical use of folk music materials had already occasioned considerable discussion in the West between the 1950s and the 1980s.[30] In addition, from at least the 1940s on, some quite widely disseminated writings by leading American and European scholars of the day expressed respect and liking for indigenous folk aesthetics of song setting and singing style, along with a firm belief that the way in which a song is sung is integral to its identity.[31] At the same time, China's neighbors to the east, Japan and South Korea, were implementing policies aimed at preserving and encouraging indigenous performing arts in self-consciously traditional rather than Western-influenced form: Japan's Cultural Properties Protection Law was a milestone in the process in 1950, while South Korea adopted a similar law in 1962.[32] Some of my Chinese colleagues active in the 1980s and early 1990s were aware of these developments in the West and in Japan and Korea, and one in particular frequently expressed regret that China was not borrowing from their experience to honor village-based arts and outstanding folk musicians.

Ethnomusicologist Yang Mu, however, relates an anecdote that suggests how difficult it was at the time to critique the status quo. Wishing to point up the contrast between carefully staged performances for a national audience on the one hand and the aesthetics and fate of the *minjian* originals in the villages on the other, he invokes a discourse of authenticity to make a rhetorical point:

> [At the conclusion of] the National Minorities Performing Arts Festival . . . held in Beijing [in October 1980], . . . I was invited, with a group of scholars, teachers and students in the field of ethnic music study, to a meeting organized by the authorities, to comment on the festival for media publicity. . . . While acknowledging the success of the festival, . . . I pointed out that these performances should not be declared by the authorities to be authentic folk arts from the people's real lives. They were actually professional theatrical products, though based more or less on raw materials obtained from real folk arts. The items were professional compositions and were performed by professional artists. While the government was spending enormous sums of money to promote this kind of art, . . . the real folk arts in ordinary people's daily lives were dying out and could not obtain government support.[33]

Not surprisingly, Yang was informed that his comments would not be published unless he emended them to fit the government guideline, which he declined to do.[34]

Yang's discourse of authenticity finds far more sympathetic echoes in Chinese publications nowadays, a quarter-century on from the festival he was critiquing. Qiao Jianzhong's recent discussion of the hot-button term "original ecology folksongs" (*yuan shengtai min'ge*) explains clearly the reasons for this transformation: alarmed by the threat to traditional village-based amateur folksinging posed by decades of "processing and modification" (*jiagong xiugai*), rejection, and marginalization, the scholarly world is finally waking up to the warning signs emitted by a beleaguered traditional culture. Just as people in China are now becoming concerned about degradation of the natural environment (figures 2.1 and 2.2), Qiao says, so are they borrowing the idea of environmental balance to apply to the embattled world of traditional music and thus emphasizing the concepts of "original ecology" (*yuan shengtai*), "[continued] existence" (*shengcun*), and "protection" (*baohu*).[35]

Figure 2.1. Billboard in the county seat of Xianggelila County (formerly Zhongdian County), Yunnan Province, March 2007. Slogan reads: "Environmental conservation benefits the nation and the people." (Photo by author)

Figure 2.2. Trilingual sign warning of high fire risk in Tibetan, Chinese, and English. Shangri-La National Park, Pu Dacuo, Xianggelila County (formerly Zhongdian County), Yunnan Province, March 2007. (Photo by author)

Back in the 1980s, however, it was not always easy for a university professor to convince his or her immediate superiors of the value of doing village-based research or of the outstanding artistry of the folk musicians discovered.[36] The notion that folk arts as performed by non-conservatory-trained local people might hold intrinsic cultural value, appeal aesthetically to those beyond their immediate "backward" or "conservative" audiences, or even manifest commercial potential would have surprised many of my Shanghai Conservatory classmates in the late 1980s.

Changes Beginning in the 1990s

Much changed in the 1990s, however. For a start, the extraordinary sounds of China's villages, small towns, rituals, and urban amateur ensembles have become accessible to a far wider audience, outside China as well as inside. As restrictions lessened and private Chinese-foreign cooperation became easier during the 1990s, Chinese scholars wanting an outlet for languishing field recordings forged partnerships with foreign companies. Convinced from the outset of the cultural and aesthetic value of "unimproved" folk music, enterprises such as Pan Records in Leiden, the Netherlands; AIMP in Geneva, Switzerland; Ode Records in New Zealand; Apsara Media in Van Nuys, California; and Wind Records in Taiwan have all issued historic field recordings by Chinese and Western ethnomusicologists alike.[37] In addition, several Western scholars benefited from ever-greater freedom of movement during this decade to research rural genres, publishing books that include audio CDs of previously inaccessible traditions.[38]

Live music, too, has acquired more mobility since the early 1990s. Village-based, ritual, and urban amateur folk and traditional musicians have increasingly been able to accept invitations to tour abroad, achieving a success that has initially perplexed some back home. The Buddhist Music Ensemble of Tianjin, which toured Britain and the Netherlands in fall 1993 (figure 2.3), was one of the first such groups to achieve international acclaim and record a CD in a foreign studio.[39] They were followed by many others, including the Suzhou Taoists who visited England and Belgium in 1994 (figure 2.4) and the spectacularly successful amateur Dayan Ancient Music Association (*Dayan guyuehui*) of Lijiang. These ethnically Naxi musicians made their first foreign trip to England, courtesy of Asian Music Circuit, in October 1995 and subsequently visited many other European and Asian countries and Seattle (figure 2.5).[40]

More recently, the splendid Hua Family Shawm Band from a village in northern Shanxi Province participated in the Smithsonian Folklife Festival of the Silk Road in summer 2002 and performed in England and the Netherlands in 2005, earning a wildly enthusiastic reception.[41] The prestigious Amsterdam China Festival, held in October 2005, featured the Hua Family Shawm Band, a Taoist group from Shanxi, an amateur urban *Jiangnan sizhu* ensemble from Shanghai, and village musicians from Yunnan, alongside professional state troupes and pop musicians, thus underlining the aesthetic validity of these indigenous local traditions in the eyes of the Dutch organizers.[42]

While most Chinese ethnomusicologists have never needed to be convinced of the intrinsic merits of such genres and their performers, the prestige of foreign success has often proved helpful in persuading officials and other Chinese citizens that there is something special, or at least useful, about them. This has helped ignite a new discourse of value (cultural, commercial, and propagandistic) in relation to folk music. For example, according to He Jiaxiu, a Communist Party official in Lijiang, before the Dayan Ancient Music Association's now legendary concert tour of England in 1995, many locals

Figure 2.3. Map of China. (Created by Jack Bishop on the basis of an original by Inne Choi.)

Figure 2.4. Publicity poster by England's Asian Music Circuit for the 1993 concert tour of the Suzhou Taoist Music Troupe. (Photo by author)

Figure 2.5. Publicity poster by England's Asian Music Circuit for the 1995 concert tour of the Dayan Ancient Music Association of Lijiang. (Photo by author)

derided their tradition as "a few old guys on their way out playing old tunes on their way out."[43] After the trip, when the previously amateur association became a multimillion-yuan-a-year enterprise that engendered huge prestige for Lijiang and the Naxi, local attitudes changed drastically, and many young people started learning the music. The general atmosphere of greater appreciation for folk arts has also resulted in what senior ethnomusicologist Qiao Jianzhong terms a "folksong craze" (*min'ge re*) evident since 2004, as television channels have shown programs and competitions featuring non-conservatory-trained village folksingers.[44]

Along with these developments have come several more, including the showcasing of local folk arts to entertain tourists, even in quite remote parts of China, and the borrowing of folk music elements in commercially successful popular music.[45] Most startling of all, starting in the early 1990s, magazines such as *Renmin yinyue* [People's music] were suddenly full of discussions of copyright, perceived infringement of cultural rights in the adaptation of traditional songs, and, lately, lawsuits relating to the use of traditional musical materials.

What caused this abrupt turnaround in attitudes toward local folk arts? I would suggest three major factors: first, the introduction in 1991 of mainland China's copyright law, which for the first time offered legal protection to creators and adaptors of musical and other works and to performers; second, the rapid development of the market economy, which has injected the possibility for individual and community profit-making, occasionally on a massive scale, into the artistic scene; and, third, a growing appreciation in intellectual and government circles of the value of local musics in their original folk forms—especially as many genres become threatened through the spread of mass media, youth indifference, and transmission crises caused by the Cultural Revolution and other extremist political movements of the 1950s and 1960s. This appreciation is certainly fostered by the prestige afforded traditional genres worldwide through UNESCO's recent program to recognize "masterpieces of the oral and intangible heritage of humanity," in which China has enthusiastically participated.

All these factors are underlaid by the general political, economic, and social liberalization underway since the late 1970s. This has, for example, made it acceptable for many traditional rituals to be celebrated in public—a huge benefit to local music, which is usually an integral part of religious festivals and life-cycle rituals.[46] The same liberalization has made it easier to voice critical opinions and enter into public disputes on the arts and has facilitated travel overseas for ordinary Chinese citizens—including rural folk artists.

Copyright, the Market Economy, and Intangible Cultural Heritage

Copyright Law

While China had dipped its toe into copyright protection as early as 1910, the first copyright law in the People's Republic was adopted only on September 7, 1990, becoming effective on June 1, 1991.[47] It covers "works" including "musical works, operatic and dramatic works, works of *quyi* [oral narrative genres] and choreographic works." Article 6 adds that "measures for the protection of copyrights in folk literary and artistic work shall be formulated separately by the State Council," although by mid-2003 in practice this had still not happened.[48] Overall, a commentator writing in *Renmin yinyue* [People's music] in 1994 concludes that "none of [the] regulations can resolve the question of copyright ownership in folk music, because what the 'Copyright Law' protects is principally professional artistic works and the legally allowable rights and interests of their copyright holders, not folk artistic works."[49]

Nevertheless, the law is not without potential benefits to people involved in various ways with folk music. For instance, of significance to collectors and arrangers of folk materials, Article 12 in this 1991 law extends protections not just to composers but also to those who adapt, translate, annotate, or collate preexisting works, provided that exercise of their right does not prejudice copyright in the original work.[50] In addition, all performers are given some protections, including provision that parties wishing to reproduce and distribute sound or video recordings need a license from the performer(s).[51] Revisions made to the law in 2001 include new clauses giving performers the right "to authorize others to reproduce or distribute sound recordings and video recordings incorporating the performance, and to receive remuneration therefor," and "to authorize others to communicate the performance to the public on information networks, and to receive remuneration therefor."[52] The performers thus protected presumably include village folk musicians.

Perhaps more significant than exactly what the law does and does not cover is its effect on people's thinking. It did not take long after 1991 for concerns over copyright and exploitation to become a hot topic among numerous scholars, composers, folk and professional performers, and others working in the realm of traditional music.[53] The backdrop to these concerns, of course, was the rapid development of China's market economy.

Folk Music and the Market Economy

In 1978, following the death of Mao and the end of the disastrous Cultural Revolution two years earlier, the Third Plenary Session of the Eleventh Chinese Communist Party Central Committee set in motion a gradually accelerating agricultural, economic, and social liberalization. Thirty years on, China's meteoric economic rise makes daily headlines, private entrepreneurship at all levels is ubiquitous, and the country is inundated with electronic gadgets. The effects of these changes on folk arts, many of which had been seriously damaged by the political campaigns of the 1950s, 1960s, and 1970s, were multifarious. In some cases, the easy availability since the 1980s of popular culture via television, boom box, and VCD (video compact disc) has turned a generation of young people away from local traditional culture; in addition, the ability to make money in private ventures has lessened leisure time to indulge in learning complex repertoires. Other genres, by contrast, that were traditionally performed on a paid basis and had become attenuated in the decades following 1949 suddenly became viable again as the market economy gradually took hold; local demand for the services of the Hua Family Shawm Band from the late 1970s on is a good example of this.[54] And as personal incomes began to improve through much of the country in the 1980s, more people had the wherewithal to patronize temples and lay ritual groups, leading to a resurgence in some forms of religious and paraliturgical music.

In addition to the revival of longstanding forms of patronage for some folk musics, however, there was soon a new and increasingly significant player in the folk arts economy. The tourist industry sputtered into life in the late 1970s, as a few hundred thousand adventurous foreigners tested the waters; it then grew steadily through the 1980s and early 1990s and has exploded since the last few years of the twentieth century as more and more Chinese citizens are able to travel for pleasure (figure 2.6).[55] As in other countries, there has been a concomitant demand for local entertainment and handicrafts to serve the visitors. Already in the mid-1980s, tourist concerts by professional, state-run ensembles were well established in large cities: performing their Western-influenced, modernized version of Chinese music, groups such as the Tang Dynasty Chang'an Music and Dance Troupe in Xi'an and the Shanghai Chinese Orchestra tailored programs especially for foreign guests.[56]

By the late 1980s, there were also stirrings of private entrepreneurship in this field. Ethnomusicologist Frederick Lau reports on the amateur Chaozhou traditional musicians in northeast Guangdong Province, who gathered most afternoons at this time to play for locals and tourists. They had an eye for overseas Chaozhounese who might feel nostalgia for the local music of their ancestral home and in particular for visitors who would donate money to help the group keep going.[57] Such local amateur groups, notes Lau, "are consciously playing up their local identity and emphasizing the folk-like style of their music and demeanor."[58]

Perhaps the most famous example of a local amateur folk group that saw the potential of tourist concerts is one already mentioned above: the Dayan Ancient Music Association of Lijiang County in northwest Yunnan Province, near the Tibetan border. Starting in summer 1988, these ethnically Naxi musicians cleverly put together a concert package that showcased deliberately un-modernized renderings of their beautiful local Dongjing ensemble repertoire, now renamed "Naxi Ancient Music" (*Naxi guyue*).[59] Their performances

Figure 2.6. Advertisement on Huaihai Central Road, Shanghai, December 2007. Directed at both Chinese and foreigners, it offers travel to the exotic destination of Tibet. (Photo by author)

retained the delicate heterophony, distinctively local instruments, and regionally inflected playing style long typical of the tradition; to this, they added a romantic setting in an old mansion, a witty English-language commentary by their charismatic leader, Xuan Ke, and a twin emphasis on their preservation of Chinese musical tradition and their exotic Naxi ethnicity. The concerts were an immediate hit with the foreign tourists visiting Lijiang and, as mentioned above, led to numerous overseas tours in the late 1990s (figure 2.7). By the early twenty-first century, the Dayan Ancient Music Association, now mainly serving domestic tourists, is big business, with a sophisticated Web site dedicated to news of the association, its music, and its leader.[60]

The role of folk and other traditional performing arts in the tourist business is a hot topic in many musicological journals, magazines, and newspapers today. Much of the commentary concentrates on how local music can be used to promote the charms of an area. Quite early on, a report for the town government written by members of the Dayan Ancient Music Association emphasized this point: in preserving, disseminating, and researching their local Dongjing music repertoire, they aimed "to help in the construction of socialist spiritual culture in Lijiang, and in the construction of material civilization; to improve the visibility of the renowned historical

Figure 2.7. Tourist concert by the Naxi musicians of the Dayan Ancient Music Association in Lijiang, May 1992. (Photo by author)

town [that is, Dayan Town]; and to contribute to the vigorous development of Lijiang's economy."[61]

The efficacy of this local Lijiang music as a tourist attraction and a means to improve the area's name-recognition was stressed a few years later in a local arts magazine by the prefectural Communist Party Propaganda Bureau chief He Jiaxiu, who had accompanied the musicians to England.[62] Inspired by the Lijiang musicians' success, many other local governments in Yunnan have sought to showcase their local Dongjing musicians—and in some cases performers of other genres too—to promote their areas.[63] Sometimes this has involved "gentrifying" the music into a less "folk" sound considered more acceptable to middle-class urban Chinese tourists; in other cases, the original flavor has been retained.

In the latter case, one may find the rhetoric of environmental and cultural purity conflated, in ways that remind us of Qiao Jianzhong's deconstruction of the term "original ecology folksong" (*yuan shengtai min'ge*). From Xinjiang Uyghur Autonomous Region in northwest China comes the following anecdote:

> The notion of an unpolluted natural environment as a sustainable asset for the tourist industry is also being introduced into the preservation of intangible ex-

> pressive arts. Concepts such as "primordial" (*yuansheng*) and "uncontaminated/pure" (*chunzheng*) are increasingly in vogue in the revival of minority cultural traditions through touristy performances and recreated festivals. For example, the most high-profile tourist show in northwest China in 2005—held at the Grand Bazaar, the hub of [the] Uyghur neighborhood in southern Urumchi—incorporated for the first time an ensemble of four Uyghur-Dolan amateur rural musicians from southwestern Xinjiang. They were told to dress in their most traditional costumes, performing their most indigenous musical styles with their instruments in the most authentic forms, to groups of cosmopolitan tourists from mainland China and foreign countries. Often perceived as coarse and uncivilized by the urban Uyghur, this repertoire, represented in this way, signifies the purity and genuineness of Uyghur heritage, something the tourist industry increasingly demands.[64]

Yunnan and Xinjiang, while considered among the most exotic domestic holiday destinations, are not the only regions where the use of folk music is advocated to promote tourism. Two tourism professors and a music professor from Shanxi University in northern China recently set out detailed suggestions for employing "cleaned up" versions of local folk music to supplement Shanxi Province's ten-year plan for tourism development.[65] CDs, VCDs, and small-scale models of local musical instruments would make wonderful souvenirs, they note. And they are probably correct: many other regions successfully exploit their local musical traditions in this manner (figures 2.8 and 2.9). The economic potential of the folk arts is in fact widely recognized. China's 2002 report to the World Intellectual Property Organization on folklore protection and legislation notes that "[s]ome regions have based their development efforts on their distinctive culture, which in turn brings along cultural industries, to promote both economic growth and cultural development."[66] Along just these lines, in May 2008, the heavily tourism-dependent province of Yunnan celebrated International Labor Day with a huge "cultural tourism festival" (*wenhua lüyou jie*). This showcased performers and food from the region in the provincial capital of Kunming (figure 2.10).

While folk music can be exploited to promote the tourist industry, some Chinese commentators—like their counterparts in many other countries—warn of the loss of cultural meaning when traditional culture is commercialized.[67] A few take a more optimistic approach, however. Ethnomusicologist Liu Yong reports on a fascinating example of "cultural tourism" (*wenhua lüyou*) in Zhaoxing Township, Liping County, Guizhou Province. This traditionally poor southwestern region is inhabited by the Dong ethnic group, who have long been famous for their choral folksongs (*ga lao* in the Dong language, better known by the Chinese term *dage*), which have recently be-

Figure 2.8. Souvenirs of Uyghur musical instruments on sale to tourists in Urumchi, Xinjiang, summer 2005. (Photo by Chuen-Fung Wong)

Figure 2.9. Conflation of natural wonders with local music at a major tourist attraction: a huge model of the iconic *sa'xian* plucked lute of the Sani ethnic group stands in front of the famed Sani homeland, the Stone Forest. Lin Youren poses for scale. Tourist performances by Sani folk artists are frequently given in the Stone Forest. Shilin County (formerly Lu'nan County), Yunnan Province, April 2008. (Photo by author)

Figure 2.10. Dancers dressed in stage versions of ethnic Yi attire perform at Jinbi Square, central Kunming, for the 2008 China Kunming International Cultural and Tourism Festival, May 2008. (Photo by author)

come a big tourist draw—so much so, Liu suggests, that "if the *dage* were to become attenuated, there would be a serious adverse impact on the development of the Dong tourism industry."[68] To keep up with demand, the head of the township's cultural station, himself a fine Dong musician, organizes classes at his office and in local schools to ensure that young people learn the tradition. Each year he sends about a hundred singers out to perform in hotels, retaining a band of around twenty close to home to service the tourism industry in the township's main village.[69] Opportunities to sing are actually greater than previously, Liu notes, since performance for visitors is added to traditional contexts; thus, "the development of the tourism industry has not only not caused Dong song transmission to fall into dire straits, on the contrary it has opened up new avenues for transmission."[70] It has also changed the manner of transmission, since the songs are now taught in schools rather than privately by a song master. Whereas before transmission was purely oral, now cipher notation is used, and the words are written down.[71] Debate over what happens to "original ecology folksongs" when they encounter new environments like this is a major topic of conversation at present in China and is intimately related to the growing fascination there with the concepts of intangible cultural heritage and cultural survival.[72]

Intangible Cultural Heritage

Concern over the likely attenuation or total demise of many folk genres was widespread among local traditional musicians and sympathetic scholars and officials with whom I worked in Yunnan Province in the early 1990s. It became clear that many genres throughout China—such as ritual music and some love songs—had been intermittently or totally disrupted through political movements in the first thirty years of Communist rule, thus breaking the all-important chain of transmission. Just as important, from the early 1980s on, as transport improved and TV and popular culture increased their impact even in rural regions, many young people who might otherwise have taken up local traditional arts instead disdained them as old-fashioned and dull.[73] Up through the early 1990s, this problem was not a particularly hot topic in the scholarly or popular press, but things have changed remarkably in the last few years. As noted above, just as concern over environmental degradation has been on the rise in China, so has discussion of protection of traditional culture.[74]

Perhaps most high-profile have been several international symposia held in Beijing and some major international collaborative projects. Spring 2003, for instance, saw the Asia-Europe Training Programme on Preservation of Traditional Music, which involved participants from twenty countries discussing case studies, methodology, archives, education, and legal issues. The foreword to the program report, by Xiao Mei, a prominent ethnomusicologist who was at the time deputy director of the Music Research Institute of the Chinese Academy of Arts, expresses succinctly some major issues with which she and her colleagues in China and elsewhere contend in the early twenty-first century: "[T]raditional music is undergoing rapid disappearing due to various factors such as globalization, rapid social changes with urbanization, adoption of written form in the education system etc. . . . There is therefore an urgency to protect, promote and preserve the transmission of traditional music."[75]

Later in 2003, an International Symposium on Preservation of the Arts Heritage of Chinese Ethnic Groups and Development of Contemporary Arts was held in Beijing, with a UNESCO representative as a major speaker and approximately 120 participants. I was fortunate enough to be invited to attend and was thus able both to hear the formal papers and to take part in the more informal discussions. Chinese participants included scholars and officials not only from Beijing-based institutions but also from provincial, prefectural, and county-level organizations. They were also ethnically diverse: over twenty of the Chinese citizens present were members of ethnic groups other than the majority Han Chinese. Many of the formal papers expressed an urgent need to find ways to protect and preserve traditional arts in different parts of China; a few papers by foreigners reported on projects conducted in other Asian/Pacific countries such as South Korea, Vietnam, and Vanuatu, providing food for comparative thought.[76]

Among Chinese speakers, there was a remarkable ferment of ideas, considerable awareness of international developments, and some sophisticated critiques of the domestic situation. At least two speakers brought up the problem of the long-term denigration of "unimproved" local folk music as "backward" (*luohou*) and of rural dwellers as "having no culture" (*meiyou wenhua*), and the deleterious effects of such labeling on people's self-esteem and regard for their local culture. Xiao Mei stressed the need to give a voice to the tradition-bearers themselves and for scholars to be self-critical in their work. Ma Tieying of the Arts College of Inner Mongolia raised the issues of using bel canto singing style for Mongolian music at his institution and of his school's tendency to teach most courses, even on Mongolian music, in Chinese. A number of papers discussed the advantages and disadvantages of exploiting traditional arts in the tourism industry.

Moving to a more international level of discussion, several Chinese speakers wanted one of their local performing arts to be nominated for the 2005 round of UNESCO's "Proclamation of the Masterpieces of the Oral and Intangible Heritage of Humanity," and a couple of participants expressed concern over the possibility that neighboring countries might get in first with cross-border genres. The closing speaker, Zhang Qingshan, vice president of the Chinese Academy of Arts, made several important points. He noted that recent UNESCO recognition of the Chinese classical opera Kunqu and seven-string zither *qin* as "Masterpieces of the Oral and Intangible Heritage of Humanity" had caused Chinese people to realize what intangible cultural heritage is and to see its value; he also commented on the concept of intellectual property and suggested that in many ways, Japan and South Korea have done a better job with preservation of traditional culture than China.[77] Perhaps most remarkable of all, the concert put on for the symposium included amateur folk performers of the Dong and Uyghur ethnic groups brought specially from their villages as well as the standard fare of state-supported song and dance troupes performing professionally staged numbers that one would normally expect at such an occasion.

International recognition and success have long been both desired outcomes and influential motivators in the Chinese cultural sphere, and Zhang Qingshan was surely correct in suggesting that UNESCO's "Masterpieces" program has heightened awareness in China of the existence and value of traditional arts. Certainly there has been a rash of initiatives in the last few years that exemplify a newly energized approach to the country's traditional cultural heritage. These initiatives have appeared at national, provincial, and local levels. National-level projects have included the digitization of historical recordings held by the Music Research Institute, funded largely by UNESCO and carried out with the technical assistance of the Vienna Phonogrammarchiv.[78] More eye-catching for the general public have been the State Council's recent designation of the second Saturday of June as annual "Cultural Heritage Day" and an exhibition in Beijing in early 2006 of intangible heritage from all over the country.[79]

While national-level projects are of course especially visible, it is perhaps the provincial- and even county-level undertakings that are most interesting and may signal a more thoroughgoing rethinking of values. In May 2000, for instance, Yunnan Province became the first region to issue regulations on traditional folk culture, seeking both to encourage and protect folk arts and to set up "ethnic traditional culture protected areas" (*chuantong wenhua baohu qu*).[80] Another recent tactic in Yunnan has been to bestow the name "home of *x*" on an area, picking the most distinctive local artistic form, and to confer the title "ethnic folk art transmitter" (*minzu minjian yishu chuancheng ren*) on outstanding local tradition-bearers.[81] And in a very significant move, the Yunnan Art Institute has experimented with implementing the principle of "nativization" (*bentuhua*) in its teaching of music, eschewing "Western-centric pedagogic concepts," since "for a long time, the mainstream of China's elite arts education has been Westernized, with the native artistic resources of each ethnic group scarcely getting a look-in."[82] In 2005, in a departure unthinkable just fifteen years previously, professors at the institute invited folk musicians into the classroom to give performance demonstrations and thus expose students to local folk arts and their aesthetic as actually found among the ordinary people.[83]

County-level officials too sometimes take initiatives to protect and use their local music. In early 2002, the government of Youyang County, a remote southwestern area under the governance of Chongqing City, invited nine specialists from Beijing's Music Research Institute (MRI) to document the rich musical heritage of the local Tujia ethnic group and to discuss their policy of "a county built on culture" (*wenhua li xian*). Suggestions from the specialists ranged from how to publicize their unique musical heritage (including creating a Web page), through the necessity of maintaining the cultural environment of the music, to paying elderly folk artists to teach their traditions. The MRI scholar who wrote up the trip also raised the possibility of using cultural properties as an economic mainstay and commented quite perspicaciously that "ethnic culture is often a non-renewable resource, but also has great [economic] development value."[84] He noted, in addition, that Youyang County was not the only one to have invited MRI specialists to give advice: apparently Taijiang County in Guizhou Province, a stronghold of the Miao (Hmong) ethnic group, did the same thing.[85]

A number of remarkable grassroots initiatives have also sprung up in the first decade of the twenty-first century to document, protect, and gain respect for local or ethnic heritages perceived as endangered. Tibetan students at Qinghai Normal University, for example, enthusiastically participate in the Tibetan Endangered Music Project: assisted by anthropology professor Gerald Roche and donations of money and equipment, they use their vacations to fan out and record the rapidly disappearing folk music of their home regions.[86] In eastern Gansu, as of 2007 a village school had invited local shadow puppet troupe members into their classrooms to teach the children to perform the tradition, since the teachers and local officials valued it highly and feared for its future.[87]

Controversies and Court Cases

With all the new developments described above, it was inevitable that some people engaged in performance, research, arrangement, and economic exploitation of folk music would encounter collisions of interest amid the new awareness of copyright, marketability, and the cultural capital of intangible cultural heritage. Indeed, such collisions of interest prove excellent bellwethers for the newly evolved climate in which Chinese traditional music exists today. Below, I outline four major sets of controversies and court cases that have achieved national discussion and set precedents since the mid-1990s.

The Wang Luobin Controversy

Perhaps most notorious in the mid-1990s was the national debate on the actions of the Beiping-educated Han Chinese composer Wang Luobin (1913–96), who in the 1930s began adapting, re-composing, and fitting new words to folksongs he collected from Turkic groups in the northwest. He continued doing this for many decades, and some of his songs became extremely popular throughout China.[88] For years, nobody objected publicly to his activities, which were quite the norm at the time. The controversy that bedeviled his last years was ignited when he licensed some of his songs for commercial use in Taiwan. It soon became known in Beijing and northwest China that Wang was thus claiming copyright in the songs and stood to make a fair amount of money from the deal. No lawsuit resulted, but the resulting polemic scorched the pages of *Renmin yinyue* [People's music], *Zhongguo yinyue* [Chinese music], and other journals and newspapers for many months in 1994 and 1995.

Some of the most enraged commentary came from people belonging to those Turkic ethnic groups whose songs Wang had adapted. They objected to an outsider profiting from their cultural patrimony, to what they considered his distortions of the texts, and, in the case of the Kazakhs, to his culturally inaccurate assumption that Kazakh folksongs did not have individually named creators, whose work he had thus plagiarized. One Kazakh scholar, Yimannali, demanded that Wang return any profits from his Kazakh-inspired songs to the Kazakhs and apologize to the Kazakh people.[89]

A particularly pertinent factor in the Wang Luobin scandal was historical context. As leading Chinese ethnomusicologist Tian Liantao notes, different standards of documentation and different concepts of transcription and arrangement prevailing in the 1940s and 1950s made it hard even for Wang himself to determine the nature of his creative input into each of his songs. Furthermore, the unconscious practices of those decades were certainly out of step with the sensibilities of the 1990s, when ethnic minorities were more able to assert their identities and demand their rights.[90] Moreover, some minority commentators admitted that their own views of Wang's work had changed over time and with circumstance: in the 1950s, they had felt pride that their songs were being disseminated to the rest of the country, but when it became obvious forty years on that publishers, performers, and Wang himself were now making money from them, they felt very differently.[91]

Guo Song and the Hezhe Folksongs

Wang Luobin certainly spent a disagreeable few months being vilified in the national musicological press for his personal exploitation of northwestern folksongs, but he escaped a lawsuit. Several years later, however, the popular singer Guo Song, together with the television company CCTV and Beijing North Star Shopping Center, found themselves the defendants in a copyright infringement suit brought by the Sipai Hezhe Nationality Township government of Raohe County, Heilongjiang Province, in China's far northeast. The plaintiff alleged that Guo Song's highly successful song "Wusuli Boat Song" (*Wusuli chuan'ge*) was based on folksongs of the Hezhe ethnic minority of Sipai Township but that he was claiming it as his own original composition and additionally that CCTV and the shopping center also profited from the song through the sale of products such as VCDs.[92] The Beijing Second Intermediate Court asked the Music Copyright Association of China for a technical analysis of the songs; three experts participated and agreed that

"Wusuli Boat Song" was indeed adapted from Hezhe folksong melodies. In December 2002, the court held that Guo Song could enjoy copyright as one of the composers of the song but that he and CCTV must clearly indicate that it was based on the Hezhe folksongs, that the Beijing North Star Shopping Center must desist from selling all publications that lacked that identification, and that the defendants must pay the plaintiff's legal expenses. The court did not support the plaintiff's demand for further monetary compensation.[93]

Two interesting precedents were set by this case. First, the principle embodied in the copyright laws of 1991 and 2001 that works of folk literature have copyright protection was upheld. This was despite the fact that as of mid-2003, the State Council had still not issued regulations as required by the law for such protection. Second, while there was as yet no clear provision as to who would have the right to represent the owners of folk arts whose copyright was infringed, the court decided that in the case of an ethnic minority, the local government of a minority area could act as the plaintiff in its capacity as political representative of a part of that minority.[94]

Sadly, as with the Wang Luobin case, Guo's version of the song had been around for several decades and had even received the approbation of the Hezhe, who turned against Guo when he claimed it as his own composition in a very public and possibly profitable forum.[95] Ever the astute commentator, ethnomusicologist Tian Liantao underlines again for his readers the crucial importance of distinguishing between original composition and arrangement—not always clearly marked in China—and endorses the court's judgement.[96]

The Curious Case of the Folksong That Wasn't

Perhaps the oddest recent copyright dispute of all concerns one of the most charming songs known throughout China today, "Xiaohe tang shui" (The babbling brook).[97] With a flowing, lyrical melody based on a pentatonic scale, its words depict a girl calling to her lover. It appears on a popular audio compilation, the third CD of *Zhongguo min'ge jinqu* [Golden Hits of Chinese Folk Songs] (1994), on which it is listed as a "Yunnan folksong." In volume 2 of the standard four-volume anthology of Chinese folksongs, *Zhongguo min'ge,* the song's origin is given as Midu, a county in west-central Yunnan.[98] The first time the song appeared in print seems to have been in 1951, when it was included in an anthology of Yunnan folksongs and identified as a Midu song. This attribution stuck to it as it achieved national popularity in the mid-1950s, thanks to its promotion by the famous Yunnanese singer Huang Hong.[99]

There matters rested for some decades. However, in 1994, a strange series of events was set in motion, which ultimately overturned everything everyone thought they knew about this song. It all started in May 1994, when Yin Yigong, a general editor of the Yunnan Nationalities Press, submitted a request to the provincial copyright bureau for acknowledgment of his rights in the song. In January 1997, the bureau issued a document recognizing him as the "collector and arranger" (*shouji zhengli*). Yin explained that "Xiaohe tang shui" was not a Midu folksong pure and simple but one that had gone through a process of "adaptation" (*gaibian*). All was quiet for over three years, until in July 2000, Gao Liang, the composer of another song, "Da tian zaiyang yang lian yang" (Transplanting seedlings in the fields), lodged an appeal with the copyright bureau, stating that the music of "Xiaohe tang shui" had been adapted from his own song, which he had composed in 1943. It wasn't a Midu folksong at all, he averred. At this point, as commentator Tian Liantao notes succinctly, "a protracted copyright dispute ensued."[100]

Tian summarizes in masterly fashion the convoluted story he uncovered. From the evidence of several witnesses, it appears that in 1943, Gao Liang did indeed compose his song and that it did not directly borrow from any local folksongs—although, ironically, the opening melodic phrase was inspired by a Mongolian folksong published in the contemporary magazine *Xin yinyue* [New music]. Next, in 1947, Yin Yigong apparently jotted Gao's melody down, not knowing it was Gao's work, when a friend of his sang it without the words. After arranging it and fitting words to it, he produced "Xiaohe tang shui." Finally, singer Huang Hong and another local arranger, Lin Zhiyin, added more words and put some finishing touches to the tune, resulting in the version widely known today. Strong proof that the famous song did not originate in Midu is provided by the fact that song collectors have repeatedly failed to find the melody in the repertoire of local village folksingers.[101] After running through the relevant articles of China's copyright law, Tian suggests that any income from the song should be divided, with Gao Liang, the "original composer," getting one-third; Yin Yigong, the "adapter of the words and music," one-half; and Huang Hong and Lin Zhiyin, "authors of the lyrics to the second section," splitting the final one-sixth between them. Noting that all four contributed to the making of this song, and thus have all rendered a service to the Chinese people, Tian urges the two parties to the dispute to adopt an objective and impartial attitude and to bring their disagreement to a "friendly and decorous conclusion."[102]

Once again, Tian is sensitive to historical context, noting that owing to the unusual circumstances of the war, it was not possible in 1943 for Gao Liang's original song to be formally published; instead, it and others he had composed slipped into common currency among the people via oral transmission and hand-copied manuscripts. Nobody here was committing deliberate plagiarism, Tian stresses; the strange situation was the product of historical circumstance.[103]

This case turns the usual situation on its head: rather than folk originators demanding redress from collector-arrangers, as we have seen with the Wang Luobin controversy and the Hezhe lawsuit, here we have a composer battling for his rights to an original composition erroneously supposed to be a folksong with no known creator. That he only bothered to do so five decades after his work slipped into the de facto public domain speaks volumes for the multiple paradigm shifts engendered through China's post–Cultural Revolution reforms. As an unintended consequence, what could have turned into one of the country's biggest musicological mysteries has been solved, thanks to the motivation and mechanisms provided by the market economy.

The Many Lawsuits of Xuan Ke

Finally, I turn to the one musician and the one traditional folk music genre that seem to have generated the greatest amount of rancorous debate and the largest number of lawsuits. As noted above, one of the most commercially successful of all Chinese traditional musics is that purveyed as "Naxi Ancient Music" by the Dayan Ancient Music Association of Lijiang County, northwest Yunnan Province, and their charismatic leader, Xuan Ke (b. 1930).

Xuan Ke's first venture into legal territory, in 1999, was to sue a rival tourist concert institution, the Dongba Palace (*Dongba gong*), for copyright violation, apparently on the basis of three traditional pieces both groups performed; the suit was withdrawn in September 2000 before any verdict was reached, possibly because any such infringement would have been hard to prove on the basis of China's copyright law and the community nature of the traditional repertoire concerned.[104] His second such foray was more spectacular and was directly linked to UNESCO's recent program of recognition of intangible cultural heritage. With each country limited to nominating one item at a time, there were numerous people in China who by 2003 were pushing for their local musical heritage to be selected for the 2005 round of nominations. In response to a campaign to promote Naxi Ancient Music, the Beijing-based journal *Yishu pinglun* [Arts criticism] published an article by the distinguished Yunnanese scholar Wu Xueyuan. Wu criticized the veracity of several aspects of Xuan's presentation of the music, in particular his claims as to the extraordinary length of its history and its local uniqueness. In effect, his article set out scholarly evidence that could have undermined the basis for a nomination. Wu also commented harshly that Xuan's presentation had pulled the wool over the eyes of numerous leaders and foreign dignitaries; he suggested that local protectionism and local people's not daring to challenge the presentation had contributed to this state of affairs. "As a result," he concluded, "cultural misrepresentation is going on, and this kind of international joke should be stopped."[105] This article is paired in the journal with another attacking Xuan's personal credibility.[106]

Predictably, Xuan sued for defamation. To few people's surprise, in December 2004 the Lijiang Intermediate Court ruled in his favor, stating that Wu's article was damaging to Xuan's reputation and that his rights were infringed. *Yishu pinglun* appealed the decision to the provincial court in Kunming, apparently in part because of accusations of local bias at the local level—some people felt that Lijiang had too much to lose to judge the case fairly. The internationally known composer Ye Xiaogang described the court's verdict as "incomprehensible," clearly agreeing with Wu's argument that the supposed antiquity and local uniqueness of the music were not supported by the historical evidence. Ye and three musician colleagues made a formal proposal to the Chinese People's Political Consultative Conference in Beijing to "protect the right of 'art criticism' in order to root out 'fake cultures.'"[107] Nevertheless, in November 2005, the Yunnan provincial court upheld Xuan's victory, although it did cut the compensation payable to him in half, bringing it down to 10,000 yuan (a little over US$1,200) for Wu Xueyuan and 50,000 yuan for *Yishu pinglun*.[108] One of the journal editors is said to have remarked that he didn't mind having lost the case, as it was good publicity for the still relatively new journal.[109]

Bizarre as this case at times appeared, the aftermath too has not lacked for legal drama. Xuan followed his initial victory in December 2004 by launching three more lawsuits for alleged defamation of himself and his family members in a variety of publications, at least one of which (according to one of the targets) was subsequently withdrawn.[110] And in May 2006, the tables were turned when an audience member named Ma Zheng reportedly sued "Lijiang Xuan Ke Naxi Ancient Music Culture Company Ltd." (Lijiang Xuan Ke Naxi guyue wenhua youxian gongsi) for cheating consumers. According to the Kunming newspaper *Chuncheng wanbao* (Spring City evening news), the plaintiff's complaint concerned the claim made at tourist concerts that pieces including the famous "Ba gua" (Eight trigrams) are ancient items from the Tang and Song dynasties (broadly, the early seventh through early thirteenth centuries). Specifically, Ma alleged that "since there is no historical material or research results [to this effect], [this claim] constitutes false advertising, and has infringed the plaintiff's right to know the situation in his capacity as a consumer."[111] Not surprisingly, Xuan is reported to have denied the allegation with vigor, responding wittily with a rhetorical question directed at the plaintiff: "Do you have some proof that 'Ba gua' is not an ancient Tang or Song piece?"[112] Should this case actually go to trial, the legal arguments on both sides should be intriguing.

For the record, China's successful 2005 nomination for UNESCO recognition went to the Muqam musical suites of the Uyghur people of Xinjiang, in the far northwest of the country, to great local rejoicing; it is unclear whether the decision was influenced at all by Wu's critique and Xuan's spirited response, though with many strong candidates among regional traditions from all over China, quite possibly their dispute made little difference anyway.[113]

Conclusion

Xuan Ke's rash of lawsuits brings together the three phenomena outlined above as factors in China's new cultural environment: the 1991 copyright law, which inspired his first, abortive lawsuit; the UNESCO recognition program, which indirectly led to his second, successful lawsuit; and the rapid development of the market economy, which has underlaid his ensemble's meteoric rise, as well as virtually every other lawsuit, dispute, and discussion of these matters since the beginning of the 1990s.

There is, however, a fourth factor at work in most of the controversies that have arisen: the majority involve traditional musics of ethnic minorities.[114] When I first started looking into this subject, I was surprised that almost every instance—other than the rather exceptional case of the "Midu folksong"—involved minority music, often being exploited (or perceived as exploited) by members of China's majority ethnic Han population. On reflection, however, this is not so surprising: ethnic minority music has often seemed exotic to Han composers and audiences and thus has been particularly susceptible to adaptation. Also, especially in the 1950s and 1960s, the desire to represent China as a united multi-ethnic country led to the frequent use of minority songs as the basis for propaganda pieces, and in the more liberal atmosphere since the 1990s, ethnic minority citizens feel freer to assert their cultural uniqueness and to claim their own heritage.

This perhaps goes some way toward alleviating the concern of legal scholar Paul Hunt (cited at the beginning of this essay) that the United Nations' framework for human rights has until recently led to group cultural rights and collective minority rights being de-emphasized. For 20 percent of the world's population at least, those rights have long had a de jure existence and in the musical context have been invoked quite frequently since the mid-1990s, with varying degrees of material result. As I trawled the literature and the Web sites, however, and discussed the issues involved with numerous interested parties, I began to wonder if one particular kind of group cultural rights is truly underemphasized, at least in terms of public rhetoric. If in early July 2006 one typed the Chinese-language phrase *wenhuaquan* (cultural rights) into the Google search engine, there were about 16,700 hits, on both domestic and international topics; clearly, Chinese-language discussion of the broad concept is quite voluminous. If one typed in the phrase *minzu wenhuaquan* (ethnic cultural rights), 347 sites came up, the first of which concerned developing education and cultural rights in Xinjiang, a heavily minority area, though international topics were also represented. When the search was further refined to *shaoshu minzu wenhuaquan* (ethnic minority cultural rights), 11 sites appeared. What did not seem to come up was material discussing cultural rights of the Han. This is hardly a scientific survey, of course, but it is at least suggestive of a trend in Chinese thinking on cultural rights that tends to focus on ethnic minorities.

It can be argued, naturally, that with the Han overwhelmingly dominant throughout China, their cultural rights are well looked after and do not need as much discussion, attention, and policy-making as those of their minority compatriots. However, I would suggest that precisely because so much attention tends to be lavished on the obviously exotic, the discourse on group cultural rights in the Chinese context may give the appearance of shortchanging the wealth of distinctive but little-known regional folk traditions belonging to those citizens classified as Han. The "kind of collectivity"[115] implied by, say, Han residents of a single small town is not easily recognizable by the legal and administrative structures in place—never mind how distinctive their dialect, performing arts, and sense of local pride may be. While nationally prominent Han traditions such as Kunqu opera and the qin—both honored by UNESCO as "masterpieces of the oral and intangible heritage of humanity"—are in no danger of being overlooked, and the government has long promoted modern, Western-influenced pan-Chinese genres such as the modern China orchestra, many wonderful Han traditions of a highly localized nature risk dropping through the cracks.[116] Even abroad, I have discovered through involvement since 1993 with concert tours and CD companies that it is often easier to interest foreign institutions in a minority folk art than in its regional Han counterpart. I found it hard to answer two elderly Han folk musicians, one from Yunnan and the other from Shanghai, who quite independently of each other essentially asked me the same question: "Why is the Naxi music group always the one invited overseas? Our music is similar and even more beautiful."

Two more instructive points arise from the contemporary Chinese situation as manifested in the world of the folk arts. First, if the United Nations has tended in the past to approach rights from the point of view of the individual citizen, as Paul Hunt and others suggest, and is only now moving toward greater consideration of community rights, then it can be argued that the People's Republic is moving in the opposite direction. Freed from the highly collectivist ideology of the pre-reform era, individuals have the opportunity as never before to become stars and entrepreneurs, to press their cases through the media and the courts, and to openly support, critique, or undermine endeavors of their own community or someone else's. As a result, potential tensions between individual and group rights and views in the cultural arena may increasingly need to be addressed. Second, along with the freedom to exploit one's folk arts or folk-inspired compositions in the free market may come an expectation of, and a need for, scrupulous honesty in any claims made for their history, originality, and ownership—an issue graphically illustrated in dramatically different ways by the Wang Luobin controversy and the legal disputes over the Hezhe folksongs, the Midu folksong, and Naxi Ancient Music. This in turn may require a new culture of careful documentation that obviously mattered far less in the past to most practicing musicians, both folk and otherwise, and is a nuance in the cultural rights discourse that may invite more discussion as time goes on. As ethnomusicologist Tian Liantao so cogently suggests, historical context is everything in so many of these folk music controversies; in practice, when the paradigm shifts, so does everything else, including the future of the musical past.[117]

Finally, in any discussion of the use and ownership of folk music in China today, one cannot forget that the various case histories cited above are the exceptions that prove the rule: most folk traditions do not in fact end up as tourist commodities, or on foreign tours, or at the center of legal disputes. Despite the numerous examples showcased in this essay, many communities continue to use their local music in longstanding ways, or to find new contexts for it that do not immediately intersect with modern concerns of copyright, tourism, the wider marketplace, or representation. For folk musicians in this position, cultural rights ideals may seem of little direct relevance to their everyday music-making, even as the United Nations' International Covenant on Economic, Social and Cultural Rights guarantees their right "to take part in cultural life" and learned commentators debate the "original ecology" of their music.

Notes

I wish to thank Martin Daughtry, Nancy Guy, Andrew Weintraub, and Bell Yung for their critical reading of various drafts of this essay. Discussions over the years with teachers and colleagues including Huang Bai, Stephen Jones, Frank Kouwenhoven, Lin Youren, Qiao Jianzhong, Antoinet Schimmelpenninck, Anthony Seeger, Larry Witzleben, Chuen-Fung Wong, Xiao Mei, Zhang Xingrong, and Zhou Zhengsong have contributed greatly to my understanding of the issues presented in this essay. Jack Bishop and Inne Choi created the map.

Romanization of Chinese place-names and terms is Pinyin, except for the city of Hong Kong. The names of residents of mainland China and of authors writing in Chinese are rendered in Pinyin. For Chinese citizens of Kazakh and Uzbek ethnicity, their names are given in the Pinyin transliteration of the Chinese transliteration that they themselves use in their own writings. For Chinese citizens of Han and all other ethnicities, names are given in customary style (surname first, given name second). Names of authors writing in English are spelled as in their own publications.

1. Qiao Jianzhong, "Hanzu chuantong yinyue yanjiu sishi nian" [Forty years of research on traditional music of the Han], in *Tudi yu ge—chuantong yinyue wenhua ji qi dili lishi beijing yanjiu* [Land and song: research on traditional music and its geographical and historical background] (Ji'nan: Shandong wenyi chubanshe, 1998), 322–48. Quote from 324, subsequent paraphrase from 322–25.

2. Tsui Yingfai, "Ensembles: The Modern Chinese Orchestra," in *Garland Encyclopedia of World Music,* vol. 7, ed. Robert C. Provine, Yosihiko Tokumaru, and J. Lawrence Witzleben (New York: Routledge, 2002), 227–32. Any definition of the term "folk music" creates gray areas (see Philip V. Bohlman, *The Study of Folk Music in the Modern World* [Bloomington: Indiana University Press, 1988], xv–xix). For example, some kinds of Chinese regional opera exist both in state-supported troupes that deliberately employ somewhat Westernized music and modern high-tech staging techniques and in a *minjian* form that largely eschews those elements. And the instrumental genre of Cantonese music, still much performed for personal pleasure by amateur aficionados, also has a century-long history of interaction with the film, recording, and radio industries and urban dance halls, resulting in a seamless integration of some Western instruments and compositional influences (Stephen Jones, *Folk Music of China: Living Instrumental Traditions* [Oxford: Clarendon Press, 1995], 344–61). The working definition I am using, however, based on an extended version of Qiao's description, is sufficient to cover the major genres discussed below.

3. Figures estimated as of July 2006, The World Factbook, http://www.cia.gov/cia/publications/factbook/rankorder/2119rank.html (accessed July 1, 2006).

4. Office of the United Nations High Commissioner for Human Rights, "Status of Ratifications of the Principal International Human Rights Treaties as of 09 June 2004," at http://www.unhchr.ch/pdf/report.pdf (accessed July 1, 2006).

5. The government of the People's Republic of China classifies all its citizens by ethnicity. It recognizes fifty-six ethnic groups (*minzu,* often translated "nationalities"). According to the 2000 national census data (About.com: Chinese Culture, http://chineseculture.about.com/library/china/china2000/ncensus2000a.htm [accessed July 4, 2006]), that year 91.59 percent of the population were members of the Han, the largest group, whose members are bearers of mainstream Chinese languages and civilization; the remaining 8.41 percent were members of the fifty-five officially recognized ethnic minorities (*shaoshu minzu,* often translated "minority nationalities" or "national minorities"), with a few tens of thousands belonging to groups yet to be officially classified. The non-Han tend to be concentrated in often rather sensitive border areas, especially Inner Mongolia and Tibet; Xinjiang and the rest of the far northwest, where Turkic peoples predominate; and the southwest, where Tibeto-Burman, Tai, Miao-Yao, and Mon-Khmer groups are found. Since 8.41 percent

of around 1.3 billion still corresponds to over 100 million people, some of whom (such as many Tibetans and Uyghur) would actively prefer independent homelands, it is not surprising that the People's Republic has gone to great lengths to classify its non-Han citizens and develop policies designed to secure their acquiescence, sometimes with quixotic results. See, for example, June Teufel Dreyer, *China's Forty Millions: Minority Nationalities and National Integration in the People's Republic of China,* Harvard East Asian Series No. 87 (Cambridge, Mass.: Harvard University Press, 1976); Stevan Harrell, ed., *Cultural Encounters on China's Ethnic Frontiers* (Seattle: University of Washington Press, 1995); and Mette Halskov Hansen, *Lessons in Being Chinese: Minority Education and Ethnic Identity in Southwest China* (Seattle: University of Washington Press, 1999).

6. Paul Hunt, "Reflections on International Human Rights Law and Cultural Rights," in *Culture, Rights, and Cultural Rights: Perspectives from the South Pacific,* ed. Margaret Wilson and Paul Hunt (Wellington, New Zealand: Huia, 2000), 25–46, cited 27–28, 37–39.

7. Anne-Christine Bloch, "Minorities and Indigenous Peoples," in *Economic, Social and Cultural Rights: A Textbook,* ed. Asbjørn Eide, Catarina Krause, and Alaan Rosas (Dordrecht: Martinus Nijhoff, 1995), 309–21; International Work Group for Indigenous Affairs, "Declaration on the Rights of Indigenous Peoples," http://www.iwgia.org/sw248.asp (accessed March 13, 2008).

8. *The Common Program and Other Documents of the First Plenary Session of the Chinese People's Political Consultative Conference* (Peking: Foreign Languages Press, 1950), 19.

9. See, for instance, Article 4 of the 1982 constitution. For an English-language translation, see "Constitution of the People's Republic of China," Hong Kong Human Rights Monitor, http://www.hkhrm.org.hk/english/law/const02.html (accessed July 1, 2006).

10. Many English-language publications treat the history and cultural lives of ethnic minorities under the People's Republic. For an overview of policy toward minority arts, see Helen Rees, *Echoes of History: Naxi Music in Modern China* (New York: Oxford University Press, 2000), 19–27. For two elegantly nuanced recent ethnographic studies, see Sara L. M. Davis, *Song and Silence: Ethnic Revival on China's Southwest Borders* (New York: Columbia University Press, 2005), and Chuen-Fung Wong, "Peripheral Sentiments: Encountering Uyghur Music in Urumchi," Ph.D. diss., University of California, Los Angeles, 2006.

11. Zheng Xiaoyun, "Lun quanqiuhua beijing xia shaoshu minzu wenhuaquan de baohu yu fazhan" [On the protection and development of ethnic minority cultural rights in the context of globalization], 2004, Sohu News, http://news.sohu.com/2004/03/25/97/news219589788.shtml (accessed June 28, 2006).

12. E.g., David N. Gellner, "From Group Rights to Individual Rights and Back: Nepalese Struggles over Culture and Equality," in *Culture and Rights: Anthropological Perspectives,* ed. Jane K. Cowan, Marie-Bénédicte Dembour, and Richard A. Wilson (Cambridge: Cambridge University Press, 2001), 177–200; Halina Niec, "Cultural Rights: At the End of the World Decade for Cultural Development," n.d. [c. 1998], De Kracht van cultuur [The Power of Culture], http://www.krachtvancultuur.nl/uk/archive/commentary/niec.html (accessed June 28, 2006); and Lance Polu, "Cultural Rights and the Individual in the Samoan Context," in *Culture, Rights, and Cultural Rights: Perspectives from the South Pacific,* ed. Margaret Wilson and Paul Hunt (Wellington, New Zealand: Huia, 2000), 57–68. See also Rodolfo Stavenhagen, "Cultural Rights and Universal Human Rights," in *Economic, Social and Cultural Rights: A Textbook,* ed. Asbjørn Eide, Catarina Krause,

and Alaan Rosas (Dordrecht: Martinus Nijhoff, 1995), 63–77; and Asbjørn Eide, "Cultural Rights as Individual Human Rights," in *Economic, Social and Cultural Rights: A Textbook,* ed. Asbjørn Eide, Catarina Krause, and Alaan Rosas (Dordrecht: Martinus Nijhoff, 1995), 229–40.

13. On the history of folksong collection in China, see Antoinet Schimmelpenninck, *Chinese Folk Songs and Folk Singers: Shan'ge Traditions in Southern Jiangsu* (Leiden, Netherlands: CHIME Foundation, 1997), 2–7; and Qiao Jianzhong, "Ecology and Transmission of Chinese Folk Songs Today—Concurrent Discussion on the Oral Version and Written Version of Folk Music," in *Preservation of Traditional Music: Report of the Asia-Europe Training Programme,* ed. Xiao Mei, Zhang Gang, and Delfin Colomé (Beijing: Chinese Academy of Arts/Asia-Europe Foundation, 2003), 33–36. Ming and Qing dynasty folksong collections are listed by Yang Yinliu, *Zhongguo gudai yinyue shigao* [Draft history of ancient Chinese music], 2 vols. (Beijing: Renmin yinyue chubanshe, 1981), 749. On the reconstructed history of a Shanghai regional opera since the eighteenth century "through the successive and overlapping stages of rural folk song, seasonal folk opera, urban ballad-singing, and finally opera," see Jonathan P. J. Stock, *Huju: Traditional Opera in Modern Shanghai* (Oxford: Oxford University Press, 2003), 30–58 (quote found on 56). For folk influences on composers, see Chan Hing-yan, "Syncretic Traditions and Western Idioms: Composers and Works," in *Garland Encyclopedia of World Music,* vol. 7, ed. Robert C. Provine, Yosihiko Tokumaru, and J. Lawrence Witzleben (New York: Routledge, 2002), 345–51; and Wang Yuhe, "New Music of China: Its Development under the Blending of Chinese and Western Cultures through the First Half of the Twentieth Century (Part 2)," trans. Liu Hongzhu, *Journal of Music in China* 3, no. 2 (2002): 187–228.

14. The published catalog, *Zhongguo yishu yanjiuyuan yinyue yanjiusuo suo cang Zhongguo yinyue yinxiang mulu (luyin cidai bufen)* [Catalog of Chinese music recordings (recorded tape portion) housed in the Music Research Institue of the Chinese Academy of Arts], is edited by Zhongguo yishu yanjiuyuan yinyue yanjiu ziliao shi (Ji'nan: Shandong youyi chubanshe, 1994). See also Shen Qia, "Ethnomusicology in China," trans. Jonathan P. J. Stock, *Journal of Music in China* 1 (1999): 7–38.

15. This process is seldom discussed explicitly, though Chin Ming ("How the Peacock Dance Reached the Stage," *China Reconstructs* 12, no. 3 [1963]: 10–11) and Colin Mackerras ("Folksongs and Dances of China's Minority Nationalities: Policy, Tradition, and Professionalization," *Modern China* 10, no. 2 [1984]: 187–226) provide information on ethnic minority regions. A similar transformative process occurred with the large-scale incorporation of folk instrumentalists into the modern European-style music conservatory system. For instance, this caused newly elevated *dizi* (flute) performers to address the lack of a solo dizi repertoire by creating a new body of solo pieces, initially by adapting the repertoire of folk ensembles from their home regions (Frederick Lau, "Forever Red: The Invention of Solo *Dizi* Music in Post-1949 China," *British Journal of Ethnomusicology* 5 [1996]: 113–31). The incorporation of the folk instrument *erhu* (two-string bowed lute) into the formal conservatory system and its repertoire is also an excellent example (Jonathan P. J. Stock, *Musical Creativity in Twentieth-Century China: Abing, His Music, and Its Changing Meanings* [Rochester, N.Y.: University of Rochester Press, 1996], 142–67).

16. Isabel K. F. Wong, "*Geming Gequ:* Songs for the Education of the Masses," in *Popular Chinese Literature and Performing Arts in the People's Republic of China 1949–1979,* ed.

Bonnie S. McDougall (Berkeley: University of California Press, 1984), 112–43; Rachel Harris, "From Shamanic Ritual to Karaoke: The (Trans)migrations of a Chinese Folksong," *Chime* 14–15 (1999–2000): 48–60.

17. Miao Tianrui, Ji Liankang, and Guo Nai'an, eds., *Zhongguo yinyue cidian* [Dictionary of Chinese music] (Beijing: Renmin yinyue chubanshe, 1985), 268.

18. For numerous instances of this, see Su de San Zheng, "From Toisan to New York: Muk'yu Songs in Folk Tradition," *Chinoperl Papers* 16 (1992–93): 165–205; and Schimmelpenninck, *Chinese Folk Songs*. 1997.

19. E.g., Wenhuabu wenxue yishu yanjiuyuan yinyue yanjiusuo, ed., *Minzu yinyue gailun* [Overview of Chinese music] (Beijing: Renmin yinyue chubanshe, 1980 [first published 1964]); Jiang Mingdun, *Hanzu min'ge gailun* [Overview of folksongs of the Han] (Shanghai: Shanghai wenyi chubanshe, 1982). The same is true of some works on instrumental folk music.

20. Liu Tieshan, letter to the editor under the heading "Shaoshu minzu gequ chuangzuo de fengge wenti he yuyan wenti" [Problems of style and language in composition of national minority songs], *Renmin yinyue* [People's music] 16 (1953): 63.

21. Du Yaxiong, "Recent Issues in Music Research in the People's Republic of China," *Association for Chinese Music Research Newsletter* 5, no. 1 (1992): 9–12, quote from 9.

22. Jiang Mingdun, *Hanzu min'ge gailun*, 14, 16.

23. Wenhuabu wenxue yishu yanjiuyuan yinyue yanjiusuo, ed., *Minzu yinyue gailun*, 5. I do not have access to the original 1964 edition of this book; I am citing the reprint from 1980, which may include small revisions.

24. For example, during my fieldwork in 1992 in Lijiang County, Yunnan Province, the fiftieth anniversary of the "Talks" was marked by a special concert given by local professional and amateur musicians. The May 1992 issue of the national magazine *Renmin yinyue* [People's music] also featured five articles memorializing the "Talks."

25. Bonnie S. McDougall, *Mao Zedong's "Talks at the Yan'an Conference on Literature and Art": A Translation of the 1943 Text with Commentary*, Michigan Monographs in Chinese Studies No. 39 (Ann Arbor: Center for Chinese Studies, University of Michigan, 1980), 105–7, 57, 75.

26. Ibid., 71, 73.

27. Ibid., 68. The tendency of urban, educated Chinese to look down on rural and oral folk arts was exacerbated by the New Culture Movement of the early twentieth century, which blamed China's backwardness on the static nature of traditional Chinese culture and advocated improving it through modern Western culture. Mao himself favored selective appropriation of Western musical principles and instruments (Mao Zedong, "A Talk to Music Workers [August 24, 1956]," *Beijing Review* 22, no. 37 [1979 (1956)]: 9–15). Influence from the Soviet Union, which pursued a policy of introducing European art music elements into folk and non-European traditional musics, was also strong (Asiya Ibadullaevna Muhambetova, "The Traditional Musical Culture of Kazakhs in the Social Context of the Twentieth Century," *World of Music* 37, no. 3 [1995]: 66–83, cited 73). Perhaps most surprisingly among Communist nations, North Korean leaders, whose longstanding policy of isolationist "self-reliance" (*juche*) might appear to militate against such an approach, also use their powerful propaganda machine to promote selective appropriation of European musical influences for improving "national" music (e.g., Kim Il Sung,

"On Creating Revolutionary Literature and Art," in *Selected Works,* vol. 4 [Pyongyang: Foreign Languages Publishing House, 1971 (1964)], 149–64, cited 161–62; Kim Jong Il, "Let Us Compose More Music Which Will Contribute to Education in the Party's Monolithic Ideology," in *Selected Works,* vol. 1 [Pyongyang: Foreign Languages Publishing House, 1992 (1967)], 195–207, cited 204; and Kim Jong Il, "On the Direction Which Musical Creation Should Take," in *Selected Works,* vol. 1 [Pyongyang: Foreign Languages Publishing House, 1992 (1968)], 390–97, cited 395).

28. One Chinese colleague described to me how he grew up in a village in the 1940s and 1950s, enjoying the traditional local folksongs, opera, and ritual music in their *minjian* form; when he entered a music conservatory, however, he learned to prefer Westernized versions of these Chinese genres that incorporated equal temperament and European harmony, since these were held up as models of modern musical development. It was only after he began doing fieldwork many years later on rural folk music that he rediscovered his ear for and love of "unimproved" traditional arts.

29. J. Lawrence Witzleben, "*Jiangnan Sizhu* Music Clubs in Shanghai: Context, Concept and Identity," *Ethnomusicology* 31, no. 2 (1987): 240–60, quote from 246. To this day, most of my middle-class urban Chinese friends—the engineers, computer scientists, businesspeople, teachers, and civil servants—find my interest in and enjoyment of folk and traditional Chinese genres in their village/unmodernized form quite inexplicable. We have had numerous friendly debates, in which they have strenuously argued the superiority of European classical music, in particular European harmony, over Chinese traditional music. Their own children learn piano or violin and enjoy popular music.

30. E.g., the International Folk Music Council, *Statement on Copyright in Folk Music Adopted by the General Assembly of the International Folk Music Council, August 26, 1957* (London: International Folk Music Council, 1957); Charles Seeger, "Who Owns Folklore?—A Rejoinder," *Western Folklore* 21, no. 2 (1962): 93–101; more than twenty entries listed by Joseph C. Hickerson and Katherine W. Johnston, "Copyright and Folksong" (Washington, D.C.: Archive of Folk Song, Library of Congress, 1978), typescript; Alan Jabbour, "Folklore Protection and National Patrimony: Developments and Dilemmas in the Legal Protection of Folklore," *Copyright Bulletin* 17, no. 1 (1983): 10–14.

31. See, for example, Charles Seeger, "Contrapuntal Style in the Three-Voice Shape-Note Hymns," *Musical Quarterly* 26, no. 4 (1940): 483–93, cited 487–88; Ruth Crawford Seeger, "Music Preface," in *Our Singing Country: A Second Volume of American Ballads and Folk Songs,* comp. John A. Lomax and Alan Lomax, ed. Ruth Crawford Seeger (New York: Macmillan, 1941), xvii–xxiv, cited xviii; and Alan Lomax, *Folk Song Style and Culture,* Publication No. 88 (Washington, D.C.: American Association for the Advancement of Science, 1968), vii. Béla Bartók also emphasizes the vital importance of "characteristic peculiarities" of folk singing style (Béla Bartók, "Hungarian Folk Music," in *Béla Bartók Essays,* ed. Benjamin Suchoff [Lincoln: University of Nebraska Press, 1976 (1929)], 3–4).

32. See Barbara E. Thornbury, *The Folk Performing Arts: Traditional Culture in Contemporary Japan* (Albany: State University of New York Press, 1997) (for Japan); and Yang Jongsung, "Folklore and Cultural Politics in Korea: Intangible Cultural Properties and Living National Treasures," Ph.D. diss., Indiana University, 1994 (for Korea). Both countries' experiences have influenced current UNESCO initiatives in cultural preservation.

33. Yang Mu, "Academic Ignorance or Political Taboo? Some Issues in China's Study of Its Folksong Culture," *Ethnomusicology* 38, no. 2 (1994): 303–20, quote from 317–18.

34. Ibid., 303–20, cited 317–18.

35. Qiao Jianzhong, "'Yuan shengtai min'ge' suoyi" [Incidental views on "original ecology folksongs"], *Renmin yinyue* [People's music] 477 (2006): 26–27.

36. Jack Body, "'One of Yunnan's Most Unique Features Is Its Music': Zhang Xingrong on His Fieldwork among Minorities in Southern China," *Chime* 8 (1995): 59–66.

37. While the commercially oriented world music market often invokes a discourse of authenticity to help market its products, it should be emphasized that none of the projects listed here was expected—or intended—to make much money. I was heavily involved in the preparation of field recordings ultimately issued by Pan, Ode, and Apsara. In the latter two cases, the company owners expressly said they were committing scarce resources because they felt the materials were of immense cultural value and should be made available. This was despite the fact that they would not make any profit from them and indeed would probably lose money on their efforts.

38. E.g., Schimmelpenninck, *Chinese Folk Songs* (folksongs of Jiangsu Province, near Shanghai); Rees, *Echoes of History* (music of the Naxi ethnic minority in Lijiang, Yunnan Province); and Stephen Jones, *Plucking the Winds: Lives of Village Musicians in Old and New China* (Leiden, Netherlands: CHIME Foundation, 2004) (village traditions from Hebei Province, near Beijing).

39. Frank Kouwenhoven, "The Tianjin Buddhist Music Ensemble's European Tour: Group Takes European Audiences by Surprise," *Chime* 7 (1993): 104–12.

40. Stephen Jones, "Suzhou Daoists in Europe," *Chime* 7 (1993): 130–31; Helen Rees, "'Naxi Ancient Music Rocks London': Validation, Presentation, and Observation in the First International Naxi Music Tour," *Ethnomusicology* 46, no. 3 (2002): 432–55.

41. "The Hua Family Shawm Band," Asian Music Circuit press release, 2005, http://www.amc.org.uk/press/pr_hua_band.pdf (accessed January 9, 2006) and author's personal observation in Amsterdam.

42. *Amsterdam China Festival Oktober 2005*, publicity brochure issued on September 15, 2005.

43. He Jiaxiu, "Naxi guyue zhenhan Ying Lun" [Naxi Ancient Music rocks London, England], *Yulong shan* [Jade Dragon Mountain] 74 (1996): 101–13, 99; quote from 113.

44. Qiao, "'Yuan shengtai min'ge' suoyi," 27.

45. Space constraints preclude a thorough examination here of the use of folk music elements in commercial mediated popular music; see, however, Rachel Harris, "Cassettes, Bazaars, and Saving the Nation: The Uyghur Music Industry in Xinjiang, China," in *Global Goes Local: Popular Culture in Asia,* ed. Timothy J. Craig and Richard King (Honolulu: University of Hawaii Press, 2002), 265–83, and Chuen-Fung Wong, "Peripheral Sentiments," on the presence of folk music elements in the Uyghur pop music industry of Xinjiang; Janet Upton, "The Poetics and Politics of *Sister Drum:* 'Tibetan' Music in the Global Marketplace," in *Global Goes Local: Popular Culture in Asia,* ed. Timothy J. Craig and Richard King, (Honolulu: University of Hawaii Press, 2002), 99–119, on a Han pop singer's appropriation of Tibetan cultural influences; and Baranovitch, *China's New Voices: Popular Music, Ethnicity, Gender, and Politics, 1978–1997* (Berkeley, Calif.: University of California Press, 2003), for various uses of Han and minority folk music materials in

China's popular music industry since 1978. For an instance of unacknowledged sampling of a field recording in a popular music CD, see Helen Rees, "The Age of Consent: Traditional Music, Intellectual Property and Changing Attitudes in the People's Republic of China," *British Journal of Ethnomusicology* 12, no. 1 (2003): 137–71, cited 151.

46. For excellent examples of the beneficial effect of the post–Cultural Revolution liberalization on ritual-based musics in northern China, see Jones, *Plucking the Winds;* and Stephen Jones, liner notes to *Walking Shrill: The Hua Family Shawm Band* CD, 2109 (Leiden, Netherlands: Pan Records, 2004).

47. On the history of copyright in China, see Qu Sanqiang, *Copyright in China* (Beijing: Foreign Languages Press, 2002). Elsewhere I have discussed in detail the effect of the law and piracy on the Chinese musical world (Rees, "Age of Consent," 145–51); here I summarize only those aspects directly relevant to folk and traditional music. The Web site of the Music Copyright Society of China is a good place to find the latest developments (www.mcsc.com.cn).

48. *IP Protection in China: The Law,* 2nd ed. (Hong Kong: Asia Law and Practice Publishing, 1998), 144–45; David Cheng, "The New Development of Intellectual Property Protection for Traditional Music in China," in *Preservation of Traditional Music: Report of the Asia-Europe Training Programme,* ed. Xiao Mei, Zhang Gang, and Delfin Colomé (Beijing: Chinese Academy of Arts/Asia-Europe Foundation, 2003), 215–20, cited 215.

49. Ju Qihong, "Minjian yinyue de xiandai chuancheng ji qi zhuzuoquan guishu" [Modern transmission of folk music and copyright ownership], *Renmin yinyue* [People's music] 348 (1994): 13–16, quote from 15.

50. *IP Protection in China,* 146.

51. Ibid., 152, 154–55.

52. Henry Huang and Lesley Lai, "New Developments of Copyright Protection in China," 2003, the International Association of Entertainment Lawyers, www.iael.org/publications/IAEL_article_Huang.pdf (accessed August 26, 2005), 2.

53. Rees, "The Age of Consent," 149–51.

54. Jones, liner notes to *Walking Shrill,* 7–8.

55. For statistics from the period 1978 to 1993, see Zhang Guangrui, "China's Tourist Development since 1978: Policies, Experiences, and Lessons Learned," in *Tourism in China: Geographical, Political, and Economic Perspectives,* ed. Alan A. Lew and Lawrence Yu (Boulder, Colo.: Westview Press, 1995), 3–18. Recent statistics are especially striking for heavily tourism-dependent provinces. For example, in 2001 domestic tourists spent 45,700,000 days in Yunnan Province, an increase of 19 percent over the previous year, while foreign visitors added a further 1,100,000 tourist days, up 9.8 percent from 2000. Income from tourism reached 26.7 billion yuan (well over US$3 billion) in 2001, representing 12.5 percent of the province's entire gross domestic product (*Yunnan nianjian 2002* [Yunnan yearbook for 2002] [Kunming: Yunnan nianjian zazhishe, 2002], 233).

56. Frederick Lau, "'Packaging Identity through Sound': Tourist Performances in Contemporary China," *Journal of Musicological Research* 17, no. 2 (1998): 113–34, cited 118–23.

57. Ibid., 123–29.

58. Ibid., 123.

59. On the Naxi, a small Tibeto-Burman group concentrated in Lijiang, and the lay ritual Dongjing music found throughout southwest China, see Rees, *Echoes of History.* Lijiang's version of Dongjing music may be heard on the CD accompanying *Echoes of History* and on the CD *Naxi Music from Lijiang: The Dayan Ancient Music Association* (Monmouth, Wales: Nimbus Records NI 5510, 1997).

60. Helen Rees, "'Authenticity' and the Foreign Audience for Traditional Music in Southwest China," *Journal of Musicological Research* 17, no. 2 (1998): 135–61; Rees, "'Naxi Ancient Music Rocks London.'" The Dayan Ancient Music Association's Web site may be found at http://www.xuanke.com.

61. Dayan guyuehui, "Baogao" [Report], manuscript, kept by Dayan Ancient Music Association (1992), 1.

62. He Jiaxiu, "Naxi guyue de jin yi bu baohu he kaifa" [Further protection and development of Naxi Ancient Music], *Yulong shan* [Jade Dragon Mountain] 74 (1996): 43–45, cited 43.

63. For instance, the authorities in Jianshui County, Yunnan, have invited their local amateur Dongjing ensembles to play from time to time in the magnificent Ming dynasty Confucian temple, the symbol of their county, to entertain passersby and tourists. Other county governments feature their local Dongjing groups on their Web sites.

64. Chuen-Fung Wong, "Peripheral Sentiments," 25.

65. Liu Zhao, Li Shuji, and Liu Shu, "Yi minjian yinyue cujin Shanxi lüyouye fazhan de shexiang" [Thoughts on promoting the development of the tourism industry in Shanxi through folk music], *Renmin yinyue* [People's music] 468 (2005): 30–31.

66. "Current Status on the Protection and Legislation of National Folklore in China," World Intellectual Property Organization, 2002, http://www.wipo.int/edocs/mdocs/tk/en/wipo_grtkf_ic_3/wipo_grtkf_ic_3_14.pdf (accessed May 19, 2008), 4.

67. Liu Yong, "Wenhua lüyou yu chuantong yinyue de chuancheng" [Cultural tourism and the transmission of traditional music], *Zhongguo yinyue* [Chinese music] 97 (2005): 109–10, cited 110.

68. Ibid., 109. I am following Liu Yong here in referring to this ethnic group by the standard Chinese term "Dong." In their own language, they refer to themselves as "Kam."

69. Ibid., 109–10.

70. Ibid., 110.

71. Ibid.

72. Qiao, "'Yuan shengtai min'ge' suoyi."

73. Body, "'One of Yunnan's Most Unique Features Is Its Music,'" 66.

74. While the emphasis in this essay is on music and other performing arts, many Chinese observers and UNESCO representatives alike are also greatly dismayed by the massive ongoing demolition of the country's architectural heritage as cities rush to modernize (Richard Spencer, "Chinese Minister Apologizes for Destroying Heritage in Rush to Modernize," *Daily Telegraph,* May 26, 2006, n.p.).

75. Xiao Mei, "Foreword," in *Preservation of Traditional Music: Report of the Asia-Europe Training Programme,* ed. by Xiao Mei, Zhang Gang, and Delfin Colomé (Beijing: Chinese Academy of Arts/Asia-Europe Foundation, 2003), 13–15, quote from 13.

76. Data on this meeting come from the volume *Zhongguo shaoshu minzu yishu yichan baohu ji dangdai yishu fazhan gouji xueshu yantaohui* [Preservation of the arts heritage of Chinese ethnic groups and development of the contemporary arts] (Beijing: Zhongguo yishu yanjiuyuan, 2003), which contains symposium abstracts, timetable, and participant list, and from my own notes made during the discussions.

77. See the UNESCO Web site, http://portal.unesco.org/culture/en/ev.php-URL_ID=2226&URL_DO=DO_TOPIC&URL_SECTION=201.html. Kunqu was nominated by China and accepted by UNESCO for listing in 2001 in the first round of nominations and the qin in 2003, in the second round.

78. "Digitization of Recordings of Traditional Chinese Music," UNESCO, http://portal.unesco.org/ci/en/ev.php-URL_ID=16294&URL_DO=DO_TOPIC&URL_SECTION=201.html (accessed January 22, 2006).

79. "Guowuyuan queding meinian liu yue de di er ge zhouliu wei wenhua yichan ri" [The State Council sets the second Saturday in June every year as Cultural Heritage Day], 2006, Zhongguo zhengfu xinwen http://gov.people.com.cn/GB/46742/4087733.html (accessed February 20, 2009); "Di yi pi guojia fei wuzhi wenhua yichan minglu yinyue lei tuijian xiangmu mingdan" [List of recommended musical items in the first national intangible cultural heritage registry], *Renmin yinyue* [People's music] 483 (2006): 53–54; Peng Shanshan, "Renlei caifu, huaxia guibao—shou jie 'Zhongguo fei wuzhi wenhua yichan baohu chengguo zhan' ji zhuanchang biaoyan guanhou" [One of the riches of humanity, and a treasure of China—the first "Exhibition of the results of protecting China's intangible cultural heritage" and special performances], *Renmin yinyue* [People's music] 483 (2006): 55–58.

80. "Yunnan sheng minzu minjian chuantong wenhua baohu tiaoli" [Regulations for the protection of Yunnan Province's ethnic folk traditional culture], 2000, Zhonghua bowu [China Art], http://www.gg-art.com/law/index.php?bookid=147 (accessed January 22, 2006).

81. Xu Facang, "Yunnan minzu minjian wenhua baohu de lifa yu shijian yanjiu" [Research on the legislation and practice of preservation of ethnic folk culture in Yunnan], *Minzu yishu yanjiu* [Studies in national art] 84 (2001): 19–23, cited 20.

82. Yunnan yishu xueyuan yinyue xueyuan, "Yunnan yishu xueyuan yinyue xueyuan tuixing 'minzu yinyue bentuhua jiaoyu' de tese ji youshi" [The Music College of Yunnan Art Institute implements the special characteristics and preference for "nativized education in ethnic music"], *Yunling gesheng* [Voice of the cloud mountains] 186 (2005): 28–30, quote from 28.

83. Ibid., 29.

84. Deng Jun, "'Wenhua li xian' yu minjian yinyue de baohu yu kaifa—Yu dongnan Youyang xian minjian yinyue wenhua ziyuan kaocha shulüe" ["Building a county on culture" and the protection and development of folk music—report on an investigation into the folk music culture resources of Youyang County in southeast Chongqing], *Renmin yinyue* [People's music] 445 (2003): 26–28, quote from 27.

85. Ibid.

86. Paul Mooney, "Digital Music Project Race to Save Tibetan Folk Songs," *National Geographic News*, June 29, 2007, http://news.nationalgeographic.com/news/2007/06/070629-tibet-music.html (accessed March 13, 2008).

87. Frank Kouwenhoven and Antoinet Schimmelpenninck, *Chinese Shadows: The Amazing World of Shadow Puppetry in Rural Northwest China,* DVD, 9607 (Leiden, Netherlands: Pan Records, 2007). Occasionally, initiatives by foundations from outside mainland China also make a contribution at local levels. The Hong Kong–based Orochen Foundation, for example, has since 2004 spearheaded efforts to help the tiny Orochen minority of northeast China with projects aimed both at cultural preservation and at raising their standard of living. See the first issue of their annual newsletter, *Uncooked* (2005), and their Web site, http://www.orochenfoundation.org (accessed July 6, 2006).

88. Some of Wang's most famous songs may be found on the CD *Xibu gewang: Wang Luobin zuopin zhuanji* [Song king of the west: special collection of Wang Luobin's works] (Shanghai: Zhongguo changpian Shanghai gongsi SCD-080, 1994). Since two detailed treatments of this case already exist in print (Rees, "Age of Consent," 151–60, and Rachel Harris, "Wang Luobin: Folk Song King of the Northwest or Song Thief? Copyright, Representation, and Chinese Folk Songs," *Modern China* 31, no. 3 [2005]: 381–408), I merely summarize here the main points relevant to this essay.

89. Rees, "Age of Consent," 156–58.

90. Tian Liantao, "Yong falü gainian shenshi Wang Luobin xibu min'ge de zhuzuoquan" [Using legal concepts to examine the copyright in Wang Luobin's western folksongs], *Renmin yinyue* [People's music] 354 (1995): 18–19; Rees, "Age of Consent," 159.

91. Xiamili Xiake'er [Xamil Xakir], "Guanyu Wang Luobin yu xibu min'ge de lai xin" [Letter concerning Wang Luobin and western folksongs], *Renmin yinyue* [People's music] 352 (1995): 19–22, cited 19.

92. Guo's singing of this song may be found on track 4 of the second volume of a three-CD set, *Zhongguo jinqu/Great Songs of the Time 1949–1999: Centenial [sic] Classical Music Album of China* (Shenzhen: Zhongguo changpian Shenzhen gongsi, n.d. [1999 or after]; 3-CD set).

93. D. Cheng, "New Development of Intellectual Property"; Tian Liantao, "Ping 'Wusuli chuan'ge' yu Hezhezu min'ge de zhuzuoquan susong" [Assessing "Wusuli Boat Song" and the copyright lawsuit over folksongs of the Hezhe ethnic group], *Renmin yinyue* [People's music] 443 (2003): 15–20.

94. Ibid.; D. Cheng, "New Development of Intellectual Property."

95. Tian, "Ping 'Wusuli chuan'ge' yu Hezhezu min'ge de zhuzuoquan susong," 15–16.

96. Ibid., 18–19.

97. I wish to thank Zhou Zhengsong for bringing this case to my attention.

98. *Zhongguo min'ge* [Chinese folksongs], vol. 2. (Shanghai: Shanghai wenyi chubanshe, 1982), 66–67. The CD *Golden Hits* is published by Bailey Records (BCD 92056, 1994).

99. Tian Liantao, "Suben qiuyuan 'Xiaohe tang shui'—jian ping gequ 'Xiaohe tang shui' de zuopin shuxing yu zhuzuoquan guishu" [Tracing the source of "The Babbling Brook": evaluating the attribution and copyright ownership of the song "The Babbling Brook"], *Renmin yinyue* [People's music] 463 (2004): 28–33, cited 28.

100. Ibid.

101. Ibid., 32.

102. Ibid., 33.

103. Ibid., 29, 31.

104. "Xuan Ke 'zhuzuoquan guansi' jiang shenqing chesu" [Xuan Ke applies to withdraw

his "copyright lawsuit"], *Chuncheng wanbao* [Spring City evening news], September 26, 2000. For detailed discussion of this case, see Rees, "Age of Consent," 161–62.

105. Wu Xueyuan, "'Naxi guyue' shi shenme dongxi?" [What Is "Naxi Archaic Music"?] *Yishu pinglun* [Arts criticism] 1 (2003): 12–26, quote from 26.

106. Liu Hongqing, "Xuan Ke shenhua" [The myth of Xuan Ke] *Yishu pinglun* [Arts criticism] 1 (2003): 27–36.

107. "Naxi Music Case Questioned by Musicians," New China News, http://news.xinhuanet.com/english/2005-03/11/content_2681718.htm (accessed March 29, 2005).

108. "'Naxi guyue' guansi zhongshen luomu, pei jingshen fuweijin jian yi ban" ["Naxi Ancient Music" lawsuit receives final judgment, and the compensation for emotional distress is halved], Xinhua Web site, http://news.xinhuanet.com/legal/2005-11/15/content_3781443.htm (accessed June 28, 2006).

109. I encountered an interesting sidelight on this case in a casual conversation with several Chinese colleagues shortly after the final verdict. While disinterested overall in their comments on what had happened, and generally in agreement with Wu Xueyuan's argument, they felt that the title of his article, literally "What [kind of] *thing* is Naxi Ancient Music?" (my emphasis), was especially provocative. In their view, the use of the word *dongxi* (thing) was deliberately insulting and may have inflamed personal and local feelings even beyond what was warranted by the content of the article.

110. "Xuan Ke fang Wang Zhi yi ma" [Xuan Ke lets Wang Zhi off], *Dushi shibao* [Capital times], January 30, 2005: A6.

111. Quoted in Cheng Zhaolin, "Cheng shangwei shoudao fayuan chuanpiao; Xuan Ke: women mei qizha" [He has not yet received the court summons; Xuan Ke: we have not cheated (anyone)], *Yunnan ribao wang* [Yunnan daily web], May 20, 2006, http://www.yndaily.com/html/20060520/news_89_172535.html (accessed June 28, 2006).

112. Ibid.

113. The official promulgation may be found at http://www.unesco.org/culture/intangible-heritage/10apa_uk.htm (accessed July 7, 2006). See Chuen-Fung Wong, "Peripheral Sentiments," 174–82, for an excellent analysis of what this honor has meant to the Uyghur.

114. For a few other minor instances in mainland China, again involving minority music, see Rees, "Age of Consent," 2003: 149–51. The most famous folk music copyright infringement case from Taiwan, too, involves sampling of aboriginal (non-Han) music without the musicians' permission (Nancy Guy, "Trafficking in Taiwan Aboriginal Voices," in *Handle with Care: Ownership and Control of Ethnographic Materials,* ed. Sjoerd R. Jaarsma [Pittsburgh: University of Pittsburgh Press, 2002], 195–209). In related vein, of the sixty-nine musical arts selected in 2006 for the first nationally designated intangible cultural heritage registry, twenty-one items—over 30 percent—are solely or primarily the province of recognized ethnic minorities, more than three times their representation in the overall Chinese population ("Di yi pi guojia fei wuzhi wenhua yichan minglu yinyue lei tuijian xiangmu mingdan" [List of recommended musical items in the first national intangible cultural heritage registry], *Renmin yinyue* [People's music] 483 [2006]:53–54).

115. Stavenhagen, "Cultural Rights and Universal Human Rights," 68.

116. Fortunately many Han genres do have local champions, which must have contributed to the inclusion of around forty Han musics on the 2006 intangible cultural heritage

list issued by the government and showcased in a national exhibition ("Di yi pi guojia fei wuzhi wenhua yichan minglu . . ."). A number of those items included on the list are canonic genres already well known from Chinese music textbooks (e.g., Cantonese music, Chaozhou music, Jiangnan Sizhu, Buddhist music from Wutai Shan, and Nanyin from Fujian Province). My concern here is more with the less well-documented Han traditions from extremely circumscribed areas.

117. I adapt this felicitous phrase from the title of the fifth chapter of Chuen-Fung Wong's Ph.D. dissertation.

3 Access and Control

A Key to Reclaiming the Right to Construct Hawaiian History

AMY KUʻULEIALOHA STILLMAN

Humpty Dumpty sat on a wall,
Humpty Dumpty had a great fall.
All the king's horses and all the king's men
. . . [Are still trying to] put Humpty together again.

Once upon a time, there lived a group of people. Everyone understood how to live harmoniously together and how to steward their environment. The people acknowledged that some higher force must have provided all that was sufficient for sustenance, and they regularly made respectful offerings of thanks. In their daily lives, all of their senses were engaged by their surroundings, their activities, and their interactions with each other. Among their activities, there were performances of what we might call music and dance. These performances were prepared by skilled performers who had been carefully trained by experienced masters. Musical performances encased poetic compositions in sonic vessels designed to enhance the poetry. Performances were even more intensified by the addition of dancing, which added a visual dimension to the words and sounds of the vocalized poetic text.

One day, a group of newcomers arrived from somewhere else. These newcomers believed that the people needed to change their lifestyles and beliefs. The people were pressured by the newcomers to give up their rituals and performance traditions (which the newcomers considered to be pagan and indecent) and to take up the newcomers' religion instead. Then more newcomers arrived with ideas about becoming wealthy by taking over the land from the people. And so it passed that the people were gradually displaced from their lands, their lifestyles were radically altered, and their cultural practices were fractured, scattering pieces on the winds of time.

When scholars finally arrived on the scene to study the people, very few elders were left who remembered much about the ancient traditions. The old times were gone; hence, knowledge of traditional lifeways had lost their utility. But scholars, being very tenacious sorts of folks, sought out the elders and asked about the traditions. Privileged information was given by elders to scholars, who, it was thought, often displayed more interest in the information than did their own descendants. Descriptions of antiquated practices were poured onto notebook pages. Over time, numerous reminiscences were retrieved from the cobwebs of memory and were recalled, recited, and recorded.

When these scholars returned home, many of them would write books about the people. But only a fraction of the information that was collected could actually be included in those books. The remainder of the information about the people's traditions, gathered on the pages of notes typed and handwritten by the scholars, eventually passed into places like libraries, archives, and museums.

Several decades later, descendants of the people began to think that the old traditions given up generations earlier were not the licentious and corrupting forces that the people from elsewhere had made them out to be; in fact, the traditions were beautiful jewels. Amidst the revival, celebration, and reinvigoration of their indigenous traditions, the descendants were excited about recovering poetic repertoire and animating pieces once again in performance onstage. Living elders gradually shared what they did remember, but they also emphasized that much more had been recorded in books now filed away in archives. So the intrepid among this new generation of performers headed off to libraries and archives in search of buried treasures.

Alas, the treasures did not come readily into view. The descendants now faced institutional rules and policies that governed the conditions under which they could see things—that is, when the archives were even in proximity to the community. Some elders could recall who the scholars were and thought they knew where their papers might be now, but who could begin to imagine that other untracked treasures might be tucked away elsewhere? The descendants were in the shoes of the proverbial king's horses and men, trying to piece together traditions that had shattered over time and scattered over space, literally around the globe.

This scenario has played out in countless indigenous communities worldwide, where the experience of colonization has brought about political and economic transformations, conversion from indigenous belief systems to one of the major world religions, the decline and disappearance of indigenous cultural practices, the popularity of new practices from elsewhere, and subsequent study by scholars. Crates of artifacts and reams of notes have made their way out of these communities. Increasingly, communities are now seeking access to those cultural resources and even repatriation to bring those resources home.

As a Native Hawaiian, I came of age in the late 1960s and early 1970s, at the dawn of what is called the "Hawaiian Renaissance." This was the name we gave to the extraordinary revival and resurgence of Hawaiian cultural practices that had nearly disappeared under two centuries of cultural erosion, colonization, and social transformation. Among our elders were some who believed that things of the past had no place in modern times and were determined to take their knowledge to the grave with them. However, most elders were thrilled at the prospect that knowledge they had received from their teachers would, after all, continue beyond them, that young folks would continue their legacies as guardians of knowledge. But aside from what our elders could recall, the stories they told about great quantities of material supposedly stored in libraries and archives took on mythic proportions.

Much of my career has been devoted to charting the heritage resources of hula performance. And yet, as exhilarating as these voyages of discovery have been for me, personally as well as professionally, there have also been some profoundly disturbing moments. It was not only that treasures had dropped out of sight but that the vacuum created by their absence had already been filled in by narratives, not all of which corresponded to the sources when those sources surfaced. Moreover, the privilege attached to my status of scholar became apparent in institutions such as archives, museums, and libraries when I realized that the access to archival resources that I enjoyed was not shared equally by the hula people, who had the most to gain from access to these resources. My research turned up numerous sources that revealed how knowledge that remained in circulation was really fragmented. But how is it possible to recognize when fragments of heritage are missing if the pieces in hand are believed to stand for the whole? And now that missing fragments are coming to light, how could these resources be claimed and reintegrated by the Hawaiian community in ways that do not disrespect the elders, either past or present?

Out of these insights came a turn to thinking strategically about archival resources related to performance traditions and ways in which those heritage resources that have been alienated from communities of origin could be reconnected with those who possess the skills to reanimate them in performance. The case of contents related to the Hawaiian performance tradition of hula offers a useful perspective on some of the stakes for indigenous communities. My purpose in this chapter is to demonstrate how archived resources for Hawaiian hula performance constitute a conceptually Hawaiian historical chronicle and how the process of performing pieces of the repertoire from archival sources engages performers and audiences alike in knowing that chronicle. From this case study, it is possible to extrapolate a compelling case for the right of indigenous communities to know their histories in the media in which those histories are embedded. When significant traces of historical chronicles have become entombed in archives and libraries and museums, performers and audiences alike are entitled to access this content in order to sing, dance, and experience those histories at will.

This chapter sits at the intersection of several discourses concerning indigenous peoples, holding institutions (including museums, archives, and libraries), performance, and repatriation. Significant advocacy for the interests of indigenous peoples has been advanced on a global scale by the United Nations Permanent Forum on Indigenous Issues (originally the UN's International Working Group on Indigenous Peoples, which began meeting in 1982) and the World Intellectual Property Organization. The adoption of the United Nations Declaration on the Rights of Indigenous Peoples in September 2007 signifies a major achievement in articulating issues related to heritage and its preservation in indigenous communities.[1] Article 31 addresses the heritage content relevant to performing arts: "Indigenous peoples have the right to maintain, control, protect and develop their cultural heritage, traditional knowledge and traditional cultural expressions. . . . They also have the right to maintain, control, protect and develop their intellectual property over such cultural heritage, traditional knowledge, and traditional cultural expressions."

As admirable as the rhetoric appears, its implementation straddles rising and ebbing tides of negotiation between communities and holding institutions that are increasingly becoming subject to legal and legislative mechanisms as well as to moral and ethical goodwill. In the United States, for example, federal legislation such as the American Indian Religious Freedom Act of 1978 and the Native American Graves Protection and Repatriation Act (NAGPRA) of 1990 govern the return of human remains to their communities of origin, along with associated artifacts of "cultural patrimony," defined as objects "having ongoing historical, traditional, or cultural importance central to the Native American group or culture itself."[2]

From within the tradition of hula practice, cultural patrimony central to the practice of hula includes not only the material artifacts such as costumes and instruments but also documentation of items of repertoire in archival resources. The operative process that concerns me here is access. Successful maintenance of the hula tradition must include community access to archival documentary resources, and holding institutions are obliged to provide and facilitate access. Exploring the multiple dimensions of access crosscuts the contentious terrain of repatriation, with its positioning of indigenous communities and institutions such as archives, libraries, and museums as champions of agendas in need of being brought into alignment. However, while archival resources related to heritage and performance could clearly be defined as cultural patrimony, much of it falls outside of the narrow sphere demarcated in NAGPRA's fine print. Continued vigilance and advocacy is required to ensure the restoration of cultural patrimony to the communities of origin.

The intangibility of performing arts contributes complexity and opportunity simultaneously to dialogues on repatriation. How can archivists, museum curators, scholars, and community members negotiate the atemporality of documents with the ephemerality of musical sound and moving bodies? Does the repatriating institution's role end when objects and information exchange hands? Or, in the case of performance, is repatriation completed only when objects and information are deinstitutionalized and resurrected back into use and circulation?[3] I propose that repatriating institutions have unique opportunities to engage with communities in ways that can enhance the programming of performance in conjunction with exhibits. On the whole, communities value opportunities to connect with heritage resources, and scholars, archivists, curators, and librarians all have important roles to play in enabling those connections.[4]

My argument, therefore, exceeds making a case for repatriation of archived resources. What is at stake is far greater: access by a given community to experiencing the historical understanding channeled through performance repertoire and acknowledgment of the loopholes in existing mechanisms by which access to cultural patrimony resources could be guaranteed. Indigenous peoples have the right to access all documentary resources related to their culture and history. Therefore, avenues of access must be developed to open these resources to their communities of origin and to enable a community's exercise of self-determination in weaving the contents of tangible archival resources back into intangible performance.

In turning to hula, I shall first present the case for why archival resources for hula matter for Hawaiians and describe briefly how archival resources came to be alienated from the Hawaiian community. Then I will consider the limitations of various ways in which access has been construed and implemented in the past. Finally, I'll explore collaborative knowledge repatriation as a means for engaging both institutions and communities in the process of access to heritage resources and the potential for curating performance that enriches both institutions and communities alike.

Why Do Archival Resources Matter to Hula?

Hula is the performance tradition of the indigenous settlers of the Hawaiian Islands and their descendants, who are referred to as Native Hawaiians. Hula is a multimedia tradition. At its core are poetic texts called *mele.* Precomposed mele are the basis for vocal and dance performance. While mele subject matter ranges from the very sacred prayers for major state gods to the very secular jesting of improvised ribaldry, the most commonly performed repertoire is made up of mele whose poets honor ruling chiefs, loved ones, meaningful events, and meaningful places. Poetic composition requires knowledge of language-based techniques and expressive conventions. Poets must exercise great care in choosing their words, because Hawaiians believe that words have power, and either poorly chosen or poorly delivered words can have negative consequences for all who come in contact—poets, performers, audiences, and those to whom mele are dedicated.

Once composed, mele poetic texts are taken by performers, whose responsibility is to create melodic and choreographic interpretations. The mele is the foundation of all performance, for it is the basis for what is delivered sonically by singers and accompanying instrumentalists and enhanced visually by dancers. Choreographers decide which aspects of the mele to illustrate, then choreographies are taught to dancers who actually execute the dance. One brief example will suffice to demonstrate how a poetic text might be rendered visually through hula gestures. In the following stanza from the song "Nani Kaua'i" ("Beautiful Is Kaua'i Island"), the italicized terms may be chosen for depiction via hand and arm gestures.

Aloha a'e au i ku'u *'āina*	I love my land
I ke kū kilakila o *Wai'ale'ale*	Mt. Wai'ale'ale stands tall

A conventional gesture for "love" is to begin with both hands pointing to the chest and palms facing inward, then extending both arms directly forward with palms facing upward. "Land" is often depicted by starting with both arms extended directly forward, hands placed at the level of the waist with palms facing down, then moving both arms outward to each respective side. In the verse above, over eight counts of music in the first line, the dancer only shows "love" and "land," without necessarily picturing "I" (implicit in the arm gesture starting from the dancer's chest), or that the land is "mine." In the second line, there are several conventional gestures that all represent "mountain" using one or both arms extended upward in front directly or at either front diagonal direction; multiple gestures are necessary because the tune takes sixteen beats. From this extremely brief example, it is clear that poetic texts are the basis for choreographed dance movements; without mele, there can be no hula.

Prior to the introduction of Christianity beginning in 1820, the Hawaiian language was entirely oral. Inherited traditions were memorized and passed from one generation to the next. Great care was taken to ensure accurate memorization and transmission of poetic texts because of the sacred power of the subject matter. This means that the tradition of mele poetic texts cumulates into a historical chronicle recording what poets of different periods chose to commemorate poetically.[5] And because repertoire remains active in performance or can be revived anew, this means that performances are moments in which the past is brought into the present, into coexistence with the living. The corpus of mele passed down from the past into the present, then, is an archive about people and times past that live in the present.[6]

The technology of literacy was introduced by Protestant missionaries who arrived in 1820. They systematized the written representation of Hawaiian-language sounds and spellings and set about teaching Hawaiians how to read and write. Translation of the Bible into Hawaiian was completed by the late 1830s. Hawaiians embraced the culture of literacy so quickly that an independent press of Hawaiian-language newspapers emerged by the 1860s and continued well into the 1940s.[7] Hawaiians who sensed that their traditions were eroding under the influence of Christianization and Westernization began using the technology of literacy to record the inherited corpus of traditions that had accumulated over centuries of oral transmission. Multitudes of tellings of epic traditions appeared in the pages of Hawaiian-language newspapers. Poets also submitted new compositions to the newspapers, which printed thousands of mele over the decades. Personal diaries and ledger books, also filled with lore and mele, passed eventually into the care of the Bishop Museum in Honolulu and later the Hawaii State Archives; I do not know how many pages of traditions may remain in private hands.

Throughout the nineteenth century, Christian hymnody and American and European popular entertainments offered raw materials for Hawaiians to take up on Hawaiian terms. By the 1880s, Hawaiian song composers had begun to engage in the commercial music industry. Copublication agreements between Honolulu and mainland-based publishers ensued. The national popularity of 'ukulele and Hawaiian guitar playing launched via the Hawaiian Pavilion at the 1915 Panama-Pacific Exposition in San Francisco empowered dozens of publishers across the Midwest and mid-Atlantic seaboard to engage in sheet music publication as well. Commercial production of sheet music, songbooks, and subsequently sound recordings all contributed to a vast archive of material artifacts. These artifacts not only document performance practices but are the very material traces of these traditions.

In the late nineteenth century, antiquarian scholars began to amass collections of lore as exemplars of a societal brilliance now on the wane. Their efforts were augmented by early-twentieth-century anthropologists and folklorists, whose collections were the outcome of ethnographic fieldwork and who used sound-recording technology to capture voices of performers. The most important of these field collections, produced in the 1920s and 1930s, passed into the Bishop Museum, where they reside alongside the most important unpublished manuscript collections of performance repertoire.

How Did Archival Resources Become Alienated from the Hawaiian Community?

The picture I am painting is one in which numerous sources of Hawaiian songs were produced since the mid-1800s. Where are all of these resources now? As a student at the University of Hawai'i in the 1970s, I acquainted myself with Honolulu's research libraries and came to understand how each library's collection represented strengths in particular traditions within Hawaiian performance. The University of Hawai'i's Hawaiian Collection is unparalleled for published literature. The Hawai'i State Archives is the repository of government documents spanning from the time of the kingdom through statehood. The Hawaiian Mission Children's Society Library is a repository of the fruits of missionary labor and thus the first stop for exploring the repertoire of Christian hymnody. The Bishop Museum Library holds unpublished manuscript material from members of the kingdom's nobility as well as reams of information culled from decades of scientific and anthropological research carried out by museum scholars. The Hawaiian Historical Society encourages historical research and dissemination.

When I began doing research in the late 1970s, I first explored collections at the Bishop Museum and the Hawai'i State Library in Honolulu. As a graduate student on the East Coast in the 1980s, I was able to visit museums and libraries with significant American sheet music collections, such as the Library of Congress and the John Hay Library at Brown University. There was much to see that I hadn't seen in Honolulu. The Library of Congress's collection was particularly rich in pre-1900 sheet music. Why? Because Hawaiian songwriters in Honolulu—including Queen Lili'uokalani—understood the mechanism of copyright. We are indeed fortunate that materials submitted for copyright registration then were subsequently accessioned into the Music Division. But how could I explain how Hawaiian sheet music came to be at

Brown University—or in the Lester Levy collection at Johns Hopkins University, the Historical American Sheet Music Collection at Duke University, and the Popular Music Archive at Middle Tennessee State University? As an active e-Bay bidder since 1999, I have watched as sellers—individuals and dealers alike—have come forward with Hawaiʻi-related materials from all over the United States, as well as Europe and Japan. And now, situated in the Midwest, I am finding regional specificity in Hawaiian music sources that are coming up in estate sales, flea markets, and antique malls. There are tons of materials, significant amounts of which are outside Hawaiʻi. Scholars might be able to figure it out, but how are Hawaiian performers supposed to patch it all together? How are Hawaiians supposed to make sense of all this?

The irony of this situation is that not everything located in Hawaiʻi was accessible to the community, either. And herein lies larger tragedies. The decline of Hawaiian language fluency within the Hawaiian community produced a shroud of opacity around the vast archives of lore published in the Hawaiian-language newspapers. Midcentury microfilming technology provided a certain extent of physical preservation of the newspapers, but even then, limited Hawaiian language instruction before the 1970s severely curtailed the number of those able to read the newspapers with much proficiency.

At the Bishop Museum, the unpublished materials housed there languished in near obscurity. Financial resources had been expended to process the ethnographic field collections, and notes and mele texts were typed up, edited, and even translated, but much of the handwritten manuscript material remained untouched. Only minimal inventory information was provided in the library's card catalog.

Public service practices underscored the institutionalized nature of these manuscripts, particularly in relation to the corpus of mele—poetic repertoire—that was the basis for performance in music and dance. There existed a separate index card file called the Mele Index that provided access to the contents of the manuscript sources. This card file was kept in a staff work area closed to the public. Librarians consulted the Mele Index on behalf of patrons. The Mele Index only included first lines; there was no subject index. So, a patron had to know about the existence of a mele in order to request it. The system did not accommodate exploration or discovery. Moreover, the preservation mandate worked to further distance patrons from mele resources. When a card recorded multiple sources for a mele, librarians often brought out only what they felt would be the most easily usable source. Sources with English translations of mele were favored over sources that contained mele only in Hawaiian, the presumption being that few Hawaiians understood the Hawaiian language. Typescripts were favored over handwritten sources. And

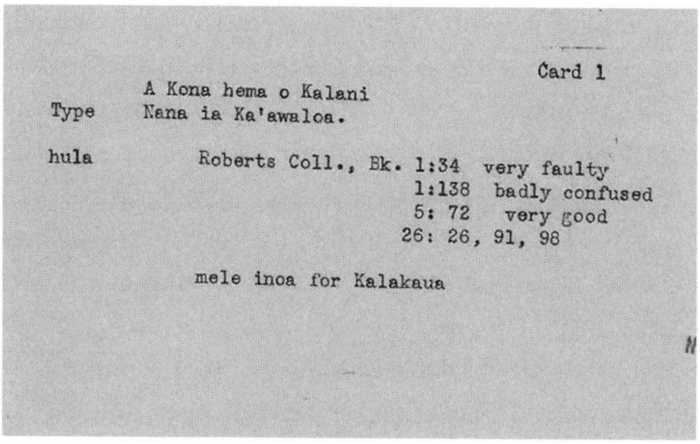

Card 1
A Kona hema o Kalani
Type Nana ia Ka'awaloa.
hula Roberts Coll., Bk. 1:34 very faulty
1:138 badly confused
5: 72 very good
26: 26, 91, 98
mele inoa for Kalakaua

a.

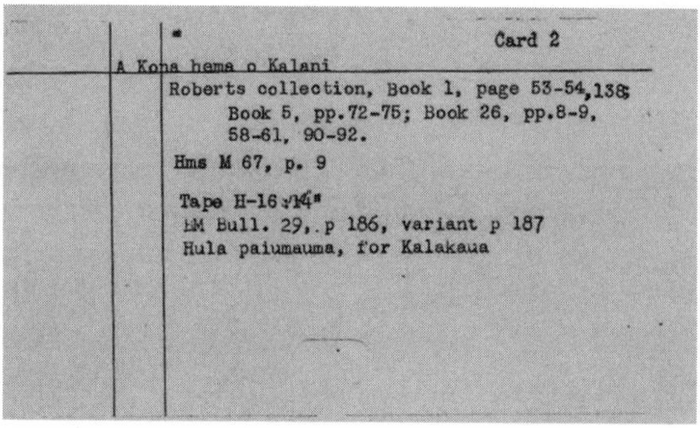

Card 2
A Kona hema o Kalani
Roberts collection, Book 1, page 53-54,138;
Book 5, pp.72-75; Book 26, pp.8-9,
58-61, 90-92.
Hms M 67, p. 9
Tape H-16 :14"
BM Bull. 29,.p 186, variant p 187
Hula paiumauma, for Kalakaua

b.

Figures 3.1a and 3.1b. Examples of cards from the original Mele Index at the Bishop Museum, Honolulu.

librarians tried, whenever possible, to avoid exposing deteriorated sources to risk of further damage. (See figures 3.1a and 3.1b.)

As the Hawaiian Renaissance of the 1970s unfolded, more performers and instructors embarked on the quest to learn what the ancestors had passed down. People who went into the Bishop Museum with one title in mind often came away with more pages photocopied, because after all, once a book is in hand, what's to stop a reader from turning the pages?

The relative accessibility of materials in the ethnographic field collections thus came to shape contemporary understandings of the corpus of mele, because this is what performers of my generation and vintage got to work with extensively. My own systematic comparison over the years of the contents of field collections and personal manuscript books has revealed that the field collections contain only fragments of what is found in the manuscripts. Ethnographers in the 1920s and 1930s mined the memories of elders who had come of age by the 1870s. The field collections represent what these performers remembered. It is only on comparison with written sources from the

1870s and 1880s that the fragmentary nature of the field recollections becomes apparent. In turn, the record of what performers remembered of mele current in the 1920s and 1930s is also shown to be greater in quantity than what my generation was taught at the beginning of the Hawaiian Renaissance in the 1970s. And thus, the historical chronicle that survived in the mele that remained in continuous circulation is finally exposed as fragmentary—despite the survival of the material artifacts that contain the much fuller chronicle that the ancestors recorded.

Issues of Access: The Humpty Dumpty Challenge

The case of hula is one in which thousands of poetic texts—which are the basis for vocal recitation melodically and interpretive hand gestures choreographically—exist in historical and archival sources, yet those in the hula community who possess the skills to render poetic texts in performance are disconnected from a major portion of this legacy. Moreover, it is not simply a matter that access to poetic texts would mean more material from which performers may select. When surveyed collectively and chronologically, the subject matter of the poetic texts present a succession of themes that inspired poets to create poetic commentary. That thematic succession is a chronicle from the perspective of distinctly Hawaiian worldviews, conveyed from within the symbolic expression of poetic convention. Moreover, the thematic succession reflects Hawaiian responses to the political, social, and economic upheavals of the nineteenth century that do not appear in English-language sources. Thus, the poetic archive, made up of expressions created with the intention of being performed, is the means for Hawaiian people to connect with a history of resilience in the face of the demise of the independent sovereign kingdom by the end of the nineteenth century, and the performance of those expressions is a potent means by which Hawaiian audiences engage with the expressions of resilience.

The alienation of the corpus of poetic repertoire preserved in archival sources from the performers who would animate the expressions, and from audiences who would engage with the subject matter, presents what can be described as a Humpty Dumpty moment: how can the pieces of the chronicle be put back together again? Because of the institutionalization of archived resources, the concept of repatriation resonates here. Archived resources are cultural patrimony, and the right to access cultural patrimony further makes possible the right to know the historical chronicles embedded within the archived sources.

In the current moment of the information economy circulating via the Internet, access to the contents of archived sources is fast eclipsing the need for access to the physical documents themselves. That said, existing avenues of access to resources institutionalized in archives, libraries, and museums require commentary and critical evaluation, particularly with respect to issues of selectivity, limitations, and institutional constraints.

For example, consider publication as one means to make content accessible. Many people think of book or article publication as a form of repatriation, despite the fact that published sources are commonly considered secondary sources rather than primary sources. Preparing a compilation of performance repertoire for publication, whether of printed texts or sound recordings, involves selecting and arranging individual items, correcting spelling mistakes, confirming or verifying locatable factual information, and creating additional explanatory notes that enhance readers' insight. When published books or articles contain collections of repertoire or reproductions of images or other kinds of documentary evidence, such publications may be considered by readers as substitutes for primary sources in the event that those readers are unable to access the primary source collection. But more fundamentally, published volumes reflect three other steps that distance readers from the primary sources. First, published volumes involve selecting items out of a collection; rarely is a collection of repertoire published in its entirety. Second, published volumes present an author's or editor's ordering and arranging of individual items. Third, published volumes often include contents drawn from multiple collections and sources that can include libraries, archives, people, attics and basements, and the like. This obscures even further a reader's sense of the comprehensiveness of each constituent collection from which selections are drawn.

Book publication about indigenous traditions has had mixed reception in indigenous communities. The scientistic language of scholarly analysis has alienated many communities, who understand clearly that they are not a target audience for the monographic writing. Accounts presented in nonscholarly trade publications are often read within the represented communities as superficial and oversimplifying. Published collections of musical notation generally fare worse, given the far lower rate of notational literacy in our contemporary era of mass media dissemination, the widespread understanding that Western staff notation is incapable of representing or describing meaningful aural aspects of non-Western traditions, and perceptions that any profits from such publications are not benefiting the community. The present-day market realities of book retailing pose further challenges for a community's ability to encounter published collections of repertoire. Publishers are increasingly unable to take on projects whose potential sales are projected to be too low to recoup production costs, and retailers are unwilling to give shelf space to products—printed products and sound recordings—with limited general appeal.

Once in circulation, it is astonishing to note how published collections of repertoire often acquire auras of comprehensiveness. In some communities, published repertoire is represented almost entirely by the publications of scholars who collected and edited the material. Where commercial publication exists, the products are frequently pedagogical materials that are clearly selections of repertoire, arranged for accessibility to performers of limited skill, and without any pretenses to comprehensiveness or even representativeness. What must be asked, then, is this: What is the relationship of published repertoire to the entirety of known repertoire?

A sobering case in Hawaiian music and hula should give us pause. The collection of sound recordings and texts of repertoire compiled by anthropologist Helen Roberts from field research in 1923–24 formed the basis for her report, *Ancient Hawaiian Music,* published in 1926, and for an edition, *Nā Mele Welo: Songs of Our Hawaiian Heritage* (1995), that presents a selection of poetic texts and translations.[8] Roberts's collection, along with collections of recordings made in the 1930s by Bishop Museum anthropologist Kenneth Emory and scholar Theodore Kelsey, formed the basis for restudy and musical analysis by Bishop Museum ethnomusicologist Elizabeth Tatar in a doctoral dissertation submitted to UCLA in 1978 and published by the Bishop Museum as *Nineteenth Century Hawaiian Chant* in 1982. In addition, Tatar compiled an anthology of recordings published in 1981 by the Bishop Museum as *Nā Leo Hawaiʻi Kahiko: Voices of the People of Old* and remastered onto compact disc in 1997 under the slightly altered title *Nā Leo Hawaiʻi Kahiko: The Master Chanters of Hawaiʻi.* Tatar also produced a videotape, *Ka Poʻe Hula Hawaiʻi Kahiko,* using films made in the 1930s by dance teacher Vivienne Huapala Mader that came to the Bishop Museum in the early 1980s.

Although such a litany of publication might suggest accessibility to the collected repertoire, in fact the opposite is closer to the truth. Helen Roberts wrote: "It was not feasible to secure the vocal music for all of the chants, nor for the longest ones. In all, about two hundred tunes were taken, enough to provide a basis for a critical study. . . . Sixty phonograph records, made for the purpose of casting into permanent form audible and exact representations of the old methods of chanting, have been set aside for preservation."[9] Out of some 200 tunes Roberts claimed to have collected, only 152 notated musical examples are included in her monograph, *Ancient Hawaiian Music.* Roberts's supposed selection of sixty phonograph records for preservation was apparently not carried out to completion, for the Curatorial Record Form (finished only in 1977 by Elizabeth Tatar) itemizes 124 pieces of repertoire on sound recordings, 15 of which were included on the recording *Nā Leo Hawaiʻi Kahiko.*

The point I am underscoring is that disparities will almost always exist between quantities of resources published and quantities within the collections from which compilers draw. Scholarly editing projects always involve decisions of selection, inclusion, ordering, and representation. Publishers' presumptions of readers' tolerance and purchasers' budgets impose practical limits on what can be included in publication and how long a published volume can be sustained, in print, in a publisher's active catalog. To force readers to rely only on published books places them in the position of not knowing what part of the whole the contents of a book represent. Let us not, therefore, fool ourselves in thinking that books can ever contain "all there is." To consider book publication a form of repatriation is accurate up to a point—as long as a book remains in print and/or accessible to people whose heritage is contained within *and* as long as there are ways of enabling users to contextualize a given collection within the broader fabric of the tradition itself.

Performers, scholars, and interested enthusiasts who seek access to collections of primary sources that have been institutionalized in libraries and archives encounter at least two kinds of issues: first, policies of access and use that will determine who gets to see what and when, and second, circumstances of curatorial commitment that will determine what is collected in the first place.

Policies of access and use are implemented by institutions for various reasons. Not all institutions have mission statements that make provisions for broad public access; for example, the Huntington Library in Pasadena, California, is devoted to scholarly research at a professional level and requires either academic affiliation or letters of introduction and recommendation in order to gain admission. The imposition of academic qualifications in order to work with collections is one kind of barrier that is antithetical to indigenous communities where access to educational attainment is still limited by access to educational opportunity!

The case of Honolulu's Bishop Museum described above presents another kind of concern that is legitimate from the perspective of the institution. Librarians who exercised the power of choice in selecting from among multiple sources for requested items were acting in part to ensure the safety and preservation of the sources in their care. But such selectivity places barriers between researchers and primary sources *when researchers may not be aware that such filters are in place.* In turn, the researcher's ability to discern the broad context of a collection in which an individual source is located is compromised. When collections are pertinent to indigenous communities, institutions must be held accountable for implementing use policies that do not inadvertently separate community members from resources.

Access into an institution and successful connection with specific resources to study depend on the user's ability to identify relevant sources. Doing so depends on the quality of the cataloging and indexing that facilitates connections between seekers and resources sought. It is only logical that a fully indexed collection is one in which the mere existence of contents is at least identifiable. However, when institutions such as archives, libraries, and museums operate under financial constraints and limited staffing, then the underdevelopment of indexing and finding aids should become a matter of wider community concern.

In the hula tradition, indexes facilitate access to the pieces of repertoire that register the surviving historical chronicle. For decades, Bishop Museum librarians relied on the Mele Index card file in rendering assistance to patrons. Complete indexing of their manuscript books was undertaken only in 1992, with federal funding provided through the Native Hawaiian Culture and Arts Program and the Hawai'i Bishop Research Institute.[10] Online access to a computerized Mele Index was launched in 1993. The ability to search by keyword has finally made it possible to explore and discover the corpus of repertoire in deeper and more powerful ways.

While this step has addressed major issues of familiarization with the corpus of repertoire, serious questions of access remain. A series of financial crises faced by the Bishop Museum has limited staffing and public service capacity to virtually a trickle. Reduced hours and the imposition of admission fees to the library in the late 1990s (but rescinded after public outcry) did not endear the Hawaiian community to the institution from which they already felt alienated. More important, once the existence of mele is identified, Hawaiians still have to go to the Bishop Museum to see the actual source. The serious inequity here is this: for Hawaiians in Honolulu, the trip to the Bishop Museum is a cross-town or cross-island car or bus ride; for Hawaiians off-island, the trip to the museum must begin with an airplane ride. Access from off-island is limited to those with the resources to travel.

This situation reverses with the existence of primary sources in institutions outside Hawai'i. In 2005, I had the opportunity to survey the papers of Nathaniel Emerson, whose two books—*Unwritten Literature of Hawaii: Sacred Songs of the Hula* of 1909 and *Pele and Hiiaka* of 1915—had achieved the status of primary sources in the absence of Emerson's papers. The papers, long out of sight, surfaced at the Huntington Library in Pasadena, California. Although the Huntington purchased the papers from a private collector in 1984, inventorying was completed only in 2002. To the Huntington's credit, the entire inventory is accessible online and is a model of comprehensiveness.[11] However, accessing the papers themselves requires going to the Huntington Library. In a delicious irony, access to Emerson's papers for Hawaiians in southern California and elsewhere on the mainland can begin with ground travel, while Hawaiians in Hawai'i must begin with an airplane ride.

Issues of access to institutions that possess collections, as well as to the collections themselves, depend on yet another underlying factor: the commitment on the part of an institution to acquire resources and develop collections in the first place. Collections come into being when someone decides to collect something. On an institutional level, curatorial commitment on the part of individual librarians, archivists, and curators is a significant factor in identifying resources that should be incorporated into an institution's holdings and amassing those resources so that patrons can access and use them. Institutional mission and policies developed in strategic planning processes are insertion points for establishing a commitment to connecting communities and resources of cultural patrimony by taking up the initiative to acquire materials in the present that will be part of the heritage legacy in the future.

In the case of Hawaiian resources, Dr. Chieko Tachihata stands out as an exemplar of foresight. Tachihata served as curator of the Hawaiian Collection at the University of Hawai'i Library from 1984 to 2000. During her tenure, she implemented numerous visionary strategies that have altered the nature of collection development at that library. Relevant to present purposes were two in particular. First, in addition to acquiring published books, Tachihata began to collect ephemera that included concert programs, tourism promotional materials, posters, and the like. The result is a far richer contextualization of the secondary source nature of published books. Second, Tachihata began to request photocopies of materials held in other institutions, both in and outside of Hawai'i. She was, in effect, conducting a repatriation program of her own, bringing into a public library in Hawai'i copies of materials that had been accessible only to far fewer people for whom access was a privilege rather than a right.

One of the "best practices" in ethnomusicology since at least the 1980s is the sharing of materials collected in fieldwork with the host community. Depositing copies of sound collections and associated documentation made during field research in a repository accessible to the community has become common practice. In tandem with this development is the recognition that scholars could also assist host communities in locating materials collected by earlier researchers that now reside in institutions worldwide. Scholars and institutions are now collaborating to assist communities with obtaining copies of published works and unpublished archival materials retrospectively.

For sound recordings, the Federal Cylinder Project at the Library of Congress is a model repatriation effort. Launched in the 1980s, the project's goal was the return of copies of recordings, made as early as the 1890s, to the communities in which those recordings were made. The recordings were made on wax cylinders—a medium that preceded the development of flat shellac and vinyl discs—which were used by researchers in the early decades of anthropological fieldwork. In the mid-twentieth century, the Library of Congress published recordings of selections from the field collections. But the Federal Cylinder Project aimed to return the entirety of the library's collections from a given community back to that community. Issues of ethics and access abounded, but staff of the Federal Cylinder Project collaborated, community by community, to effect the repatriation of voices and repertoire back to the descendants of the performers recorded.[12]

But having possession of recordings is little more than fetishism if there are no institutional provisions that allow access to the voices and sounds on the recordings! Institutions with audio and film/video recordings must provide facilities for listening and viewing. To limit audiences to brief excerpts in exhibit kiosks amounts to withholding the completeness of thoughts voiced on the original recordings.

The dramatically expanding storage capacity of the Internet is altering the terms on which we connect virtually with people, places, and things. What is particularly exciting about online opportunities is the ability to transcend institutional boundaries, to break free from the limits of any one institution's holdings. The screen shot reproduced in figure 3.2 is from Hulapages.com, a Web site maintained by collector Keith Emmons, who has generously shared thumbnail images of sheet music from his personal collection for our viewing pleasure. The view of Hawaiian sheet music from this collector's Web site contrasts greatly with the view one gets by searching through individual institution holdings, such as the Lester Levy Sheet Music Collection at Johns Hopkins University or the Historical American Sheet Music Collection at Duke University. A similar project to this collector's effort is the virtual library of nineteenth-century California sheet music that catalogs and presents over two thousand pieces of sheet music from at least ten participating libraries.[13] Granted, we face daunting legal issues of licensing and copyright. However, projects that bring together encyclopedic information collections make it possible now to envision creating channels of access that link up existing resources that exceed those of any one individual institution. In my mind, it is about creating resources that represent a community rather than X, Y, and Z institutions' holdings about that community.

In a parallel development, two digitizing projects are underway to place the entire archives of Hawaiian-language newspapers online. Although the thousands of items of poetic repertoire published in various newspapers

Figure 3.2. A screen shot from www.hulapages.com, "Hawaiian and Tropical Vintage Sheet Music Image Archive" (accessed May 21, 2008), maintained by Keith Emmons. Used with permission.

are of immense significance for Hawaiian performance, access for many decades has been via aging microfilm held by a small number of institutions in Hawai'i. The pilot project "Hawaiian Language Newspapers," undertaken by the University of Hawai'i Library and posted online in its Image Archive, has been superseded by the "Ho'olaupa'i Hawaiian Nūpepa Collection," a tri-institutional collaboration between Alu Like, Inc., and the Bishop Museum in Honolulu and Hale Kuamo'o of Ka Haka 'Ula o Ke'elikolani College of Hawaiian Language at the University of Hawai'i in Hilo.[14] The newspaper archive is now part of the Web site Ulukau: The Hawaiian Electronic Library.[15] Using optical character recognition technology modeled on Maori OCR software, the Ho'olaupa'i project is producing a searchable text database along with the scanned images of newspaper pages. Creation of an online archive of the Hawaiian-language newspapers now opens access to this important resource to anyone with an Internet connection.

The advent of digital technology has also facilitated the ability to restore sound recordings on older media. The technical means now exist for communities to access the thousands of hours of voices on cylinders, discs, and magnetic tape. When sound recordings can be linked to associated or relevant printed sources of repertoire, then published sources will cease to be texts divorced from temporal sonic contexts. Two examples from New Zealand illustrate this vividly. First, a collection of poetic texts commonly referred to as *Ngā Mōteatea,* originally published by Sir George Grey in 1853, was translated by Maori statesman and scholar Sir Apirana Ngata between the 1920s and 1950s and published in four volumes after Ngata's death by the Polynesian Society between 1958 and 1990. Since 2004, a completely reset edition of volumes 1 and 2 has reappeared. Both volumes contain CDs with field recordings made in the 1950s and 1960s of items that had remained in continuous practice. The inclusion of the sound recordings with the printed texts offers readers the means to access the words on the page temporally via the voices of singers. Second, the volume *Traditional Songs of the Maori* by ethnomusicologist Mervyn McLean and literary scholar Margaret Orbell was first published in 1975. Unlike *Ngā Mōteatea, Traditional Songs* includes musical transcription of tunes.[16] Initially scorned by scholars and community alike as a heritage item only for scholars, the heritage value of the volume within the Maori community has increased with the passing of the elders whose knowledge is represented therein. The third edition, issued in 2004, includes for the first time two CDs with the recorded performances that were the basis of the transcriptions. Readers of *Traditional Songs* may now access the words sonically, delivered in the voices of singers who entrusted those songs to Mervyn McLean decades ago.

Knowledge Repatriation

The concept of knowledge repatriation is a useful rubric for thinking through the dynamics of linking communities and information. At its core, the enterprise of repatriation involves a return of a physical resource to the community of its origin. It behooves us, however, to be aware of multiple distinctions. The presence of a source in the community does not, in and of itself, guarantee the ability of community members to access its contents. And access to the information content of sources should not be conflated with a community's ability to fully experience the knowledge encased therein as it was intended to be presented and consumed.

"Knowledge repatriation" gestures usefully toward the collaborative nature of information return and emphasizes the facilitation of interaction and engagement with the returned contents. My cue for this concept derives from a heritage initiative named The Beringian Yupik Heritage Project

(1998–2000). Launched by three Yupik scholars and a Smithsonian curator, the project involved taking stock of historical documentary records—"written knowledge"—that "remains poorly known to the very people it portrayed." The process of engaging with documents led to the insight that returning documents was distinct from the one-way returns that characterized the repatriation of human remains and burial objects. "Knowledge repatriation," as it was named, was found to be "about *sharing* rather than giving back." On consulting Yupik elders on fact-checking, memories were recalled and more stories were related, recorded, and added to the archive: "This is the most productive form of exchange, when knowledge collected many decades ago produces more knowledge today."[17]

In the Hawaiian hula context, the repatriation of knowledge exceeds mere accessibility of the resources needed for performance. I argue that knowledge is repatriated when the contents of what poets have chronicled are experienced in the way that they were intended to be consumed: via vocal recitation of the poetic texts embellished by melodic setting and choreographic interpretation. When skilled hula masters have access to the poetic texts and animate those texts via song and dance onstage in performance, then performers and audience alike are able to experience the expressions in the medium in which they were intended to be delivered.

Repatriating knowledge back into performance can make for powerful experiences. In April 2004, the organization Kūlia i ka Pūnāwai (Kumu Hula Association of Southern California) produced a concert of hula in Los Angeles. It was no ordinary concert, however. Several years prior, I had proposed that the group might collectively stage mele from archival sources. Although it was a widespread practice in the 1800s to compose mele in sets, contemporary events such as hula competitions that impose time limitations require performing troupes to present only single items. A concert produced by an association, however, was an opportunity to present historical sets in their entirety. Each member of this association was a director of an individual hula troupe; thus, the labor of reconstruction could be distributed and worked through collaboratively.

Because of members' residence in California, they had limited opportunities to access libraries and archives in Honolulu. I pulled out mele that I had collected during research in manuscript sources and from the Hawaiian-language newspapers of the 1880s. The group chose one set of fifteen mele that were performed on the occasion of King Kalakaua's birthday jubilee on November 16, 1886. To prepare for the concert, the group worked out individual settings of individual mele and also the staging to move entire troupes onstage and offstage in sequence. To increase audience appreciation of the subject matter of the mele, the narration script was augmented by a PowerPoint presentation that included images of places and people referred to in the mele and of the primary documents from which the group worked. From the audience, appreciative feedback affirmed that the presentation was informative as well as entertaining. But more so, among the performers, there was a clear sense that what happened onstage that day was, in some way, an extraordinary connection with a vision originally created over a hundred years ago. Importantly, the performers grasped that the scale of presentation in that day's performance—of a set of fifteen mele in its entirety—was clearly befitting of a beloved ruling monarch, of his ability to inspire poetic composition on such a scale, and of the continued relevance of animating that poetry in performance in a community of Hawaiians now residing away from the ancestral homeland. The organization has since released a CD of studio recordings of that repertoire; all texts and translations are included in the liner notes.[18]

Bringing archival resources back to life in performance signifies a kind of closure, of reuniting resources with performers who possess the skills to realize the visions of the resources' creators. Even more so, presenting performance repertoire onstage allows audiences once again to engage with the subject matter and to reconnect with a legacy handed down from the past. Chronicles cast in poetic texts intended for vocal and dance presentation fell out of public view, not because the Hawaiian community did not value those chronicles but because the community had been cut off from many chronicles by the circumstances of language loss and policies of archival accessibility. The successful revitalization of the Hawaiian language over the past two decades means that more performers and audiences are able to grasp the poets' perspectives directly when those chronicles are accessible to those who would animate the expressions the chronicles record.

Conclusion

Is the right of a group of people to know their history undeniable? This, it seems to me, is the central question. For from this question flow all moral and material imperatives to address the widespread alienation of people from sources in which their histories are embedded.

For Native Hawaiians, the orientation to past and future runs exactly opposite to what is commonly conceptualized. Namely, the future lies in back of us; it comes upon us from behind. It is the past that lies before us, in full view, and it guides us as the unknown comes upon us. This is why hula is so significant to Native Hawaiian people: it articulates and enacts the chronicles that explain how and why the gods and chiefs cared for their people and how and why we must now care for each other. This is why we need to restore knowledge of the chronicle contained in mele, poetic texts that are the basis for sonic and movement interpretation in performance. By enacting visions of the world that was, performance enables Hawaiians to envision the world as it could be. Reconnecting performers with the cultural patrimony inherent in archived poetic traditions will enable the hula to connect Hawaiians to the ancestors and the future.

This case casts sharp light on the stakes involved in reconnecting people and heritage resources. As such, it highlights a gap between existing legal mechanisms that govern repatriation efforts and heritage preservation initiatives (including digitization projects) that promise to democratize access to heritage resources while navigating the turbulent waters of community empowerment and intellectual property. The World Intellectual Property Organization's Creative Heritage Project seeks to develop "best practices and guidelines for managing IP issues when recording, digitizing and disseminating intangible cultural heritage."[19]

When heritage resources are already institutionalized, community access requires institutional cooperation and collaboration. Institutions such as museums, archives, and libraries have a serious responsibility to indigenous peoples whose traditions are represented among the holdings. In fact, institutional mission statements that articulate presentation, education, outreach, and accessibility should be held to applying those principles to the subjects of their collections as well as to their audiences. Moreover, the revenue-generating capacity from admissions, duplication, and photocopying must never be allowed to preempt the development of avenues of access that may reduce the revenues—a factor actually among the arguments made against online digital archives.[20]

The concept of cultural memory has garnered much attention across many fields in the humanities, the social sciences, and information technology, and there is consensus that archives can be construed as memory keepers. The case of Hawaiian hula illustrates clearly how one avenue for activating cultural memory is in the performance of poetic repertoire. Accessing the subject matter chronicled in poetic repertoire is one means by which Hawaiians can know what our ancestors prioritized to be remembered. More important, experiencing that knowledge through performance honors the intentions of the chroniclers who chose the medium of poetry to deliver their thoughts and commentary. In this situation, accessing archival resources is key to knowing and experiencing history.

Historian Greg Dening penned a line in what remains one of the most moving histories I have ever read: "To have no history is an awful dispossession."[21] I wonder how many other ruptured traditions are out there, lying in archives, libraries, and museums? And I wonder how many other peoples are out there whose chronicles exist, but out of sight?

Notes

I am grateful to Ray Silverman and Bradley Taylor of the University of Michigan Museum Studies Program for the invitation to present an earlier version of this paper in the Museum Studies Colloquium series, "Ownership, Appropriation, Repatriation: Museum Collections in a Changing World," in March 2005, and for the valuable discussion that the presentation generated.

1. United Nations Permanent Forum on Indigenous Issues, http://www.un.org/esa/socdev/unpfii/ (accessed February 13, 2008); World Intellectual Property Organization, http://www.wipo.int/portal/index.html.en (accessed February 13, 2008); United Nations Declaration on the Rights of Indigenous People, http://www.un.org/esa/socdev/unpfii/en/declaration.html (accessed January 23, 2009).

2. The full texts of both acts are available online at the National Park Services site, http://www.cr.nps.gov/hps/laws/religious.htm and http://www.cr.nps.gov/nagpra/ (accessed February 13, 2008). "Cultural patrimony . . . shall mean an object having ongoing historical, traditional, or cultural importance central to the Native American group or culture itself, rather than property owned by an individual Native American, and which, therefore, cannot be alienated, appropriated, or conveyed by any individual regardless of whether or not the individual is a member of the Indian tribe or Native Hawaiian organization, and such object shall have been considered inalienable by such Native American group at the time the object was separated from such group."

3. Amy Kuʻuleialoha Stillman, "Resurrecting Archival Poetic Repertoire for Hawaiian Hula," in *Handle with Care: Ownership and Control of Ethnographic Materials,* ed. Sjoerd Jaarsma (Pittsburgh: University of Pittsburgh Press, 2002), 142.

4. There are, however, circumstances in which a community may decline opportunities to receive repatriated materials, in order to avoid divisive contestation over the control of resources; see Brian P. Oles, "Dangerous Data from Mokil Atoll," in *Handle with Care: Ownership and Control of Ethnographic Materials,* ed. Sjoerd Jaarsma (Pittsburgh: University of Pittsburgh Press, 2002), 174–94.

5. See Amy Stillman, "Of the People Who Love the Land: Vernacular History in the Poetry of Modern Hawaiian Hula," *Amerasia* 28, no. 3 (2002): 85–108.

6. These processes are theorized in the abundance of scholarship on collective and social memory; especially useful are Paul Connerton, *How Societies Remember* (Cambridge: Cambridge University Press, 1989); James Fentress and Chris Wickham, *Social Memory: New Perspectives on the Past* (Oxford: Blackwell, 1992); and Paul Ricoeur's magisterial *Memory, History, Forgetting,* trans. Kathleen Blamey and David Pellauer (Chicago: University of Chicago Press, 2004). In music studies, see George Lipsitz, *Time Passages: Collective Memory and American Popular Culture* (Minneapolis: University of Minnesota Press, 1990); and Kay Kaufman Shelemay, *Let Jasmine Rain Down: Song and Remembrance among Syrian Jews* (Chicago: University of Chicago Press, 1998).

7. Esther K. Mookini, *The Hawaiian Newspapers* (Honolulu: Topgallant, 1974); Helen G. Chapin, *Guide to Newspapers of Hawai'i 1834–2000* (Honolulu: Hawaiian Historical Society, 2000). A comprehensive historical survey is available in Chapin, *Shaping History: The Role of Newspapers in Hawai'i* (Honolulu: University of Hawai'i Press, 1996). Below, I discuss digitizing projects underway to increase access to the newspaper resources.

8. This work is bibliographically confusing. It is a selection of pieces from the Roberts collection, with translations from Hawaiian to English by Mary Kawena Pukui; it is arranged and edited by Pat Namaka Bacon and Nathan Napoka. However, the publisher did not print Bacon and Napoka's names on the cover page, and the University of Hawai'i library cataloging entry did not enter any of those names in either author or editor fields.

9. Helen H. Roberts, *Ancient Hawaiian Music* (Honolulu: Bishop Museum, 1926), 11.

10. *Folktales of Hawai'i*, collected and trans. Mary Kawena Pukui and Laura C. S. Green (Honolulu: Bishop Museum Press, 1995), xvi.

11. The inventory of the Nathaniel Bright Emerson Papers is accessible through the Online Archive of California, http://www.oac.cdlib.org/ (accessed February 13, 2008).

12. Erika Brady, *A Spiral Way: How the Phonograph Changed Ethnography* (Jackson: University of Mississippi Press, 1999). Brady was a sound technician who carried out the dubbing of sound from cylinders to tape.

13. Mary Kay Duggan, "19th-Century California Sheet Music," http://people.ischool.berkeley.edu/~mkduggan/neh.html (accessed January 23, 2009).

14. "Ho'olaupa'i Hawaiian Nūpepa Collection," http://www.nupepa.org (accessed January 23, 2009), part of Ulukau: The Hawaiian Electronic Library, http://www.ulukau.org (accessed January 23, 2009).

15. Ulukau: The Hawaiian Electronic Library, http://ulukau.org (accessed January 23, 2009).

16. The 1853 title used the orthographic convention of that time to indicate the phonemic lengthened vowel by doubling it in print: Ngaa. Twentieth-century orthography replaced the double vowel by adding a macron over a single vowel—Ngā—which is how the title appears in the twentieth-century edition with translations.

17. Igor Krupnik and Lars Krutak, *Akuzilleput Igaqullghet: Our Words Put to Paper* (Washington, D.C.: Arctic Studies Center, National Museum of Natural History, Smithsonian Institution, 2002), 19.

18. *Kalākaua* CD, Daniel Ho Creations, 2006.

19. World Intellectual Property Organization, *Creative Heritage Project*, brochure (WIPO Publication No. L934E/TCH), http://www.wipo.int/export/sites/www/tk/en/folklore/culturalheritage/pdf/creative_heritage_brochure.pdf (accessed May 12, 2008).

20. Barry Barclay, *Mana Tuturu: Maori Treasures and Intellectual Property Rights* (Honolulu: University of Hawai'i Press, 2005), 100.

21. Greg Dening, *Islands and Beaches: Discourse on a Silent Land, Marquesas 1774–1880* (Honolulu: University Press of Hawai'i, 1980), 309.

4 National Patrimony and Cultural Policy

The Case of the Afroperuvian Cajón

JAVIER F. LEÓN

You were born on the coast of Peru
race and rhythm brother
of the conga and the batá
cajón, cajón

—"Anthem to the Peruvian Cajón," words and music by Victor Merino and Isabel Alvarez

On August 2, 2001, the Peruvian National Institute of Culture (INC) issued National Directorial Resolution (RDN) No. 798 declaring the *cajón,* an idiophone from the coastal region of Peru, as Cultural Patrimony of the Nation. The text of the resolution explained "that the Peruvian cajón has its origin in the Colonial Period, when a population of African origin arrived in Peruvian lands and began to make music in community, accompanying itself with simple wooden crates, gradually establishing the form that is known today and that transformed it into the main percussion instrument for many Peruvian rhythms like the festejo, landó, zamacueca, marinera and others, additionally [the cajón] being a unique instrument of its kind worldwide."[1] The document also noted the need for further study regarding the instrument's history and cultural significance while at the same time reminding the reader that, as cultural patrimony, the instrument was under the guardianship of the state and the individuals who formed the Peruvian nation, who also had the duty to protect it.

While still relatively new, declarations such as this have become increasingly common in Peru, a way of identifying particular forms of expressive culture and safeguarding them for the good of society at large. They can be seen as an example of how larger social and economic changes that are taking place in Peru (and in many other parts of the world) are redefining the relationship between local musics (in this case, Afroperuvian music), the state, and civil society. These types of changes are transforming the way in which individuals, groups, and various civil society organizations invoke culture, increasingly giving the concept a pragmatic edge in order to achieve a particular goal.[2] As Ana María Ochoa suggests, in this environment, culture and the arts become more important for their potential to be deployed to achieve political rather than aesthetic ends.[3] In some respects, the declaration of the cajón can be seen as a similar example of cultural expediency. After all, the passing of RDN No. 798 was the result of an advocacy campaign seeking to claim the instrument as uniquely Peruvian at a time when some individuals in Peru felt that the instrument was in danger of being appropriated by foreign interests. From this perspective, it can be said that the cajón campaign was fairly successful. In the intervening years, there has been a fair amount of activity surrounding the cajón, including the proliferation of workshops, teaching methods, concerts, festivals, and competitions; a growing local cajón industry; musical experimentation with new instruments inspired by the cajón; and the promotion of the cajón abroad as a national cultural product.

At the same time, it is more difficult to ascertain whether all of this activity can have a lasting and tangible impact on the Afroperuvian community with which the cajón has historically been associated. Much of the discourse surrounding the cajón has been aimed at validating its Peruvian rather than Afroperuvian origins. Therefore, there is a need to ask whether such moves aid in the recognition of a population that has been excluded from the Peruvian national imagination or contribute to its further disfranchisement. This is an important consideration, given that music and dance practices associated with the cajón have been the principal markers of that which distinguishes the Afroperuvian community from other communities on the Peruvian coast. This distinction allows members of this community to call for specific collective or group rights. The question takes on further relevance when one considers the social and cultural environment in which notions of cultural difference have become increasingly appropriated by capitalist interests and have been often used to validate those identity projects that have the most potential for the development of mainstream society. Against this backdrop, the discussion that follows will assess the potential relevance that the declaration of the cajón as cultural patrimony of the nation has had for members of the Afroperuvian community. To this end, I will first give an overview of the historical relationship of Afroperuvian music and musicians to cultural agencies like the INC and will evaluate how recent changes in cultural policy have affected this relationship. Second, I will chronicle the circumstances that led to the passing of RDN No. 798 and discuss how the role played by those individuals most closely associated with its formulation and promotion were tied to the desire to develop a series of cultural industries surrounding the cajón. Finally, I will examine the subsequent types of musical and cultural production associated with the cajón and analyze the degree to which these have had an impact in raising awareness about the instrument and the community that it represents.

The Cajón in the Age of Neoliberal Cultural Policy

Recent Latin American scholarship suggests that globalization and the adoption of neoliberal economic policies, as part of the process of re-democratization of the last fifteen years, have had a tangible impact on local urban and rural communities in the region.[4] More specifically, there has been a debate focused on whether the push toward privatizing various local industries (among them the culture industry), the weakening of the state, and the strengthening of civil society have had a positive or negative effect on people's ability to assert their cultural rights. In the case of music and dance, it can be argued that, on the one hand, less state intervention can lead to the emergence of more alternatives to the type of institutionalized "official" music and dance ensembles that have been commonplace in the region.[5] On the other, shifting this activity away from state-sponsored institutions can place an undue burden on private citizens, community groups, and/or grassroots organizations seeking to promote the cultivation of particular forms of artistic expression. This is especially the case when the forms of musical expression in question are associated with marginal groups that often lack the political, social, and economic capital necessary to embark on such a project on their own. Consequently, as Víctor Vich points out, in this neoliberal setting there is often a gap that is produced by the state's inability to continue to create persuasive modes of identification and particular communities' ability to generate those forms of identification on their own.[6]

One such case is that of the Afroperuvian community. In a country where issues of race, ethnicity, and national identity have always been informed by debates regarding the place that indigenous and/or mestizo voices should have in the national imaginary, the contributions of Afroperuvians to the development of a modern Peruvian nation remain little more than a footnote in the national narrative.[7] Artists, activists, and scholars give a number of reasons for that absence. Chiefly among them are a) the comparatively small size of the Afroperuvian population vis-à-vis indigenous groups; b) the historical association of descendants of Africans with the very institutions of colonization rather than with the pre-Columbian past; c) the creolized character of Afroperuvian cultural practices, many of which overlap quite significantly with those of the dominant criollo coastal culture; and d) the social pressure that has existed for Afroperuvians to integrate into the aforementioned dominant culture as a means of gaining some amount of social acceptance.[8] This social invisibility, as it has come to be known in recent years, has provided some challenges when invoking Afroperuvian cultural rights. As anthropologist Shane Greene observes, there has been a tendency to "[portray] indigenous people as inevitably 'rooted' in a semi-sovereign soil (the 'Americas') while Afro-descendants are presented as 'uprooted' from their only 'legitimate' sovereign soil on the other side of the Atlantic ('Africa')."[9]

A notable exception to this social invisibility has been in the realm of music and dance, where musicians, artists, and intellectuals have been able to promote these forms of cultural expression as the primary symbols of Afroperuvian identity. The movement started in the 1950s and 1960s with a series of attempts at reviving, revitalizing, and in some cases re-Africanizing a repertoire that was little known outside particular families of musicians.[10] In the decade that followed, these artists were able to take advantage of cultural policies that emphasized regional diversity and developed relationships with state-sponsored cultural organizations such as the INC, which eventually led to the recognition of the revival repertoire as an official form of regional folklore in Peru.[11] While effective at one level, the institutionalization of Afroperuvian music was not without its problems. Chief among them was the canonization of the revival repertoire into a relatively inflexible standard that came to be adopted as part of the curriculum of folklore academies and music and arts programs at schools and universities. This development helped to reinforce the standing of those musicians who had a hand in the development of such a standard, but it also led to the exclusion of younger voices under the charge that their lack of intimate knowledge of the Afroperuvian repertoire threatened to dilute or distort the Afroperuvian musical legacy.[12] Nevertheless, the popularization of Afroperuvian music and dance from the 1970s on has led most Peruvians to recognize these practices as indicative of the cultural distinctiveness of the Afroperuvian community.

Unfortunately, this recognition has yet to translate into larger positive outcomes, particularly in terms of political representation and the ability of some individuals outside the aforementioned musical, artistic, and intellectual circles to identify with these musical practices as being a part of their cultural heritage. Peruvian cultural policy experts suggest that one of the ways of bridging this gap is through an effective and decentralized cultural policy that mediates not only the relationship between the state and these various civil society actors but also the relationship of these two to an increasingly independent culture industry.[13] From this perspective, having an Afroperuvian musical instrument officially recognized as Cultural Patrimony of the Nation can be seen as taking a step in that direction. This is a view that was consistently expressed to me during interviews with current and former INC officials, all of which saw RDN No. 798 as indicative of positive changes in the realm of cultural policy. Since the creation of the INC in 1971, the overwhelming number of declarations regarding cultural patrimony has been tied in one way or another to land and property (archaeological sites, historical buildings, monuments, and the like). In this sense, the concept of cultural patrimony has been fairly static and linked to that of ownership. It has been a way of laying claim to key portions of territory that contained tangible evidence of the historical legacy that defines the Peruvian nation—pre-Columbian ceramics, Inca temples, colonial-era churches, republicanera forts, and so on. In contrast, the cajón constitutes one of the first items associated with a living tradition, and, despite it being a physical object, the language of the declaration defines the cajón less as a relic or museum piece and more as what the United Nations Educational, Scientific, and Cultural Organization (UNESCO) would eventually designate as "intangible cultural heritage," that is, the "practices, representations, expressions, knowledge, skills—as well as the instruments, objects, artifacts and cultural spaces associated therewith—that communities, groups and, in some cases, individuals recognize as part of their cultural heritage."[14] The association of the cajón with the notion of intangible cultural heritage is important because of the emphasis that the UNESCO convention places on a community's ability to define this cultural heritage in that community's own terms. Technically, RDN No. 798 predates UNESCO's Convention for the Safeguarding of Intangible Cultural Heritage in 2003.[15] However, since then, Peru has passed its own legislation in support of the protection of intangible cultural heritage (2004), and consequently, the instrument has come to be seen as a potential test case of the active role that local communities can have on the protection of cultural patrimony.[16]

This shift in cultural policy toward the acknowledgment of living traditions is a marked change from decades past where the norm was for state cultural agencies like the INC to follow a top-down model based on the establishment and enforcement of standards designed to protect the integrity of particular cultural products and forms of cultural production.[17] Moving away from the implicit paternalism of this latter approach, the more recent trend has been to assert that the various communities that contribute to Peru's diverse cultural landscape should have the autonomy to determine what aspects of their cultural production need to be protected and how. The change is not only philosophical but economic. Throughout its three and a half decades of existence, the INC's social and political capital has steadily decreased. Lacking legislative and enforcing power, the INC has had to adapt by developing partnerships with those for whom the organization purported to speak in the past. Soledad Mujica, director of the INC's Directorate of Registration and Study of Culture in Contemporary Peru, suggests that declarations such as that regarding the cajón are good examples of how these partnerships can be mutually beneficial. From her perspective, the recognition of intangible cultural heritage has the potential to empower communities, since it provides the type of official validation that can lead to the more proactive promotion and protection of forms of cultural expression that have always been important to that group of people but have not always been valued as such. This process of validation is also considered to give communities more agency, since it is up to each one to determine which of its forms of cultural expression should be declared part of the intangible cultural patrimony of the nation.[18] In theory, giving a community the ability to register its own forms of cultural expression as patrimony and to be able to request the INC to intervene on the community's behalf when deemed necessary can provide a mechanism through which groups and individuals can assert their cultural rights.[19]

Outside the realm of cultural policy, living up to the potential of such partnerships can be fairly complicated. Some of the challenges are logistical and procedural. At this point, much of the implementation of policies regarding intangible cultural heritage is still in its infancy.[20] There are also deeper questions that are tied to the issue of ownership, such as, who are the individuals deemed to be representatives of "the community" to which a particular intangible cultural patrimony belongs? In the case of the cajón, there are multiple contenders. The prominence that music and dance have had as symbols of Afroperuvian identity suggests that the most likely candidates would be musicians, namely professional musicians and other artists and intellectuals associated with the Afroperuvian music environment in Lima. In many respects, this is quite an appropriate choice. After all, the popularization of the cajón in the second part of the twentieth century is due in large part to the prominent role that the instrument took as a result of the Afroperuvian revival. On the other hand, the association of the Afroperuvian community with this particular group of individuals tends to erase important distinctions within the Afroperuvian communities, such as social and cultural differences between rural communities on the southern coast, rural communities on the northern coast, and urban communities within the capital.[21] This can be difficult given that, as the director of an Afroperuvian non-governmental organization (NGO) pointed out, many of the outlying rural communities, particularly those in the north, have musical practices of their own that in many cases are only peripheral to Peruvian collective memory of what sounds Afroperuvian.[22] Furthermore, today the cajón is not only associated with the Afroperuvian community but has become commonplace in a variety of other musical genres, including criollo popular music, jazz, and more recently some Andean popular musics, thus suggesting a community that is not necessarily bound by a single ethnic, regional, or cultural heritage.

The multiplicity of communities that can lay claim to the cajón can pose problems when it comes to determining whose interests RDN No. 798 best serves. In theory, the fact that all Peruvians are charged with the promotion of an instrument whose origins are still firmly rooted in the experiences of descendants of Africans in Peru speaks to the desired integration of the Afroperuvian community into the larger Peruvian national context. In practice, however, such claims of ownership are often mediated through a complex web of political and economic interests that places some individuals and groups in more privileged positions than others. This gap between who has more and who has less ability to lay claim to the cajón is the product of a logic that rewards those whose invocation of cultural difference can best contribute to the further development of neoliberal social and economic interests. The quest to have the cajón declared cultural patrimony of the nation speaks to that logic and to the potential economic interest that the cajón has come to represent.

Getting a Birth Certificate for the Cajón

The cajón, as it is known in Peru, is a wooden idiophone that developed on the coast and has historically been associated predominantly, but not exclusively, with the Afroperuvian community. The instrument is a wooden box with a round sound hole in the rear and a plywood face that is struck with bare hands by a performer who sits on top of the instrument. Over the years, musicians, artists, and intellectuals have offered a number of theories regarding both the way in which the instrument was developed and the exact time period in which this development took place. The connections that the instrument has to populations of African descent have led some to posit that the cajón may have been originally fashioned out of fruit crates, shipping containers, or pieces of furniture as a substitute for more conventional membranophones that could no longer be fashioned, either because of a scarcity of materials or because of instrument bans imposed by the colonial authority. There are also those who suggest that the cajón may be a direct descendant from West African box membranophones like the *gome* that could have been brought to Peru as a result of the slave trade.[23] The earliest written historical references to the cajón date from the middle of the nineteenth century and are usually found within descriptions of a popular couples' dance known as the *zamacueca,* which, although often associated with descendants of Africans, was also practiced by other populations on the coast.[24]

By the first part of the twentieth century, the cajón was perhaps best known as an accompaniment instrument for the *marinera,* a descendant of the zamacueca that today is considered to be Peru's national dance. The cajón also remained an instrument associated with Afroperuvian communities in general, particularly those in the area of Lima and on the central and southern coast, and it appears to have been used to accompany a number of other music and dance genres, although not as consistently as was the case with the marinera.[25] During the second part of the twentieth century, the cajón became a central element of the Afroperuvian revival movement, and the instrument became increasingly used to accompany a variety of revitalized and reconstructed genres. Along the way, more complex and distinct accompaniment patterns were developed for each genre, and in many cases the cajón became not only an accompaniment instrument but the instrument in charge of providing various cues to other musicians and dancers as well as a solo virtuoso instrument. At the same time, the increasing popularity of Afroperuvian music also led to the proliferation of the cajón to accompany criollo genres like the *vals* and polka, and the instrument is now considered essential to the performance of any criollo or Afroperuvian performance.[26]

Awareness of the existence of other types of cajón outside of Peru is commonplace among Afroperuvian musicians and music aficionados. Afroperuvian musicians have historically been well versed in Afro-Cuban traditions, and many of them have known of the existence of the Cuban instruments by the same name (of different shapes and sizes) for decades due to their experience in performing these genres and the various trips that many of them have taken to Cuba.[27] In recent years, a number of musicians have become aware of the appearance of a similar instrument in the region of Veracruz in Mexico.[28] Then there is the story of how the cajón was adapted to be used in flamenco, a story to which many musicians find a personal connection, given that a number of them know someone who witnessed the event firsthand. In 1977, during a visit to Peru, flamenco artist Paco de Lucía saw a local musician play a cajón at a party that the Spanish embassy had organized in de Lucía's honor. The percussionist was Carlos "Caitro" Soto, one of the founding members of Perú Negro and also a longtime collaborator of criollo composer Chabuca Granda. The Spanish guitarist was intrigued by the instrument's sound and ended up obtaining a cajón from Soto, which was subsequently adapted for use in flamenco by one of de Lucía's band members, Brazilian percussionist Rubem Dantas. Over time, flamenco percussionists developed their own accompaniment patterns and playing styles, and the instrument became quite popular within the contemporary or modern flamenco movement. According to Rafael Santa Cruz, the widespread popularity of the cajón in Spain, the establishment of a local cajón-making industry, and the lack of knowledge regarding the existence of descendants of Africans in Peru led to the assumption that the cajón was an instrument of European origin.[29] It is this uninformed assumption regarding the origins of the cajón more than the existence of instruments by the name in other parts of the world that led to the crusade to declare the cajón as indigenous to Peru.

Although María del Carmen Dongo is the individual most associated with the campaign to vindicate the cajón as uniquely Peruvian, a number of other individuals were invested in similar projects, some of them predating Dongo's much-publicized efforts in the year leading up to the passing of RDN No. 798. Throughout the 1990s, singer Susana Baca had to contend with the aforementioned misconception each time she toured Europe. As the first and probably best-known Afroperuvian artist to enter the international world music scene, Baca often found herself having to correct audiences and members of the press, retelling the story of how Caitro Soto gave Paco de Lucía his first cajón.[30] For Baca, this was a matter of national pride, as she explained during a newspaper interview. "It happens the same as it did with the pisco sour," said the singer, invoking the well-known dispute between Peruvians and Chileans regarding the origin of the alcoholic beverage; "it is because we are generous and we give everything away."[31] Baca's rising popularity on the international stage brought attention to the issue of the origins of the cajón and led to the subsequent and repeated acknowledgment of the instrument's origins by a number of prominent flamenco artists, including de Lucía. In Peru, however, little was known of these events as Baca's career was largely aimed at an international audience and market, and her music and activities abroad were not well known back at home.

María del Carmen Dongo began a similar campaign within Peru. Dongo first became aware of the need to defend the origins of the cajón in 1997 while she was conducting a series of workshops under the direction of guitarist Félix Casaverde at the National University of Costa Rica.[32] However, her project did not begin to form until March 2000, when she returned to Peru after working for a time in Mexico with singer Tania Libertad.[33] At that time, Libertad, a Peruvian singer who has lived in Mexico for more than twenty years and who is best known for singing boleros and *nueva trova,* was in the process of reinventing herself as a performer of Afroperuvian genres in the hopes of entering the world music circuit, much like Susana Baca had done. Dongo had noticed that Libertad's new emphasis on Afroperuvian music and the use of the cajón was being well received by audiences in Mexico and the United States and decided that the time was right to return to Peru and begin her project.[34] For the following year, Dongo taught workshops and gave lectures on the subject. Her efforts were supplemented by the Web site El Rincón Musical Peruano (The Peruvian Musical Corner), an online community of Peruvian music aficionados living predominantly in the United States who devoted a series of pages to documenting the history and various debates regarding the origins of the instrument.[35] Having had prior experience with various arts organizations in Lima, she began to garner the support necessary to bring attention to her cause in those circles. Her workshops at the Catholic University's Cultural Center were well attended, and in the course of one year she graduated 120 young *cajoneros*, many of whom became her tireless supporters. Although still a fairly localized movement, the attention began to pay off. In late May 2001, the French news wire agency Agence France Presse reported that during a concert by flamenco dancer Joaquín Cortés in Lima, a number of the audience members (presumably some of Dongo's supporters) insisted to the members of the press that the *cajones* on stage originally belonged to Peruvian musicians because they had been invented by Afroperuvian slaves.[36]

All of this informal attention began to coalesce into a more visible movement. On June 1, Dongo made a case for the protection of the cajón as part of a series of conferences on tourism organized by the Tourism and Telecommunications Commission of the Congress of the Republic of Peru.[37] A newspaper article written a few weeks later by one of Dongo's students, who also happened to be a journalist, gave the broad strokes of what must have been Dongo's presentation. Playing into preexisting concerns that Peru often does not appreciate its own cultural expressions until they are either praised or appropriated by foreigners, the article sought to fan righteous nationalist indignation and garner support for the project. It began by relating the birth of the cajón to the banning of "drums with leather heads" (*tambores de parche*) by the Spanish Inquisition during the colonial period and remarked on the irony that the very people who sought to ban drums now sold the instrument all over the world, claiming it to be a "flamenco cajón."[38] The quotation marks around the term were used throughout the article to denote the lack of legitimacy of the Spanish instrument. This was also reinforced by the comment that there were insufficient formal construction differences to claim that the flamenco version is a different instrument or a patentable innovation.[39] Using phrases like "cultural theft" and "Spanish re-conquest," the article told readers of the multiple Web sites out of Spain and other parts of Europe that sell cajones without acknowledging the Peruvian origin of the instrument and about the indignation that one should feel at the prospect of people thinking that the best cajones in the world are German-made.[40] Readers were also made aware of Dongo's appeal to the Congress and her call for the promotion of the cajón in Peru by integrating its instruction into educational curricula; sponsoring concerts, festivals, and competitions both in Peru and abroad; and subsidizing a local cajón-making industry.[41]

The Tourism and Telecommunications Commission did not follow up on the matter, but the growing publicity around the cajón did draw the attention of Luis Repetto Málaga, former director of the INC. Throughout the 1990s, the INC's effectiveness in the promotion of various types of cultural activity had waned. In response to the economic crisis of the late 1980s and early 1990s, the Fujimori government restructured and downsized the INC to the point that it was reduced to a largely ineffectual and bureaucratic organization.[42] Emphasis was given to more pragmatic and profitable endeavors that were outside of the INC's jurisdiction, such as the promotion of tourism and the exportation of pottery, textiles, and other crafts.[43] During Repetto's tenure, the INC began to reassert itself in the area of protection of cultural patrimony. More important, despite the fact that the then current cultural policies and constitutional norms did not make room for the notion of intangible heritage, the INC tried to keep up with international developments in cultural policy and began to identify potential candidates nearly four years before the ratification of the UNESCO convention by the Peruvian congress.[44] As Repetto recalls, the cajón seemed like a natural choice, given the instrument's popularity throughout Peru and because most people realized Afroperuvian music's potential to crossover internationally and thus promote Peru abroad.[45] Having been aware of the important role that musicians had had historically in the promotion of Afroperuvian culture and seeking to support Dongo's efforts, Repetto petitioned the current head of the INC, Enrique González Carré, to begin working on the cajón declaration.[46]

RDN No. 798 was passed a few months later, and as Rafael Santa Cruz puts it, the Peruvian state gave the cajón its long-awaited official birth certificate.[47] At the time, the cajón was one of the first in a string of cultural goods—including the Peruvian *paso* horse, the *caballito de totora, seviche,* and the pisco sour—targeted for official recognition.[48] In the previous section, it was noted that even though these products qualified as forms of intangible cultural heritage, the mechanisms for the protection and promotion of such goods did not come into place until after the ratification of UNESCO's Convention for the Safeguarding of Intangible Cultural Heritage in 2004.

This, however, does not mean that there were not other tangible reasons why passing the declaration would be considered advantageous. Both the language surrounding the "cajón controversy," as it was dubbed by Dongo and her collaborators, and the very text of the resolution suggest that RDN No. 798 was also envisioned as a sort of copyright. After a decade of economic reforms emphasizing free trade and privatization, many Peruvians had become increasingly wary of neoliberalism.[49] Although it had tapered off in the mid-1990s, foreign investment in Peru was still sizable, and it was common for people to complain about the proliferation of foreign-owned businesses and industries in all realms of Peruvian society.[50] In this climate, the notion that foreigners could profit from Peruvian ingenuity infuriated many, much to the benefit of Dongo's crusade, and therefore it is no surprise that calls for the support of this resolution were consistently couched in terms of the development of specific cultural industries, particularly those centered on live performance, education, and manufacturing.

Developing cultural industries surrounding the cajón could be an effective way of creating a sustainable infrastructure for the further promotion of the instrument. Speaking to this, Repetto points out that developing effective cajón pedagogy is an important aspect of how knowledge of and interest in the cajón can be imparted to a population seeking new ways of actively engaging with the notion of being Peruvian.[51] Similarly, having musicians travel abroad as cultural envoys and allowing local makers to introduce their instruments in the North American and European markets can further sustain that infrastructure. Three decades ago, at the height of popularity of the Afroperuvian revival repertoire, it would have been the role of the state to spearhead these initiatives through subsidies, trade regulations, and the like. In fact, there were few cases of such successful initiatives at that time, most notably, perhaps, the state's patronage of Perú Negro during the 1970s.[52] Today, the bulk of this role is left to a variety of social actors within Peruvian civil society (individual artists, university and neighborhood cultural centers, grassroots organizations, NGOs, and so on). While in theory this implies a greater potential for agency, in practice this has not proven to be the case. As Santiago Alfaro Rotondo observes, the persistence of uneven development under neoliberalism cannot be ignored; otherwise, "we would have to negate the existence of power relations between members of different cultures and assume that all us citizens have the same opportunities to realize our life projects."[53] Consequently, attempts at developing cultural industries around the cajón have been equally uneven, often benefiting some individuals more than others and not always engaging with the broader Afroperuvian community.

The Cajón and the Afroperuvian Cultural Industry

In the context of this discussion, the term "cultural industry" has come to mean those areas of society that produce and disseminate products and knowledge that in one way or another are associated with the pursuit of cultural endeavors such as music (both live and recorded), film, art, literature, and so on.[54] Within the realm of cultural policy in Peru, the cultural industry has generally been thought of as the local network of mass production and distribution of CDs, DVDs, television programs, and books, both national and international, with or without an explicit educational purpose. It has also come to include what are at times called small and medium cultural industries—musical instruments, masks and costumes, pottery and crafts (what in Latin America is often called *artesanías*), tourism, live performances, educational workshops, local and regional festivals, and so on. Much of the interest in these networks has been aimed at determining and improving their effectiveness at providing goods and services that can promote cultural activity on a large scale. There are many facets to these discussions, most of them concerned with the relationship that these cultural industries have with various local and transnational market interests. These range from figuring out ways of improving the content and quality of these aforementioned goods and services to discussion regarding the best ways to capitalize on and protect local cultural industries that may be at a competitive disadvantage with their transnational counterparts.[55] Less attention, however, has been given to the producers themselves, often leading to the impression that those who are the most visible are individuals who are adequate representatives of the communities with which a particular type of cultural production is associated.

Situating Afroperuvian musical production within this series of networks can be complicated. Despite the fact that the popularization of Afroperuvian music, particularly the revival repertoire, was due to its successful dissemination through the mass media during the 1970s, that panorama has markedly changed. Today, Afroperuvian music occupies a relatively small but nonetheless visible and stable niche within a popular music environment that is generally dominated by salsa, *techno cumbia, reggaetón,* and a variety of Andean vernacular musics. The majority of individuals who actively engage with this music are urban middle or working class from a variety of ages and cultural backgrounds and with different levels of investment in Afroperuvian music, depending on the place that such music has in their own personal identities. On the other hand, many of the producers of Afroperuvian cultural products such as music are individuals of African descent but from a variety of different backgrounds. Some have grown up within families with long and strong traditions of music-making, while others have come to music relatively late and learned how to sing, dance, or play a musical instrument by taking private instruction or attending a folklore academy. There are also differences in terms of social class, with some producers being working-class musicians who make ends meet by accepting any opportunity that comes their way, while others are relatively well-established middle-class performers whose access to better economic and educational opportunities have also allowed them to try on many roles, including those of educators, producers, promoters, venue owners, and the like. There are also those individuals who do not necessarily self-identify as Afroperuvian but rather as having a mixed background or being criollos or mestizos; nonetheless, they have grown up in musical environments where Afroperuvian music is actively practiced or have managed to master that knowledge through other means. Consequently, Afroperuvian musical production is defined by a number of social actors ranging from "rank-and-file" workingclass musicians employed at restaurants and nightclubs, to freelance music and dance instructors, to college and professional school students taking classes and moonlighting in a number of amateur and semiprofessional groups, to street performers, to professional studio musicians, to influential celebrities and recordings artists.

In one way or another, all of these individuals form a part of the Afroperuvian artistic community and are therefore contributors to the generation and promotion of Afroperuvian music. Their differences, however, can have an influence on whose cultural production is most visible. While Alfaro's comments regarding uneven development refer to an unlevel playing field within the broader realm of cultural production (for example, the disproportionate advantage that Hollywood films have over small independent films), many of the same observations apply to the diverse groups of individuals involved with one particular environment. Differences in terms of an individual's ability to accumulate and favorably spend his or her social, cultural, and economic capital are therefore important in understanding how this particular field of cultural production operates.[56] From this perspective, it should be clear that Dongo's activities surrounding the declaration of the cajón constitute a series of moves to consolidate her own cultural capital within the realm of Afroperuvian musical production. This has been a necessary strategy given that, although she is recognized as a skilled percussionist, she is not considered by many to be an Afroperuvian musical community insider. Rather, her visibility within this realm of cultural production has been the result of her connection to prominent artists with whom she has worked over the years, such as Eva Ayllón and Tania Libertad, and because of the prominence that she has been able to gain within particular sectors of Limeño society since the declaration of the cajón as cultural patrimony.

In the year following the passing of RDN No. 798, pictures of Dongo playing her cajón began to appear in a variety of blogs and Web sites along with news of the resolution and excerpted text fragments culled from the pages of *El Rincón Musical Peruano* and from newspaper articles. These sites also chronicled the series of concerts and events that she organized in an effort to continue bringing attention to the cajón. On October 31, 2001, the Day of Criollo Song, Dongo organized a large concert at the Nicomedes Santa Cruz Auditorium in Lima's Grand Park that featured scores of well-known cajoneros as special guests and brought together important figures of criollo and Afroperuvian music like Arturo "Zambo" Cavero, Pepe Villalobos, and an elderly Caitro Soto, the musician who nearly three decades earlier had given a cajón to Paco de Lucía.[57] The concert was broadcast over the Internet by the Web site Peru.com and featured as another of its centerpieces the premiere of "Himno al Cajón Peruano" (Anthem to the Peruvian Cajón). The connection that was made between the resolution and Dongo's efforts to promote the cajón soon led to her becoming one of the state's favorite cultural ambassadors and defenders of intangible cultural patrimony. In this capacity, Dongo and her group, Manomadera, were invited by the INC and PromPerú, the state's tourism agency, to represent Peru in the Second Encounter for the Promotion and Diffusion of the Folkloric Patrimony of the Ibero-American Countries, which was sponsored by UNESCO in Santa Ana de Coro, Venezuela.[58] The theme for the encounter was "African Influences on Traditional Andean Cultures," and during the closing ceremonies, the participants ratified the cajón's national origin as being Peruvian. In the months and years that followed, Dongo and her group continued to receive invitations from PromPerú to travel and perform in various parts of the world, including the International Percussion Festival in Puerto Rico, which as one of its themes honored the work of women percussionists, and UNESCO-sponsored festivals in Brazil and Spain.

The events of 2001 served as the inspiration for two elaborate concert productions that used the cajón as a centerpiece: "El cajón es del Perú" (The Cajón is from Perú) in 2002 and "Cajón peruano: A golpe de tierra" (Peruvian Cajón: To the beat of earth) in 2006. Both productions featured Dongo with more than twenty of her students playing the cajón in perfect synchronicity while accompanying a dance troupe whose choreographies provided modern dance reinterpretations of Afroperuvian dances like the *festejo, landó,* and zamacueca. The productions also spun off multimedia CD-ROMs, CDs, and DVDs, which included materials regarding the instrument's history, the "controversy," and Dongo's efforts to promote its Peruvian origins as well as T-shirts and, of course, cajones. Dongo's music has been received favorably by most audiences, although some Afroperuvian music aficionados find the productions most effective either through live performances or video. The emphasis that the presentations have on visuals does not translate as well to CD, where many of the long percussion breaks feel a bit monotonous, as do the at times relentless *guapeos,* usually calling out either "Perú!" or "cajón!" or some variation of both.[59] Sensing that the cajón campaign is reaching its limits, Dongo is in the process of developing a new show that promises to be a bit more varied. She also continues to travel abroad and teach cajón workshops, and in recent years Dongo has begun to develop a type of rhythm therapy centered on Afroperuvian rhythmic patterns.

For the most part, Dongo's project has attracted the attention of middle-class and upper-middle-class criollo audiences. Within this realm, her activities are well appreciated not only because she integrates her students into her presentations but also because of the emphasis that she gives to the fact that anyone, regardless of cultural background or, perhaps more important, gender, can learn to play the instrument. This approach is consistent with the idea that the cajón is a musical instrument that belongs to *all* Peruvians, regardless of class or cultural background. It also supports the notion that today there is a need for a more progressive and cosmopolitan conceptualization of tradition that moves away from the type of orthodoxy that dictates that cajones should be played only by Afroperuvian males, because that is perceived to be more "authentic." This latter point is echoed by cultural policy officials who in recent years have come to informally use the phrase "cultural Talibans" to refer to those who have yet to embrace the more recent discourse of intangible cultural patrimony, living tradition, and multiculturalism.[60] For them, Dongo and Manomadera have come to personify the new face of multicultural arts in Peru, at least as envisioned by cultural centers and performing arts organizations associated with the INC and the decidedly urban, cosmopolitan audiences that patronize their activities.

This environment, however, does not map itself directly over the field of Afroperuvian musical production. To be sure, historically there have been overlaps, particularly when it comes to prominent artists and celebrities like Nicomedes and Victoria Santa Cruz, Perú Negro, Eva Ayllón, and Susana Baca. But generally speaking, there has been a gap between the types of public programs and institutional initiatives promoted by the state and the Afroperuvian community whose cultural production these programs and initiatives seek to promote. This is particularly evident from the INC's first published *Directory of Arts and Culture in Peru* (2006), which sought to provide a complete registry of individuals, venues, institutions, ensembles, and mass media programs devoted to cultural endeavors. Aside from Dongo and Manomadera, the publication omits nearly every major Afroperuvian artist who is currently active in Lima, not to mention the countless number of working musicians, neighborhood associations, grassroots organizations, and NGOs devoted to the promotion of Afroperuvian music and dance.[61] It is this lack of representation in the legitimate realm of "the cultural" that poses problems for the Afroperuvian community. As Gisela Cánepa Koch points out, "In the framework of discourses and politics that promote the concept of Peru as a brand name, according to which all forms of cultural expression are potentially an economic resource, the mere act of having a distinguishable cultural repertoire and the capacity to represent it transforms their practitioners into potential agents of development of the city and the nation."[62] The cajón has become that distinguishable cultural repertoire, and Dongo's association with the passing of RDN No. 798 and the efforts to copyright the cajón as Peruvian cultural property have given her the expediency necessary to be recognized as an authority on all cajón-related matters.

Generally speaking, most musicians have been appreciative of the fact that the cajón has received official recognition, but there has been strong ambivalence about associating the project exclusively with Dongo. As suggested earlier, most individuals who are "in the know" regarding Afroperuvian musical matters have been aware of how the cajón got to Spain for decades; from their perspective, the "controversy" was nothing new. Furthermore, it was not something that many found worth contesting. After all, if the same logic applied across the board, then Afroperuvian musicians would be forced to disclaim that the conga drums, bongos, and cowbells that they routinely use in their performances are originally Afro-Cuban or Afro-Caribbean, to say nothing of the *batá* drums and *djembes* that have become popular in recent years and that Dongo herself uses in her presentations. The fact that Dongo invited a number of well-known percussionists to participate in the concert that she organized in Lima's Grand Park was perceived as an expression of solidarity. However, a number of them were disappointed when they arrived at the technical rehearsal and saw how all the guest cajoneros had been arranged in a pyramid shape with Dongo sitting at the very top. Some considered this an insult, given that among the guest artists were individuals who came from families that had been playing the cajón for generations, while they saw Dongo as an outsider, someone who started playing *nueva canción* and rose through the ranks of the salsa circuit before playing mostly auxiliary percussion, congas, and bongos for artists like Ayllón and Libertad. There was also resentment from some of the performers involved in the recording of "Himno al cajón peruano" who alleged that they were not credited for their participation and had to complain to Dongo's production company in order to gain recognition.[63] This lack of acknowledgment was especially mortifying for the singer of a well-known local group who had to step in and sing lead during the session because the Manomadera member who was supposed to do it had been unable to learn her part. In her case, no acknowledgment was ever made, despite the fact that the anthem became one of Dongo's trademarks and this singer's unaccredited voice became the centerpiece of the subsequent production "El cajón es del Perú" and the accompanying multimedia CD-ROM.

This is not to say that other members of the Afroperuvian musical community have not been able to benefit from the attention that the cajón has received as of late. Over the last few years, there has been a growing interest in the instrument, something that has opened up a number of performing and teaching opportunities for local musicians. Parallel to the cajón declaration, there has also been what guitarist Yuri Juárez refers to as a change of conscience among Afroperuvian musicians regarding the place that tradition should have in contemporary music-making.[64] Increasingly, more conservative attitudes that advocated the adherence to strict stylistic codes that were deemed to make music more "authentic" have given way to an interest in innovation that seeks to reflect musicians' multiple interests in different types of world music, jazz, electronica, and so on. This turn is tied to larger societal changes that have been taking place in Peru and that, as suggested earlier, are placing more of an emphasis on cosmopolitan and multicultural interests. At the same time, however, these musicians are still concerned with producing a type of music that remains uniquely Peruvian. The cajón has proven useful in this regard, given its distinctive sound and the fact that musicians can evoke a certain Peruvian character in their compositions by using the various Afroperuvian rhythms associated with the instrument. Some musicians have also developed an interest in Cuban and Spanish versions of the instrument, and, unlike Dongo's more nationalistically inflected music, these artists actively incorporate elements of the musics associated with those instruments into their reinterpretation of the Afroperuvian repertoire.

The concept of the cajón as an autochthonous instrument has helped in the legitimization of some of these musical borrowings through the adoption of a series of cajón-like instruments. Adapting rhythmic patterns from musical traditions outside of Peru and applying them to arrangements of landós or festejos has been commonplace for a number of decades. In the 1970s, Perú Negro, in collaboration with Cuban percussionist Guillermo Nicasio Regeira—"El Niño"— helped popularize the use of Cuban *tumbadoras,* bongos, and cowbells.[65] Similarly, in the 1990s, guitarist and arranger Walter "Jocho" Velásquez became known for adding Afro-Cuban batá drums to Eva Ayllón's arrangements. However, such incorporations, although popular—particularly in the case of the tumbadoras and bongos—were never fully accepted as part of the Afroperuvian tradition, and in some cases, they were dismissed by critics who found such approaches as being "too commercial." In the last few years, however, such moves have become more permissible, particularly when the aforementioned rhythmic patterns are performed not on batá drums, congas, bongos, or djembes but on locally built, all-wooden versions of the same instruments. These instruments, particularly those built by A tempo Percusión, have become extremely popular among professional groups and, as A tempo founder Alexis Castañeda points out, are starting to become considered an integral part of contemporary Afroperuvian music.[66] Some of these instruments, like the *batajón* (a wooden version of a batá drum), are local variations of instruments that were already commercially available in the United States through companies like Fat Conga, while others, like the *caja udu* (a reinterpretation of the Nigerian *udu*), are Castañeda's own invention. This is not merely an issue of buying locally made instruments and thus supporting local industries but also an attempt at using particular construction techniques associated with the cajón as a means of claiming other musical instruments as Peruvian. A number of well-known percussionists and other artists, both from Peru and abroad, have come to endorse Castañeda's instruments, including Eva Ayllón, Perú Negro, Leonardo "Gigio" Parodi, members of Susana Baca's and Marc Anthony's bands, and Chilean singer/songwriter Joe Vasconcellos. Some musicians like Rony Campos, director of Perú Negro, even make an aesthetic argument in favor of these instruments, suggesting that the timbre of an all-wooden percussion ensemble gives their music a uniquely Peruvian sound.[67]

At the same time, a greater appreciation for the cajón has also generated more interest in the history of the instrument. While Dongo's promotional materials and various Web sites that were used to promote her activities provided some information regarding the origins of the instrument, nationalist agendas and the desire to prove that the first cajón was created in Peru led to a number of unsubstantiated claims that traced the origins of the instrument to the sixteenth century or in some cases to Africa. As a response to all of this misinformation, Rafael Santa Cruz, nephew of the noted Nicomedes and Victoria Santa Cruz and a well-known musician, actor, and educator, embarked on a research project that yielded the book *El Cajón Afro Peruano* (The Afro Peruvian Cajón).[68] According to him, the motivations for writing the book were multiple; among them were his attempt to sort through all the versions and claims that were being made about the instrument and to recognize the importance of the cajón not only as a cultural product but as a symbol of black cultural resistance in Peru.[69] Since the publication of the first edition in January 2004, the book has become immensely popular because of its meticulous attention to historical sources, musical transcriptions of rhythmic patterns associated with the cajón, and an emphasis on a wide variety of construction and playing styles, many of which are demonstrated by a number of prominent Afroperuvian musicians in an accompanying CD. Santa Cruz's work has been well received by other members of the musical community, largely due to his efforts at recognizing the contributions of other percussionists and to his interest in situating the cajón within a larger international context that led to the dialogue between Peruvian, Spanish, and Cuban musicians. In the last few years, Santa Cruz has also become well known in the educational workshop circuit and has traveled to Brazil, Chile, France, and Spain to give lectures on the history of the cajón. His expertise was also prominently featured in the documentary *El cajón con alma negra* (The cajón with its black soul) by Claudia Ruiz (2007).

Unfortunately, invoking the cajón and its cultural legacy as an effective resource has proven to be more difficult for those who are less visible within the field of Afroperuvian musical production. Professional musicians like María del Carmen Dongo, Rafael Santa Cruz, Susana Baca, and members of Perú Negro have been able to invoke the cajón as resource largely because of their perceived status as celebrities within the Peruvian public sphere and/or culture bearers within the Afroperuvian community. This visibility translates into a possibility that their activities will yield some sort of return from which the broader Peruvian society can benefit, whether it is an increase in the number of middle-class professionals who decide to enroll in cajón classes at their local cultural center or improved visibility of local industries abroad through the association of these products with Latin Grammy-winning and Grammy-nominated artists. This is precisely the reason why the campaign to promote the cajón has been primarily couched as an issue of ownership, with Peru seeking to legitimize its right to the instrument and, in the process, reaping any revenue that such ownership might yield. In this light, the notion that any members of the Afroperuvian community can lay equal claim to the cajón and appeal to the state (via the INC) if they feel someone else has misappropriated their cultural heritage appears compromised. One can too easily imagine a situation in which objections to a particular use of the cajón by members of the Afroperuvian community would fall on deaf ears if resolving the situation in their favor were to somehow compromise the increase in cultural activity surrounding the cajón that has taken place in the last few years. This is, in fact, part of the reason why no attempts were made to openly challenge Dongo's cajón campaign, despite the reservations that some had regarding her self-characterization as a central cajón figure within the Afroperuvian community and her unwillingness to share the spotlight with other musicians. At some level or another, people assumed that Dongo's close connection with the state rendered meaningless any claims that they may have against her.

Outside the realm of professional musicians, it is fair to say that the cajón has become more visible than in previous years. Today, many events having to deal with a celebration of Afroperuvian, Limeño, or coastal culture feature an event involving the cajón. This was the case with the First National Cajón competition held between July 12 and July 19, 2007, to commemorate the third anniversary of Caitro Soto's death; with the free cajón workshops offered as part of the Peruvian National Library's 473rd Anniversary of the City of the Kings (Lima) that took place on January 18, 2008; and with the Second Regional Competition of Peruvian Cajón that was held in the northern departments of Piura and Tumbes on September 27, 2007. These events were made possible due to partnerships between national and regional offices of the INC, corporate sponsors, regional governments and municipalities, local school districts, television and radio stations, grassroots organizations, and NGOs. They also constitute successful examples of the type of collaboration envisioned by INC officials when it comes to the protection and promotion of intangible cultural patrimony.

However, these initiatives appear to have had limited reach within the broader Afroperuvian community. As Oswaldo Bilbao, director of the NGO the Center for Ethnic Development (CEDET) observes, the cajón and the Afroperuvian genres associated with it are an important aspect of Afroperuvian identity with people in the region of Lima, in the communities in the southern districts of Chincha and Cañete to the south, and to a degree in the northern community of Zaña in the north.[70] Outside of those areas—for example, in the southern areas of Ica and Nazca or in the northern settlements of Yapatera and Morropón—people do not recognize the instrument nor revival genres like the festejo or landó as being a part of their daily lives.[71] Consequently, some of these communities have begun to look for their own symbols. In the case of the northern communities in the area of Piura, this led to the declaration of the *cumanana,* a local poetic/song form, as national cultural patrimony.[72] Most recently, at the behest of Rafael Santa Cruz, RDN No. 1765 (December 28, 2007) declared the Afroperuvian *cajita* national patrimony of the nation, this time defining the instrument as being uniquely Afroperuvian rather than a "shared" instrument, as became the case when the cajón was officially labeled the "Peruvian cajón."[73] It is unlikely that either one of these initiatives will become a more appropriate symbol of the Afroperuvian community given that both the cumanana and the cajita are not as widely known and are generally associated with specific subgroups rather than with the whole community.

Conclusion

To suggest that the declaration of the cajón as cultural patrimony has amounted to little more than an appropriation of an Afroperuvian symbol by the hegemonic sectors of Peruvian society would be to ignore the tangible effect that the passing of RDN No. 798 also has had on the Afroperuvian musical environment. At the same time, it is also fair to point out that the results of the campaign to promote the cajón have been mixed. As suggested above, within Lima's urban environment, the issue of ownership of the cajón is complex and cuts across class, cultural, and ethnic boundaries. Different sets of social actors within both the realm of Afroperuvian musical production and the broader Limeño public sphere can lay claim to the cajón for a variety of different reasons, ranging from those who see the instrument as a symbol of their ethnic and cultural heritage to those who have come to embrace it as a contemporary manifestation of an increasingly cosmopolitan and multicultural society. The impact of the declaration has probably been most visible with the predominantly non-Afroperuvian urban middle class whose more active engagement with the instrument has gone on to validate to a certain extent the historical contributions of Afroperuvians to the development of Peruvian coastal culture. In this context, María del Carmen Dongo and her sizable cohort of women performers have also helped question more traditional gender roles, making it not only acceptable but empowering to take up the cajón.

Within the Afroperuvian musical environment, ownership of the cajón and who has the right to be a spokesperson for the Afroperuvian community have been more contested issues. Despite the optimistic and egalitarian vision associated with the protection and promotion of intangible cultural heritage, in practice the social and cultural space within which cultural policy is realized is partially structured by neoliberal interests that reward those performances of difference that are deemed to provide more of a return investment for Peruvian society at large. Accordingly, Dongo's campaign to consecrate the cajón as a Peruvian national product, her advocacy for the development of local industries supporting the cultivation of the cajón, the close ties that she was able to develop with state organizations such as the INC and PromPerú, and the appeal that her project had for the urban middle class placed her in a privileged position in this regard, leading to the perception by some members of the Afroperuvian musical community that the cajón had been co-opted by someone who was not considered to be an insider in that community. While there was not a direct challenge of Dongo's various projects, other influential individuals within the community have been able to carve out a space for alternate representations of the cajón as a symbol of Afroperuvian identity. Among these we find an increased interest in scholarship regarding the instrument as well as experimentation with cajón-inspired instruments, both attempts at relocating Afroperuvian cultural production within the Afroperuvian musical community. Regrettably, the cajón has yet to prove an effective symbol of identity beyond the two above-mentioned environments. This has been due largely to the inability of cultural policy to reach more marginal spaces within Peruvian society effectively and provide the people in those spaces with symbols that they find relevant to their own experiences.

Notes

I would like to thank Dan Sharp and Steve Selka for comments on an earlier draft of this piece. I would also like to thank Shane Greene for some of the discussions we've had on the topic of Afroperuvian rights, Estevan Azcona for his expertise on *son jarocho,* and Molly Burke for her help with copyediting my drafts.

1. Instituto Nacional de Cultura (INC), "Resolución Directoral Nacional No. 798/INC" (Cajón peruano declarado Patrimonio Cultural de la Nación), August 2, 2001, *El Peruano,* August 10, 2001: Normas Legales, p. 208594.

2. George Yúdice, *The Expediency of Culture: Uses of Culture in the Global Era* (Durham, N.C.: Duke University Press, 2003).

3. Ana María Ochoa, *Entre los deseos y los derechos: Un ensayo crítico sobre políticas culturales* (Bogotá: Instituto Colombiano de Antropología e Histori a, 2003), 52–53.

4. See, for example, Charles R. Hale, "Neoliberal Multiculturalism: The Remaking of Cultural Rights and Racial Dominance in Central America," *Political and Legal Anthropology Review* 28, no. 1 (2005): 10–28; and Yun-Joo Park and Patricia Richards, "Negotiating Neoliberal Multiculturalism: Mapuche Workers in the Chilean State," *Social Forces* 85, no. 3 (2007): 1319–39.

5. For examples of these types of groups, see T. M. Scruggs, "Cultural Capital, Appropriate Transformations, and Transfer by Appropriation in Western Nicaragua: 'El baile de marimba,'" *Latin American Music Review* 19, no. 1 (1998): 1–30; Katherine J. Hagedorn, *Divine Utterances: The Performance of Afro-Cuban Santeria* (Washington, D.C.: Smithsonian Institution Press, 2001), 136–72; and Heidi Carolyn Feldman, *Black Rhythms of Peru: Reviving African Musical Heritage in the Black Pacific* (Middletown, Conn.: Wesleyan University Press, 2006), 125–70.

6. Víctor Vich, "Gestionar riesgos: Agencia y maniobra en la política cultural," in *Políticas culturales: Ensayos críticos,* ed. Guillermo Cortés and Víctor Vich (Lima: Instituto de Estudios Peruanos, 2006), 45–70.

7. See, for example, Mark Thurner, *From Two Republics to One Divided: Contradictions of Postcolonial Nationmaking in Andean Peru* (Durham, N.C.: Duke University Press, 1997); and Marisol de la Cadena, *Indigenous Mestizos: The Politics of Race and Culture in Cuzco, Peru, 1919–1991* (Durham, N.C.: Duke University Press, 2000).

8. Recent estimates are that Afroperuvians make up 4 to 8 percent of the total national population (28.5 million), while indigenous groups make up approximately 40 percent (Margarita Sánchez, Maurice Bryan, and MRG Partners, "Afro-Descendants, Discrimination and Economic Exclusion in Latin America," Minority Rights Group International, http://www.minorityrights.org [accessed January 27, 2008]).

The term "criollo" is one that is historically quite complex. For the purposes of this piece, the term will refer to those social and musical practices that are considered to be part of the dominant or mainstream coastal culture and the individuals who identify with them. While this sense of the term tends to assume a primarily Spanish/European cultural base informed by Afroperuvian and some mestizo influences, it should be noted that not all people who consider themselves criollo are predominantly of European descent. That tends to be the case with the upper and upper-middle classes in urban areas such as Lima. Among working-class and middle-class individuals, however, the term applies to a far more ethnically diverse constituency.

There are a number of scholars, many of them ethnomusicologists, who have discussed some of these factors. See, for example, Feldman, *Black Rhythms of Peru,* 2–3; Raúl R. Romero, "Black Music and Identity in Peru: Reconstruction and Revival of Afro-Peruvian Musical Traditions," in *Music and Black Ethnicity in the Caribbean and Latin America,* ed. Gerard H. Béhague (Miami: University of Miami North-South Center, 1994), 309–12; and William David Tompkins, "The Musical Traditions of the Blacks of Coastal Peru," Ph.D. diss., University of California, Los Angeles, 1981, 367–68.

9. Shane Greene, "Entre lo indio, lo negro, y lo incaico: The Spatial Hierarchies of Difference in Multicultural Peru," *Journal of Latin American and Caribbean Anthropology* 12, no. 2 (2007): 444.

10. Romero, "Black Music and Identity in Peru"; Feldman, *Black Rhythms of Peru.*

11. Probably the two most notable examples are that of Victoria Santa Cruz, who became director of the National School of Folklore and the National Folklore Ensemble, and the dance company Perú Negro, which was largely subsidized by the government after the members became Cultural Ambassadors of Peru.

12. Javier León, "The 'Danza de las Cañas': Music, Theatre and Afroperuvian Modernity," *Ethnomusicology Forum* 16, no. 1 (2007): 133–36.

13. See, for example, the recent collection by Guillermo Cortés and Víctor Vich, *Políticas culturales: Ensayos críticos* (Lima: Instituto de Estudios Peruanos, 2006).

14. "Convention for the Safeguarding of the Intangible Cultural Heritage," UNESCO .org, October 17, 2003, http://www.unesco.org/culture/ich/index.php?pg=00022 (accessed January 16, 2008).

15. The latter was passed on October 17, 2003, in Paris.

16. Law No. 28296, passed on June 21, 2004, called for the development of guidelines

regarding the protection of intangible cultural heritage. This was followed up by RDN No. 1207 in November 2004, which recognized contemporary cultural manifestations as part of the Cultural Patrimony of the Nation and adopted much of the language of the UNESCO convention into its text. Finally, with Law No. 28555, passed on June 1, 2005, the Peruvian congress formally recognized the convention. Soledad Mujica Bayly, interview by author, June 14, 2007, tape recording; Luis Repetto Málaga, interview by author, June 10, 2007, tape recording.

17. Perhaps the best known of these attempts at regularization is the process of qualification that was first established by José María Arguedas when he was director of the Casa de la Cultura in the 1960s and that came to be adopted upon the creation of the INC in 1974. The process of qualification required musicians to register and be evaluated by a commission in order to ensure that their music, choreography, and dress was consistent with those norms deemed standard and authentic with a particular regional tradition (Raúl R. Romero, *Debating the Past: Music, Memory and Identity in the Andes* [New York: Oxford University Press, 2001], 98–101).

18. Mujica interview.

19. During an interview with Mujica, she cited a recent case involving a local cell phone company that had shot some footage of an Andean dance for a commercial. The audio track of the original footage, taken at a local celebration, was of poor quality, so the production company was forced to overdub similar music for the final version of the commercial. When the commercial aired, members of the community complained to the local INC office that the cell phone company was using music performed by the correct group of performers but for a different festivity, and, even though the music was similar, it misrepresented a cultural practice that was part of the national patrimony; members of the community demanded action. The INC interceded on behalf of the community and requested that the cell phone company overdub the audio track of the commercial once again with pre-recorded music selected by the members of the community as culturally appropriate. The cell phone company complied, and all parties were satisfied.

20. Santiago Alfaro Rotondo, "Estado del arte del patrimonio inmaterial en el Perú," 2005, Lo Centro Regional para la Salvaguardia del Patrimonio Cultural Inmaterial de América Latina (CRESPIAL), http://www.crespial.org/web/peru.php (accessed January 23, 2008); Luis Guillermo Lumbreras, "El papel del Estado en el campo de la cultura," in *Políticas culturales: Ensayos críticos*, ed. Guillermo Cortés and Víctor Vich (Lima: Instituto de Estudios Peruanos, 2006), 71–111. A survey of RDNs issued by the INC between August 21, 1997, and January 19, 2008, shows that out of 873 cultural patrimony declarations, 634 (72.62 percent) were for archaeological sites and 200 (22.91 percent) for monuments and historical buildings, and the remaining 39 (4.47 percent) in one way or another can be considered some type of intangible cultural heritage.

21. This latter point was brought to my attention by the work of Shane Greene, who discusses how, within the context of activist-seeking political representation, the same types of regional and class difference among Afroperuvians complicate what is often conceived as one homogeneous Afroperuvian community, often leading to various internal conflicts ("Entre lo indio," 449–50). See also the work of Park and Richards dealing with the challenges that differences in social class can bring for Mapuche activists in Chile ("Negotiating Neoliberal Multiculturalism").

22. Oswaldo Bilbao Lobatón, interview by author, December 18, 2007, tape recording.

23. While many of these theories are certainly plausible, there is little evidence to support them. Colonial sources describing musical instruments associated with enslaved Africans mention a wide variety of instruments, among them many membranophones (Tompkins, "Musical Traditions," 147–51). This suggests that neither were materials for the construction of these instruments scarce nor that membranophones were banned in any sort of systematic way by the Spanish. Furthermore, these descriptions do not make mention of any instrument resembling the cajón either in shape or construction materials.

24. Tompkins, "Musical Traditions," 143–44; Rafael Santa Cruz Castillo, *El cajón afro peruano*, 2nd ed. (Lima: RSANTACRUZ Ediciones, 2006), 64–69.

25. On the northern coast, particularly in the region of Piura, many musicians use an instrument known as the *checo*—a large gourd bottom that is placed in between the knees and played like a drum—as a substitute for the cajón.

26. Javier F. León, "El que no tiene de inga, tiene de mandinga: Negotiating Tradition and Ethnicity in Peruvian Criollo Popular Music," master's thesis, University of Texas at Austin, 1997, 136–37; Santa Cruz, *El cajón afro peruano*, 76.

27. Feldman, *Black Rhythms of Peru*, 147–50; Javier F. León, "Mass Culture, Commodification, and the Consolidation of the Afro-Peruvian Festejo," *Black Music Research Journal* 26, no. 2 (2006): 230–32. The Cuban version of the instrument comes in three different sizes and is occasionally used as part of a set of drums that accompanies particular types of rumba. These instruments tend to vary in shape but generally differ from those found in Peru due to the fact that they are held between the knees or placed on the floor in front of a performer, who is sitting on a chair. Cuban cajones also have a tendency to produce a more definite pitch than those used in Peru and are usually played by beating on the top face (rather than the side face) of the instrument (Santa Cruz, *El cajón afro peruano*, 34–36). In fact, I first learned of the existence of such instruments while visiting Susana Baca's home in Lima in 1996 as she had acquired a set of instruments during a recent trip to Cuba. Over the following weeks, informal conversations with a number of percussionists, including Juan Medrano Cotito, Hugo Bravo, Juan Carlos "Juanchi" Vásquez, and Rafael Santa Cruz confirmed that this was common knowledge.

28. Rafael Santa Cruz mentions this Mexican version of the instrument in passing rather than devotes a chapter to it, as he does to the Cuban and flamenco versions (*El cajón afro peruano*, 32). During an interview in 2007, he remarked that this instrument is a rather recent development that was inspired by Mexican musicians' awareness of Afroperuvian music. He describes the instrument as a five-sided box (the bottom is open) that is placed on the ground and upon which performers tap-dance various rhythms (interview by author, December 13, 2007, tape recording). The description of this object bears resemblance to the type of *tarima* (wooden dance platform) that appears photographed in the inside cover of the self-titled 1998 album by the *son jarocho* group Son de madera. Ethnomusicologist Estevan Azcona confirms that this instrument is in fact a tarima. Azcona also points out that in recent years, son jarocho groups have been invested in recovering the African roots of their music. As part of that project, some jarocho musicians have introduced African diasporic instruments like the jawbone, Brazilian *pandeiro*, and most recently the cajón (Estevan César Azcona, telephone conversation with author, February 11, 2008).

29. Santa Cruz, *El cajón afro peruano*, 46–47.

30. Susana Baca and Ricardo Pereira, interview by author, March 27, 1995, tape recording; Susana Baca, interview by author, July 4, 2007.

31. Cited in Isabel Gálvez, "El cajón peruano," 2001, El Rincón Musical Peruano, http://www.musicaperuana.com/cajon/ (accessed January 25, 2008).

32. María del Carmen Dongo, *El cajón es del Perú*, CD-ROM Multimedia (Lima: Dongo Producciones, 2003).

33. Dongo credits Libertad with giving her her first professional break fifteen years earlier when the percussionist was touring through Mexico as part of a cultural delegation called "Perú, Today and Always" (Dongo, *El cajón es del Perú*).

34. Ibid.

35. According to the liner notes of Dongo's CD, *A golpe de tierra*, the creators of the site approached Dongo during a concert she was giving in San Francisco in July 2000 and formally requested that she launch a campaign to rescue the cajón with their support (Milagros Salazar, liner notes to *Cajón peruano: A golpe de tierra* CD by María del Carmen Dongo y Manomadera [Lima: Play Music & Video, 2006]).

36. Luis Jaime Cisneros, "Joaquín Cortés deja una estela de furia y pasión flamenca en Lima," Agence France Presse, May 30, 2001, LexisNexis Academic, www.lexisnexis.com/us/lnacademic/ (accessed January 27, 2008). This event apparently made an impression on Cortés. During a return visit to Peru in 2006, the dancer gave a press conference where he declared that "wherever we go we are asked about that wooden box. We tell them that it is a Peruvian cajón and that we play it, although I don't know if I do it well, but I like its sound" ("Bailaor Cortés admira el cajón peruano porque se integra a pasión flamenco," Agence France Presse, October 2, 2006, LexisNexis Academic, www.lexisnexis.com/us/lnacademic/ [accessed January 27, 2008]).

37. Gálvez, "El cajón peruano"; Comisión de Turismo y Telecomunicaciones, Sesión Ordinaria No. 23, May 8, 2001, Acta aprobada, Congreso de la República del Perú, http://www.congreso.gob.pe/out_of_domain.asp?URL=/comisiones/2000/turismo.htm (accessed January 27, 2008).

38. This is based largely on the theory proposed by jazz percussionist Manongo Mujica that posits that the Spanish Inquisition permanently banned the use of all African drums during the colonial period (Manuel "Manongo" Mujica, personal communication with Javier León, June 26, 2007). While there is no doubt that such bans took place from time to time in the Americas, it is difficult to substantiate whether this led to the origins of the cajón. Historical records of colonial life describe quite a variety of membranophones of different types throughout the colonial period in Peru (see note 23), thus contradicting Mujica's theory.

39. The general shape and construction of both instruments is basically the same, although it has become more common for flamenco cajones to have snares stretched across the inside of the front face of the instrument (or sometimes small pieces of metal or jingle bells), which give the upper register a brighter sound. This, however, is not a unique trait. The use of snares in particular makes the instrument a little easier on the hands (one doesn't need to strike the cajón as hard to obtain a crisp cracking sound from the instrument), and so it is also possible to find similar devices built into cajones used in Peru, although these tend to be more associated with amateur cajoneros and seen as

a relatively recent trend in cajones used on the northern coast of Peru (Santa Cruz, *El cajón afro peruano*, 88–89).

40. From my perusal of many of these sites, I have been able to find only one that claims that the instrument is originally from Spain. The great majority of sites are selling instruments to flamenco musicians and do not offer any information one way or another regarding the origin of these instruments. It may be that in the interim, some of these sites may have taken those types of claims down, but I find that somewhat unlikely. Much of this nationalist rhetoric does not seem to have gone beyond Peru and the Peruvian expatriate community.

41. Reproduced in Dongo, *El cajón es del Perú*.

42. Lumbreras, "El papel del Estado en el campo de la cultura," 104–6.

43. Alfaro, "Estado del arte del patrimonio inmaterial en el Perú," 11–13.

44. Ibid., 24–26.

45. Repetto interview.

46. Luis Repetto Málaga, personal communication with Javier León, June 3, 2007; Gálvez 2001.

47. Santa Cruz, *El cajón afro peruano*, 79.

48. The *caballito de totora* is a type of fishing vessel made out of bundled dried reeds. Seviche is a traditional dish made of fish marinated in lime juice, onions, herbs, and spices. The resolution uses the colonial spelling of the dish rather than its contemporary variations ("ceviche" or "cebiche"). A pisco sour is a mixed drink made out of pisco, simple syrup, lime juice, an egg white, and bitters. It seems that there was not an attempt to declare pisco itself a cultural patrimony, most likely because Chile managed to obtain a Certificate of Origin for the spirit in the 1930s and Peru is still contesting its legitimacy within a number of international trade organizations.

49. Robert R. Barr, "The Persistence of Neopopulism in Peru? From Fujimori to Toledo," *Third World Quarterly* 24, no. 6 (2003): 1161–78.

50. Moisés Arce, "The Sustainability of Economic Reform in a Most Likely Case: Peru," *Comparative Politics* 35, no. 3 (2003): 335–54. Although many of these companies were from Mexico, Europe, and the United States, much of the Peruvian public fixated on the Chilean corporations. Paralleling the Spanish reconquest scenario associated with the cajón, it became common in some Limeño circles for people to be outraged over what they saw as the Chilean economic occupation of Peru, a type of discourse that rhetorically recalled the occupation of Lima in the aftermath of the War of the Pacific (1879–83). To be sure, since approximately that time there has been an explosion of Chilean-owned grocery, discount, and department stores, and a number of formerly Peruvian-owned businesses like AeroPerú and, most recently, Wong supermarkets have become subsidiaries of Chilean corporations. This resentment has also been fueled by ongoing trade disputes between the two countries regarding products like the aforementioned pisco and the redefinition of fishing rights and maritime borders.

51. Repetto interview.

52. Feldman, *Black Rhythms of Peru*, 127–28.

53. "Uneven development" is the notion that under capitalism, not all realms of society develop at the same rate, which in turn perpetuates if not deepens social and economic inequalities. Santiago Alfaro Rotondo, "El lugar de las industrias culturales en las políticas

públicas," in *Políticas culturales: Ensayos críticos,* ed. Guillermo Cortés and Víctor Vich (Lima: Instituto de Estudios Peruanos, 2006), 165.

54. This term is not to be confused with the term "culture industry" proposed by Horkheimer and Adorno, which assumes that all forms of mass cultural production coalesce into a sort of opiate for the masses that turn them all into passive and receptive consumers (Max Horkheimer and Theodor W. Adorno, *Dialectic of Enlightenment,* ed. Gunzelin Schmid Noerr, trans. Edmund Jephcott [Palo Alto, Calif.: Stanford University Press, 2002]). In this article, I am referring to specific networks of production, and, although some scholars find a great deal of overlap between the two concepts, I would like, for the purposes of this discussion, to set aside the implicit value judgment and maintain the distinction between the two.

55. See, for example, Teresa Quiroz, "Políticas e industrias culturales en las políticas públicas," in *Políticas culturales: Ensayos críticos,* ed. Guillermo Cortés and Víctor Vich (Lima: Instituto de Estudios Peruanos, 2006), 113–35; Vich, "Gestionar riesgos," 45–70; and Alfaro, "El lugar de las industrias culturales en las políticas públicas," 137–75.

56. See Pierre Bourdieu, "The Field of Cultural Production, or: The Economic World Reversed," in *The Field of Cultural Production,* ed. Randal Johnson (New York: Columbia University Press, 1993), 29–73.

57. The Day of Criollo Song was created by President Manuel Prado in 1944 as a nationalist attempt to combat the rising popularity of Halloween among Limeños. Since then it has become a date that is usually celebrated by a series of concerts featuring criollo, Afroperuvian, and most recently different types of Andean and Amazonian musics.

58. "Manomadera" is a combination of the words *mano* (hand) and *madera* (wood). Dongo, *El cajón es del Perú;* Salazar, *Cajón peruano;* Repetto interview.

59. *Guapeos* are rhythmic shouts of encouragement that are often improvised by Afroperuvian percussionists.

60. E.g., Repetto interview.

61. The publication acknowledges the existence of more individuals and organizations than those listed. It cites a number of the challenges that the institution experienced in gathering the information, including logistical, budgetary, and time constraints and people's unwillingness to give their personal information to an agency of the state (Instituto Nacional de Cultural [INC], *Directorio de la cultura y las artes en el Perú* [Lima: Instituto Nacional de Cultura, 2006], 7).

62. Gisela Cánepa Koch, "La ciudadanía en escena: fiesta andina, patrimonio y agencia cultural," in *Mirando la esfera pública desde la cultura en el Perú,* ed. Gisela Cánepa Koch and María Eugenia Ulfe Young (Lima: Consejo Nacional de Ciencia, Tecnología e Innovación Tecnológica, 2006), 237.

63. This song and a number of other pieces were recorded ahead of time and were played over the P.A. system during live performances, allowing the percussionists on stage to play along.

64. Yuri Juárez, interview by author, June 22, 2007.

65. Feldman, *Black Rhythms of Peru,* 158–59.

66. Alexis Castañeda, interview by author, December 17, 2007, tape recording.

67. Rony Campos, interview by author, June 11, 2007, tape recording.

68. Santa Cruz, *El cajón afro peruano.*

69. Santa Cruz interview.

70. Bilbao points out that in Zaña, the cajón is considered of secondary importance in comparison to the checo (see note 25 for a definition of this instrument) (Bilbao interview).

71. Bilbao interview.

72. Instituto Nacional de Cultural (INC), "Resolución Directoral Nacional No. 1255/INC" (Declaran Patrimonio Cultural de la Nación a la Cumanana), November 26, 2004, *El Peruano,* December 13, 2004: Normas Legales, p. 282277. At the same time, however, this symbol is not one that is exclusively associated with an Afroperuvian identity. Rather, acknowledging the heterogeneous ethnic makeup of the region and the historical connections of the *cumanana* to old Spanish poetic forms such as the *copla,* the text of the declaration defines the cumanana as a form of expression of European origin but that was made unique by the contributions of Afroperuvian and indigenous performers (Instituto Nacional de Cultura, "Resolución Directoral Nacional No. 1255/INC").

73. Instituto Nacional de Cultural (INC), "Resolución Directoral Nacional No. 1765/INC" (Declaran Patrimonio Cultural de la Nación a la Cajita Rítmica Afroperuana), December 28, 2007, *El Peruano,* January 13, 2008: Normas Legales, p. 383905. The *cajita* is a wooden box that hangs from the performer's neck. The instrument is played by alternating strikes on the sides of the instrument with a wooden clapper while using the other hand to slam the lid of the box shut. The instrument is predominantly associated with a dance known as the *son de los diablos* in Lima and was introduced into other genres like the *festejo* during the Afroperuvian revival movement.

5 Historical Legacy and the Contemporary World

UNESCO and China's Qin *Music in the Twenty-first Century*

BELL YUNG

Interest in cultural rights has largely focused on contemporary folk and popular music and their various hybrids and on minorities and groups outside of mainstream societies, as evidenced by the many contributions in this volume. This chapter deals with a different kind of subject matter: a musical tradition that is old and revered and has been perpetuated by the society elites for centuries. Practiced by China's literati class, the *qin* tradition has a long and continuous history of over two millennia that is documented in written words, musical notation, and iconic images and material culture from archaeological discoveries.[1] Until recently, the qin tradition has remained relatively stable to such an extent that notation from six centuries ago can be read without difficulty. In this long history, there existed two contrasting ideologies. The first one emphasized musical function for self-cultivation and was advocated mainly by the literati; the second, emphasizing musical sound in performance, was advocated mainly by professional musicians. The advocates of each vied for representation and control of the tradition, and it was the former that dominated received wisdom, thanks to the prestige of written words, produced mainly by the literati. However, China has witnessed tumultuous changes in the last three decades, particularly since the beginning of the twenty-first century, changes that altered the playing field for the struggle between the two ideologies.

This chapter examines the two ideologies of the qin musical tradition by first reviewing its historical background and then tracing the changes it has undergone after the fall of the last imperial dynasty, in the last three decades since China liberalized its political and economic policies in the late 1970s, and particularly in the first few years of the new millennium after the United Nations Educational, Scientific, and Cultural Organization (UNESCO) proclaimed qin music a "Masterpiece of the Oral and Intangible Heritage of Humanity" in 2003. What were these changes? What were the factors that induced and produced and continue to affect these changes? What do changes in this long-standing musical tradition tell us about contemporary Chinese society? How and why are these questions relevant to cultural rights? What was UNESCO's role? A debate over these questions has been raging among Chinese qin players in the last few years, and they deserve attention from Western scholars and activists.

The Qin and Its Music

The musical tradition of the qin is in many ways unique in China and in the world. The very first sentence in Robert van Gulik's now classic study of the qin, *The Lore of the Chinese Lute*, the most influential in the English language, reads: "The music of the ancient lute as a solo instrument is widely different from all other sorts of Chinese music: it stands entirely alone, both in its character and in the important place it occupies in the life of the literati class."[2] The long and uninterrupted history of the qin spans at least two millennia, as evidenced by archaeological and literary evidence.[3] While many instruments in the world are as old, few can claim the unbroken continuity of the qin tradition to the present day, a continuity that underscores its generally conservative nature. Until the last century, the qin tradition retained much that was archaic, including the repertory, notational system, performance practice, aesthetic ideals, and social context. Hence, the transformation of the qin tradition in this Internet age and globalized world provides a particularly interesting case for analysis and interpretation. A small community of qin players who grew up in the first half of the twentieth century are now confronting contemporary qin music and a musical environment that they hardly recognize or comprehend.

The qin tradition has been extensively written about in the English language.[4] Still, it may be helpful to give a summary of its major characteristics.

The conservative nature of the tradition is most obvious in the construction of the instrument, which is a long wooden half-tube zither with seven strings. Its basic playing technique consists of the right-hand fingers plucking the strings near the right end of the instrument while the left-hand fingers move along the entire board to produce stopped notes or harmonic notes and occasionally also to pluck the strings. Thirteen inlaid markers (usually made of mother-of-pearl, gold leaf, or precious stone) run along the upper surface at the outer edge from near the extreme right (marker one) to near the extreme left (marker thirteen) to help the left hand find its place. The entire wooden surface is finely lacquered; varying among individual instruments, the color of the finish ranges from black to reddish brown. Strings are traditionally made of silk; each is made up of a large number of silk strands tightly wound into different thicknesses. The one farthest from the player, string one, is the thickest; the one closest, string seven, is the thinnest.

As represented in historical documents and popular culture, qin music has always been cultivated almost exclusively by China's small and elite class of literati, and it is identified closely with the refinement and sophistication of this social group.[5] Until recent times, the great majority of China's population had little chance to hear this music, although many were familiar with the name of the instrument because it is often mentioned in popular performing genres such as storytelling and opera, where it functions as a symbol of the literati. It is also a common subject in paintings that depict the reclusive scholar contemplating the serenity and grandeur of nature while playing the instrument or strolling on a mountain path followed by a servant boy carrying his qin.

The qin's long history has produced a rich lore concerning the instrument and its music. The physical parts of the instrument and many of the individual finger techniques have come to bear symbolic significance, while individual pieces in the vast repertory are laden with extra-musical content. The symbolism and lore are related to the history, myths, legends, philosophy, and religion of China, especially as cultivated and transmitted by the literati. Thus, along with poetry, calligraphy, and painting, the qin and its music form a microcosm of China's elite and refined culture. Gulik writes that the qin is "one of the indispensable paraphernalia of the library of the Chinese scholar."[6] A large body of writings from generations of qin scholars and musicians bears on the instrument and its music, performance technique, and lore and philosophy. The notational system used for performance today was established in the twelfth century C.E. or earlier and has remained essentially unchanged.[7] The relative stability of the notation makes music written down centuries ago accessible to a modern musician. A repertory of over three thousand items, mostly from the last five and a half centuries, is extant today.

The instrument was used as part of an ensemble for ritual music and as an accompaniment to the singing of refined poetry. But its outstanding role in performance has always been as a solo instrument. As such, the music is complex in structure and refined and subtle in its aesthetics. The extreme quietness of its tone requires a serene environment and the full and undivided attention of the player as well as the listener; it takes a sensitive and cultivated ear to appreciate the many shades of timbre and dynamics, varying within a small range that are produced by minute differences in finger techniques. The fact that most compositions have extra-musical content that relate to the history, philosophy, and religion of China poses yet another challenge to player and listener alike.

The characteristics summarized above render the qin tradition "art music" par excellence; it has enjoyed such longevity in part because it has for centuries catered to the elite literati class, who, serving as court and government officials, held enormous power, possessed great wealth, and enjoyed lofty social status. So long as the privileges of this class remained unchanged, the qin tradition and its special characteristics were sustained. Despite China's turbulent history in the last two millennia, as dynasties rose and fell, the power and prestige of the literati remained essentially unchanged. It follows that the longevity and continuity of the qin tradition were maintained.

Nevertheless, no music stays unchanged, and the qin tradition, despite its overall conservative nature, underwent slow changes that were documented in the literature. These changes were not only in the playing technique, repertory, and musical styles but also in the degree of emphasis given to two opposing ideologies through the long history of the tradition. China's recent political liberalization and economic development, coupled with technological advancement and the ubiquity of the mass media, brought the conflict between these two ideologies to the forefront. Before I discuss the changes in recent decades, it is important to place them in their historical context. To that end, I shall first outline the changes that took place in the distant past.

The Literati's Qin and the Artists' Qin

The two opposing ideologies differed in the degree of emphasis each laid on what may be termed, for convenience, musical function and musical sound. The two ideologies have been advocated and practiced by the literati and by the professional musicians, respectively. Xu Jian, in his influential book *Qinshi chubian* (First study of qin history), identifies them as *wenren qinjia* (literati qin connoisseurs) and *zhuanye qinshi* (professional qin masters). He specifically mentions that it was during the Sui and Tang dynasties (sixth to tenth centuries C.E.) when the "professional" (*zhuanye*) qin players became increasingly important and served the literati, who admired and appreciated their performances.[8] Liu Chenghua, a historian of aesthetics, calls the two ideologies "Literati's Qin" (*wenrenqin*) and "Artists' Qin" (*yirenqin*).[9] Liu outlines the differences in their philosophy, performance practice, and artistic and social goals, which may be summarized as pairs of opposites:

LITERATI'S QIN

- stresses playing for oneself (*yuji*)
- stresses the effect of music on oneself
- stresses the player's own realization of the function of the music
- requires a relatively simple and plain playing technique, with modest energy
- stresses the qin as essentially an instrument to cultivate one's inner enlightenment
- celebrates the musician's moral character and personal virtue more than the music

ARTISTS' QIN

- stresses playing for an audience (*yuren*)
- stresses the effect of the music on the audience
- stresses communicating the musical sound to the audience
- pursues technical development and expressive power
- stresses the qin as essentially an instrument to make music
- celebrates the music being performed more than the musician's personal attributes

The critically important pair in the above list is the first—playing for oneself or playing for an audience—for the difference epitomizes and explains the other pairs. Liu explains that playing for oneself was based upon two basic principles that are linked to two Chinese philosophies. The first, which Liu dates to the pre-Han period (before the second century B.C.E.), stems from what later generations attributed to Confucianism. Among its tenets, the most relevant to qin playing is the ideal summarized in four words, *zhong, zheng, ping, he,* which may be translated as "balance, correctness, calmness, harmony." Music historian Liu Minglan writes: "The principle of *zhong, zheng, ping, he* was the Confucian ideal for one's cultivation of moral character . . . but it also served as an aesthetic criterion. . . . It not only served qin music, but was also China's dominant aesthetic principle for the arts, one that the literati pursued as a common goal."[10] The goal of playing the qin is to strengthen one's moral character; the physical sound of the music is of less concern.[11]

The second principle stems from the philosophy of Taoism, which, among its tenets related to music, states that "the objective of qin music is spiritual communion with nature and to achieve oneness with the universe."[12] In explaining this principle, contemporary musicologist Miao Jianhua quotes Zhuang Zi (369–286 B.C.E.), considered one of Taoism's founders, who said,

"A person uses language in order to capture meaning; but if he already comprehends meaning, language is no longer of concern."[13] The principle, when applied specifically to qin music, is explained by Gulik, referencing an extreme case of a hypothetical qin musician who emphasized musical function to such an extent as to ignore musical sound totally: "He might point to the great poet of the Chin [Jin] period T'ao Ch'ien [Tao Qian] who, according to tradition, had a lute without strings or studs hanging on the wall, and who in one of his poems said: 'I have acquired the deeper significance of the lute; why should I strive after the sound of the strings?' This attitude, though it may be well founded from a philosophical point of view, discouraged scholars from aspiring to become accomplished performers on the lute. Therefore this attitude was sharply criticized by real lute players."[14]

While most qin players did not go to the extreme example of Tao Qian, or even near it, there was a tendency among some to de-emphasize, even denigrate, virtuosic techniques but aspire to loftier ideals of using the musical sound as merely a vehicle to achieve the function of the music. Since the significance in playing is in self-enlightenment and communion with nature, there would be no purpose to play for anyone else. Influenced by this principle, the qin player strove for an aesthetic of musical sound that emphasized tranquillity and calmness rather than overt expressivity. The depiction in many Chinese landscape paintings of a qin musician playing alone amid the beauty and grandeur of serene natural surroundings of mountains and streams, away from other people, underscores this ideology. Whether the goal was for the cultivation of moral character in Confucianism or for the pursuit of communion with nature in Taoism, the proponents of this ideology were almost all literati, hence the designation of "Literati's Qin."

Literati's Qin persisted through the ages, as evidenced by an extensive body of philosophical and aesthetic treatises. For example, the writer Cui Zundu (954–1020) emphasized the ideals of *jing* and *yuan* in qin music, which may be translated as "still" and "remote."[15] Most influential in recent centuries was Yan Cheng (1547–1625), who advocated the principle of *qing, wei, dan, yuan* (clear, subtle, quiet, remote). Yan was particularly important because he founded a school of qin playing called Yushan that developed into other influential schools and has had many followers up to the present day. Some members of these schools were the core founders of a twentieth-century qin musicians' group called Jinyu qinshe (Jinyu qin society, where "Jinyu" means "Contemporary Yushan"), established in 1936, which was widely recognized as the most important group of its kind in that century.[16] Yan's principle was followed by his disciples and quoted by many contemporary writers. For example, musicologist and qin musician Cheung Sai-bung (1943–76) wrote:

"At the end of the Ming dynasty, Yan Cheng proposed the principle of *qing, wei, dan, yuan,* which truly revived the ancient ideals of qin players from the 2nd century B.C. and earlier: a pursuit of lofty state of mind (*yijing*)."[17]

Because it was the literati who wrote books and essays, historical documents tend to emphasize Literati's Qin. However, beginning in the Tang dynasty (618–907), there was increasing reference to the Artists' Qin that stressed musical sound and that was identified with prominent qin performers. These references were often couched in negative terms by advocates of Literati's Qin. For example, poems by the eminent poet and qin musician Bo Juyi (772–846) lamented the loss of qin music from antiquity in his time, one of which reads:

> Silk and Tong wood combined to make the qin;
> In it we hear the sound of antiquity.
> The sound of antiquity is now considered plain and without flavor;
> It doesn't appeal to today's listeners.
> The jade markers have lost their splendor,
> The vermilion strings are covered with dust.
> Having been long abandoned,
> The echoes of the old music linger on faintly.
> I shall gladly play the qin for you,
> Even though people would not care to listen.
> What caused this to happen?
> The music of the Qiang flute and the Qin zither![18]

The poem expresses the frustration and despair of the advocates of Literati's Qin because their music was considered "plain and without flavor" and not worth listening to. The "Qiang flute and the Qin zither" were used as stand-ins for Artists' Qin.

In sum, the advocates of the Literati's Qin valued the contemplative aspects of the music and the self-realization of its function and significance; they did not cater to an audience and were "amateur" musicians in the best sense of the word. In contrast, those of the Artists' Qin sought to develop virtuosic technique and expressive means; as professionals, they by necessity and expectation reached out to communicate with an audience.

According to Liu Chenghua, one side or the other held the dominant position in different periods. From about the third century B.C.E. to the sixth century C.E., the Literati's Qin reigned supreme; during the next four centuries (the Sui and Tang dynasties), the Artists' Qin rose to a prominent position, eclipsing the other side. From the tenth to the twelfth centuries (the Northern Song dynasty), the two ideologies rivaled one another in equal dominance. Finally, from that point until the twentieth century, the two merged: qin players recognized the importance of both ideologies. Thus, musicians of the Literati's Qin tradition, though they continued to stress playing for oneself, paid attention to the technical aspects of performance, and musicians of the Artists' Qin tradition, while continuing to stress playing for an audience, recognized and strove for the importance of literary meaning of the music and self-cultivation.[19]

The Fall and Rise of the Qin Tradition in the Twentieth Century

The revolution in 1911 ended the last imperial dynasty and dissolved the long-standing political structure; in so doing it spelled the end of the literati class, whose fall from the pedestal and loss of political power resulted in an inevitable collapse of a style of living. Qin music lost its patronage but survived among the literati who had to earn a living. Social unrest continued after the revolution; major upheavals included the infighting among political-military factions that controlled various parts of the country (the so-called warlords), the Japanese invasion and occupation of much of China—a period that spanned the 1930s through the mid-1940s—and the civil war between the Communists and the Nationalists that persisted from the birth of the Communist Party in 1921 to the establishment of the Communist regime of the People's Republic of China (PRC) in 1949. Despite these trying circumstances, a small number of qin musicians continued to practice their art, particularly in the Yangzi (or Yangtze) River delta region where qin music had long flourished. For example, two prominent groups were formed that exerted a lasting influence in the following decades: the Mei'an Qin Society (Mei'an qinshe) of Nantong (near Nanjing), founded in 1929, and the aforementioned Jinyu Qin Society of Shanghai, founded in 1936. The membership list of the Jinyu Qin Society shows that their professions included people from education, industry, business, and government bureaucracy.[20]

After the founding of the PRC, the early years of the 1950s saw a flourishing of scholarly activities in qin conducted mainly by the Music Research Institute of Beijing (Yinyue yanjiusuo), established in 1954. These included the compilation of lists of information after surveying the activities of qin musicians and old instruments, the collection and reprinting of old qin handbooks with musical scores, and the recording of performances by distinguished musicians of the time. The Beijing Guqin Research Association (Beijing guqin yanjiuhui) was also established in 1954. The Jinyu Qin Society of Shanghai continued to be active among a small number of players. However, the young government suffered a series of political movements from the late 1950s until the late 1970s, during which time the radical "leftist" political ideology dominated. These movements had an enormous impact on the arts, in particular on qin music, since the qin tradition, being closely linked with the literati class, was considered to be totally unacceptable in a "classless" society in the Communist ideology.

The Communist ideological position regarding the arts may be best represented by the widely known document called "Talks at the Yan'an Conference on Literature and Art" by Mao Zedong (Mao Tse-tung), who held supreme power for many decades until his death in 1976. The "Talks" were delivered in May 1942 and were subsequently published in many editions and reprintings.[21] Their influence on the literary and artistic scene in China has been enormous.[22] Briefly, Mao asserted that literature and art should serve the masses, specifically "the workers, peasants, soldiers and the urban petty bourgeoisie."[23] Thus, the qin tradition, in which the elite class of literati had for centuries indulged themselves, was forced to adjust.[24] As David Ming-yüeh Liang wrote in the 1980s: "In the present socialist society of modern China, the qin, with all its associations with the past literary tradition and philosophically imbued music, has not found a comfortable position within society."[25] The situation was particularly dire during the chaotic period of the Cultural Revolution (1966–76), when some qin players destroyed their old instruments and musical scores in order to avoid persecution. It was the darkest period of the qin's long history.

After the Cultural Revolution ended in 1976, qin musicians resumed their activities cautiously, but performance practice noticeably changed.

> Mao Zedong has said that the artist needs to remold his thinking and feeling, and pay attention to the songs of the masses if he wishes his performance to win their acceptance. As a response, qin music has stepped out of the privacy and intimacy of the scholar-gentleman's study and climbed onto the stage of the public concert hall. In so doing, qin music has become like other kinds of music: its main function is to please a large, public audience. . . . On the stage of a concert hall, however, he is judged by an audience—the workers, peasants, soldiers—who are, for historical reasons, relatively uninitiated in the music and its literary content. In order for the music to be accepted and understood by such an audience, it must be modified.[26]

The modifications took several forms, including the use of strings made of a steel core wound with nylon threads instead of silk strings for better sound projection and stability in tuning, changes of repertory that either shortened existing compositions or introduced new compositions with ideologically correct content, and the exaggeration of physical movement and facial expression in performance. In short, the emphasis shifted from the Literati's Qin to the Artists' Qin: from the cultivation of oneself to the entertainment of a mass audience.

Beginning in the late 1970s, the government instituted a policy of "reform and opening" (*gaige kaifang*), which began the liberalization of China's economy. Various reforms included the permission to have private ownership of housing and business and the permission and even encouragement to amass personal wealth through industry, commerce, and service. A market economy soon emerged and flourished, feeding the growth of a middle class with disposable income. At the same time, the rapid advancement of technology first introduced mass media in the forms of radio, television, and the recording industry and then later, in the 1990s, Internet technology. Thus, in a relatively short period of a decade or so, external factors affecting the ideology of the qin switched from political ideology to commercialism and mass consumption. The transformation from Literati's Qin to Artists' Qin that had begun in earlier decades through shifts in political ideology proceeded even more rapidly in order to satisfy the demand of a growing audience of consumers.

The social and economic environment did not automatically lead to making the esoteric qin tradition appealing to a larger audience. There was also a cultural factor. As China's economy grew and as the emerging middle class possessed greater amounts of both disposable income and leisure time, there was naturally a demand for entertainment. The government's increasingly liberal cultural policy, particularly after the student demonstration in Tian'anmen Square in 1989, helped to satisfy such demands. The majority population turned to popular culture rooted in the West, such as films, television, pop songs, light fiction, and tabloid journalism. However, a small minority sought out traditional Chinese arts, many of which had been greatly suppressed during the Cultural Revolution of the previous decade. Their return to traditional culture was a direct consequence of their disillusionment at seeing the collapse of Socialist ideals, which they had wholeheartedly embraced in earlier decades. A spiritual vacuum ensued that, to some, could be filled only by a return to the roots of Chinese culture. Among the various traditional Chinese arts, qin music held a great attraction because of its age, its ideology, the abundance of historical documents regarding it, and its association with the literati of earlier centuries.

Thus, the new social, economic, technological, and ideological environment opened up opportunities for enterprising qin musicians to develop a market for their art. A small number of them have become nationally known through concertizing and, more important, through their recordings. Many qin conferences and concerts have been held, and an increasing number of qin societies have been formed. The two major hubs of activity are Beijing and Shanghai, centering on elite musical institutions. In Beijing, the Music Research Institute publishes scores and research articles and is the home of qin scholars, while the Central Conservatory of Music (Zhongyang yinyue xueyuan) and the China Conservatory of Music (Zhongguo yinyue xueyuan) have on their faculty some of the most prominent qin performers. Monthly *yaji* have been held since the mid-1990s by the newly revived Beijing Guqin Research Association, which also publishes a monthly newsletter called *Beijing Qin Bulletin* (*Beijing qinxun*).[27] In Shanghai, the Shanghai Conservatory of Music (Shanghai yinyue xueyuan) has on its faculty prominent qin players who revitalized the famous Jinyu Qin Society in 1980 and have been holding regular yaji. In addition, qin activities in Nanjing, Chengdu, Yangzhou, Hangzhou, and Guangzhou have also expanded.[28]

Probably the most significant development in qin music has been the proliferation of commercial CDs. One survey reported that 73 commercial CDs of qin music were released between 1988 and 1996.[29] Other signs of the spread of qin music include the establishment in 2001 of the Peking University Qin Society in the most prestigious of China's institutions of higher education. It was reported that when French president Jacques Chirac visited Beijing in 2000, his host, Jiang Zemin, entertained the esteemed guest with a concert of qin music.[30] This burst of activities and interest led some musicians to form a national organization for the purpose of overseeing and guiding the future of the qin. Hence the Committee of Guqin Professionals of the Association of Chinese National Orchestral Music Research (Zhongguo minzu guanxianyue xuehui guqin zhuanye weiyuanhui), or China Qin Committee (Zhongguo qinhui), was established in 2001; its first president was Wu Zhao, a senior qin musician and scholar from the Music Research Institute.[31]

Outside of China, various qin groups have been formed in recent years. Among them, the more active include the California-based North American Guqin Association, established in 1999; the New York Qin Society, established in 2000; and the London-based Youlan Qin Society, established in 2003, as well as others in Toronto, Vancouver, and San Diego. The first Internet-based guqin yaji was held by the North American Guqin Association on February 16, 2002. Another live online guqin concert was held July 9, 2002, in Beijing, sponsored by the Internet site people.com.cn (one of China's news sites) and the North American Guqin Association.[32]

But no one foresaw the sudden and even greater changes that were to happen in the twenty-first century, changes that would dwarf those of the previous two decades.

UNESCO's Proclamation and the Qin in the Twenty-first Century

On November 7, 2003, UNESCO proclaimed China's qin music as one of twenty-eight "Masterpieces of the Oral and Intangible Heritage of Humanity."[33] The Masterpieces were selected on the basis of six criteria: (1) they possessed outstanding value as a Masterpiece of the human creative genius; (2) they were rooted in the cultural tradition or cultural history of the community concerned; (3) they played a role as a means of affirming the cultural identity of the community concerned; (4) they were distinguished by excellence in the application of skills and technical qualities displayed; (5) they constituted a unique testimony of a living cultural tradition; and (6) they were threatened with disappearance due to insufficient means for safeguarding or to processes of rapid change. Furthermore, candidacy files had to include a solid action plan for the safeguarding and promotion of the proposed expression or cultural space.[34] The selections depict diverse forms of "heritage" and were spread to represent many member states within UNESCO.[35]

The news that qin music was selected in 2003 was reported instantly and widely in China's mass media and aroused great interest around the country. For example, the *Beijing Morning News* (*Beijing chenbao*) reported the news on November 9, 2003, and added, "The Chinese qin is one of the oldest plucked musical instruments in the world with a 3000 year history. The art of qin influenced China's music history, art history, social and cultural history, intellectual history, etc. It is a major musical representation of ancient Chinese civilization and its spirit."[36] Since then, writings on the qin, whether news releases, concert announcements, or CD marketing, make frequent reference to the UNESCO proclamation.

Indeed, almost two years before the proclamation, news circulated that qin music would be nominated by the PRC's Department of Culture to UNESCO as a candidate for the honor; the reaction from many qin musicians was immediate and jubilant. For example, an article published on December 14, 2001, entitled "Guqin Is No Longer Silent" ("Guqin buzai chenmo"), announcing that a new organization called the China Qin Society (Zhongguo qinhui) was formally established on November 20, 2001, in Beijing, concludes with a final paragraph that reads: "Besides the establishment of the China Qin Society, the qin tradition has another favorable piece of news. Following the 2001 proclamation by UNESCO that Kunqu opera was selected as a Masterpiece of the Oral and Intangible Heritage of Humanity, China's qin will also receive this extraordinary honor in 2003. So much good fortune in the new millennium will surely bring this ancient Chinese musical instrument new glory."[37]

In early 2003, the North American Guqin Association based in San Francisco asked its members to vote for the "Top 10 Qin News Items of 2002." Among the nineteen items to be voted on, the first on the list was "The guqin was nominated by the China Culture Department as the subject of the United Nations Educational, Scientific and Cultural Organization . . . 'Masterpieces of the Oral and Intangible Heritage of Humanity' for 2003."[38] Thus, even though the proclamation did not occur until November 2003, the anticipation that it would be named aroused great interest and commotion almost two years before the actual announcement.

The unusual response could be explained partly by the Chinese craving for international attention and recognition for their achievements; the nation had endured more than a century of humiliation militarily, politically, scientifically, and culturally at the hands of powers from Europe, Japan, and America. An honor bestowed upon the arts aroused great pride and jubilation, just as when the country had breakthroughs in weaponry (its first nuclear bomb in 1964), science and technology (its first native-made rocket that sent a satellite into space in 1990), sports (its winning the right to host the 2008 Olympics Games), and other areas.

The reaction to the UNESCO proclamation from the qin community and the related industrial and political organizations was immediate and phenomenal. All the activities that had burgeoned in the 1990s were multiplied manyfold, including new qin societies, the publication of articles and CDs, concerts, and yaji. The significance of the qin in Chinese culture, having been now officially recognized by a major international organization, was quickly seized upon for promotion and caught the attention of the wider public. Most qin musicians hailed the beginning of a new age of qin music; the general populace, which up until then considered the qin and its music as ancient, esoteric, and difficult to comprehend, concluded that if foreigners could appreciate it, surely the Chinese people could too, and should. It became a symbol of the best in China's own music and a way to counteract the rampant dominance of pop music, an import from the West. The exponential increase of Internet providers and users in China in the last few years was effectively tapped by promoters of qin activities.[39] Significantly, one of the major Web sites devoted to the qin, called Chinese Qin News (Zhongguo guqin xinwenwang), uses as its logo a combination of the Beijing 2008 Olympic Games in red and the UNESCO logo in blue. Underneath is the phrase in Chinese script: "Qin—Oral and Intangible Heritage of Humanity."[40]

Among the most notable activities on the national scale to promote the qin before the general populace was the first "Grand Competition of Chinese Guqin" ("Zhongguo guqin dasai"), organized by the China Qin Society and held in Beijing in July and August 2004. The stated purpose of the competition was "to advance the socialist civil society, to promote Chinese traditional culture, to advance the dissemination and development of the art of qin, and to discover and select talented qin musicians."[41] The competition was divided into four age groups: over thirty-six, eighteen to thirty-six, twelve to eighteen, and under twelve. It was reported later that over two hundred people participated, including some from Hong Kong, Taiwan, and the United States. A total of thirty-three gold, silver, and bronze medals from each age group were given. But controversy arose, as some participants complained about flaws in the judging standards and others accused the organizers of conducting the competition unethically. Other competitions used different names under different sponsorship. For example, it was reported that the first Youlan-Yangchun Qin Festival was held August 18–20, 2006, in the city of Tianjin (near Beijing).[42] According to its Web site, the competitors are placed in two groups: *shaonian* (teenager) and *qingnian* (young adult).[43] Each group has awards:

- One first prize (called Youlan) of a 20,000–yuan-value qin made by Zhang Yuxin, showing cracks in the paint
- Two second prizes (called Yilan) of a 10,000–yuan-value qin made by Zhang Yuxin
- Six third prizes (called Peilan) of a 3,000–yuan-value qin made by Chen Shuyuan[44]

In addition, there are six merit prizes, one "special" prize, one prize for best *qinge* (poems sung to accompaniment of the qin), and one prize for best accompaniment.

In addition to competitions of this kind, qin players can also sign up to pass examinations not unlike those offered worldwide by the Associated Board of the Royal Schools of Music (London). Sponsored and organized again by the China Qin Society, the examinations offer ten levels of difficulty and are held in many cities of China, with examiners being sent from Beijing or appointed by the China Qin Society locally. In a single week in August 2006, qin examinations were held in Kunming in Yunnan Province on the nineteenth, Chefeng in Inner Mongolia on the twenty-third, and Beijing on the twenty-fourth. Passing the examination wins the qin player a certificate, which gives him or her the authority and legitimacy to teach students.[45]

The rising prominence of the qin has resulted in unexpected disputes among cities, with each claiming to be the origin of qin music. Thus, an article argues that Huangshan (Yellow Mountain) in Anhui Province should be designated as the origin of the qin, as opposed to two other theories that proposed Lishan of Hubei Province and Changshu of Jiangsu Province.[46] The attraction of tourist income, with potential international clientele because of UNESCO's proclamation, is too difficult for town and city officials to resist.

The qin not only has been promoted out of financial consideration but also has been exploited for political ends. It was reported that, as part of the celebration of the fifty-sixth anniversary of the establishment of the PRC, a grand event was held at the Juyong Pass of the Great Wall on August 26, 2005: fifty-six musicians, wearing the national dresses of the fifty-six ethnic groups of China, played on fifty-six qin in unison.[47] (See figure 5.1.)

Figure 5.1. Playing the qin on the Great Wall, August 26, 2005, to celebrate the fifty-sixth anniversary of the establishment of the People's Republic of China. (CNSIMAGES, used with permission.)

The use of the ultimate symbol of traditional China to represent national unity in a pageant staged, apparently without irony, atop an iconic artifact that owes its construction to division and separation reflects how much China has changed. But it also shows that the qin has undergone a complete reversal of fortune since the days of the Cultural Revolution, when instruments were smashed because they supposedly represented the worst of old China.

Along with the Great Wall, the qin continues to be exploited by politicians and entrepreneurs. Most recently, as China prepared for the 2008 Olympics, a lavishly staged event was held on August 8, 2007, in Beijing to begin the one-year countdown. The BBC News on the Internet reports that among those events was a staged performance by 999 costumed students from across the country gathered at the Great Wall to play the qin and other Chinese traditional musical instruments.[48]

Another indication of the intense attention paid to the qin after UNESCO's proclamation (or rather, the nomination two years earlier) was the sudden increase in the number of scholarly articles since 2002. A survey of academic journals showed a jump in the number of articles in 2002–03, as is indicated by table 5.1. These articles, most of them by serious and well-respected qin scholars and musicians, have contributed greatly to furthering the under-

Figure 5.2. Playing the qin on the Great Wall, August 8, 2007, to begin the one-year countdown to the Beijing Olympics. (Getty Images, used with permission.)

Table 5.1. Number of journal articles about the qin, 1994–2005.

Years	Number of articles
1994–1995	60
1996–1997	48
1998–1999	50
2000–2001	74
2002–2003	134
2004–2005	160

Source: China Academic Journals Full-Text Database.

standing of the tradition.[49] Many of these articles reflect the authors' responses to the sudden and rapid change of the qin tradition in recent years. Subtly or overtly, the authors let their views be known on the development.

Representation, Control, and Historical Legacy

The reactions from qin musicians and scholars to the recent changes have by no means been uniform; indeed, the long historical debate between the advocates of Artists' Qin and of Literati's Qin on such issues as intended audience, expressivity versus meditation, and content versus form has sharpened in recent years. This is evident from scholarly conferences, published articles, public opinion expressed on the Internet, and my personal conversations with musicians. On one side are a small number of qin musicians who are widely recognized by the public as "masters"; these musicians set yardsticks on what is considered "good" performance through their teachings, concerts, CDs, and popular as well as scholarly writings. They promote examinations and competitions and serve as examiners and adjudicators, thereby further disseminating their aesthetic standards. On the other side are those, some equally well regarded as musicians among qin circles, who steadfastly adhere to the qin ideology that they have read about in historical documents and learned from their teachers; as a matter of principle, they keep aloof from public display and from the limelight.

The publicly recognized "masters" actively promote the modernization and wide dissemination of the qin, and they criticize the musicians and scholars who oppose the inevitable artistic changes that occur as society changes. The foremost voice has been Li Xiangting, considered one of the great masters today, who is also an accomplished writer, calligrapher, and artist. In his book on qin aesthetics in the Tang dynasty, he postulates that, by the time of the Tang, there existed two distinctive qin ideologies, which he calls *yishuqin* and *wenrenqin*, meaning, respectively, "Artistic Qin" and "Literati Qin."[50] By focusing on qin music rather than on the musician, as Liu Chenghua's and Xu Jian's terminologies did, Li carefully avoids the negative implication of a *yiren* (artist) or *zhuanye* (professional).[51] In defending and promoting Artistic Qin, Li theorizes that during the Tang dynasty, the Artistic Qin, which emphasized expressivity and communication to an audience, reigned supreme. Li uses colorful metaphors to denigrate those who adhere to the "traditional" performance practice, comparing it to other old practices of China that need "improvement" in the modern age, such as the weaving of "pigtails" by men, with their long hair in a single braid hanging down their backs, a symbol of ridicule and backwardness, or the binding of women's feet, universally abhorred as barbaric.[52] He invokes the Darwinian theory of natural selection: "History cannot be stopped, unless you kill it and preserve it as a stuffed animal or a mummy. History changes according to nature. . . . Human society progresses forward naturally, following the law of natural selection."[53] Thus, Li advocates a progressive attitude toward change but at the same time legitimizes the change by claiming that it is a return to an even older performance practice in the Tang dynasty. Li creates an ancestry and genealogy for the tradition that he wants to promote in modern times.

Another prominent qin master is Gong Yi, whose credentials include the post of Premier Performer in the Shanghai Chinese Orchestra, a visiting professorship at the Shanghai Conservatory of Music, and a certificate authorizing him to supervise doctoral students. Gong has concertized and taught widely, has recorded many CDs, and also publishes in scholarly and popular journals. A representative expression of his views on the debate can be found in the article "Qin Competition and the Development of the Qin Tradition as an Integral Part of Society."[54] An avid promoter of qin competition and the popularization of the qin, Gong defends his position by arguing for the need for experimentation in qin music as a means to catering to evolving society, particularly in view of the multiple needs of contemporary cultural life, the speed of media of communication, and the development of technology. He discusses the need for new compositions; the need for new performance formats, such as ensemble playing with other instruments and a "concerto" form with a large orchestra; and new performance practices including examinations, competitions, class instruction, banquet entertainment, qin Web sites, and so on. He cites examples of experimentation from history and also quotes prominent music historian Huang Xiangpeng as saying that "Chinese musical tradition is not a narrow and closed system, but it continually moves, absorbs, appropriates, and changes, thus extending its life."[55]

The views and arguments on the other side of the debate can be best represented by qin scholar and performer Wu Zhao, whose academic standing is reflected in his positions as a researcher at the Chinese Academy of the Arts, president of the Beijing Society of Qin Research, and certified supervisor for doctoral students. In his article entitled "Tradition and Modernity: The Challenges to the Art of Guqin," he points out the philosophical roots of the qin in Confucianism and Taoism but adds that, since the mid–Tang dynasty, but especially after the Song dynasty (960–1279), Zen Buddhism exerted a strong influence on qin music.[56] Addressing directly Li's promotion of expressivity in Tang dynasty qin music, Wu writes that "while it is not easy to play with passion, it is nevertheless easy to make an impression with such music. Conversely, to play quietly yet in a manner pregnant with meaning may appear to be easy, but it is in fact more difficult to achieve."[57] Wu claims: "Qin music is all about the art of *xiexin* (expression of the heart). Such music is rich in Eastern philosophical content and cannot be compared to other kinds of music. As the artistic essence of our civilization, it is unique and is irreplaceable."[58]

Wu acknowledges musical development but insists that it must be multidirectional. In the case of the qin, individual musicians are certainly free to find their own paths of development according to their liking, including those who promote the "modernization of qin music" by adopting elements of Western classical music, Western contemporary music, and mainstream Chinese music. He writes that, while qin musicians have the right to create new compositions or to perform abbreviated versions of compositions from the old repertory, it would be a grave mistake to use these activities as the guiding principle for the future development of qin tradition or as a standard by which to judge levels of achievement among contemporary and young qin players. He specifically criticizes qin competitions and examinations, activities that have been greatly promoted by the other side. He invokes the UNESCO proclamation by saying that if China were to safeguard qin music as a "heritage," then it would be the people's responsibility to preserve the qin's unique characteristics and ensure its being transmitted to future generations. He does not object to new compositions but states that "if one merely strives for newness and originality, allowing qin music to develop in the same direction as guitar, *guzheng* [a Chinese bridged zither], or piano, and simplistically follows the paths of the development of other Chinese traditional instruments, without seeking nutrition from the rich soil that had nurtured qin music . . . that would not be meaningful."[59]

The debate outlined above reflects a struggle between two long-standing ideologies. Each side of the debate constructs a history to present the past, invoking selected historical periods, philosophical thoughts, and performance practices and choosing terminologies with subtle positive or negative implications. In doing so, each side claims legitimacy for the present and argues for a voice in constructing the future. In short, each side is exercising its cultural rights to represent and to control.

While the opposing ideologies have long existed, today's debate is unlike any that might have occurred in the past. As already pointed out, the factors that make the situation different include the collapse of the literati class in the early part of the twentieth century, the creation of a market economy, and the advancement of technology. However, one may point to one other factor that reflects upon the broader change in Chinese people's political development.

The early twentieth century saw enormous spread and growth of literacy throughout the country. Western ideas of education and democracy, Marxism, and other political philosophies were introduced, in particular by an increasing number of Chinese students who studied abroad and returned to hold leadership positions in education, government, and industry. These new ideas awakened people's sense that it was possible to assert an individual identity, exercise choice, and control their own future.

The liberalization of government policy beginning in the late 1970s propelled a rapid development of the market economy and a growing middle class of consumers. The new social and economic environment has been conducive to the commercialization and popularization of many artistic products. Packaging and branding have become important tools in developing a new audience base. As qin music becomes a commodity to be bought and sold, the Chinese people can use their purchases to determine the direction of cultural development, thus obviating the need for any debate. In short, economic power enables the citizenry to exercise choice.

The last critical factor for the change in qin music was the emergence of mass media due to technological advancement, particularly nonprint media, including radio, television and film, CDs and iPods, and in particular the Internet. Such media have increased the scope and speed of communication in many parts of the country. The wide dissemination and accessibility of information facilitated consumers' scope of choice. The question is no longer who is winning the debate but who is playing the qin and in what manner.

In short, the political, social, economic, and technological transformations within China have not only enabled such debates to flourish but also encouraged the citizenry to exercise their personal choices of artistic expression, freeing themselves from the shackles of the opinions of social elites. While the transformation of qin music in society may be viewed as yet another reflection of the country as it moves toward a more progressive era, it also reflects upon the increasing commodification of the arts, with qin music as the last frontier to be conquered. Ironically, the "selling" of the qin tradition successfully attaches itself to the roots of elite culture with its refinement and sophistication. Almost all popular writings on the qin allude to its "three thousand-year-old history" and hail it as being the "oldest and most refined" of China's musical types.

When UNESCO made its proclamation in 2003, it introduced yet another external factor.

The Irony in UNESCO's Proclamation

UNESCO's concern for intangible cultural heritage has a long history and has undergone several stages of development. The germ of the idea can be dated to 1966, when the General Conference adopted the Declaration on the Principles of International Cultural Cooperation, which provided the basis for the development of cultural policies within UNESCO. Next came the Convention Concerning the Protection of the World Cultural and Natural Heritage, adopted in 1972, at which point several member states expressed an interest in the importance of safeguarding what was later to be called intangible heritage. An important step in 1973 was the addition of the protection of folklore to the Universal Copyright Convention; some years later, in 1982, the Committee of Experts on Safeguarding of Folklore was set up. In 1989, the General Conference adopted the Recommendation on the Safeguarding of Traditional Culture and Folklore, and in 1994, the Program of Living Human Treasures was launched. In 1997–98, the Proclamation of Masterpieces of the Oral and Intangible Heritage of Humanity was established, which led to the first proclamation of the nineteen Masterpieces in May 2001. Meanwhile, the Convention for the Safeguarding of Intangible Cultural Heritage was adopted by the Twenty-third General Conference of UNESCO on November 3, 2003, signed by the president and the director-general. (The convention was subsequently "entered into force" on April 20, 2006.) Thus, the 2003 Proclamation of Masterpieces of the Oral and Intangible Heritage of Humanity was particularly significant because it immediately followed the convention, a fact noted by the Chinese media in reporting the proclamation.

UNESCO's efforts to "protect and safeguard" masterpieces were carried out with preparations at every step of the way toward arriving at the first proclamation, along with the adoption of the convention two years later. Though the term "cultural rights" was never used, UNESCO's intention and effort coincided with the emerging use of the term in public discourse as expounded in this volume. That an international and august institution such as UNESCO made such high-profile pronouncements in its convention and proclamations about specific musical genres naturally caught the world's attention, particularly in developing countries. The steady increase in the number of masterpieces from one proclamation to the next shows increasing attention from member states. It should be noted that the nation-states nominate their own choice of artistic genres as candidates; the nominations are very likely affected by internal political and cultural considerations. Whether or not a nation's nomination in fact fulfills UNESCO's intention to "safeguard oral and intangible heritage," particularly if it is eventually selected, would be an interesting question to explore and examine.

When UNESCO bestowed the honor to qin music in 2003, it was perceived by many as a strong signal that distinguished qin from other kinds of Chinese music.[60] The advocates of Artists' Qin can now claim that qin music is important not only within Chinese culture but for all of "humanity." In a 2004 article, Li Xiangting promotes the wider dissemination of qin music by invoking UNESCO's proclamation, saying, "Our most esoteric, oldest, and most refined living musical tradition has formally begun to be recognized, appreciated, and shared by all humanity as a cultural wealth."[61] Catering to national pride, UNESCO's proclamation has been particularly effective in winning new audiences and supporters.

The advocates of Literati's Qin do not object to wider dissemination such as large-scale concerts, CDs, examinations, or competitions per se but rather to the tools that such practices require, which inevitably exploit the expressiveness of musical sound as a means of appealing to an uninitiated audience at the cost of educating them about literary and philosophical content. The result, they feel, is the loss of the qin tradition's unique characteristics. Though the issue of commercialism is seldom raised, one senses an unspoken criticism that the movement to popularize is driven in part by the profit motive—absolutely unacceptable in the literati tradition. They also take the social higher ground by using the designation of *yiren* for those who advocate Artists' Qin, which greatly irks them because the word has derogatory implications as denoting a profession that is of service to the literati.

The irony that UNESCO's proclamation has added fuel to the fierce debate and contributed to the rapid changes in the ideology and performance practice of the qin is not lost on qin musicians and observers. At a conference on the qin held in Hong Kong in November 2006 entitled "Chuanchen yu kaituo" (To inherit and to develop), sponsored by the City University of Hong Kong, the participants included prominent qin musicians and scholars from China, the Mainland, Taiwan, and abroad, including both Li Xiangting and Gong Yi; Wu Zhao, though invited, did not attend. The debate was both frank and heated. One of the most thoughtful papers was by Lau Chor Wah, qin musician and professor of Chinese literature and philosophy at the Hong Kong Baptist University. She urged the Department of Culture of the Beijing government to explain its original intention in submitting the nomination of the qin to UNESCO and divulge its understanding of the meaning of "Masterpieces of the Oral and Intangible Heritage of Humanity," because "such an explanation may clear up misunderstandings, and reduce the damage that the proclamation has caused to qin culture." She also called for an examination of qin activities in the post-proclamation period.[62]

In a brief report on the conference, writer Zhong Wenxin summarized the central point of debate in the opening paragraph, which is worth quoting in its entirety:

> On November 7, 2003, China's qin was proclaimed by UNESCO as the second group of "Masterpieces of Oral and Intangible Heritage of Humanity." In 2002, the UNESCO raised some queries about the nomination. The following one in particular attracted attention: "[Musical traditions] face extinction because of a lack of policies for their protection and safeguarding as a result of rapid changes, of urbanization, and of the influence of foreign cultures." Under the influence of economic reform, "[We need to create] legal measures to protect and safeguard [the traditions] from being exploited irresponsibly as cultural representation."[63] Today, shortly after the success of the nomination, many civic organizations and institutions have raised the banner of dissemination and wide recognition of the art of the Chinese qin. They use it as a great opportunity for publicity to enhance commercial success. They discover the market value of the claims "to modernize qin, and to use aesthetic experience and standard gained from contemporary music to promote the qin." In the process of "development" and "creativity," qin music and its tradition degenerated into mere formulaic pronouncements; many of its traditional artistic characteristics have lost their value. This is truly a historical irony.[64]

The "irony" is made clearer by reading the official text of the proclamation, which begins: "The Chinese zither, called guqin, has existed for over 3,000 years and represents China's foremost solo musical instrument tradition. Described in early literary sources and corroborated by archaeological finds, this ancient instrument is inseparable from Chinese intellectual history. Guqin playing developed as an elite art form, practiced by noblemen and scholars in intimate settings, and was therefore never intended for public performance. Furthermore, the guqin was one of the four arts—along with calligraphy, painting, and an ancient form of chess—that Chinese scholars were expected to master. According to tradition, twenty years of training were required to attain proficiency."[65]

As this passage makes explicit, the raison d'être of qin's nomination, and no doubt of its acceptance by UNESCO, lies in its age, its association with "noblemen and scholars," and its relationship with the other elite arts—factors that distinguish it from other musical traditions. Yet the result of the proclamation has been to destroy exactly what it was lauded for.

The musicians who defend the qin tradition they inherited from their teachers may not use the term "cultural rights," but in fact they feel that, if the qin tradition can claim a "right" to exist, that right is being eroded and violated. They sense the serious threat that, if the current trend continues and its effects snowball, the younger generation developing an interest in the qin will be exposed to a new and different qin tradition. The special characteristics that have made the qin so special in Chinese and world musical culture are disappearing in the name of "modernization" and "popularization." These musicians watch helplessly as the qin tradition takes on a new identity yet clings to descriptive words that have made it special, while in reality it is no longer unique but has become just like many other kinds of music.

The despair is articulated by a qin player and scholar from Hong Kong, now living in Vancouver, who wrote a personal e-mail to his friends in October 2006. It summarizes the feelings of some qin musicians as they reflect upon the UNESCO proclamation:

> Chinese civilization has experienced one hundred years of destruction, and is currently at its nadir. The rich cultural legacy left to us by our ancestors has been greatly damaged by people who have wiped out almost everything, both material and spiritual. What is left is but a pile of words. In order to exploit whatever still remains, they now rely upon foreigners to proclaim "Masterpieces of Humanity." In so doing we trade away even our self-respect. My friends, you have read the classics written by the sages. We learned from their writings the true spirit of our culture. Viewed from the long perspective of history, the chaos we are witnessing today may in fact be the first step of a cultural renaissance. We need to treat what is happening around us as nothing extraordinary but hold onto what we have so that the spirit of our civilization may continue into the future. Then the day of revitalization will arrive.[66]

Notes

1. Qin is also known as *guqin,* often referred to in the West as the seven-string zither. Gulik called it a "lute," which is organologically wrong.

2. Robert van Gulik, *The Lore of the Chinese Lute: An Essay on Qin Ideology,* Monumenta Nipponica, no. 3 (1940; repr., Tokyo: Sophia University Press/Charles E. Tuttle Company, 1969), 1.

3. In recent scholarly and popular literature of China, the span is claimed to be three millennia. The difference in opinion depends upon the definition of what a qin is. The more conservative figure is based upon the stability of the construction of the instrument since around 200 B.C.E.

4. E.g., Gulik, *Lore of the Chinese Lute;* Rulan Chao Pian, *Sonq Dynasty Musical Sources*

and Their Interpretation (Cambridge, Mass.: Harvard University Press, 1967); Tsun-yuan Lui, "A Short Guide to Ch'in," *Selected Reports of the UCLA Institute of Ethnomusicology* 1, no. 2 (1968): 179–204; David Ming-yüeh Liang, *Music of the Billion: An Introduction to Chinese Musical Culture* (New York: Heinrichshofen Edition, 1985); Fredric Lieberman, *A Chinese Zither Tutor: The Mei-an Ch'in-p'u* (Seattle: University of Washington Press, 1977); James Watt, "The Qin and the Chinese Literati," *Orientation* 12 (1981): 38–49; and Bell Yung, "Choreographic and Kinesthetic Elements in Performance on the Chinese Seven-String Zither," *Ethnomusicology* 28, no. 3 (1984): 505–17.

5. The literati were the educated class, particularly in the Confucian classics, who passed civil service examinations; most of them served as government officials.

6. Gulik, *Lore of the Chinese Lute,* 17.

7. An earlier notational system from which this one developed dates to the sixth century. A single composition has survived from that period. There is strong evidence that many such notational samples existed in that period and earlier but did not survive.

8. Xu Jian, *Qinshi chubian* [First study of qin history] (Beijing: Renmin yinyue chubanshe, 1982), 58.

9. The Chinese word *yi* in *yiren* is universally translated as "art" in English; hence "yiren" is naturally translated as "artist." The problem is that the Chinese term "yiren" and the English word "artist" connote different sociological meanings. In China, "yiren" has a slightly derogatory tone to refer to someone who practices an artistic profession for the service of others, while in the West, "artist," though also implying a professional, denotes individuality, originality, and creativity, connotations that are less obvious in the Chinese term.

10. Liu Minglan, "Kongzi de wenrou dunhou dui guqin yinyue de yingxiang" [The influence of the Confucius ideal of *wenrou dunhou* on the music of qin], in *Jinyu qinkan xu: Jinian Jinyu qinshe chengli liushinian* [Jinyu Qin Journal, Supplement: In memory of the 60th anniversary of the establishment of Jinyu Qin Society] (Shanghai: Jinyu qinshe, 1996), 35.

11. Confucius (551–479 B.C.E.) himself reputedly played the qin, and his main goal in playing was for self-cultivation, with no intention of serving anyone else but himself (Liu Chenghua, "Wenrenqin yu yirenqin guanxi de lishi yanbian" [Historical changes of the relationship between the literati's qin and the artists' qin], *Zhongguo yinyue* [Chinese music] 98 [2005]: 11). Whether or not Confucius actually played the qin is disputable, for extant sources appeared several centuries after his time. Historical "facts" here are taken to equate with collective memory and commonly accepted wisdom that have been in existence for millennia.

12. See Liang, *Music of the Billion,* 208.

13. Miao Jianhua, "Guqin meixuezhong de ru dao fuo sixiang" [The Confucian, Daoist, and Buddhist philosophies in the aesthetics of qin], *Yinyue yanjiu* [Music research] 105 (2002): 10. Translated by the author.

14. Gulik, *Lore of the Chinese Lute,* 19. T'ao Ch'ien (365–427) is Romanized today as Tao Qian and is also called Tao Yuanming, one of the most celebrated poets of China. The original quote of his reads "dande qinzhongqu, helao xianshangsheng."

15. Lü Ji, "Lüelun qixianqin yinyue yichan" [Brief discussion of the legacy of qin music], in *Qinqu jicheng* [Compendium of qin compositions], ed. Zhongyang yinyue xueyuan

Zhongguo yinyue yanjiusuo [Chinese Music Research Institute, Central Conservatory of Music] and Beijing guqin yanjiuhui [Beijing Society of Qin Research] (Beijing: Zhonghua shuju, 1962), 15.

16. Dai Xiaolian, "Jinyuqinshe sheming de laili" [The origin of the name Jinyu qin society], in *Jinyu qinkan xu: Jinian Jinyu qinshe chengli liushinian* [Jinyu Qin Journal, supplement: In memory of the 60th anniversary of the establishment of Jinyu qin society] (Shanghai: Jinyu qinshe, 1996), 9.

17. Cheung Sai-bung, *Zhongguo yinyueshi lunshugao* [Historical studies of Chinese music] (Hong Kong: Union Press, 1975), 436.

18. Original Chinese quoted from Liu Chenghua, "Wenrenqin yu yirenqin guanxi de lishi yanbian," 14; translated by the author. The word "Qin" in the last line does not refer to the instrument but to the kingdom of Qin during the Warring States period, considered to be the originator of the instrument *zheng* (zither).

19. Liu Chenghua, "Wenrenqin yu yirenqin guanxi de lishi yanbian," 18.

20. "Qinren timinglu" [List of qin players], *Jinyu qinkan* [Journal of Jinyu Qin Society] (1937): 235–53.

21. The official publication from the PRC is Mao Tse-tung [Mao Zedong], *Talks at the Yenan Forum on Literature and Art* (1942; Peking: Foreign Languages Press, 1967).

22. See Bonnie S. McDougall, *Mao Zedong's "Talks at the Yan'an Conference on Literature and Art": A Translation of the 1943 Text with Commentary,* Michigan Monographs in Chinese Studies No. 39 (Ann Arbor: Center for Chinese Studies, University of Michigan, 1980).

23. Mao, *Talks at the Yenan Forum,* 10–12.

24. Qin music was not the only genre that was forced to make adjustments. See Bonnie S. McDougall, ed., *Popular Chinese Literature and Performing Arts in the People's Republic of China, 1949–1979* (Berkeley: University of California Press, 1984).

25. Liang, *Music of the Billion,* 199–200.

26. Bell Yung, "Music of Qin: From the Scholar's Study to the Concert Stage," *ACMR Reports* (Journal of the Association for Chinese Music Research) 11 (1998): 5. Originally published as "La musique du guqin: du cabinet du lettré à la scéne de concert," in *Cahiers de musiques tranditionnelles 2: Instrumental* (1989): 31–62.

27. *Yaji,* or "elegant gathering," refers to occasions when scholars meet to carry out activities in the elite arts such as qin music, Kunqu opera, calligraphy, and poetry as they enjoy wine and food.

28. Qiao Jianzhong, "Xiandai qinxue lungang" [Outline of contemporary qin research], *Tianjin yinyue xueyuan xuebao* [Journal of the Tianjin Conservatory of Music] 2 (2000): 4–9, reprinted in Qiao Jianzhong, *Yongtan bainian: Qiao Jianzhong yinyuexue yanjiu wenji* [Collected articles in musicology by Qiao Jianzhong] (Ji'nan: Shandong wenyi chubanshe, 2002), 202–13.

29. Luo Haolin, "Guqin yinyue CD changpian mulu huibian" [A list of CD recordings of qin music], in *Jinyu qinkan xu: Jinian Jinyu qinshe chengli liushinian* [Jinyu qin journal, supplement: In memory of the 60th anniversary of the establishment of Jinyu Qin Society] (Shanghai: Jinyu qinshe, 1996), 120–21.

30. See color plate with caption "Jiang zongshuji qingxi guangling qinshe" [General Secretary Jiang's affectionate link with Guangling Qin Society], *Qixianqin yinyue yishu*

[The art of the seven-string qin] 10 (2002): color plates between pp. 63 and 64. Jiang was China's supreme leader by serving as general secretary of the Communist Party of China from 1989 to 2002 and as president of the People's Republic from 1993 to 2003.

31. In 1996, Cheng Yu, based upon interviews with members of the Beijing Guqin Research Association, expressed pessimism about the future of qin music despite renewed activities in yaji, concerts, and publications since the end of the Cultural Revolution. See Cheng Yu, "The Precarious State of the Qin in Contemporary China," *Chime* 10/11 (1997): 50–61. He writes, "While this survey may give the impression that the number of qin supports is on the increase, the overall situation of qin culture in China remains precarious, as the case of the Beijing Guqin Research Association exemplifies" (58). He specifically mentions that "[qin players] lack sufficient funding to carry out any major research or organize performances on a regular basis, and there is little recognition or involvement on the part of society at large" (58–59) and laments "public and governmental neglect shown towards one of the oldest and most precious parts of the country's musical heritage" (59). Such concerns for funding, "recognition or involvement on the part of society at large," and governmental support underscore a major shift in attitude of qin players in the 1990s from those of several generations earlier. It also foreshadows the rise of Artists' Qin in the next millennium.

32. See the Web site of the North American Guqin Association at www.chineseculture.net/guqin/ under "News and Events."

33. This proclamation came after the first one in 2001, when nineteen Masterpieces were selected, and was subsequently followed in 2005 by a third proclamation numbering forty-three selections.

34. *Masterpieces of the Oral and Intangible Heritage of Humanity: Proclamations 2001, 2003 and 2005* (Paris: Intangible Heritage Section, Division of Cultural Heritage, UNESCO, 2006), 4.

35. For example, the nineteen selections in 2001 range from "The Oruro Festival" of Bolivia and "The Gbofe of Afounkaha: The Music of the Transverse Horns of the Tagbana Community" of Cote d'Ivoire to "The Cultural Space and Oral Culture of the Semeiskie" of Russia. For China, the "Kunqu Opera" was included in the 2001 selections and "The Art of Uyghur Maqam of Xinjiang" and the "Urtiin Duu: Traditional Folk Long Song" in the 2005 list.

36. *Beijing Morning News,* November 9, 2003, htech.sina.com.cn/other/2003-11-09/0904253816.shtml (accessed April 9, 2008).

37. Published in *Yinyue zhoubao* [Music weekly] in Beijing, December 14, 2001.

38. "Top 10 Qin News Items for 2002," www.chineseculture.net/guqin/newsletters/2002qinitems.htm (accessed April 9, 2008).

39. For example, Zhongguo guqin xinwenwang [Chinese qin news], www.guqinnews.com.cn/; Mei'an qinyuan [Qin center of Mei'an], www.china-qin.com/; and Chinese guqin, www.chineseguqin.com.

40. See www.guqinnews.com.cn/. The logo appeared when accessed on September 2, 2007. When accessed April 9, 2008, the logo had changed.

41. "2004 nian shoujie zhongguo guqin dasai zhangcheng" [Rules and regulations on the first grand competition of Chinese guqin in 2004], www.folkmusic.org.cn/show.asp?id=1678.

42. "Youlan" (Elegant orchid) and "Yangchun" (Sunny spring) are two qin compositions that are considered to be among the oldest and most refined.

43. Hanwang [Han Internet], http://www.hanminzu.com /bbS/dispbbs.asp? boardid=157 &id=115969.

44. Prizes are all named after the word *lan,* meaning orchid.

45. "Guqin kaoji xuzhi" [Information on guqin examinations], www.guqinnews.com .cn/news/phopic/2008/124/0812421441598B0H8B4AH8EE5KFCF2.html.

46. "Guqin youpiao yuandi yingyou huangshan" [Guqin postage stamp should have Huangshan as guqin's place of origin], www.guqinnews.com.cn/Search.html?Keyword= %BB%c6%c9%BD&Subsys=NS&SearchSubmit_Foosun=%B1%BE%D5%BE%CB%D1% CB%F7.

47. Zhongguo changcheng wang [The China Great Wall net], www.chinagreatwall.org/ detail/news_detail.jsp?info_id=1100112076&cust_id=greatwall.

48. "In Pictures: China Celebrates Olympics," http://news.bbc.co.uk/2/hi/in_ pictures/6936707.stm.

49. Miao Jianhua, "Guqin meixuezhong de ru dao fuo sixiang"; Qin Xu, "Qinyue shiyige buduan biange fazhan de duoyuan kaifang xitong" [The qin tradition is an open system that is ever changing and developing], *Zhongguo yinyuexue* [Chinese musicology] 72 (2003): 5–20; Fei Denghong, "Dui guqin yishu zhenxing qianjing de chuangxin gouxiang" [A creative envisioning of the future of the revival of qin musical art], *Zhongguo yinyue* [Chinese music] 95 (2004): 21–27; Li Xiangting, "Guqin yishu yinggai chengwei meige zhongguoren de jichu zhishi zhiyi" [The art of qin should be among the fundamental knowledge of every Chinese], *Renmin yinyue* [People's music] 456 (2004): 36–37; Gong Yi, "Guqin bisai jiqi shehuihua fazhan" [Qin competition and the development of the qin tradition as an integral part of society], *Renmin yinyue* [People's music] 470 (2005): 25–27; Liu Chenghua, "Wenrenqin yu yirenqin guanxi de lishi yanbian"; Wu Zhao, "Chuantong yu xiandai: Zhongguo guqin yishu mianlin de tiaozhan" [Tradition and modernity: The challenges to the art of guqin], *Renmin yinyue* [People's music] 470 (2005): 22–24.

50. Li Xiangting, *Tangdai guqin yanzou meixue ji yinyue sixiang yanjiu* [Study of the aesthetics of qin performance and musical ideology in the Tang dynasty] (Taipei: Wenhua jianshe weiyuanhui, 2003).

51. See note 9. The word *zhuanye* has the equally derogatory implication as *yiren.*

52. Li as quoted in Zheng Peikai, ed., *Kouchuan xinshou yu wenhua chuancheng* [Oral transmission and cultural continuity] (Guilin: Guangxi Normal University Press, 2006), 73.

53. Ibid., 75.

54. Gong Yi, "Guqin bisai jiqi shehuihua fazhan." The original term *shehuihua* in the Chinese title is best understood as "becoming integrated into society."

55. Ibid, 27.

56. Wu Zhao, "Chuantong yu xiandai: Zhongguo guqin yishu mianlin de tiaozhan."

57. Ibid., 23.

58. Ibid.

59. Ibid., 24.

60. With the exception of Kunqu opera, which was given the same honor two years earlier in 2001. Notably and revealingly, Kunqu opera, a musical genre very much like

qin music in being considered a refined art and catering to the literati class, did not stir up as much debate and controversy as qin music did. One reason is the importance of its libretto, which is difficult for anyone without a classical literary education to appreciate, a "handicap" that qin music does not have.

61. Li Xiangting, "Guqin yishu yinggai chengwei meige zhongguoren de jichu zhishi zhiyi," 36.

62. Quoted in "Chuancheng yu kaituo" [To inherit and to develop], conference held on November 1–2, 2006, City University of Hong Kong. Conference booklet, p. 4.

63. Not the original wording, but translation back to English from the Chinese version of the UNESCO document that the author, Zhong Wenxin, quotes. The quote echoes two of the "main objectives" of the proclamation: to raise awareness on the importance of the oral and intangible heritage and the need to safeguard it, and to encourage countries to establish national inventories and to take legal and administrative measures for the protection of their oral and intangible heritage. See *Masterpieces of the Oral and Intangible Heritage of Humanity,* 4.

64. Zhong Wenxin, "Chuancheng yu kaituo" [To inherit and to develop], *Mingpao Monthly* (Dec. 2006): 119.

65. *Masterpieces of the Oral and Intangible Heritage of Humanity,* 29.

66. Huang Shuzhi, personal communication. Quoted with permission.

6 Representation and Intracultural Dynamics

Romani Musicians and Cultural Rights Discourse in Ukraine

ADRIANA HELBIG

In cultural development practices of post-socialist Eastern Europe, cultural rights function as an interchangeable concept with minority rights, in which ethnicity figures as a central framework for political and social equality. Policy initiatives and projects funded by government agencies and international non-governmental organizations (NGOs) address minority rights issues through a lens of ethnic homogeneity that, in most cases, completely overlooks those issues of gender, class, and education that work together to influence relative cultural agency and powers of representation within a community and in society at large. It follows that many cultural policies implemented by local and international NGOs obscure processes of social exclusion and economic and political marginalization within communities where cultural development initiatives are funded.[1] Who has the "right" to choose which cultural practices are to be sustained and promoted? How do public presentations of culture draw general awareness to certain agendas and individuals within particular communities? What is the role and responsibility of the ethnographer who researches representational practices in contexts where cultural expression is highly politicized?

With regard to Romani groups in Ukraine, government and international non-governmental initiatives throughout the 1990s and well into the twenty-first century have continued to perpetuate Soviet-era cultural stereotypes of "Roma" as "Gypsies," musicians, and entertainers. Various cultural initiatives, publications, concerts, ensembles, and recording studios have been funded, as have education programs that incorporate music and dance into their curricula. The funding is predominantly channeled into Romani communities through local Romani NGOs. An essentialized, performance-focused identity unites the Romani rights movement and helps present a top-down homogenized cultural image of linguistically diverse Romani groups. Moreover, certain images are more strongly perpetuated by Romani community leaders and politicians than others. "High-class" professional musicians signify the acceptable norm for Romani musical stereotypes. They appear on Ukrainian television as part of minority festivals or in segments of cultural programs. Romani community leaders use images of prevalent poverty only when targeting group discrimination in light of European Union–based Romani development initiatives funded by local government and international philanthropic project grants. In this dynamic, impoverished Romani musicians appear in photographs of philanthropic reports but are silenced within the Romani rights movement by Romani rights activists, scholars, cultural workers, and economically privileged Romani musicians. Less wealthy Roma are deprived of access to the types of local and international financial support from which more affluent Roma are able to benefit. The argument and/or justification for the exclusion of poor musicians is rooted in their alleged loss of traditional culture and their cultural and linguistic assimilation into non-Romani society.

Romani poor are deemed by "their own" as having "no culture" and thus have no political power within the ethnically driven Romani rights movement in Ukraine. The crux of the issue lies in the fusion of two notions of culture that prevail in the post-socialist sphere: culture as artistic expression of group identity and culture as a marker of civilization, both delineated by the same word, *kultura.* The two definitions of kultura are neither mutually exclusive nor always complementary. The ethnographic analysis that follows examines the types of representative agency to which poorer segments of marginalized ethnic groups have access within the myriad contradictions of current cultural rights movements and projects in the post-socialist context. In other words, this chapter analyzes the impact of cultural rights discourse on Romani members of the economically poorest strata of society in Ukraine.

The Romani Rights Movement in Ukraine

In philanthropic discourse, culturally and linguistically diverse Romani groups are categorized by the catchall term "Roma of Ukraine." Roma, traditionally referred to in Ukrainian as "Tsyhany" (Gypsies), are the thirteenth largest minority in Ukraine and number from 40,000 to 100,000 among a population of 48 million. Servy, the largest Romani group within Ukrainian territories, are descendants of migrants from Wallachia and Moldova who settled in eastern and southern Ukraine in the sixteenth and seventeenth centuries. Kelderara and Lovara groups migrated from territories within the Austro-Hungarian empire at the beginning of the twentieth century. Ruska Roma, also known as Khaladitka Roma, constitute yet another linguistic group in Ukrainian territories and are descendants of migrants who came to the Tsardom of Russia in the sixteenth and seventeenth centuries from Germany through Poland and Lithuania. The Crimean Peninsula, which became a part of the Ukrainian Soviet Socialist Republic (SSR) in 1954, is home to Krimuria, or Krimchi Roma, who practice Islam. Southern Ukraine is also home to groups from Moldavia and Linhurari, migrants from Romania.

In the mid-1990s, Western philanthropic organizations initiated cultural development grants to help incorporate minorities into the ethnically fragmented post-socialist realm. The culture-based model aimed to diffuse ethnic strife that marked the immediate post-independence era in Ukraine. Many Romani musicians in Transcarpathia, fluent in Hungarian, the language of donors from the Open Society Institute in Budapest, capitalized on incoming financial opportunities to stage music festivals, open Romani Sunday schools, and publish literature, news, memoirs, and *rozmovnyky,* books that list Romani words and phrases with Ukrainian or Russian translations. Varied forms of funding have helped mobilize a viable Romani rights movement, a loosely organized public relations campaign presently supported through a network of more than sixty Romani NGOs throughout Ukraine. Activists within the movement strive to break historical cultural stereotypes regarding Tsyhany as lazy, thieving, politically apathetic musicians, entertainers, and dark-skinned people who possess magical powers to frighten and manipulate the local non-Romani population. These stereotypes are common throughout Europe and the Soviet Union and are often drawn on by non-Roma to justify Romani marginalization, poverty, illiteracy, and housing shortages, as well as police brutality toward them. Today, the Romani rights movement has shifted its weight to Kyiv, the capital of Ukraine, where Romani public figures lobby for minority rights and fair representation in the Verkhovna Rada (Parliament). They also organize commemorations for Romani victims of the Holodomor and the Holocaust.[2] Nonetheless, festivals of Romani music and dance are the most effective means for drawing public awareness to Roma in the territories of Ukraine.

The Post-socialist Landscape of Poverty

Ukraine experienced its most drastic economic recession in the mid-1990s following the breakup of the Soviet Union. In 2000, at the time of my first visit, people were making ends meet with the help of a barter system rooted in an elaborate network of personal exchanges called *blat* held over from the Soviet era.[3] The barter system was particularly evident in the villages of Transcarpathia, Ukraine's westernmost region, which, perhaps even more than other parts of the country, had been overrun by politically linked mafia businessmen. Roads, agricultural structures, and other social, medical, and educational institutions were in desperate need of an overhaul. Because train and bus transportation in 2000 was difficult and dangerous, I rode a bicycle from village to village and witnessed the trauma of sudden drastic poverty among Romani communities caught in the turmoil of post-socialist economic transition. At that time, it was more common for a university professor to be found selling family heirlooms on the black market than to be working at the university, where his or her salary was often withheld for six months at a time. A prominent ethnochoreologist made it through this period by breeding and selling little fish in her kitchen. With the bazaars overrun with people of all socioeconomic and ethnic backgrounds, Romani traders became the target of heightened discrimination and were quickly pushed out. Frequently in my fieldnotes I wrote down the names of Romani musicians I suspected would die from malnutrition or tuberculosis before my next visit.

It was in this context that a Romani interlocutor in the Transcarpathian village of Osii encouraged me to travel from the villages to Uzhhorod, the administrative capital of the region, to work with a person she colloquially referred to as the "president of Roma." I dismissed the suggestion, believing I would be a more effective advocate against Romani poverty in the West by documenting it in the villages. Arriving in desolate Romani communities, I often did not even unpack my recording equipment but rather went directly to the local market to purchase food, oftentimes for the whole community. Even in 2000, five U.S. dollars could buy enough rice to feed fifty people.

I further dismissed the idea of moving to Uzhhorod because I thought that my interlocutor, in referencing the hierarchical position of "president," was in fact referring to a culturally defined system of Romani barons—family and Romani settlement leaders—that was as much historically rooted as it was self-ascribed in the then-prevalent context of mafia big men. I assumed the "president of Roma" probably drove the latest model of Mercedes, a sure sign of mafia connections, and was a member of a network I attempted to avoid out of general fear of the violence associated with people in power. The president of Roma, however, a musician by profession, acquired his ascribed title (and, perhaps, his Mercedes) because he was the director of the largest Romani NGO in Transcarpathia. When I traveled to Uzhhorod for my year of fieldwork in 2002, I realized our paths would cross constantly, and I eventually came to work for him as an English translator for a Romani rights newspaper written by his non-Romani NGO staff funded by the Open

Society Institute in Budapest. From 2002 to 2004, I translated the newspaper for the Internet—where my English translations ensured further funding from donors in the West—in exchange for information and access to Romani communities, made possible through his connections. Though twenty years my senior, he called himself my brother and drove me in his Mercedes to take newspaper pictures of impoverished Romani settlements similar to the ones I had visited on my bicycle, but now as a fully integrated actor in the processual objectification of Romani culture for political means. It was a fieldwork experience drenched in ironies.

Performing Culture, Inscribing Status

Taking into account the numerous Romani communities I have worked with and visited over the years in Transcarpathia's villages and towns, it would be difficult for me to say that much has improved for them despite the fact that the number of internationally funded Romani NGOs in Uzhhorod alone grew to twelve by 2002 and all local Romani NGO projects and philanthropic activities, on paper at least, were geared toward helping the relatively poorer Roma in Ukraine—Transcarpathia in particular. It seems that the continued neglect of the Romani poor is socially and culturally perpetuated among more affluent Roma throughout the country.

Elite justifications for the continued marginalization of the Romani poor are rooted in complex binary understandings of civilized/uncivilized Roma and linguistically pure/assimilated Romani groups. Such conceptualizations are couched in a post-socialist concern with cultural authenticity as manifested in performance practices. Moreover, they are closely intertwined with the history of Romani cultural development projects and Romani sociocultural integration within a Soviet-socialist paradigm.

Romani music and dance, as performed on stages for both Romani and non-Romani audiences in urban contexts and in the media, are extremely important for Ukraine's Romani elite and stem from the high visibility of Moscow's Theatre "Romen" during the Soviet era. Theatre "Romen," founded in 1931, is a theater of music and drama that features traditional Romani culture in stylized form. It continues to be viewed by Romani performers and audiences throughout Russia and Ukraine as the pinnacle of Romani musical excellence and stylistic achievement. Thus, even after the collapse of the Soviet Union, the images and performance styles fostered in Moscow continue in full force on the Romani stages of Ukraine.

Many festivals and concerts have been produced with the help of philanthropic aid from the International Renaissance Foundation (IRF), as evidenced in the performances of Kyiv's Theatre "Romans," established in 1998 by Ihor Krykunov, a former performer with Moscow's Theatre "Romen." Performance aesthetics promoted on the stages of Kyiv are similar to what audiences can see in cities from Kharkiv in the east to Uzhhorod in the west. This is an important point to make in a country such as Ukraine, where the ethnic and linguistic differences between the eastern and western regions are so varied among both majority and minority ethnic groups and where they reflect such strong influences of past imperial rule, whether Russian in the east or, to a lesser extent, Austrian (as well as Polish and Hungarian) in the west. Here, the Soviet-era ensembles, which simultaneously promote regional variation yet stylistically homogenize them, serve as a force that performatively unifies east and west.[4] In my fieldwork in Uzhhorod among Romani music and dance ensembles associated with NGOs that wished to revive waning local musical traditions in the wake of post-socialist economic hardship, I often encountered dance steps and songs that were more consistent with styles perpetuated by Moscow-based Romani musicians than with styles that were representative of the more Hungarian- and Slovak-influenced local Romani styles I witnessed in Transcarpathia in nonstaged contexts such as weddings.

Performers from Moscow's Theatre "Romen" are often featured guests at Romani music and dance festivals in eastern cities such as Kyiv and Kharkiv. These performers' personal and musical connections with musically and culturally elite families, such as that of Nikolai Slichenko (1934–2004), former director of Moscow's Theatre "Romen" and winner of numerous cultural awards from Russia and the USSR, validate the persistence of certain aesthetics of vocal production, instrumental arrangements, choreographies, costumes, and modes of self-representation prevalent among affluent Romani families in Ukraine.

These elements carry equal importance in Transcarpathia, and some musicians still perform in professional venues that mirror the aesthetics promoted by Moscow's Theatre "Romen." Historically, however, Romani musicians in the strongly Hungarian-influenced province played in restaurants and were part of an elaborate network of musicians who provided entertainment for non-Romani patrons. Following the breakup of the Soviet Union, the restaurants closed, and a number of Romani musicians lost their jobs. In the wake of economic collapse, many sold their instruments. It is rare to find musicians in rural and urban Romani settlements who still own instruments or whose instruments are not in bad need of repair. During my fieldwork, I often traveled with an accordion, a violin, and a guitar throughout the villages in order to be able to make musical recordings, as in the village of Sobatyno, seen in Figure 6.1.

Figure 6.1. Author with Romani musicians in the village of Sobatyno, central Transcarpathia, 2000. (Author's collection)

In the last few years, non-Romani families who have regained some economic status in Transcarpathian villages have begun to invite Romani musicians, such as the ensemble from the village of Sobatyno, to perform certain elements of wedding rituals, such as playing at the gate of the bride's home as the groom "buys" her from her family with gifts and money. Such instances have been more exceptions than the norm, and it has been extremely difficult for local Romani musicians to pass on their craft to younger musicians, let alone make a living from music.

This does not mean, however, that a viable local music scene among Romani communities in Transcarpathia does not exist. It simply exists in forms that vary from those of the Soviet era. Evangelical churches have played an instrumental role in forging new musical repertoires in Romani communities. Having attended numerous services of the Church of the Living God in Mukachevo, Uzhhorod, and Korolevo, I witnessed popular melodies being infused with religious texts and the beat of the songs diffused into a more hymnlike sonic structure so as to make popular songs more conducive to church services. At the weddings I frequented in Uzhhorod, one of the highlights of certain celebrations was a Slovak tune; paying money to dance with the bride, each community member welcomed her in her new social role within the community. Members of more affluent Romani groups in eastern Ukraine often interpret such musical appropriations as signs of cultural assimilation into non-Romani society. Among the cultural elite, lines between cultural practices deemed Romani or non-Romani are often very strict, particularly regarding gender roles. In one memorable case, a close friend who was able to make a living as a wedding singer took me to another town to introduce me to her somewhat more affluent relatives (the gradation in wealth was minimal). Though she wore jeans during our everyday interactions in Uzhhorod, for the trip she tossed a long skirt into her bag. She changed on the train and explained that her choice of outfit was a sign of respect for her family at home and for the family we were visiting. She said that they would view her jeans as a sign of *gadje* (non-Roma) culture and would think that her father had become poor and could not provide for the family in a way that would ensure their adherence to elite Romani cultural norms. Many affluent Romani men throughout eastern Ukraine have explained to me that financial stability allows women to practice all necessary traditions that constitute Romani culture. In such families, however, I had few opportunities to speak privately with women or could not get them to express their opinion on the subject.

As evidenced by the jeans episode, however, it seems that many cultural norms, particularly with regard to gendered propriety, are constituted by social, familial, and community contexts. During my 2007 trip to Kyiv and Kharkiv, affluent Romani men repeatedly echoed non-Romani stereotypes concerning Romani poor in Transcarpathia, calling them dirty, uneducated, assimilated, and thus uncultured (*nekulturni*). On the one hand, this meant that the poor were uncivilized people who did not act in accordance with progressive social norms, and on the other hand, they were assimilated and not adhering to traditional forms of Romani cultural behavior. To create greater distance between themselves and the poor in Transcarpathia, the more affluent Roma called the latter "Tsyhany," distinguishing them from other Roma (the current politically correct term for Gypsies increasingly used in Ukrainian politics, though not in the media). At an international ethnomusicology conference that same summer, I was surprised when such attitudes toward the Romani poor in Transcarpathia were informally echoed by a prominent scholar who argued that they are not worthy of study because they lack authentic cultural expression. In other words, kultura functions as a marker of, from one side, cultural distinction and, from the other, civilization, based on the modernization discourses promoted under Soviet nationalities policies with regard to various ethnic groups.[5] In theory, ethnic groups such as Roma had equal rights in the eyes of the socialist state but were deemed backward and were forced to alter their kultura (in both senses of the word) to better integrate into a "progressive" society that reflected the political ideals of Soviet advancement.

In the post-socialist sphere, the Soviet notion of culture as modernization and the Western notion of culture as the embodiment of traditions that need to be saved have fostered a complex duality within the Romani rights movement itself. Essentially, Romani elites and non-Roma alike deem "high-class" Romani musical expression professionalized during the Soviet era to be representative of Romani "traditional" cultural expression and, at the same time, a marker of kultura as civilization. Thus, the interpretation of kultura as solely that of professional musicianship allows scholars and Romani elite within NGO circles to dismiss the 50,000 impoverished Roma in Transcarpathia as not worthy of serious ethnographic research for its own sake and as only a population from which to gather poverty statistics for development reports.[6]

In such a context of delineation between Romani groups that are constituted as "real Roma" and communities of people who are not the "right" kind of Roma, what is the role and positioning of the ethnographer, such as myself, who chooses not to research the "right" kind of people in a particular fieldwork environment? My experiences have been greatly determined by my own role within this complex terrain of Romani identity as it has been defined for me by Romani interlocutors in different parts of Ukraine, Europe, and the United States. I had entered the field at the time when Romani NGOs were being established throughout the country and were vying for regional power. Language, kinship, gender, age, and myriad political and economic factors determined an internal hierarchy among Romani NGO representatives and public figures within the burgeoning Romani rights movement. Over the years, I have played a game of negotiated neutrality among opposing Romani NGO leaders. However, what seemed to be my fluid positioning between two political camps eventually backfired because of the tense political struggles in Ukraine during and immediately following the 2004 Orange Revolution and prevented me from visiting my fieldwork site for one year.[7] It was not until my return to Ukraine in 2007 that I fully realized my own complex status in the public representation of Romani identity—Romani leaders in Kyiv dismissed their opponents in Transcarpathia, and me along with them, stating that since I had chosen to work with the poor initially in 2000, I should continue to work only with "my people" in Transcarpathia. The ironies have layered themselves one on top of another only to be complicated even further by politically motivated discourses that aim to drive Transcarpathian Roma out of the political picture altogether due to their poverty. Ironically, their endemic poverty is the primary catalyst propelling the philanthropic machine and Western development aid from which Romani NGO leaders throughout the country continue to benefit economically and politically. Thus, it seems that a cultural debate over kultura reaches far beyond a question of who has a "true" culture and/or what constitutes it.

The Marketing of Cultural Stereotypes

Anthropologist Alaina Lemon has argued that stereotypes among non-Roma regarding Roma emerge because non-Roma engage Roma only in certain contexts.[8] My own experiences have suggested that representatives from elite Romani groups share non-Romani stereotypes about poorer Roma, a dynamic that has perhaps always existed but is most certainly exacerbated by the contemporary cultural, musical, and development structures that lump all "Roma" into one category indivisible by class, gender, occupation, or generation.

Music and dance play a significant role in this discourse because the most common stereotype among non-Roma, and one that is actively promoted by all Roma, poor and elite, is that they have a penchant for the expressive arts. This has been, by far, the only relatively positive stereotype expressed by non-Romani interlocutors regarding any Romani group throughout the duration of my research. Music festivals in Ukraine such as the International Arts Festival of National Minorities "Amala," established by the Gypsy Musical and Drama Theatre "Romans" in Kyiv, as well as popular CD compilations produced in the West such as *Road of the Gypsies* (Network, 1996), *La Route des Gitans: The Gypsy Road* (Auvidis/Ethnic, 1999), and *Gypsy Caravan* (Putumayo World Music, 2001), to name just a few, stress the common heritage of all Romani groups worldwide based on an allegedly shared historical migration from India. Kyiv's "Amala" festival and such CD compilations feature musical groups from countries in Europe that have a significant "Romani" population. Though scholars have begun to show that many different cultural and linguistic groups experienced this migration from India for varying reasons more than one thousand years ago, the play on words between "routes" and "roots," as evidenced in the Gipsy Kings recording *Roots* (Nonesuch, 2004), is an excellent example of the prevalence of the now-common marketing tactic that unites all "Roma" and/or all "Gypsies" through the trope of historical nomadism.[9] Significant in this discourse is the use of the "road" image in the names of Romani NGOs in various parts of Ukraine: Romano Drom (Romani Road) in Poltava and Vynohradiv, and Uzhhorod-based Amaro Drom (Our Road), Amaro Drom Ternenhero (Our Road of the Youth), and Terne Chaya Po Nevo Drom (Young Women on a New Road).

While world music CDs and Romani NGOs promote a transnationally established, top-down "Romani" identity and imply a collective hurdle of historical exclusion and marginalization, intragroup dynamics among Romani communities in Ukraine reveal a somewhat different picture—the Romani rights literature published by philanthropic organizations such as the IRF and the Open Society Institute strongly promotes this sense of unity but does not put it into practice. As a case in point, the *Romani Yag* (Romani Fire) newspaper based in Uzhhorod published the same timeline, noting the appearance of the first Roma on the European continent in the fourteenth century, over and over. By publishing the events that occurred to Roma in various European countries, the newspaper editors sent to their readers the message that these are common identifiers, namely dates known to all Roma who know their own history. Due to lack of scholarship on Romani history in Ukraine, dates from events that happened to Roma in other European countries filled in the empty blanks of Ukrainian Romani history.

But the actual practice of such trans-ethnic connections and inclusive affiliations has been far from evident in the territories of Ukraine. A famous popular Romani singer in Kyiv dismissed any formal cultural connection to Romani poor in Transcarpathia in an interview with me in 2007, stating that they are not "true" Roma because they do not speak Romanes and have lost Romani cultural traditions as a result of extreme poverty, which prevents them from holding on to their cultural practices. However, his music album features the song "Loli Phabay" (The Red Apple), which was popularized through the 1975 Mosfilm *Tabor Ukhodyt v Nebo* (Camp Ascends to the Heavens), directed by Emil Loteanu. The song and the film are both strongly associated with Romani musicians in the Carpathian region, many of whom claim the melody as their own, which they support with the fact that Transcarpathian Romani musicians appear as extras in the film. Thus, while certain musical expressions, divorced from the music's original performers, function as an acceptable form of representation in certain contexts, direct links to Romani poor in the realm of cultural expression are dismissed by Romani elite.

The argument over which groups have retained the truer Romani identity today revolves largely around language ideologies. Servy Roma, also commonly known as Ukrainian Roma, speak a dialect that is often described by members of the Lovary group as a mixture of Romanes and *surzhyk* (a combination of Russian and Ukrainian, spoken commonly in more Russified parts of eastern Ukraine). Lovary in Transcarpathia and in cities such as Kharkiv view their language as less Russified and thus more European and closer to the language of Romani groups in the Balkans, from where Lovary are said to have migrated generations ago. According to a Servy musician from Kyiv who married into a Lovar family in Kharkiv, "When I learned the Lovar tongue, Europe opened up to me."[10] The positioning of Europe as more developed and more advanced in relation to Ukraine itself reveals a pull among Romani intelligentsia for validation and connection with Roma and non-Roma in the West. The same template, as already argued, exists in relation to Russia, which is also considered by Romani elite to be more culturally developed than Ukraine. To express his affinity to Russia, the previously mentioned Romani NGO director referred to by local Roma as the "president of Roma" had the melody of the second post-Soviet Russian anthem programmed as his cell-phone ringtone.[11] At the "Amala" festival, produced by the director of the aforementioned Theatre "Romans" in Kyiv, Romani musicians billed as being from Norway, Poland, Belgium, or Slovakia are often friends and family members who emigrated from Ukraine but now represent "Europe" to Ukrainian audiences and imbue such Western place-based identities with great importance. Positioning language on a scale of more civilized versus less civilized allows certain Romani groups to create intergroup hierarchies and to push those who speak no Romanes lower on the comparative scale of cultural purity. Subjective understandings of authentic kultura validate intergroup elite status.

On the other hand, non-Roma perceive poor and rich Roma as two sides of the same coin. While Romani poor in Transcarpathia are useful for Romani elite in terms of justifying international philanthropic aid for "Roma," they simultaneously embody the more negative and often more damaging non-Romani stereotypes regarding Roma. They also serve as a reminder that despite class distinctions, non-Romani stereotypes tend not to distinguish between poor and rich Roma. A poor Romani person is feared for his or her alleged potential to steal and trick and manipulate, while the rich Romani man is feared for alleged participation in illegal activities such as drug dealing. Members of the Romani upper class believe that through disassociation with lower class Tsyhany, negative stereotypes toward Romani elite that prevail among gadje will dissipate.

The Cultural Impact of Philanthropic Aid

Processes of intragroup identification in Ukraine have been complicated by the presence of philanthropic aid programs from the West that, for the past twenty years, have been alloting aid to Romani communities. Philanthropic programs do not distinguish between various Romani groups and classes but rather cast all members who in some way fit Western understandings of "Gypsies" and "Roma" into one homogeneous category. Philanthropic programs, however, do distinguish between educated and non-educated persons within these communities by allotting grants to those who submit applications, usually older urban males who present themselves as working in the interest of "all Roma." According to a grants manager at the IRF in Kyiv, "As long as a person of Romani ethnicity submits a reasonable budget plan and sends timely reports on monies spent, he will receive a grant from us."[12]

In the opinions of philanthropic agencies such as the IRF, monies are allotted for "Roma" because they are deemed poor and marginalized. Conditions of the very poor are used as statistics, but monies are distributed to those who might not be in relative need. Studies conducted by scholars in Ukraine and published by the Open Society Institute concentrate solely on the poorest communities and provide the abysmal statistics of per capita income, education level, number of children, types of diseases most prevalent in such communities, and descriptions of living conditions. Couched within these statistics is a critique of cultural practices among poor Roma regarding early marriage and the alleged lack of family planning that leads to multi-child households that perpetuate the cycle of poverty. I recall that in the village of Bilky, Transcarpathia, a one-story wooden house with only three walls was home to thirty people. When I inquired about the lack of the fourth wall, the male head of household simply replied, "There are so many of us here we'd need a revolving wall." This metaphorical revolving wall always spins in favor of Romani elite and leaves the impoverished Roma in the cold.

Many of the pictures I took in such communities were published in the *Romani Yag* newspaper, which lost funding from the Open Society Institute in 2006 and has not been published regularly since.[13] However, a photo that I took of amateur female Romani dancers in Moscow's Theatre "Romen"–like costumes playing in the Uzh River near a Romani settlement in Uzhhorod appeared on the Web site of the Ukrainian BBC, part of the BBC's February 14, 2007, article on Romani poverty and socioeconomic marginalization. The article was accompanied by a photo series titled "Tsyhanske Schastia" ("Gypsy Fate" or "Gypsy Happiness," depending on contextual interpretation of the Ukrainian word).[14] The eight pictures featured members of Uzhhorod's poorest Romani settlement participating in projects sponsored by the International Organization for Migration. Seven photos featured the dirty, tragic living conditions in the far reaches of the settlement in which I lived during my fieldwork; the eighth was my picture of the dancers in the river.

I took the picture in 2002 when a television crew came to the settlement to film the ensemble because of its participation in a regional minority music and dance festival. As in many instances throughout my fieldwork, such occasions were apt to be exotified. The crew members found what they expected—quaint, colorful Roma in a self-essentialized environment. The ensemble members dressed themselves and community members in costumes, rented a horse, borrowed my guitar because the synthesizers they perform on clashed with the natural aesthetic of the river setting, and built a traditional nomadic

Figure 6.2. Photograph taken by author in Uzhhorod, Transcarpathia, 2002, and published by the Ukrainian BBC without author's permission in 2007. The smokestack was cropped in the BBC photo to position the dancers in a more "natural" setting.

caravan to give the filming a more authentic "Gypsy" feel. When the gadje film crew left the settlement, the ensemble leader asked me to take a series of pictures featuring the girls dancing and posing in their costumes to use as concert promotional material. The informal shot of the girls playing in the water at the end of the hot summer day was published in the *Romani Yag* newspaper and later scanned from the black-and-white newspaper article and republished on the Internet with the caption "Members of the Association 'Roma' dance ensemble in Transcarpathia following a performance." Given the fact that no reporter (or researcher) can do interviews in a rural or segregated urban Romani community without permission and the presence of the Romani settlement leader (or director of a Romani NGO), I initially assumed that the choice of pictures for the BBC article was influenced by the local Romani NGO leader who wished to feature Romani poverty (and not his own affluent house in the center of the settlement) alongside an example of cultural expression, which has become such a fundamental factor within the Romani rights movement in Ukraine. Recently, however, I learned that the "culture" picture was submitted to the BBC by a non-Romani person affiliated with the International Organization for Migration affiliate office in Kyiv. This reinforces the fact that philanthropic and development organizations play a significant role in defining, influencing, and manipulating cultural rights discourse.

Within the arguments of this chapter, the inclusion of this picture as part of the BBC feature article is significant because it represents the core issue regarding representation within the Romani rights movement—that "Gypsies" without "culture" aren't Roma. In this sense, "culture" represents artistic expression but is fused with understandings of kultura in the form of civilization, meaning upper-class, cosmopolitan, staged representations of Romani identity. The picture serves as a validation of the argument that the impoverished communities are worthy of inclusion in the Romani rights movement because they have a music and dance ensemble that proves their alleged retainment of distinct cultural traditions. Significant to note is that each Romani NGO in Transcarpathia that I had encounters with, whatever its broader mission and goal, sponsored a music and dance ensemble that promoted the aesthetics of Moscow's Theatre "Romen" and/or Kyiv's Theatre "Romans." The positioning of the picture alongside the Romani poor functions as a way through which marginalized Tsyhany are incorporated in the Romani rights movement.

Cultural Rights as Interpretive Framework for Fieldwork

Cultural rights are not synonymous with other aspects of human rights. Ethnomusicologists Dan Lundberg, Krister Malm, and Owe Ronström have pointed out that the cultural diversity paradigm conflicts with the multicultural paradigm.[15] The former focuses on individual freedom while the latter focuses on recognition through collective heritage. Under the guise of protection and promotion of cultural rights, an intricate power struggle takes place regarding who has the authority to define culture, who attributes value to certain traditions, who gets the money, and who remains poor. Most often this occurs within discourses of authenticity, while in other cases it is much more complicated and nuanced, with answers lying well beyond the realms of actual cultural expression.

When scholars select certain groups to work with, they choose them over others and imbue them with a certain value. Such actions are often interpreted locally with respect or anger. What role do ethnographers play in molding the discourses and actions that shape attitudes and actions toward cultural rights and cultural development agendas in the communities we study? How does the increasingly prominent cultural rights discourse shape the ethnographic contexts in which ethnomusicologists work? In what instances does an overt cultural rights agenda overshadow scholarly objectivity? Should a scholar advocate for certain groups within culturally constituted intergroup relationships on behalf of persons with less group agency or power, such as women or members of a culturally untouchable caste?

There is a growing literature dealing with these questions, since scholars increasingly must struggle with them in fieldwork contexts where cultural rights advocacy has become the normative discourse among interlocutors involved in and influenced by transnationally mediated human, women's, minority, and/or cultural rights movements.[16] It is vital that ethnomusicologists recognize the extent to which such processes frame our own positioning and influence the musical traditions we study. Understandings of and motivations behind rights agendas vary by sociopolitical locale and are interpreted differently by various sectors of society.

The disjunctures between institutional discourses and life as lived on the ground for poor Romani musicians raise broader questions regarding cultural representation, ethnicity as a marker for the distribution of aid, and intragroup agency that may be brought to bear on other aid projects throughout the world. Western institutions play a highly significant role in establishing and perpetuating global frameworks through which cultural expressions are mediated. Shifts within these Western networks transform and determine what people on both sides of the equation understand by the notion of culture and what they do, protect, and promote in its name.

Notes

1. Julie Hemment, *Empowering Women in Russia: Activism, Aid, and NGOs* (Bloomington: Indiana University Press, 2007); Michele Rivkin-Fish, *Women's Health in Post-Soviet Russia: The Politics of Intervention* (Bloomington: Indiana University Press, 2005); Valerie Sperling, *Organizing Women in Contemporary Russia: Engendering Transition* (Cambridge: Cambridge University Press, 1999).

2. "Holodomor" derives from the Ukrainian words *moryty holodom,* "to inflict death by hunger," and refers to the Famine of 1932–33 in the Ukrainian SSR induced by Stalin to weaken Ukrainian peasant rebellion against collectivization and to gain Soviet control over Ukrainian agricultural lands. Seven to ten million people perished, among them countless Roma. Romani activist Volodymyr Bambula published the first Romani Holodomor memoir in 2002, *Tsyhanska Dolia—Yak Viter u Poli* [Gypsy Fate—Like Wind in the Steppe] (Pereiaslav-Khmelnytsk, Ukraine: Karpuk Press, 2002). In 1941, Nazi forces massacred between 100,000 and 200,000 Kyiv citizens at Babyn Yar, among them Jews, Ukrainians, Russians, Poles, and Roma. Romani activists organize annual commemorations at Babyn Yar and publish oral history accounts of Romani Holocaust survivors. See Aladar Adam, Evheniia Navrotska, and Yulia Zeikan, *Bilyi Kamin z Chornoi Kativni* [White Rock from the Black Prison] (Uzhhorod, Ukraine: Uzhhorod City Press, 2006).

3. *Blat,* or *po platu,* refers to exchanges of favors with neighbors, school friends, and coworkers, incorporating access to hard-to-obtain material objects or social services.

4. There is a significant amount of literature in ethnomusicology that addresses the ways the stylization of folklore was used to both foster and suppress ethnic difference within socialist cultural policy. For Bulgaria, see Donna A. Buchanan, *Performing Democracy: Bulgarian Music and Musicians in Transition* (Chicago: University of Chicago Press, 2006); and Timothy Rice, *May It Fill Your Soul: Experiencing Bulgarian Music* (Chicago: University of Chicago Press, 1994). For Poland, see Timothy Cooley, *Making Music in the Polish Tatras: Tourists, Ethnographers, and Mountain Musicians* (Bloomington: Indiana University Press, 2005). For Russia, see Laura Olson, *Performing Russia: Folk Revival and Russian Identity* (London: RoutledgeCurzon, 2004); and Anthony Shay, *Choreographic Politics: State Folk Dance Companies, Representation, and Power* (Middletown, Conn.: Wesleyan University Press, 2002).

5. Contemporary UNESCO discourses regarding intangible cultural heritage also focus on distinction and recognize only one community/nation as the bearer of a particular musical tradition. Regarding issues surrounding the nomination of Croatia's "Istrian Ethnomusical Microcosm" to UNESCO's "Masterpieces of the Oral and Intangible Heritage of Humanity" program, see Naila Ceribašić, "Musical Faces of Croatian Multiculturality," *Yearbook for Traditional Music* 39 (2007): 1–26. For an analysis regarding Georgia's preference for polyphony as an exclusive musical symbol of the Georgian nation and ethnicity and the consequential exclusion of *duduki* music from Georgia's national narratives, a dynamic validated and reinforced through UNESCO's naming of Georgian polyphony to the "Masterpieces" program in 2001, see Nino Tsitsishvili, "Social and Political Constructions of Nation-Making in Relation to the Musical Styles and Discourses of Georgian Duduki Ensembles," *Journal of Musicological Research*, 26, nos. 2–3 (2007): 241–80.

6. Romani NGO directors argue that there are 350,000 Roma in Ukraine, 50,000 of whom live in Transcarpathia. According to the official 2001 Ukrainian census report, there are 47,600 Roma in Ukraine. However, this figure is suspiciously low and too similar to the 1989 Soviet census that identifies 47,917 Tsyhany in the Ukrainian SSR. Because they fear discrimination, Roma often reject the social stigma associated with Tsyhany and hide their ethnic identity on official documents. Self-negation in light of the rising ethnic strife in the post-socialist context explains, in part, the lower census figures for Roma in Ukraine in 2001. However, Roma mostly accuse 2001 census takers of omitting Romani communities completely from the census and claim that officials accepted bribes to write Roma off as members of other ethnicities. Accusations of wrongdoing are plausible because, as one government official in Uzhhorod pointed out to me, "Where there are no Tsyhany, the government has no problems," implying that the government does not have to pump extra funds into programs to help alleviate Romani poverty, unemployment, and illiteracy if there is no official record of Roma in the region. Compare Hryhorii Iemets, *Tsyhany Zakarpattia* [The Gypsies of Transcarpathia] (Uzhhorod: Karpaty Press, 1993); L. P. Malyk, M. I. Pitiulych, O. S. Peredrij, and B. A. Shynkar, *Tsyhany Zakarpattia: Problemy, Shliakhy Vyrishennia* [Gypsies of Transcarpathia: Problems, Ways to Solutions] (Uzhhorod: Carpathian Division of the International Institute of Management, Uzhhorod National University, 1991); and O. O. Yaremenko and O. H. Levtsun, *Osoblyvosti Sposobu Zhyttia ta Problem Sotsialnoii Intehratsiii Romiv v Ukraiini: Analitychnyi Zvit za Rezultatamy Sotsiolohichnoho Doslidzhennia* [Lifestyle Characteristics and Problems of Romani Social Integration in Ukraine: An Analytical Report Based on the Results of

Sociological Surveys] (Kyiv: Ukrainian Institute of Sociological Studies, International Renaissance Foundation, 2003).

7. Adriana Helbig, "Ethnomusicology and Advocacy Research: Theory and Action among Romani NGOs in Ukraine," *Anthropology for East Europe Review: Special Issue on Roma and Gadje* 25, no. 2 (2007): 78–83. For a detailed discussion regarding the role of music in these protests, see Adriana Helbig, "The Cyberpolitics of Music in Ukraine's 2004 Orange Revolution," *Current Musicology* 82 (2006): 81–101.

8. Lemon discusses the influence of theatrical and musical performance on non-Romani perceptions of Roma in Russia. See Alaina Lemon, *Between Two Fires: Gypsy Performance and Romani Memory from Pushkin to Post-Socialism* (Durham: Duke University Press, 2000).

9. David Malvinni, *The Gypsy Caravan: From Real Roma to Imaginary Gypsies in Western Music and Film* (New York: Routledge, 2004).

10. Personal communication with a young Romani accordion player and songwriter, Kharkiv, June 20, 2007.

11. The second post-Soviet Russian anthem, adopted by President Vladimir Putin in 2000, shares the same melody as the anthem of the former Soviet Union. J. Martin Daughtry, "Russia's New Anthem and the Negotiation of National Identity," *Ethnomusicology* 47, no. 1 (2003): 42–67.

12. Interview with a grants manager (identity withheld) at the International Renaissance Foundation in Kyiv, September 4, 2006.

13. Eugene Hutz and the group Gogol Bordello held a benefit concert in Irving Plaza on June 9, 2006, to help finance the continued publication of the *Romani Yag* newspaper.

14. "Does Racism towards Gypsies Exist in Ukraine?," BBCUkrainian.com, http://www.bbc.co.uk/ukrainian/forum/story/2007/02/070213_gypsies_gallery_it.shtml.

15. Dan Lundberg, Krister Malm, and Owe Ronström, *Music—Media—Multiculture: Changing Musicscapes* (Stockholm: Svenskt visarkiv, 2003), 33–43.

16. Helbig, "Ethnomusicology and Advocacy Research"; Ursula Hemetek, "Applied Ethnomusicology in the Process of the Political Recognition of a Minority: A Case Study of the Austrian Roma," *Yearbook for Traditional Music* 38 (2006): 35–57; Angela Impey, "Culture, Conservation and Community Reconstruction: Explorations in Advocacy Ethnomusicology and Participatory Action Research in Northern KwaZulu Natal," *Yearbook for Traditional Music* 34 (2002): 9–24; Svanibor Pettan, *Roma muszikusok koszovóban: Kölcsönhatás és kreativitás/Rom Musicians in Kosovo: Interaction and Creativity* (Budapest: Magyar Tudományos Akadémia Zenetudományi Intézet, 2002).

7 Representing Tibet in the Global Cultural Market

The Case of Chinese-Tibetan Musician Han Hong

NIMROD BARANOVITCH

In the discussion of cultural rights, references are often made to the position of ethnic minorities within modern nation-states. The underlying framework is usually made of two distinct cultures, a majority culture and a minority one, and of the need to protect the latter from being assimilated by and in some cases from being destroyed or annihilated by the former. The case of Tibet in particular, the focus of this chapter, provides multiple examples of such discourse. Indeed, few in the West have not heard of the calls to "save Tibet" and its culture from annihilation by the Chinese state.[1]

While fully recognizing the validity and importance of this concern to protect minority cultures, and while acknowledging the severe cultural loss that some ethnic minorities in China have experienced in recent decades, this chapter aims to shift the focus to the gray area that lies in between cultures and to the people and identities that inhabit it. This area reminds us that cultures are not homogeneous monoliths, that they do not necessarily exist in isolation from one another or in conflict with one another, and that they do not remain unchanged.

Indeed, millions of minority people today in China, whose ancestors maintained rich cultures that were very distinct and independent from (Han) Chinese culture, are culturally integrated into the latter. Some of these people cannot speak the language of their ethnic groups and know very little about the history and customs of their ancestors. Some were born in modern Chinese cities and were educated in Chinese schools. And still others are of mixed blood with one of their parents being of minority origin while the other is Han Chinese. Among these people are those who have given up their minority identity and have been practically assimilated. But there are many who insist on identifying themselves as minority people and engage in a constant struggle to redefine their ethnic identity. In this chapter, I refer to these people as "integrated minority people."

The following monologue of a Tibetan artist named Gonkar Gyatso, who grew up in China and now lives in London, raises some of the main issues addressed in this chapter. Gonkar Gyatso was trained in China in traditional Chinese calligraphy and landscape painting and started to incorporate elements from traditional Tibetan art into his work relatively late in his career as a part of a personal roots-seeking journey. Although Tibetan, he feels strongly connected to Chinese culture and defines his creative work as a blend of cultures and identities:

> I grew up in a Tibet of Chinese occupation, a land where history had been almost erased. But I am involved in Chinese culture in a very deep way through my years as a student and as a teacher at [the] university. As a Tibetan, my Tibetanness . . . comes very naturally: It is in my blood, it's my essence, so I have no other choice but to draw on my own cultural tradition. . . . I use Tibetan elements, but not in a traditional way, which is difficult for my Tibetan audiences to understand. . . . At the same time, conservative Tibetan and Western intellectuals criticize me for revisionism. This is the dilemma I face because of the isolation and . . . incomprehension between different cultures. I still feel culturally displaced. . . . [Once] on a return flight to Lhasa, I had an important realization: I felt like a Chinese person looking at Tibet. . . . When I heard the Dalai Lama's account of Tibetan history and our status as an independent nation, it motivated me to try to create something "Tibetan." However, at that time I had no knowledge of Tibetan techniques such as *thangka* painting, so my first attempt of portraying the Tibetan environment was still in the stylistic mould of Sino-Realism.[2]

In the late 1980s, as part of his roots-seeking journey, Gonkar Gyatso left China for Dharamsala, the center of the exiled Tibetan community. There, however, he realized that although being Tibetan, he could not reach out to his fellow Tibetans living in India. He found himself feeling very much like an outsider and realized that his art was rejected in Dharamsala because it was seen as Chinese:

> As an artist who had created a new style in the TAR [Tibet Autonomous Region], I soon discovered that no-one knew where I was coming from; no-one understood my art. In Dharamsala—it is seen as yet another foreign art style inspired by China, which suggests a treacherous inclination on the part of the

> artist. In Tibet my modernist style had been a survival tactic, but in exile it was unmarketable and led to marginalization and rejection. I took up *thangka* painting but it became part of a process of accommodation into a cultural system that I did not have access to in Tibet. My appreciation of my heritage was, however, filtered through a different aesthetic. I feel like I am more of an outsider, observing Tibetan culture from a distance. My predicament is that I do not share the same philosophy of the Tibetan exiled culture because it is dedicated to what Tibet once was: and they could not understand my images of Tibet.[3]

This monologue highlights the complex sense of identity of many minority artists and writers living in China today and points to some of the major themes that accompany this sense of identity; the sense of distance that these individuals feel vis-à-vis the traditional culture of their minority groups; the strong influence of Chinese culture on their creative work and sense of identity; their engagement with the question of how to express their complex identity through their art and literature; and their experience of marginalization by many of their fellow people, Western intellectuals, and the Western market.

Using Gonkar Gyatso's monologue as a starting point, the main focus of this chapter is a half-Tibetan, half–(Han) Chinese pop musician named Han Hong, who has emerged in recent years as one of China's most famous pop stars, thanks mainly to her many songs about Tibet. Han Hong will be examined here as a representative case of an integrated minority artist. I will analyze the different representations and receptions of Han Hong's music in four different locations—among Han Chinese in China, among Tibetans living in China, among Tibetans living outside China, and in the West—and will argue that each of these is intimately linked to the different perceptions of Tibet that exist in each of the four locations. In particular, I will show that in sharp contrast to her extreme popularity in China, Han Hong has been totally excluded from the music market in the West. I will propose that this exclusion derives from the fact that Han Hong and her music do not fit the two elements that dominate the Western attitude toward Tibet, namely, the romanticized spiritual image and the ideological cause of Free Tibet. In the context of the latter, Tibet is seen as independent from China, and any Chinese influence is perceived as reflecting Chinese occupation. To support my claim, I will show how, in sharp contrast to Han Hong, Tibetan musicians who do conform to the Western vision of Tibet enjoy considerable popularity in the Western music market.

I will also propose that the representation of Tibet in the West is dominated by Tibetan exiles, among whom Han Hong is practically ignored, in large part because she is so popular in China, something that implies that she is either not authentic enough or a collaborator with the oppressive Chinese regime. Arguing that these political implications also constitute a major factor in the exclusion of Han Hong from the Western music market, I also suggest that the different receptions of Han Hong among the four different audiences mentioned above are intimately connected to one another and influence one another. Within this theoretical framework, the ambivalence with which Han Hong is seen by Tibetans living in China, as opposed to her total rejection by Tibetans living outside China, is understood in this chapter as an important indicator of the significant influence that mainstream Chinese culture has exerted on Tibetans living in China and of the hybrid sense of identity that these Tibetans have developed as a result of this influence.

The main theoretical focus of this chapter is cultural representation in the context of globalization, and it is based on the understanding that such representation constitutes a major cultural right. Because representation in the global cultural landscape today depends to a large extent on access to and participation in the global cultural market, I consider access to the cultural market to be another important cultural right, despite the apparent discrepancy between the idea of cultural rights and the commercial character of the market. Based on these two propositions, I argue that the exclusion of Han Hong and other integrated minority artists from China from representation in the Western cultural market constitutes a violation of their right to representation. Moreover, since Han Hong's hybrid identity is shared by many Tibetans living in China today, I also propose that the violation of her right to representation implies that the cultural rights of a whole cultural community of integrated Tibetans is also violated.

A Short Biography of Han Hong

Han Hong, who in her childhood was also called in Tibetan Kelsang Dolma (Chinese: Gesangzhuoma), was born in 1971 in Shigatse (Chinese: Rikaze), the second largest city in the Tibetan Autonomous Region, to a Tibetan mother and a Han Chinese father. The former, named Yongxi (in transliteration to Chinese), was a singer who gained some fame during the late 1960s and early 1970s with her rendition of the revolutionary "Tibetan" classic "On Beijing's Golden Mountain" (Chinese: "Beijing de jin shan shang").[4] Following the unexpected death of her father, Han Hong moved to Beijing when she was nine to live with her grandmother (from her father's side) and has remained there ever since. After moving to Beijing, she essentially lost contact with her mother and her Tibetan relatives and did not return to Tibet until the mid-1990s.[5]

Right after her arrival in Beijing, Han Hong joined a local children's choir, and in 1987, when she was sixteen, she joined the army as a singer. She remained a soldier until 2003, but since 1993, along with her work in the army, she began writing music and lyrics for herself and for others in a pop and rock style and thus started to develop an independent career as a pop musician. In 1995, she made her first national appearance as a singer, when she performed her song "Himalaya" (Chinese: "Ximalaya") on China's Central Television (CCTV). "Himalaya" incorporated elements from traditional Tibetan music, the most important of which was the low and raspy sound of the Tibetan ritual long horns (used by monks in monasteries). The video clip for the song was shot in Tibet, and in its lyrics, which depict the beauty of the Tibetan landscape, Han Hong states that she was born in Tibet and grew up there. This song marked the beginning of Han Hong's bright career, at the center of which were her many songs about Tibet.

Since 1998, Han Hong released five solo albums (for details, see the discography at the end of the chapter), and several of her songs became hits and occupied top places in dozens of billboard charts all over China, sometimes for several consecutive weeks. She also won numerous prizes in China and East Asia, including awards by CCTV, MTV Asia, and Channel V. Some of the most important awards included nomination for MTV Asia's "Best Chinese Female Singer" in 2002, the "Most Popular Female Artist Award" in the ninth Channel V Chinese Music Awards in 2003, and the "Best Female Artist of the Year" in China in the seventh CCTV-MTV Music Honors in 2005. Since the late 1990s, Han Hong has sung extensively all over China, and in 2003 she joined the short list of Chinese musicians who had the privilege of performing a solo concert in Beijing's Capital Gymnasium (Shoudu tiyuguan).

Han Hong's Musical Identity: A Chinese-Tibetan Blend

Han Hong's ethnic pop songs about Tibet share several common characteristics: their lyrics are usually about the beauty of Tibet's natural landscape but sometimes refer also to typical Tibetan places and sites, customs, and objects. The following lines are representative:

> HIMALAYA
>
> *(Lyrics and music by Han Hong)*
>
> I come from the Himalayas
> Embracing the Potala [Palace]
> I come from the foot of the snowy mountains
> I grew up in beautiful Lhasa

I was nurtured by yak butter and *tsampa*[6]
The water of the Yalu Tsangpo River washed clean my long hair
My beloved ones put on me a pure white *khata*[7]
They reminded me not to forget to return to our Lhasa . . .

Musically, the most recognizably Tibetan component in these songs is Han Hong's powerful and piercing, high-pitched singing, which most Chinese would immediately identify as Tibetan singing. This singing style, which became one of Han Hong's most important artistic trademarks, includes typical ornaments and vocal effects that add to the Tibetan flavor of her music. In many of her songs about Tibet, Han Hong also employs melodic material borrowed from Tibetan folksongs over which she lays her own compositions (for example, "Singing 2002" [Chinese: "Gechang 2002"] from the album *Singing*). According to Han Hong, she collected some of this material during her visits to Tibet and other Tibetan-inhabited areas in China, visits during which she met and recorded local musicians.[8] In her later songs, Han Hong also incorporates a substantial amount of singing in Tibetan, some of which she performs herself (for example, "End of the World" [Chinese: "Tianya"] from the album *Singing*), while some is performed by other Tibetan singers who accompany her in characteristic Tibetan group singing (for example, "Love of Langla Mountain" [Chinese: "Langlashan qing"] from the album *Singing*). Besides these ethnic markers, Han Hong employs in some of her songs a slow tempo and long, misty synthesized sounds, to which hand drums are added. These elements create the stereotypical atmosphere of mysterious spirituality, which conforms to the popular image of Tibet that developed in China in the early 1990s.[9]

In addition to the lyrics and the sonic elements, Han Hong also constructs and asserts her Tibetanness visually. As already mentioned, some of her video clips were shot in Tibet and celebrate the typical landscape of snowy mountains. Photographs from Tibet also decorate two of her albums. Moreover, on her 2002 album, *Singing*, which celebrates Tibetanness to an unprecedented extent, the lyrics of some of the songs are printed in the accompanying pamphlet in both Chinese and Tibetan. On its cover, Han Hong's name appears in Chinese characters that are written in a Tibetanized form and look like a Tibetan script.

In another expression of her Tibetan identity, Han Hong has also performed and recorded famous songs about Tibet written and originally performed by others. These include two of the most popular Tibetan revolutionary songs from the Maoist era, "On Beijing's Golden Mountain" (the song for which Han Hong's mother won fame more than three decades ago) and "The Emancipated Serfs Sing a Song" (Chinese: "Fanshen nongnu ba ge chang"), both of which were popularized all over China by famous Tibetan female singer Tseten Dolma (Chinese: Caidanzhuoma); a popular hit about Tibet from the 1990s called "The Qinghai-Tibet Plateau" (Chinese: "Qingzang gaoyuan"), which was originally performed by famous Han female singer Li Na; and, most recently, a song titled "Heavenly Path" (Chinese: "Tian lu"), which was written in 2001 to commemorate the construction of the new railway to Lhasa.[10] Originally sung by female Tibetan singer Pasang (Chinese: Basang), "Heavenly Path" was performed by Han Hong on the CCTV's *Spring Festival Party* (Chinese: *Chunjie lianhuan wanhui*) in early 2005 and immediately became a nationwide hit.[11]

However, notwithstanding the emphasis on Tibetanness in some of Han Hong's songs, the Tibetan elements are always incorporated into the framework of mainstream Chinese music. Indeed, with the exceptions of a few songs and a few excerpts in other songs, Han Hong performs her songs in Chinese, and the overall style of her music often shows the conspicuous influence of mainstream Chinese pop and rock music. Moreover, she has not limited herself to performing songs only about Tibet, and many of her songs show no signs whatsoever of her minority identity.[12]

Han Hong is completely aware of her complex identity as a mixed-blood person and of her complicated relationship with her Tibetan origins. Nonetheless, despite the fact that her father is Han Chinese, and although she can speak very little Tibetan, she has chosen, at least since her first album was released, to identify herself as Tibetan (Chinese: Zangzu) rather than as half-Tibetan, half–Han Chinese, or as Han Chinese.[13] While this identification as Tibetan may be a calculated attempt to claim authenticity for her songs about Tibet, which have catapulted her to fame, there are nevertheless many indications that Han Hong not only prefers to represent herself as Tibetan but also feels Tibetan. One such indication is her missionary zeal about Tibetan music and its image. Han Hong feels that she is playing an important role in changing people's attitude toward Tibetan music. She believes that before her appearance on the Chinese pop scene, most people thought that Tibetan music was monotonous, that it had nothing unique about it besides very high pitch, and that it was rustic. Thus, many Han Chinese, especially young ones between the ages of sixteen and twenty-two, did not like Tibetan music. However, after her appearance, many people changed their attitude, and Tibetan music became very popular.

Another powerful indication that Han Hong feels Tibetan was her reply when I asked if she would like to change her identity and not be a person of mixed blood if she had the chance to be reborn. Han Hong suggested to me that in her view, mixed-blood children are very smart. Yet, after acknowledging that she was only half-Tibetan and that one part of her was already sinicized (Chinese: *Hanhua*), she nonetheless expressed her strong wish to marry a Tibetan rather than a Han man; otherwise, her child would be completely sinicized.

Han Hong's concern for maintaining her Tibetan identity and Tibetan identity at large, however, does not necessarily mean that she is particularly concerned about preserving traditional Tibetan culture. In fact, what appears as one of the most important elements in her artistic work is her creation of what she refers to as "modern" Tibetan music. As if to make a statement, Han Hong has deliberately avoided the popular habit among many minority singers in China, especially those who work for official minority song-and-dance troupes, of performing in the traditional-style costumes of her minority group. Furthermore, since the turn of the twenty-first century, she has adopted many of the most updated features of contemporary Western pop and rock culture, such as short hair smeared with gel and sometimes dyed, fashionable sunglasses, casual unisex (sometimes overtly masculine) clothes, and "wild" behavior on stage, including screams and bold, rhythmic body movements.

When I asked Han Hong why she never wears traditional-style Tibetan costumes in her performances, she replied that there was no need for her to do so, because the moment she opens her mouth, everyone knows she is a Tibetan. Following this answer, Han Hong started to sing several phrases in a powerful, piercing, high-pitched voice to prove her point. Then she added that many people in China think that minority people can make only their own non-fashionable music, and she wanted to prove that as a Tibetan, she could create very good pop (Chinese: *liuxing*) music. To my question of what differentiates her music from the songs of Tseten Dolma and her mother, Han Hong replied that she herself was "pop" whereas they were traditional. Clearly, by "pop," Han Hong actually meant "modern" music, and her statements indicated that she considered being modern as one of the most important components in her creative work and personal and artistic identity.

While perpetuating many of the Han-created stereotypes of Tibetanness in her songs and discourse, Han Hong in her insistence on modernity was also resisting the most basic stereotype, namely that of backwardness (Chinese: *luohou*), which has become almost synonymous for Tibetan identity in China.[14] The quest for modernity is quite typical of the new generation of integrated minority artists who participate in mainstream Chinese culture. Given that most minorities are still perceived and represented in China as backward if not primitive, for these artists, who often see themselves (and can hardly escape being seen by others) as representatives of their entire ethnic group, this quest for modernity is a quest for normality and equality.[15] However, as I will argue below, at the same time that Han Hong's insistence on modernity clearly challenges the popular Chinese view that Tibetans are extremely primitive, paradoxically, perhaps, it is also a major reason for her success in China.

The Different Representations and Receptions of Han Hong and Her Music

The Representation and Reception of Han Hong among Han Chinese

Han Hong's appearance on the Chinese pop scene in 1995 with her song "Himalaya" was closely linked to a "Tibet fever" (Chinese: *Xizang re*) that swept the country in the mid-1990s. This "fever" was brought to a climax in 1994 with a rock song named "Return to Lhasa" (Chinese: "Hui dao Lasa") by Han male musician Zheng Jun, which became a nationwide hit soon after its release.[16] With its line "return to our Lhasa," there is little doubt that Han Hong's "Himalaya" was directly influenced by this particular song. Another important product of the "Tibet fever" was the album *Sister Drum* (Chinese: *A jie gu*) by Han female singer Zhu Zheqin. Released in 1995, this album immediately became a top seller in China and met with unprecedented success internationally.[17]

The "Tibet fever" was part of a general ethnic revival that started in China in the early 1980s and has intensified ever since. It was also linked to the general global fascination in recent years with ethnic things. As elsewhere in the affluent world, as the Chinese economy started to soar and a new Chinese middle class emerged in the rapidly growing Chinese cities, many young urbanites started looking for exotic alternatives to enrich their standardized modern lives. The celebration of ethnic things in China reached unprecedented heights in the mid-1990s as the country was swept by a tide of capitalist consumption. Within this context, China's hitherto peripheral minority cultures became "in" and turned into an exotic cultural commodity. The new trend manifested itself most clearly in the domain of tourism, where many Han Chinese urbanites started to travel to minority areas. In the mid-1990s, Tibet in particular became a popular destination for many Han urban youngsters who traveled to the region to find inspiration and to "look for themselves."[18]

The new trend was also evident in popular culture. For many young Han middle-class urbanites, Zheng Jun's song, Zhu Zheqin's album, and, later, many of Han Hong's songs were the equivalent of Western world music. They offered this audience something different and refreshing, authentic, simple, natural, and free, something full of tranquillity and spirituality on one hand and "primitive" force on the other, all of which enabled them to escape the stress, alienation, and chaos of modernity and the standardized, oppressive mainstream. The two songs translated below, "The Radiating Light of the Land of Snow" (Chinese: "Xue yu guangmang") and "Hometown" (Chinese: "Jiaxiang"), nicely illustrate many of these points. The former is the first song on Han Hong's first album (from 1998) and the one that gave the album its name. The latter is the second song on the same album and one of Han Hong's most popular songs to date:

THE RADIATING LIGHT OF THE LAND OF SNOW

(Lyrics and music by Han Hong)

Run away, break loose from the ropes that bind you
Rediscover the freedom that you have yearned for for so long . . .

If you're the powerful eagle, you ought to unfold your wings and fly
at the high plateau
Let the singing pierce through the layers of clouds . . .

HOMETOWN

(Lyrics and music by Han Hong)

My hometown is in Shigatse
There is a beautiful river over there
Mother says that the mountain slopes are full of cattle and sheep
Because of the protection and blessing of Buddha

Om mani padme hum
Om mani padme hum . . .

In celebrating the powerful beauty of unspoiled nature, these two songs provide the urban Han Chinese audience with a fantasy of another world. To this celebration, "Hometown" also adds a rare pinch of religious spirituality by integrating the famous Tibetan Buddhist mantra *Om mani padme hum,* which is set in the song to a sweet melody and used as a refrain.[19] The alternative world that the songs construct is reinforced by their music. "The Radiating Light of the Land of Snow" opens in slow, free rhythm, with the long, misty synthesized sounds mentioned earlier. The melody shows the conspicuous influence of Tibetan folksongs, and as in "Himalaya," it is sung in a style that draws upon the powerful, high-pitched traditional Tibetan singing with its many typical ornaments. At the end of each stanza, unintelligible screams by a male singer that sound as if they come from a distance add to the general atmosphere of a wild and primitive world, which is further enhanced by the powerful beats of a hand drum.

The ethereal synthesizer and the screams of the male singer in "The Radiating Light of the Land of Snow" suggest that Han Hong has not limited herself in her ethnic pop songs (as opposed to her more orthodox pop and rock songs) to drawing only upon traditional Tibetan music. A song called "Lover" (Chinese: "Qingren") from her 1998 album, for example, draws heavily upon Indian music both in its melody and accompaniment, featuring sitar, Indian flute, and tabla drums.[20] Likewise, in "Hometown," one can clearly hear a *darbuka* drum in addition to acoustic and classical guitars and a Western flute. These examples reflect Han Hong's general interest in "world music" and "unplugged music" and in the fusion of musical elements from various sources, all of which clearly help to enhance the sense of otherness that her music aims to communicate. This otherness, however, is almost always incorporated into the standard pop and rock framework of a regular 4/4 beat, electric lead and rhythm guitars, bass guitar, drum set and keyboard, and the most up-to-date sound technology. These make her songs sound modern and familiar for the young urban Han Chinese audience. And clearly, as was also the case with Zheng Jun's "Return to Lhasa" and Zhu Zheqin's *Sister Drum,* it is this modern sonic framework (and overall packaging) that makes Han Hong's musical celebration of primordial and exotic Tibet appealing to the modern ears (and eyes) of Han Chinese urbanites.

Another important reason behind the "Tibet fever" of the mid-1990s and the popularity of Han Hong's songs, which has increased ever since, was the growing influence of globalization in China, something that came hand-in-hand with the rise of ethnicity in the country. The dramatic increase since the early 1990s of the influx of Western cultural artifacts, images, and sounds from Hong Kong, Taiwan, and the West caused many mainland artists and audiences to look for something that was uniquely Chinese with which they could assert their distinct identity and, in the case of the artists, also compete with non-mainland artists in the music market.

The flooding of China by Western culture also caused Chinese officials to look for something with which to promote China's distinct national character. The solution was found in the images and sounds of China's minorities. In addition to providing something different and exotic, they also offered the kind of imagined primordial authenticity that was necessary for the construction of a unique national essence. Celebrating the traditional cultures of China's minorities was an excellent solution to the threat of globalization, because it did not damage the modern image of the Han majority and probably even strengthened it.[21] Chinese officials, however, were at the same time very careful also to encourage modern representations of China's minorities. With her modern ethnic pop, Han Hong proved that China's minorities are not only encouraged to maintain their different ethnicity and are able to celebrate it in public to much acclaim but are also enjoying in the People's Republic of China (PRC) unprecedented modernity.[22]

Indeed, the "Tibet fever," like every popular "fever" in China, was closely connected to state politics, and it could not have persisted for so long without official encouragement.[23] The fact that the "fever" was brought to a climax just a few years after a series of pro-independence demonstrations broke out in Lhasa (between 1987 and 1989, and again in 1993) and after the Dalai Lama was awarded the Nobel Peace Prize (in 1989) was more than sheer coincidence. Promoting cultural expressions that dealt with Tibet was the government's way to promote unity and integration between Tibet and China. It was also a way to claim ownership and assert control symbolically over the rebellious region and a way to neutralize the challenge that the latter posed to the authority and legitimacy of Chinese rule. In this respect, the "Tibet fever" of the 1990s reminds one of the enhanced production of artistic works relating to Tibet that was evident in China immediately after the Tibetan uprising of 1959 and its brutal suppression by the Chinese army.

It was in this general context that Han Hong became a star in China. Han Hong and her music included all the right political ingredients from the point of view of the Han Chinese audience, who consumed the music, and of Chinese officialdom, which helped to propagate it through the state-run media and large-scale concerts. With the possible exception of "The Radiating Light of the Land of Snow," which could be read as a criticism of the lack of freedom in China and perhaps, albeit less likely, even as a call directed at Tibetans to free themselves, Han Hong's lyrics did not show any sign of resistance or discontent and presented a happy and peaceful Tibet. Furthermore, while her own songs were not overtly political, and thus had the effect of depoliticizing Tibet, Han Hong, by performing some of the most politicized, official propaganda songs about Tibet ("On Beijing's Golden Mountain," "The Emancipated Serfs Sing a Song," and "Heavenly Path"), was simultaneously asserting her loyalty to the Chinese state and reaffirming in the most direct form the widely accepted notions among Han Chinese that Tibet was part of China, that the Tibetans were liberated by the Chinese, and that the Chinese had brought great happiness and prosperity to Tibet. To be sure, most Han Chinese identified with the messages conveyed in the lyrics of these political songs, and it was also clear that many gained pleasure from listening to them, especially after they were rearranged by Han Hong, who performed them in a modern pop and rock style.

Finally, Han Hong was a "real" Tibetan—born in Tibet to a Tibetan mother, used Tibetan in her songs, and could sing like a Tibetan—and simultaneously 100 percent Chinese, who had a Han Chinese father, lived in Beijing, behaved like a Chinese, and sang her songs in fluent Chinese. She was different, but not too different, so that her otherness did not pose a threat to the orthodox notion in China that despite differences, all the different ethnic groups in the country share a common identity and origin and have been part of the Chinese nation (Chinese: *Zhonghua minzu*) since antiquity. Moreover, with her highly sinicized celebration of minority identity, she was also living embodiment and proof of both the politically correct notion that Chinese culture is a fusion (Chinese: *ronghe*) of the different ethnic cultures in the country and also of the less politically correct but extremely popular notion that Han Chinese culture is actually superior and dominant and that it possesses an irresistible assimilating power.

The Representation and Reception of Han Hong among Tibetans Outside China

In sharp contrast to her extreme popularity in mainstream Chinese culture, among Tibetans living outside China, Han Hong was either completely unknown, deliberately ignored, unacknowledged as Tibetan, or treated with conspicuous hostility. A search under Han Hong's name conducted in February 2005 on Internet sites of Tibetans living outside China yielded only one result. This was a brief reference in a recent report by the Tibetan government in exile protesting the persecution of Tibetan writer Woeser (Chinese: Wei Se) in China.[24] In this report, Han Hong was mentioned only in passing and was not identified as Tibetan: "Woeser has participated in a number of petitions calling for preservation of traditional Tibetan culture and respect for ethnic values. One of her petitions resulted in the Han swimmer Zhang Jian abandoning his plans to swim across Namtso Lake, one of the three sacred lakes of Tibet. Another campaign resulted in the cancellation of a concert by the singer Han Hong planned at Lhasa's Potala Palace."[25] Interestingly, while Zhang Jian is identified in this report as a "Han swimmer," Han Hong is only identified as a "singer." This seems to suggest that the writer was well aware of Han Hong's mixed identity and therefore avoided identifying her as Han. Nevertheless, in sharp contrast to the many articles on Han Hong in the Chinese press, which usually identify her as Tibetan, the Tibetan reporter seemed to have self-consciously avoided identifying her as such. Thus, Han Hong ends up in this short report as another "other," very much like the Han swimmer Zhang Jian.

The marginality of Han Hong in the Tibetan diaspora was also evident when a student of mine asked about her in a popular Tibetan Web forum that serves mainly Tibetans living outside China (Phayul.com). Very few people responded to the query, and one of them expressed the following view: "Han is a mixed blood full person. Her mother is from Shigatse and was a singer. Her father is a Han Chinese. Han Hong was raised up in China and she speaks little Tibetan. She sings about Tibet, but she hates to recognize herself as a Tibetan. Therefore, many Tibetans do not like her. . . . Han Hong is . . . one of . . . those who make profit in the name of Tibet but refuse to take Tibetan identity."[26] It is not difficult to understand why Tibetans who live in exile and know Han Hong marginalize her and even treat her with hostility. From the point of view of these Tibetans, many of whom aspire to gain independence from China and make every effort to preserve their traditional culture, Han Hong embodies what they fear the most, namely, the loss of Tibetan identity and culture and giving up the idea of an independent Tibet. Indeed, by singing in Chinese, the language of the colonizers, and participating in China's cultural system, Han Hong has crossed the cultural and political boundaries that these Tibetans have been struggling for years to keep.[27]

This attitude toward Han Hong seems to be representative of a general attitude among many Tibetans living in exile toward Tibetan artists and writers who grew up in the PRC and were influenced by Chinese culture. When known in the Tibetan diaspora, these artists and writers, some of whom have already left China, have often been criticized for being sinicized, and in the case of those still in China, sometimes also for catering to Han Chinese audiences and for internalizing the denigrating attitude that Han Chinese have toward Tibetans. The monologue of Gonkar Gyatso with which I opened this chapter and in which the artist describes how his Chinese-inspired art was seen in Dharamsala as "treacherous" provides one good example of this attitude. Another example is the not-so-positive experience of Tibetan female singer Dadon (full name in Tibetan: Dawa Dolma; Chinese: Dazhen) in Dharamsala in the early 1990s. Dadon is considered to be Tibet's first pop star, and she enjoyed extreme popularity among Tibetans in China in the late 1980s and 1990s. Despite her enormous success in China, which included winning top prizes in national song competitions, she fled the country in 1992 and arrived in Dharamsala. There, however, she did not find her place, because her singing style, which was heavily influenced by mainstream Chinese pop music, was considered too sinicized.[28] Soon afterward, Dadon left Dharamsala and moved to the United States, where she still performs occasionally.[29]

Another good example of this negative attitude toward Tibetan writers and artists who have been influenced by Chinese culture is found in a review written by a Tibetan writer and filmmaker living in India of *The Dust Settles* (Chinese: *Chen'ai luo ding*), a novel written in Chinese by Alai, a Tibetan writer living in China.[30] Describing the life of the Tibetan chieftains who inhabited the border area between China and Tibet before 1949, this novel, published in 1998, was awarded the Mao Dun Prize, China's most prestigious literary award, in 2000. A few years later, it was arranged into a twenty-five-part television serial that was broadcast nationwide. The reviewer, Tenzing Sonam, writes: "Alai's picture of pre-Communist life is so relentlessly barbaric, so over-the-top, that it loses all sense of reality and becomes a grotesque caricature. Is Alai simply a victim of his Chinese upbringing, faithfully spewing out the party line, unable to distinguish the truth from lies, or is there some deeper, more subtle, agenda?"[31] After pointing to some ambiguities in the text, the reviewer nevertheless clearly implies that there is no deeper or more subtle agenda and that Alai is indeed a victim of his Chinese upbringing. The review ends by suggesting that the ambiguities come "too late to save the book" and by criticizing Alai for producing a "two dimensional cartoon world of the [Tibetan] chieftains."[32]

The Representation and Reception of Han Hong among Tibetans in China

Whereas Han Hong clearly occupies diametrically opposite positions in mainstream Chinese culture and in the transnational Tibetan diaspora culture, her position among Tibetans living inside China is much more complex and ambiguous. Based upon conversations with Tibetans from various parts of China whom I have met in Beijing since the turn of the twenty-first century and on one field trip to Lhasa that I carried out in the summer of 2005, it became clear to me that though Han Hong was not the most popular singer among Tibetans in China, she was certainly popular among a considerable number of them. In contrast to the situation in the Tibetan diaspora, most of the Tibetans whom I met in China knew Han Hong. This is not surprising, considering that she appears regularly on Chinese television, her songs are broadcast regularly on the radio, her CDs are offered for sale in most music shops around China, and she has also performed in the Tibetan areas (including Lhasa). While a few people thought that she was Han Chinese, most knew not only that she was born in Tibet but also that her mother was Tibetan and her father was Han Chinese. Whereas some of the latter could not decide whether in the final analysis she was Tibetan or Han Chinese, others insisted, often with a pinch of pride, that she was Tibetan. Similar to the diverse opinions regarding her ethnic identity, the opinions regarding Han Hong as a musician and regarding her music were also quite diverse. While some Tibetans shared the negative view of the Tibetan netizen quoted above (although nobody said that Han Hong was loath to recognize her Tibetan identity), others admired her and considered her one of their favorite musicians and one of the most important Tibetan pop stars in China.

Spread along the narrow alleys of the old Tibetan quarter of Lhasa, near the Jokhang Temple and the Barkhor, are many music stands, which seem to serve mainly local Tibetans of lower socioeconomic background and Tibetan pilgrims who come to Lhasa from rural Tibetan areas. In them, I did not see many recordings of Han Hong, and the ones that I saw were pirated albums that also included songs by other female Tibetan pop singers such as Chungshol Dolma (Chinese: Qiongxuezhuoma) and Dechen Wangmo (Chinese: Deqianwangmu). These stands had some recordings of Hindi film music, mainstream Chinese pop, and modern Tibetan pop, but most of the recordings that they offered for sale were clearly of Tibetan artists who performed almost exclusively in Tibetan and in a style that was very close in its melodies, rhythms, and singing style to traditional Tibetan folk music (for example, Dube [Chinese: Debai] and Riga). Many of these songs were accompanied only by a single plucked instrument, in most cases a mandolin, while in others a *dranyen* (traditional Tibetan lute) or a Western guitar could be heard. Some songs had a more modern arrangement, but this was usually limited to the basic accompaniment of electric organ and synthesized drum machine, used in many recordings of third-world pop songs.

The traditional flavor of these songs was reinforced by their video clips. Indeed, despite their traditional style, many of these songs were recorded on VCDs (video compact discs) and were accompanied by clips that one could watch while shopping. Most of these clips showed the performers in traditional-style costumes, and many featured traditional-style dances, some of which were filmed in the context of local folk festivities.[33] Besides celebrating Tibetan festivities, many of the clips also celebrated the Tibetan landscape, while others featured more religious themes, showing temples, lamas, and monks. The latter were often grouped together in albums that were dedicated to one particular important religious person, whose face was shown repeatedly in the clip and also on the CD cover.

When I asked one Tibetan stand owner in her forties, dressed in traditional-style costume, if she had any recordings of Han Hong, she made it clear to me that Han Hong was not her cup of tea. Then, pointing at the television screen in front of her, where several Tibetans dressed in traditional-style costumes were singing and dancing in a circle, and simultaneously mimicking with her body and voice the playing of *dranyen,* she indicated with pride that this was her favorite music. When I asked another Tibetan stand owner of about the same age why she did not have any recordings of Han Hong, she replied that she sold only songs that are sung in Tibetan and that Han Hong did not sing in Tibetan. Nevertheless, this woman indicated that she herself liked Han Hong, then started to sing the refrain from Han Hong's "Hometown" to prove that she really was familiar with her songs.

While clearly not so popular in this part of Lhasa, Han Hong was very popular in other parts of the city. For example, in a newly opened modern-style café near Tibet University, which was owned by Tibetans and attended mainly by Tibetan students, Han Hong's entire albums were played nonstop for more than an hour on the two occasions that I visited. When I asked the young Tibetan attendants in the café and several young Tibetan customers what they felt about Han Hong, they indicated that they really liked her. Han Hong was also quite popular in the more established music shops in the Tibetan area of Lhasa. In one of these shops on Beijing Donglu, the young owner, a Tibetan teenager who had just graduated from high school, told me that he liked Han Hong very much, even more than Yadong, who is doubtless the most popular Tibetan pop singer today in China. When I asked why, the teenager replied that Han Hong was "more modern." This young man was later visited by some of his male and female schoolmates who also indicated that they liked Han Hong. Interestingly, when I asked this group of youngsters which kind of music they liked the most, all of them mentioned the names of famous Chinese mainstream pop singers.

My observations and interviews in Lhasa and Beijing suggest that, generally speaking, those Tibetans who liked Han Hong tended to be educated and modern young urbanites who could speak Chinese. In contrast, those Tibetans who did not like her or did not know her tended to be less educated, more traditional, older, and from rural areas and spoke little if any Chinese. This division, however, is very generalized and not clear-cut. I met quite a few young Tibetans who came from rural areas, were not educated, and knew very little Chinese but who liked Han Hong. And conversely, I also met quite a few Tibetan intellectuals who were very antagonistic toward Han Hong. Some of the latter suggested that they really liked to listen to Han Hong's songs until they heard about her plan to give a large-scale solo concert in front of the Potala Palace and that she was planning to start the concert after descending from a helicopter. One Tibetan university student explained to me that this plan reflected a total disrespect for Tibetan cultural and religious values and a complete lack of understanding of Tibetan culture on Han Hong's part. While this student was willing to "forgive" Han Hong, because she did not go through with her planned concert, and said that he still liked listening to her, others suggested that they had stopped listening to her music ever since they heard about her plan.[34] However, not everyone felt the same way about Han Hong's plans. When I asked one eighteen-year-old educated Tibetan youth what he thought about Han Hong's intended concert, he replied with obvious delight that not only was there nothing wrong with it but in fact it was quite "stylish" (Chinese: *fengge*).

Han Hong was clearly not the most popular pop singer among Tibetans in China. However, she was certainly popular, despite her fame among Han Chinese, despite the fact that she knew little Tibetan and sang most of her songs in Chinese, despite the fact that her father was Han Chinese and she had grown up in Beijing, and despite the fact that she had spent years in the army and sang some of the most official songs about Tibet. From a nationalistic/patriotic Tibetan point of view, all of these factors should have made her an anathema, but this was clearly not the case, even though she did become controversial after publicizing her plan to perform in front of the Potala Palace.

Han Hong's popularity among Tibetans, however, should not be surprising if one considers the general characteristics of contemporary Tibetan popular music in China. Clearly, the relationship between this music and mainstream Chinese popular music is a complex one. Yadong, for instance, whose songs are said to "encapsulate the soul of Tibet" and who is considered to be a "Tibetan patriot," ironically sings most of his songs in Chinese.[35] Paradoxically, and this is an important point that has seldom been mentioned, it is Chinese that allows Yadong and many other Tibetan pop stars to communicate with Tibetans from different areas in China who speak different Tibetan dialects, and it is often Chinese that helps other Tibetans from various parts of China to communicate among themselves. In addition to the use of Chinese in a number of contemporary Tibetan pop songs, many of these songs also show the conspicuous influence of Chinese music in their melodies, arrangements, and accompaniment, as well as in the singing style and body movement of their performers.

Another good example of the complex relationship in China between Tibetan pop and Chinese pop can be found in the *nangma* (Chinese: *langma*) bars in Lhasa (sometimes referred to as "karaoke bars"). Even in the most Tibetan nangma bars that I visited, which had very few or no Han Chinese at all in them, I heard quite a few mainstream Chinese pop songs, both played and performed live by local Tibetan singers.[36] In one of these bars, I also heard songs by Han Chinese musician Zheng Jun, whose famous song "Return to Lhasa" contains lines that could be readily interpreted as an expression of Han Chinese colonialist imagination.[37] This, however, should come as no surprise if one considers the fact that even the most politicized songs about Tibet from the Maoist era, most notably "On Beijing's Golden

Mountain," while hated by some Tibetans for their lyrics, still enjoy some degree of popularity among others.[38]

Another manifestation of the significant overlap between Tibetan pop and Chinese pop is the fact that Tibetan singers often participate in national song competitions in hopes of gaining recognition and success beyond their native region. Indeed, some of the most famous Tibetan pop singers, most notably Chungshol Dolma, have even moved recently to Beijing in hopes of becoming national stars.[39] Since in post-socialist China, being a star implies not only fame but also wealth, many Tibetan singers choose to sing in Chinese to appeal to the huge Chinese pop market. In addition, and no less important, more than once in music shops in Lhasa, I saw Tibetans buying albums of Chinese superstars. All these details suggest that modern Tibetan popular music is a hybrid that cannot be separated from contemporary Chinese popular music. Certainly, the former is heavily influenced by the latter. At the same time, however, by participating in mainstream Chinese pop culture, Tibetan musicians have also been able to influence this culture to an unprecedented degree.

The Representation and Reception of Han Hong in the West

Very much like her representation and reception in the Tibetan diaspora, the representation and reception of Han Hong in the West has been the complete antithesis of her popularity in mainstream Chinese culture. Han Hong has never performed in the West, and the only information on her in English until very recently was a few short articles published on the official Chinese Web site on Tibet.[40] Most important, a search for Han Hong's music on the Web sites of Amazon, J&R Music, or Tower Records yielded no results at the time of this writing, despite the fact that under "Tibetan music," one finds dozens of albums. The selection of Tibetan music marketed to Westerners is conspicuously dominated by collections of ritual and sacred music performed by groups of monks from various monasteries (most notably the Gyuto Monks). There are also several solo albums of individual musicians, one of whom is famous Tibetan singer Yungchen Lhamo, who is often referred to in the Western media as "the voice of Tibet."[41]

Yungchen Lhamo is considered the best-known Tibetan singer in the West, and in the spring of 2005, her two albums were listed as second and fifth in the top sellers list of Tibetan music on J&R Music's Web site. Born and raised in Tibet, she fled to India on foot in 1989, immigrated to Australia in 1993, and now lives in New York City. Since the release of her first album, *Tibetan Prayer* (1995), and her second album, *Tibet, Tibet* (1996), Yungchen Lhamo has toured the world extensively and performed in dozens of countries. She has performed twice in New York's Carnegie Hall and in many concerts that were held in the West in support of Free Tibet. Her music also appears on the soundtrack of the popular film *Seven Years in Tibet.* In 1998, she released a third album, *Coming Home,* and in 2006 a fourth one, *Ama.*[42]

Most of Yungchen Lhamo's songs, which, with the exception of a few songs in English, she sings in Tibetan, are slow and serene devotional songs performed a cappella in a traditional-like style. The strong atmosphere of tradition and otherworldly religious spirituality that these songs create is sometimes reinforced by samples of ritual chants performed by Tibetan monks, which are heard in the background of Yungchen Lhamo's singing. Spirituality is also communicated through the texts that accompany her CDs and the articles that discuss her music, which stress her links to Tibetan Buddhism and to the Dalai Lama. The motif of tradition and spirituality is also communicated visually. In the photographs accompanying her CDs and Web site and in the articles that discuss her music, Yungchen Lhamo, is seen with very long hair, wearing traditional-style Tibetan robes and holding *mala* prayer beads. In addition, in her CDs, one can also find photos of religious objects such as prayer wheels, oil lamps, and bells.

Another important motif in Yungchen Lhamo's music and representation, in addition to spirituality and tradition, is politics. In her third album in particular, many songs engage directly with the theme of exile and the related subjects of yearning for return, oppression and freedom, and the cause of Free Tibet. These themes are also highlighted in the preface to her third album and in the various texts that depict her biography and provide background to her creative work.

While fully acknowledging the integrity of Yungchen Lhamo's artistic work and sympathizing with her pain and loss, I suggest that her success in the West cannot be separated from the fact that her music and image, with their emphasis on spirituality and tradition, difference, ethnicity, and authenticity (read: non-Western source), fit very well with the highly romanticized Western image of Tibet as the mystical Shangri-La and also with the Western aesthetics and ideologies of New Age and "world music."[43] Indeed, like most of the Tibetan music albums famous in the West and presented as "authentic," her albums too were produced by Western "world music" producers (Real World Records) and feature some of the better-known "world music" musicians (Peter Gabriel and Hector Zazou, to mention only two).

Another crucial element in the success of Yungchen Lhamo's albums in the West, however, is the fact that her music and image also fit well with the cause of Free Tibet, which dominates the Western popular political attitude toward this region. The cause of Free Tibet cannot be separated from the romantic image of Tibet in the West or from the ideological and aesthetic preferences of "world music" audiences. Clearly, most of the Westerners who have some kind of interest in Tibet also have some knowledge of and interest in the politics of Tibet and support Tibetan independence. Indeed, the politics of Tibet, specifically the popular knowledge that Tibetans are victims of brutal occupation and oppression and that Tibetan culture is endangered because of this situation, is another source of the appeal of Tibet in the West and an inseparable part of the Western Tibetan experience.[44] In other words, the extreme popularity that Tibet enjoys in the West could be attributed to the fact that it offers many Westerners a powerful and concentrated focal point onto which they can project not only their Western Orientalistic fantasies and Western postmodern aesthetic preferences (for premodern things) but also, and no less significantly, important Western values such as freedom, democracy, and concern for cultural protection and human rights.

In light of all these points, it is easier to understand now why Han Hong has not been embraced by Western music lovers and Western fans of Tibet. To begin with, although containing many markers of Tibetanness, Han Hong's songs about Tibet are nevertheless in the style of mainstream pop and rock music, and as such, they are too modern, Westernized, and familiar or, conversely, not sufficiently authentic (traditional), exotic, or spiritual. In addition, with their Chinese lyrics, obvious Chinese musical influence, and Han Hong's Chinese background, they are also too sinicized and as such contradict the Free Tibet agenda that has gained increased popularity in the West in recent years as well as the Western values projected onto this political agenda.

It is interesting to note the strong correlation between the exclusion of Han Hong from the Western music market and her marginalization among exiled Tibetans. While this correlation could be seen as a case of "ideological convergence," I would argue that it also reflects the close relations and dialectical influence that exist between Westerners interested in Tibet and exiled Tibetans.[45] The latter are influenced by the former and in many respects try to fit themselves into the popular Western visions of Tibet in hopes of winning not just international support for their political struggle but also economic gain.[46] At the same time, however, exiled Tibetans also play an active role in influencing Western attitudes that relate to Tibet and Tibetans, especially where questions of authenticity are concerned.[47] The role that exiled Tibetans played in the mid- and late 1990s in blocking the marketing of the popular Chinese album *Sister Drum* in the West on the grounds that it was an offensive Chinese appropriation of Tibetan culture is an excellent case in point.[48] Thus, the exclusion of Han Hong from the Western music market, like the exclusion of other Tibetan artists and writers living and working in China (most notably Yadong), could also be attributed at least in part to the fact that the representation of Tibet in the West is dominated today by Tibetan exiles and refugees.[49]

Judging from the content of live concerts of Tibetan music that are held in the West, as well as from the various albums of Tibetan music that are offered for sale in the West, it is quite clear that the Western music market has not been too attentive to the many academic critics who have repeatedly pointed to the gap between the "virtual Tibet," which exists mainly in the minds of many Westerners and in the Western media, and the real Tibet.[50] However, Han Hong's absence from the West, like the absence of Yadong and other Tibetan pop musicians from China, is not limited to the Western music market alone. It also extends to Western scholarship, where interestingly, in sharp contrast to Tibetan traditional music, to date very little has been written on contemporary Tibetan popular music. It is perhaps not incidental that the first in-depth study of contemporary Tibetan popular music (and the only one until 2004) focuses on Tibetans who live in exile in Dharamsala rather than on Tibetans who live in Tibet itself.[51] Indeed, it seems that the Tibetan exile community has been quite successful in convincing Westerners that they are the authentic voice of Tibet and that Tibetans from Tibet itself are too sinicized to claim authenticity.

Finally, to complete the picture, it should be noted that Yungchen Lhamo (like Nawang Khechog and other Tibetan musicians who enjoy popularity in the West) is almost totally unknown among Tibetans living in China. Among the many dozens of Tibetans whom I interviewed in China, only two have heard of her, one of whom has studied in the United States and the other of whom had only come across her name on the Internet. While this situation could be attributed in part to the difficulties in importing and disseminating popular music from the Tibetan diaspora in China, I should emphasize that I did find in Lhasa quite a few recordings of exiled Tibetan musicians (for example, the above-mentioned Dadon, the San Francisco–based Techung, and Tibetan music from Nepal).[52] Hence, the absence of Yungchen Lhamo from the Tibetan music market in Tibet may also be an indication that her music caters mainly to Western New Agers and "world music" fans rather than to her own people.

Conclusion

Han Hong and her music raise important questions that relate to authenticity. Can her music be considered Tibetan, or is it just another case of appropriation of Tibetan music for artistic and commercial ends? Does Han Hong's music represent Tibetan culture and identity and can it be considered an authentic Tibetan voice, or is it the voice of the Chinese state (and of the Han majority) pretending to be the vox populi of the Tibetan people and using the mouth of an individual minority artist who was made to collaborate with the regime? This chapter does not offer clear-cut answers to any of these questions, but it does suggest that perhaps the categories and dichotomies on which these questions are based are somewhat oversimplified and ignore a complex reality that exists in China today.

This chapter proposes that Han Hong and her music are a manifestation of a hybrid identity, which, although greatly influenced by the dominant Chinese culture, is still Tibetan, or at least a manifestation of one particular kind of Tibetan identity that could be best referred to as Chinese-Tibetan, following the pattern of hyphened identities that is widely used in the United States. On a more general level, I also suggest that it is perhaps time that the representation of China's minorities in the West (especially of Tibetans) be expanded to include other aspects and forms of interaction, such as integration, dialogue and coexistence, fusion, creativity, and change, in addition to the traditional emphasis on conflict, oppression, resistance, and cultural loss.

On a continuum that ranges from total isolation and cultural purity to total integration and cultural fusion, Han Hong probably stands very close to the maximum integration end. This is because one of her parents is Han Chinese, because she can speak little Tibetan, and because she has lived in Beijing most of her life. Nevertheless, the trend of integration and fusion is a general one that applies to many other Tibetans living in China today. To be sure, there is still a lot of continuity with the Tibetan musical tradition, especially in the rural areas, and there is also quite a lot of conscious resistance to Chinese influence, especially among intellectuals. However, the fact remains that at least where contemporary Tibetan urban popular culture is concerned, the influence of Chinese popular culture is profound.

Whether we like it or not, it is becoming increasingly difficult to treat contemporary minority cultures in China as totally separated from mainstream Han Chinese culture, as if they existed in isolation from one another. It is also difficult, if not impossible, to gain a full understanding of the contemporary cultures of China's minorities without recognizing the important role that creative individuals who were educated in Chinese, perform or write in Chinese, or live in Chinese cities far away from their communities have played in the construction of these cultures.

Writers such as Alai, Tashi Dawa, and Woeser, to give just a few notable examples, all belong to this group of creative individuals.[53] Alai lives today in

Chengdu, the capital of Sichuan Province, is married to a Han Chinese woman, and works on the staff of the Chinese magazine *Science Fiction World*.[54] Tashi Dawa, currently the chairman of the Tibetan Writers Association, and Woeser, who served until recently as an editor of the magazine *Tibetan Literature,* are both of mixed origin, the former being a son of a Tibetan father and a Han Chinese mother, and the latter reportedly being three-quarters Tibetan and one-quarter Chinese. Alai, Tashi Dawa, and Woeser were all educated in Chinese schools, had a close relationship with the Chinese cultural establishment for years, and, most significantly, write only in Chinese. All of them, however, identify themselves as Tibetans and focus much of their writings on the land of Tibet, Tibetan history, and Tibetan culture.

To this list of people, we can also add Tibetan pop musicians such as Yadong and Yungdrung Gyal (Chinese: Rongzhongerjia), both of whom enjoy wide popularity among Tibetans in China despite the fact that they sing many of their songs (most, in the case of Yadong) in Chinese, have a close relationship with the Chinese establishment, and have been heavily influenced in their music by mainstream Chinese music. Many of these individuals were born in the Tibetan-inhabited areas of Sichuan Province, areas that came under Chinese control and influence long before the "peaceful liberation" of Tibet in 1951. Despite their popularity in China and many years of creative work, some of these people are still completely unknown in the West, while others have gained only limited recognition and only very recently.[55]

I suggest that this marginalization and exclusion from the cultural landscape in the West is closely linked to certain notions that exist in the West as to what Tibetanness means or should mean and to a popular tendency to isolate Tibet and Tibetan culture from China and Chinese culture. The Western record market in particular also tends to extol the image of an exotic, mysterious, and spiritual Tibet that exists almost unchanged in time (and in space). This trend seems to be closely related to the general aesthetics of "world music," which tends to prize "traditional," "authentic," and "different" sounds and to reject and exclude more modernized and Westernized "world music." The exclusion is also connected to world politics, specifically to the agenda of protecting and saving Tibetan culture from annihilation by the Chinese. This agenda is part of the broader agenda of Free Tibet, which has become increasingly popular in the West in recent years. However, while trying to represent and give voice to an authentic, oppressed, and endangered Tibet, such representations too often marginalize, exclude, and silence important Tibetan voices that do not fit the Free Tibet agenda.

Integration into mainstream Chinese culture and the concomitant exclusion from the cultural landscape in the West is not limited only to Tibetan artists.

Famous pop musicians such as Teng Ge'er and Siqin'gerile (Mongol) and Askar and Erkin (Uyghur) and the famous group Shan ying (Yi), to give just a few examples, all live and work today in Beijing and sing mainly in Chinese. While they are looked upon with ambivalence by some of their fellow minority people because of their "sinicization," they are nevertheless considered idols by many other members of their minority group. Indeed, these artists are admired in part at least because they are "modern," because they can sing in fluent Chinese, and because they have made it in the national sphere. In the West, however, these artists have remained practically unknown.

Proceeding from the understanding that recognition and representation are basic cultural rights, my main argument in this chapter is that it is time for people in the West to recognize the cultural rights of integrated minority artists and writers from China and to stop ignoring them or treating them as not authentic enough or, alternatively, as collaborators with the Chinese regime. Han Hong and other integrated minority artists may not advance the agenda of independent Tibet, Eastern Turkistan, or a unified Mongolia and may be correctly perceived as a threat to the struggle of some of their fellow people to preserve their traditional culture and protect it from undergoing sinicization. However, we also have to recognize that after half a century of a powerful Chinese presence (and in some cases centuries of direct influence), many minority people today in China, including Tibetans, have already lost much of their traditional culture, have been strongly influenced by Chinese culture, have an entirely different sense of identity from their ancestors, and may have a completely different agenda from those who struggle to preserve their traditional cultures and/or to achieve independence.[56] These people, many of whom often identify themselves spontaneously as Chinese in addition to their minority identity, may actually aspire to achieve more integration, equality, respect, representation, and the freedom to reform and modernize their traditional cultures and represent their otherness in ways that make sense for them in the context of their changing lives in China.

Western scholars, those engaged in the cultural market, and the general public should fully recognize and respect the cultural rights of Tibetans who struggle to preserve their culture and who, to that end, marginalize and exclude any cultural or artistic expression that shows signs of sinicization. However, at the same time, we should also recognize and respect the cultural rights of many Tibetans living in China for whom marginalizing Chinese culture is no longer a viable option, and perhaps not even a desirable one. Many Tibetans and other minority people in China today cannot really avoid being bilingual and in many cases being more fluent in Chinese than in their mother tongue. Moreover, we cannot and should not expect minority people in China to isolate themselves in cultural ghettos and to reject participation in the general cultural trends that surround them. We should also recognize that to develop and to be modern today in China requires some degree of sinicization. It is the right of integrated minority artists in China, Tibetan or others, to be recognized as full representatives of their ethnic cultures and to have full representation as such for themselves and for their artistic and literary works in the global cultural scene.

Finally, the above emphasis on the cultural rights of integrated minority artists and the need to protect these rights should by no means imply that these artists are powerless. These people deserve the most serious attention because of the merits inherent in the unique and original new culture that they create, because of the important possibilities that are embodied in their art, and precisely because they are active participants in the Chinese mainstream. Functioning at the center of Chinese culture, these people have been able to assert their different identity in their own terms; to achieve recognition, more understanding, and respect for their ethnic cultures; and to carve a respectful niche for these cultures and identities in contemporary Chinese culture. They have been able to expand the range of expressions traditionally allocated to minorities in mainstream Chinese culture and to enrich the discursive universe and repertory of narratives and images that relate to minority identities in China. And no less important, by their participation in the system, these artists have also been promoting a peaceful dialogue between different ethnic groups in China, helping to overcome suspicion and hostility and to bring distinct identities and peoples closer to one another.

Discography

Han Hong. *Gandong* [Moved]. 2005. Available online at http://www.56.com/u75/v_MzglNjg5Njg.html; http://www.56.com/u74/v_MzkxNzE5NDM.html; and others (accessed February 9, 2009).

———. *Gechang* [Singing]. ISRC CN-A51-02-428-00/A.J6. Beijing: Jingwen changpian [Jingwen Records], 2002.

———. *Hong* [Red]. ISRC CN-A51-03-381-00/A.J6. Beijing: Jingwen changpian [Jingwen Records], 2003.

———. *Xing le* [Awakening]. ISRC CN-E04-00-355–00/A.J6. Beijing: Qilin tong wenhua [Kirin Kid Productions], 2001.

———. *Xue yu guangmang* [The radiating light of the land of snow]. ISRC CN-A07-98-307-00/A.J6. Beijing: Qilin tong wenhua [Kirin Kid Productions], 1998.

Yungchen Lhamo. *Ama.* Real World Records, 2006.

———. *Coming Home.* CDRW72. Real World Records, 1998.

———. *Tibet, Tibet.* CDRW59. Real World Records, 1996.

Notes

I am grateful to Avital Pollak and Michal Zelcer for their help in the research for this essay. I am also grateful to Thierry Dodin, Alana Guarnieri, and Nanjia Cairang for their help in the transliteration of Tibetan names. The research for this essay was supported by THE ISRAEL SCIENCE FOUNDATION (Grant No. 903/03).

1. A Google search under "save Tibet" in March 2006 yielded 3,270,000 results. The call to "save Tibet" appears in numerous articles and titles of various Tibet-related events and Tibet-related products, and it is also used in the name of various organizations and Web sites that are dedicated to the Tibetan cause. For the latter, see, for example, the Save Tibet Web site of the International Campaign for Tibet (ICT) at http://www.savetibet.org.

2. "Artists in Exile: Gonkar Gyatso," http://www.refugeesonline.org.uk/artistsinexile/artists/gonkar.htm (accessed February 23, 2005).

3. Ibid. For more information on Gonkar Gyatso, see Clare Harris, "Struggling with Shangri-La: A Tibetan Artist in Exile," in *Constructing Tibetan Culture: Contemporary Perspectives,* ed. Frank J. Korom (Quebec: World Heritage Press, 1997), 160–77.

4. For more information concerning "On Beijing's Golden Mountain," see Nimrod Baranovitch, *China's New Voices: Popular Music, Ethnicity, Gender, and Politics, 1978–1997* (Berkeley: University of California Press, 2003), 60–68, 100; and Tibet Information Network (TIN), *Unity and Discord: Music and Politics in Contemporary Tibet* (London: Tibet Information Network, 2004), 101.

5. The section on Han Hong's biography is based on several conversations that we had between 2001 and 2004, one formal interview that I conducted with her on August 17, 2004, newspaper articles, and articles from the Internet. For the latter two, see, for instance, Ding Kaishan, "Han Hong, women ai ni" [Han Hong, we love you], *Beijing qingnian bao* [Beijing youth daily] March 15, 2000; "Han Hong: Dreaming of Tibet," China-Tibet Information Center, http://www.tibetinfor.com.cn/tibetzt-en/zyfy/zyfy_3_si_hanhong_d.htm (accessed August 4, 2004); and "Han Hong 'gechang' rensheng" [Han Hong "sings" life], http://www.ir188.com/tmp/dchd200301-02/hd01/htm (accessed March 26, 2005).

6. *Tsampa* is a roasted barley flour used in Tibet as the staple food and also in religious ceremonies. For an interesting discussion of the use of tsampa as a symbol of Tibetan identity, see Robert Barnett, "Symbols and Protest: The Iconography of Demonstrations in Tibet, 1987–1990," in *Resistance and Reform in Tibet,* ed. Robert Barnett and Shirin Akiner (Bloomington: Indiana University Press, 1994), 252.

7. *Khata* is a white ceremonial scarf often made of silk. Presented as a gesture of greeting and also used in religious contexts, it is one of the best-known signs of Tibetanness in China today.

8. Han Hong, personal communication, 2001, 2004.

9. The association of Tibet in contemporary China with desired spirituality is a relatively new phenomenon and stands in sharp contrast to the total negation of Tibetan religion among Han Chinese until recently. For more about this change in attitude, see Janet L. Upton, "The Poetics and Politics of *Sister Drum:* 'Tibetan' Music in the Global Market Place," in *Global Goes Local: Popular Culture in Asia,* ed. Timothy J. Craig and Richard King (Honolulu: Association for Asian Studies and University of Hawai'i Press, 2002), 103–4, 115; and Baranovitch, *China's New Voices,* 99–100.

10. For more information on Tseten Dolma, see Isabelle Henrion-Dourcy, "Women in the Performing Arts: Portraits of Six Contemporary Singers," in *Women in Tibet,* ed. Janet Gyatso and Hanna Havnevik (New York: Columbia University Press, 2005), 226–34.

11. The *Spring Festival Party* is one of the most popular televised events in China. A colorful variety show that includes songs, dances, skits, and other artistic performances, it is broadcast nationwide on CCTV on the eve of the Chinese New Year and features China's most famous performing artists. Songs performed on CCTV's *Spring Festival Party* often become hits all over China immediately after the program. The music and lyrics in Chinese of "On Beijing's Golden Mountain," "The Emancipated Serfs Sing a Song," "The Qinghai-Tibet Plateau," and "Heavenly Path" can be found in Xizang zizhiqu dangwei xuanchuanbu wenyichu, eds., *Chang gei taiyang de ge* [Songs sung for the sun] (Lhasa: Xizang renmin chubanshe, 2003).

12. One of Han Hong's best-known songs, which gained her great fame but has nothing to do with Tibet, is called "It's Dawn" (Chinese: "Tianliang le"). Performed by Han Hong for the first time on March 15, 2000, on CCTV, this song tells the story of a tragic cable-car crash that occurred in 1999 in Guizhou, in which a two-year-old baby boy lost his two parents. For more information on the song and the accident, see Tong Fengyan, "Han Hong liulei chang 'Tianliang'" [Han Hong sings "It's Dawn" in tears], *Beijing chen bao* [Beijing morning post], March 15, 2000.

13. Since the release of her first album in 1998, Han Hong has been identified in the Chinese media as a "Tibetan singer" (Chinese: *Zangzu geshou*). See, for example, Zhan Hua, "Han Hong: xue yu fang guangmang" [Han Hong: the snowy region shines with brilliant rays], *Xiju dianying bao* [Film and drama post], September 24, 1998.

14. For more information on the Han Chinese visions of Tibet and the representation of Tibet and Tibetans in Chinese art and literature, see Paul Clark, *Chinese Cinema: Culture and Politics since 1949* (Cambridge: Cambridge University Press, 1987), 96–99, and "Ethnic Minorities in Chinese Films: Cinema and the Exotic," *East-West Film Journal* 1, no. 2 (1987): 20–21, 28; Dru C. Gladney, "Tian Zhuangzhuang, the Fifth Generation, and Minorities Film in China," *Public Culture* 8, no. 1 (1995): 161–75; Thomas Heberer, "Old Tibet a Hell on Earth? The Myth of Tibet and Tibetans in Chinese Art and Propaganda," in *Imagining Tibet: Perceptions, Projections, and Fantasies,* ed. Thierry Dodin and Heinz Räther (Boston: Wisdom Publications, 2001); Tsering Shakya, "Foreword: Language, Literature, and Representation in Tibet," in *Tales of Tibet: Sky Burials, Prayer Wheels, and Wind Horses,* ed. and trans. Herbert J. Batt (Lanham, Md.: Rowman and Littlefield, 2001), xi–xxiii; Baranovitch, *China's New Voices,* 57–58, 64–65; Patricia Schiaffini, "Book Review: *Tales of Tibet: Sky Burials, Prayer Wheels, and Wind Horses,*" *Persimmon: Asian Literature, Arts, and Culture* 4, no. 2 (2003), http://www.persimmon-mag.com/summer2003/Bookreview10.htm (accessed January 3, 2005); and Tibet Information Network, *Unity and Discord,* 94–136.

15. See Dru C. Gladney, "Representing Nationality in China: Refiguring Majority/Minority Identities," *Journal of Asian Studies* 53, no. 1 (1994): 92–123; and Stevan Harrell, "Introduction: Civilizing Projects and the Reaction to Them," in *Cultural Encounters on China's Ethnic Frontiers,* ed. Stevan Harrell (Seattle: University of Washington Press, 1995). For discussions of other integrated minority musicians who participate in the mainstream Chinese pop scene, see the following by Nimrod Baranovitch: "Between Alterity and

Identity: New Voices of Minority People in China," *Modern China* 27, no. 3 (2001): 359–401; *China's New Voices,* 54–107; "From the Margins to the Centre: The Uyghur Challenge in Beijing," *China Quarterly* 175 (2003): 736–38; "From Resistance to Adaptation: Uyghur Popular Music and Changing Attitudes among Uyghur Youth," *China Journal* 58 (2007): 59–82; "Inverted Exile: Uyghur Writers and Artists in Beijing and the Political Implications of Their Work," *Modern China* 33, no. 4 (2007): 469–84; and "Compliance, Autonomy, and Resistance of a 'State Artist': The Case of Chinese-Mongolian Musician Teng Ge'er," in *Lives in Chinese Music,* ed. Helen Rees (Urbana: University of Illinois Press, 2009), 173–212.

16. See Baranovitch, *China's New Voices,* 98–105.

17. See Upton, "Poetics and Politics of *Sister Drum.*"

18. For a discussion of the historical roots of the "Tibet fever," see ibid., 107–10.

19. Han Hong was not the first in China to incorporate this famous mantra into a pop song. For two earlier incorporations, see Henrion-Dourcy, "Women in the Performing Arts," 238.

20. While clearly not Tibetan-inspired, the use of Indian musical elements may nevertheless be related to Han Hong's Tibetan identity if we consider the geographical proximity between Tibet and India, the fact that most of the Tibetans who live outside China live in India, and the popularity of Indian popular music in Tibet.

21. Gladney, "Representing Nationality in China."

22. For a similar argument, see Tibet Information Network, *Unity and Discord,* 62.

23. The important role that official organs played in promoting the "fever" was manifested, for example, in the frequent broadcasting of Han Hong's "Himalaya" on CCTV. It was also evident in the decision of CCTV officials to broadcast Zheng Jun's "Return to Lhasa" despite the general ban that CCTV imposed on rock songs at that time. For more details on the latter, see Baranovitch, *China's New Voices,* 104.

24. Woeser was persecuted in late 2004 after being accused of expressing reverence for the Dalai Lama and describing some unpleasant aspects of Tibetan life under Chinese rule in her book *Notes on Tibet* (Chinese: *Xizang biji*). In addition to the banning of her book, she was reportedly fired from her work unit, had to leave her state-owned apartment, and was deprived of her social welfare benefits. She was also prohibited from applying for a passport and was requested to renounce her religious beliefs. For more information, see Office of Tibet, "CTA Concerned by Tibetan Writer's Fate in Tibet," Tibet.com, October 29, 2004, http://www.tibet.com/NewsRoom/tibwriter1.htm (accessed March 1, 2005).

25. Ibid.

26. See Phayul.com at http://www.phayul.com/forums/showPost.aspx?postID=84106.

27. Diehl suggests that despite the clear agenda of the Tibetan government in exile of preserving traditional Tibetan music (and dance), an agenda that is most evident in the activities of the Tibetan Institute for Performing Arts (TIPA) in Dharamsala, the musical landscape in Dharamsala also includes influences of Hindi film music, Western rock and roll, and Nepali pop. But, as for Chinese-influenced Tibetan pop, this "[has] been explicitly rejected on political grounds by all but the newest arrivals in exile." Kiela Diehl, "Tibetan Diaspora," in *Continuum Encyclopedia of Popular Music of the World,* vol. 5, *Asia and Oceania,* ed. John Shepherd, David Horn, and Dave Laing (London: Continuum, 2005), 25. For more information on the marginalization or "ostracization"

in Dharamsala of Chinese-influenced music as well as of Tibetan pilgrims and newly arrived refugees from Tibet, see Kiela Diehl, *Echoes from Dharamsala: Music in the Life of a Tibetan Refugee Community* (Berkeley: University of California Press, 2002), 64–65, 67, 83–84, 87–88, 92, 95. Notwithstanding this rejection, the reception of Tibetan pop from China among the Tibetan diaspora community is not homogeneous, as indicated, for example, by Tenzin Tsundue, "Semshook: My Zeden Lhamo," http://www.phayul.com/news/article/aspx?id=6832&t=1&c=4 (accessed July 12, 2005).

28. Diehl, *Echoes from Dharamsala,* 84, 87; Tibet Information Network, *Unity and Discord,* 83–84.

29. Dadon's recordings were reportedly banned in China after she fled to Dharamsala in 1992. Nonetheless, in the summer of 2005 I was still able to find two of her famous cassettes in the music stalls in the old Tibetan quarter of Lhasa. For more information on Dadon, see Henrion-Dourcy, "Women in the Performing Arts," 234–46; Tibet Information Network, *Unity and Discord,* 83–84; and International Tibet Independence Movement, "Who Is Dadon?," http://www.rangzen.org/archive/97/march/dadon.htm (accessed August 16, 2005). Dadon played the leading role in Paul Wagner's 1998 film *Windhorse,* which tells a story close to her own life story of a successful and highly sinicized Tibetan pop singer who just before being fully incorporated by the Chinese media escapes to India.

30. The novel was translated into English and published in 2002 under the title *Red Poppies: A Novel of Tibet.*

31. Tenzing Sonam, "Grotesque Caricature," Hindu, November 17, 2002, http://www.hinduonnet.com/thehindu/mag/2002/11/17/stories/2002111700600300.htm (accessed May 13, 2003).

32. Ibid. For another example of this negative reception among Tibetan exiles of Tibetan artists and writers who live in China and participate in the Chinese cultural system, see Steven J. Venturino's comments on the half-Tibetan, half-Han Chinese writer Tashi Dawa (Chinese: Zhaxi Dawa), "Where Is Tibet in World Literature?" *World Literature Today* 78 (2004): 54.

33. I am using the word "traditional-style" instead of "traditional" because, at least according to exiled Tibetans, even these are heavily sinicized. See Diehl, *Echoes from Dharamsala,* 92.

34. For more information on Han Hong's plan to perform in front of the Potala Palace and on the possible reasons for her inability to realize her plan, see "Han Hong Lasa gechang zaidu liuchan. Budalagong jujue shangye" [Han Hong's Lhasa solo concert was aborted once again. The Potala Palace rejects commerce], http://gb.cri.cn/4221/2004/07/10/1002@226663.htm (accessed January 17, 2009).

35. Interviews in Lhasa, 2005; Tibet Information Network, *Unity and Discord,* 88–89.

36. For an article that describes in more detail the situation in karaoke bars in Lhasa during the mid-1990s, see Vincanne Adams, "Karaoke as Modern Lhasa, Tibet: Western Encounters with Cultural Politics," *Cultural Anthropology* 11, no. 4 (1996): 510–46. Adams rightly suggests that for many Lhasa Tibetans, karaoke is "a significant symbol of modernity" (512). He also points to the fact that Chinese pop songs not only dominated these bars but were actually liked by many Tibetans (513–14, 528–29).

37. I am referring here particularly to the lines "[It] feels like home. . . . Come, come, let's return together to Lhasa, return to the home from which we've long been separated."

It must have been these lines that caused CCTV officials in 1995 to decide to broadcast Zheng Jun's song despite the general ban that was imposed on rock at that time and later to invite Zheng Jun to Lhasa to participate in an official televised celebration of the thirtieth anniversary of the establishment of the Tibetan Autonomous Region (TAR). For more details, see Baranovitch, *China's New Voices,* 104.

38. Interviews in Lhasa; see also Tibet Information Network, *Unity and Discord,* 101. "On Beijing's Golden Mountain" is based on a Tibetan folk song and was very popular in China during the Cultural Revolution (Tibet Information Network, *Unity and Discord,* 101). For translation and analysis of the lyrics of this song, see Baranovitch, *China's New Voices,* 63–64.

39. Personal communication with Chungshol Dolma, Beijing, 2004.

40. See, for example, the China-Tibet Information Center Web site. This situation, however, changed around 2006.

41. See, for example, Chris Nickson, "Yungchen Lhamo," MP3.com, http://www.mp3.com/yungchen-lhamo/artists/172777/biography.html (accessed March 7, 2005). Other individual Tibetan musicians who enjoy wide popularity in the West include the nun Chöying Dolma and flutist Nawang Khechog. For more information on the former, see Henrion-Dourcy, "Women in the Performing Arts," 252–53, and the musician's own Web site at http://www.choying.com. For more information on the latter, see his Web site at http://www.nawangkhechog.com.

42. For more information on Yungchen Lhamo, see Henrion-Dourcy, "Women in the Performing Arts," 246–57; and the musician's Web site, http://www.yungchenlhamo.com.

43. Yungchen Lhamo's albums also fit well with the tendency in "world music" circles to promote "endangered" or "disappearing" music.

44. See, for example, Adams, "Karaoke as Modern Lhasa, Tibet," 510–46.

45. Christiaan P. Klieger, "Shangri-La and Hyperreality: A Collision in Tibetan Refugee Expression," in *Proceedings of the 7th Seminar of the International Association for Tibetan Studies: Graz 1995,* vol. 4, *Tibetan Culture in the Diaspora,* ed. Frank J. Korom (Wien: Österreichischen Akademie Der Wissenschaften, 1997), 61.

46. See, for example, Adams, "Karaoke as Modern Lhasa, Tibet"; Donald S. Lopez Jr., *Prisoners of Shangri-La: Tibetan Buddhism and the West* (Chicago: University of Chicago Press, 1998); and Dibyesh Anand, "(Re)imagining Nationalism: Identity and Representation in the Tibetan Diaspora of South Asia," *Contemporary South Asia* 9, no. 3 (2000): 272, 277, 279, 280.

47. Anand, "(Re)imagining Nationalism," 274–75.

48. See Upton, "Politics and Poetics of *Sister Drum,*" 100, 112–13.

49. For an article describing how Tibetan performing troupes from Tibet and Dharamsala competed with one another in the international arena between the mid-1970s and early 1990s, see Marcia S. Calkowski, "The Tibetan Diaspora and the Politics of Performance," in *Proceedings of the 7th Seminar of the International Association for Tibetan Studies: Graz 1995,* vol. 4, *Tibetan Culture in the Diaspora,* ed. Frank J. Korom (Wien: Österreichischen Akademie Der Wissenschaften, 1997), 51–57.

50. Orville Schell, *Virtual Tibet: Searching for Shangri-La from the Himalayas to Hollywood* (New York: Henry Holt, 2001); Jamyang Norbu, "Dances with Yaks: Tibet in Film, Fiction and Fantasy of the West," *Tibetan Review,* January 1998, 18–23; Peter Bishop, *The*

Myth of Shangri-La: Tibet, Travel Writing, and the Western Creation of a Sacred Landscape (Berkeley: University of California Press, 1989); Peter Bishop, *Dreams of Power: Tibetan Buddhism and the Western Imagination* (London: Athlone Press, 1993); Donald S. Lopez Jr., "New Age Orientalism: The Case of Tibet," *Tricycle: The Buddhist Review* 3, no. 3 (1994): 37–43; Lopez, *Prisoners of Shangri-La;* Lee Feigon, *Demystifying Tibet: Unlocking the Secrets of the Land of the Snows* (Chicago: Ivan R. Dee, 1998); Thierry Dodin and Heinz Räther, eds., *Imagining Tibet: Perception, Projections, and Fantasies* (Boston: Wisdom Publications, 2001).

51. See Kiela Diehl's excellent book from 2002, *Echoes from Dharamsala: Music in the Life of a Tibetan Refugee Community.* The first and only in-depth study of contemporary Tibetan popular music in Tibet to date is the collectively authored *Unity and Discord: Music and Politics in Contemporary Tibet,* which was published in 2004 by Tibet Information Network, an independent international organization based in London.

52. Techung (the artistic name of Tashi Dhondup) is probably the most popular Tibetan musician today among diaspora Tibetans, performing both traditional and modern original music. For more information, see his Web site at http://techung.com.

53. The list can go on and on to include Sebo, Meizhuo, Geyang, Yangdon, and many other Tibetan writers.

54. Herbert J. Batt, ed. and trans., *Tales of Tibet: Sky Burials, Prayer Wheels, and Wind Horses* (Lanham, Md.: Rowman and Littlefield, 2001), 259–60.

55. Similar to the case of Tibetan music, the book market in the West has clearly preferred books by Tibetan exiles about Tibetan religion and philosophy and about the oppression of Tibetans by the Chinese regime.

56. For an instructive and highly relevant discussion of the nature of integration and resistance among Mongols in China today, see Uradyn E. Bulag, "Ethnic Resistance with Socialist Characteristics," in *Chinese Society: Change, Conflict and Resistance,* ed. Elizabeth J. Perry and Mark Selden (London: Routledge, 2000), 178–97.

8 Music and Human Rights

The AfroReggae Cultural Group and the Youth from the Favelas *as Responses to Violence in Brazil*

SILVIA RAMOS AND ANA MARÍA OCHOA

Brazil has one of the world's highest rates of violent death.[1] Young people are at the heart of the problem, either as victims or as perpetrators of violence—especially poor black youth who dwell in slums and urban outskirts. The responses of both the state and civil society in Brazil to the problem of criminality and violence have been slow and unsatisfactory. Nonetheless, in the 1990s, several cities witnessed artistic and cultural initiatives led by the young people themselves of the city peripheries. Although heterogeneous and not articulated with one another, these experiences have proven to be important and successful endeavors that create alternatives of sociability, subjectivity, and representation of youth from the periphery in the wider Brazilian social arena, in opposition to the dynamics of urban conflicts. In this chapter, we propose that, on the one hand, it is possible to draw parallels and continuities between these groups and previous histories of art as a site for political struggle in Brazil, such as that of politically committed song of the 1960s (engagé) and Tropicália. Yet, at the same time, these groups challenge many assumptions about modes of activism developed by art, non-governmental organizations (NGOs), social movements, unions, and the Left. Crucial to this new form of activism is the emergence of a new political figure in Brazil in the 1990s: the youth from the *favela* (*jovem de favela*), who has challenged many assumptions about the mediations between art and politics.

This chapter is broadly divided in two parts. In the first, we aim to present a panorama of urban violence in the country through a detailed analysis that includes the statistics, geography, age, gender, and racial distribution of violence as well as a brief description of police structures in Brazil. One of the most problematic intellectual contemporary issues under the aegis of present-day culturalism is the relationship between what are deemed political rights proper and what has come to be ascribed to the field of "cultural rights," among them the political dynamics of cultural expressions such as music. In his book *The Expediency of Culture,* George Yúdice clearly identifies the increasing role of culture as a mediator of political and social conflicts, to the point that he assigns it the power of a new episteme, that is, of a new historical mode of mediating the relation between words and things.[2] Yet, cultural recognition of different social groups and cultural activism do not frequently or easily translate into recognition of economic, political, and juridical rights.[3]

Presenting a detailed analysis of the distribution of violence in Brazil is crucial to understanding the network of social, geographical, and political networks upon which the assemblages of artistic youth groups have emerged in the last decade. In the second part of this chapter, we aim to identify, in the Brazilian political and cultural scenario, the emergence of groups that work with art as a primary medium of social intervention and explain why we see them as "new mediators" in society and what the significance is of art in this mediation. Although music is a primary locus of intervention, in the practice of these groups, as we shall see, it is impossible to create a clear-cut dichotomy between the different kinds of art. In particular, we shall describe the case of the AfroReggae Cultural Group from Rio de Janeiro, which uses music and other artistic activities to promote basic human rights. Together with the Center for Studies on Public Security and Citizenship (Centro de Estudos de Segurança e Cidadania, or CESeC) from Candido Mendes University in Rio de Janeiro, the group has been involved since 2004 in a unique pilot experience inside military-police barracks, the Youth and the Police project, which we will also present here.

Lethal Violence in Brazil

Every year, approximately 50,000 people are murdered in Brazil. While Western Europe homicide rates range from 1 to 3 homicides per 100,000 inhabitants, Brazilian homicide rates have been higher than 25 homicides per 100,000 inhabitants, as shown in figure 8.1. In some Brazilian states, the rates are well above the national average, as is the case in the state of Rio de Janeiro, with homicide rates of 50 per 100,000. Violent deaths are concentrated in the poor areas of the big and medium-sized cities and primarily affect youngsters in the age bracket of fifteen to twenty-four years, mostly male and black.

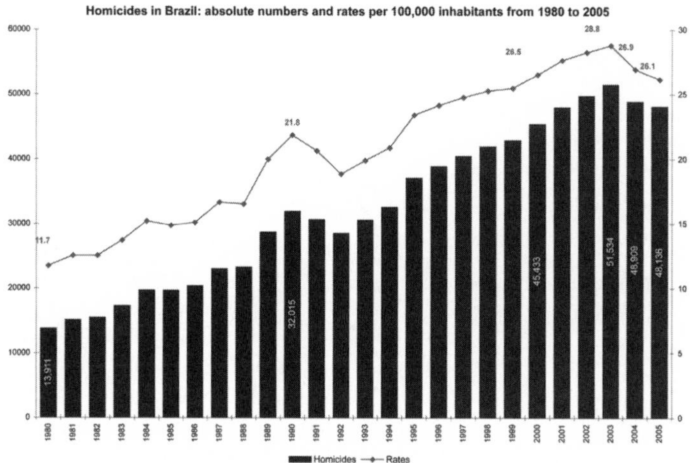

Figure 8.1. Homicides in Brazil: Absolute numbers and rates per 100,000 inhabitants, 1980–2005. (Source: Mortality Information System—Datasus)

The distribution of violent deaths in Brazil presents well-defined characteristics that need to be studied if we are to understand the profile and quality of public policies designed to deal with the problem of violence and the answers that civil society has been providing throughout this period.

The Age of Death

An intense and alarming characteristic of the Brazilian panorama is the high concentration of homicides among the young. In the fifteen- to twenty-four-year-old age bracket, the rates are extraordinarily higher than those registered for the population as a whole. As can be seen in figure 8.2, the tendency is national and also occurs in the states with the lowest rates of lethal violence. When we examine some poor urban areas and focus on the young, we come across rates of over 200 criminal homicides per 100,000 inhabitants. The gender relation of the homicide victims in the Brazilian profile follows the international pattern: 93% are male and 7% are female.

The Color of Death

Studies have also revealed the existence of a dramatic concentration of violent deaths among the black population (the total of individuals classified as black and mulatto), indicating that the uneven distribution of wealth and social

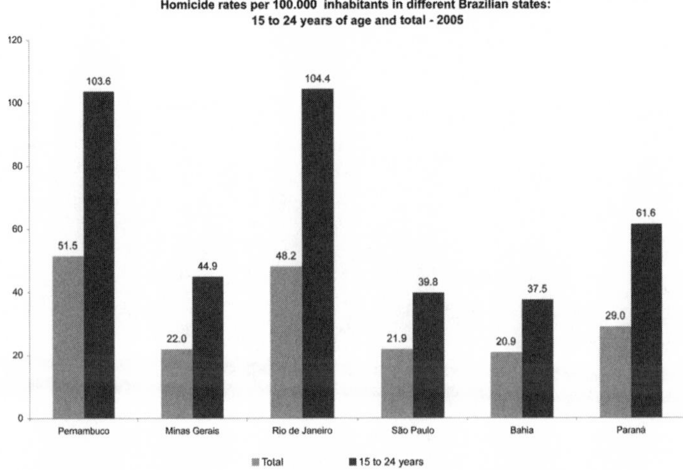

Figure 8.2. Homicides per 100,000 inhabitants in different Brazilian states: Young and total, 2005. (Source: Mortality Information System—Datasus)

resources like education, health, and sanitation among blacks and whites in Brazil eventually provokes another type of inequality, namely, the uneven distribution of violent death. Accordingly, the most common victims of lethal violence are blacks, and among these, the young. In some states, like Rio de Janeiro, as can be seen in figure 8.3, the homicide rate of young black men reaches 400 per 100,000.

The color and age variables, when seen together, are also a factor when people are considered suspects by the police. The predominantly black and poor young people who live in slums and in the periphery of big cities are the preferential suspects of the police. A survey carried out by the Center for Studies on Public Security and Citizenship in the city of Rio de Janeiro in 2003 revealed that of all people stopped in police approaches, blacks are frisked 55% of the time, compared to 32.6% of the time when whites are approached.[4] The distribution of police operations varies by neighborhood, with a predominance of approaches on foot in the street (with frisking) in poor neighborhoods and of police blockades (almost always without frisking) in the better-off districts.

The Geography of Death: Fractured Cities

In the metropolitan regions of the country, violent crime has grown predominantly in slums and poor neighborhoods on the periphery of big cities.

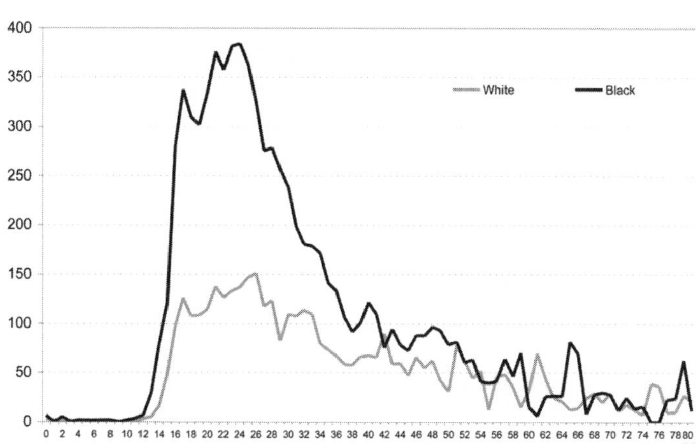

Figure 8.3. Homicides in relation to all deaths by race and age in the state of Rio de Janeiro, 2005. (Source: Mortality Information System—Datasus)

Especially in the 1980s, when drug trafficking began to emerge in these areas, conflicts between rival gangs over the control of a highly profitable market became routine. Police violence and corruption also grew over the years, closely tied to the drug trade. These poor territories that lack social services are the ones with the highest rates of lethal violence registered. In the most violent Brazilian cities, one sees evidence of a geography of death in which the majority of the victims are poor young black people.

Figure 8.4 illustrates the inequality in distribution of lethal violence in various neighborhoods in the city of Rio de Janeiro. The map shows the division of the municipality into Integrated Public Security Areas (AISPs). AISPs 2, 19, and 23, which embrace the neighborhoods of the south side of the city (Copacabana, Ipanema, Leblon, Barra) where there is a concentration of residents with greater buying power, present the lowest rates of homicide. Rates varying between 4.7 and 10 homicides per 100,000 inhabitants, close to the North American pattern, are common there. As for AISPs 27 and 9, situated in the west side and the suburbs and gathering together poor neighborhoods and regions full of slums such as Vigário Geral and Complexo do Alemão, rates as high as 72 homicides per 100,000 inhabitants are registered. This means that in different parts of the city, just forty minutes away from each other, very different daily relations to violence coexist, as if there were different countries within the same fractured city.

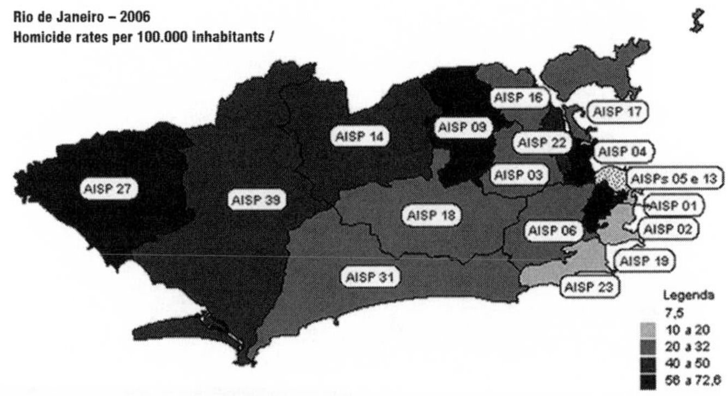

Figure 8.4. Homicide rates per 100,000 inhabitants, city of Rio de Janeiro, 2006. Source: CESeC—Candido Mendes University based on official data of the Rio de Janeiro Police.

Some analysts believe that what is underway is a veritable genocide of the young poor and predominantly black members of the population as a result of the rapid expansion of specific criminal dynamics and unlimited access to firearms. It is unquestionable that the explosive combination of arms and drugs has been a determinant in the escalation of the rates of violent crime in the large urban centers. In 1980, deaths caused by firearms totaled 43% of all homicides in the country. In 2006, the percentage had soared to 74%.[5]

Much of the violence that has become entrenched over the last few decades started within the networks of illegal drug trafficking. The accelerated growth of violent deaths in slums and poor neighborhoods may be explained by a combination of factors: the advent of cocaine in urban centers, the increase in violent and repressive police action, fighting between rival gangs for the control of the points for distributing and selling drugs, and the use of military weapons. The absence of public powers (especially an efficient and honest police force) in these areas has favored the establishment and spread of territorial control by armed groups. Since the 1980s, drug traffickers established themselves in poor areas of the city from which they command their business in a heavily armed fashion. In the late 1990s, a new phenomenon emerged: groups of off-duty policemen or ex-policemen organizing themselves to occupy territories, often disputing those areas in open armed conflicts with drug gangs. Initially, these groups were seen as a parallel police force and today are known as "militia."

Many young people see in the rapid profits and the glamorous life allowed by the power and presence of arms an attractive way out of poverty and exclusion. The drug market environment, the search for quick profit, the glamorous life, and the violence described earlier feed a context where despotism, machismo, homophobia, misogyny, and arms predominate; this context affects many young people in these places, even those who are not directly connected to the armed groups that hold the territorial control.

The Brazilian Police and Security Policies

What are the public security policies with which the country has responded to urban violence? During the more than twenty years that have elapsed since the process of transition that ended the military dictatorship in 1985, the sector that has made the least progress in relation to its modernization and democratization is that of the criminal justice system, in particular that of police institutions.[6] The first systematic efforts to design public security policies based on contemporary perspectives, identified by a combination of efficiency and human rights, began to be registered only during the second half of the 1990s. Until then, public security policies were relegated, by the majority of the governments, to the corporate spheres of the police.[7] The silence surrounding the escalation of lethal violence also predominated among large sectors of intellectuals, the media, and even NGOs during the 1980s and first half of the 1990s. In fact, in academic and university contexts, with rare exceptions, the creation of research centers dealing with the theme of violence and its relation to public security is relatively recent. The socioeconomic profile and the low capacity of political pressure of the main victims of violence may help to explain the slow awakening of successive federal administrations and civil society to the notion of public security and to the need to modernize, control, and democratize the police.

As a result of the absence of investments and rational public policies, the majority of the police forces in the country have become degraded, and many have grown violent and inefficient. The organized crime structured around drugs and arms has corrupted broad segments of the police, in some cases reaching into the upper ranks of the hierarchy.[8] In some states, police violence has become a serious problem that directly affects the poor population of slums and the urban periphery who find themselves caught between the violence of the armed groups of traffickers on one side and police corruption and police violence on the other.

Figure 8.5 shows the number of homicides by the police force in Rio de Janeiro (1997–2007), approximately 20% of all homicides. As with the rates of homicide in the city, police violence also obeys a specific geography and is strongly concentrated in the west side and suburban neighborhoods, which are the poorest areas in the city. The scant presence of civil rights organizations in these areas, together with the "naturalization" of the idea

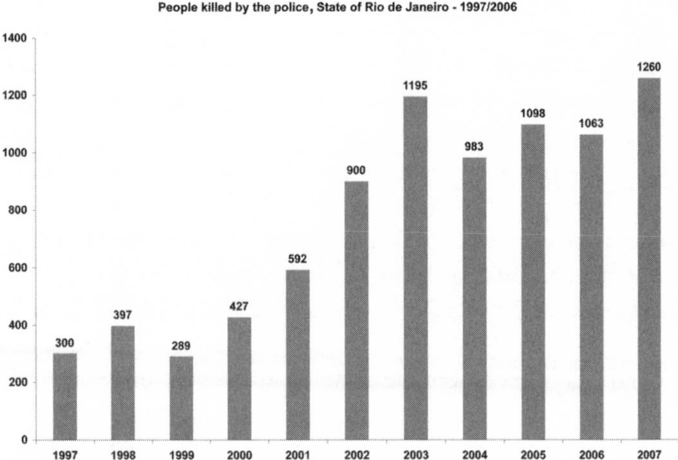

Figure 8.5. People killed by the police in the state of Rio de Janeiro, 1997–2007. The data for September through December 2007 are partial and relate only to the computerized police precincts. (Source: Secretary on Public Security of Rio de Janeiro)

that conflicts in slums provoke civil victims, may help in understanding why these figures are so appallingly high.

In Brazil, deaths that result from police action are called by the police themselves "deaths in confrontation," and it is important to understand the term's dynamics. A 1996 study of several of these cases reveals that the victims are by and large young males (aged fifteen to twenty-nine, especially the twenty- to twenty-four-year-old bracket) and that 64% are black, a significant number when one considers that blacks make up 39% of the city's population. This same study also shows that police action is six times higher inside slums than outside, considering the percentage of the population who live in slums in Rio de Janeiro. Furthermore, the mentioned analysis discloses that nearly half the victims were shot four times or more and that 65% of the corpses presented at least one shot in the back or head, thereby configuring obvious cases of summary executions among the "deaths in confrontation."[9]

With rare exceptions, the predominant response of the governments to the phenomenon of violence—regardless of partisan orientation on the federal, state, and municipal levels—seems to be inertia: a slowness in responding and a naturalization of violence when this affects marginalized segments of the population. This inertia is translated into a void where civil society and youth organization groups intervene.

The AfroReggae Cultural Group and AfroReggae Band

The AfroReggae Cultural Group is an NGO founded in 1993 and based in the Vigário Geral slum in the city of Rio de Janeiro. The group was created in the same year as the terrible slaughter in Vigário Geral, when twenty-one residents were killed by police in an illegal operation, and initially emerged as a direct response to it.[10] The objective of the group is to offer cultural and artistic training to young slum dwellers so that they have the means to construct their citizenship and escape from the path of the drug racket and joblessness; the group also seeks to multiply alternative possibilities of identification and activities for other young people. In the words of the group itself, its objective is to "promote social inclusion and justice by using art, Afro-Brazilian culture and education as tools to create bridges that span differences and serve as pillars to sustain and exercise citizenship." The group wishes to be seen "as an organization that fights for social transformation by making dreams come true through awakening the potential and self-esteem of the poorer layers of society."[11] The main activities developed by the organization are workshops dedicated to percussion, theater, the circus, *capoeira* (a Brazilian martial arts form), video, and information technology in the slums of Vigário Geral, Parada de Lucas, Cantagalo, and Complexo do Alemão in Rio de Janeiro. But the group not only works within the favela but seeks to create mediations between the middle class and the dwellers in the slums. As such, the AfroReggae Cultural Group is what Silvia Ramos labels a "new mediator." It contributes to bringing the slums closer to the middle class but also works in the opposite direction. With its "Urban Connections" project (big music concerts in the slums with the presence of leading members of the Brazilian musical world), AfroReggae takes the most important musicians and bands in the country inside the slums and at the same time "presents" the slums to musicians and guests who have never been inside a poor community. Some of the musicians who have performed for the Urban Connections project are Caetano Veloso, Gilberto Gil, Daniela Mercuri, Ivete Sangalo, Marisa Monte, Adriana Calcanahoto, Frejat, Elba Ramalho, and Fernanda Abreu, among others. Thus, while the group has gained wide experience working with low-income adolescents and children, its language and music reaches out to the youth of different social classes.

The group has created a professional band, the AfroReggae Band, that plays in large concerts in Brazil and has appeared frequently overseas. The band was founded in 1995 and initially emerged from the percussion, capoeira, and circus workshops that the AfroReggae Cultural Group organized in Vigário Geral. After future band members began to do presentations in schools and small venues around Rio in 1997, they realized that they sounded like a percussion and dance workshop but not like a full-fledged music group and so began to work earnestly on consolidating their sound. As José Junior, the director of the AfroReggae Cultural Group, states: "They saw the need of moving from a pedagogical project to a performative one. . . . The process of change began with the creation of scenic movements. The members of the band had to be complete artists: musicians, dancers, actors and fighters. The rehearsals lasted all day and involved physical, mental and psychological preparation. No drugs, alcohol or cigarettes. Besides being part of a healthy generation, they had to be conscious of their role as artists and social enterpreneurs."[12]

These are cultural activists concerned with producing a quality sound that has a commitment to a solid musical aesthetic as much as to cultural activism. Aware that they will succumb to a highly competitive market if they stay within the limited perspective of using culture at the service of the social, they have continually made great efforts to qualify as professional artists. Thus, the professionalization of the sound and scenic presentation of the band is a crucial dimension that mediates its social significance. Today, the AfroReggae Band has become a highly recognized music group both nationally and internationally. Its stage show features three rappers and two backing vocalists, five percussionists, three brass instruments, a bass, a lead guitar, keyboards, and a DJ. They have released two CDs, *Nova Cara* (New Face), produced by Universal in 2001, and *Nenhum Motivo Explica a Guerra* (There Is No Motive for War), produced by Geléia Geral in 2006.

Through the AfroReggae Band, the AfroReggae Cultural Group has a great deal of visibility in the media and often appears on television. The band enjoys the support of leading artists in Brazil such as Caetano Veloso (who is seen by band members as their godfather because of the support he gave them in the beginning), Gilberto Gil, Jorge Mautner, and Regina Casé and of international artists such as Manu Chao and British rappers Ty and Estelle, who appear on their latest CD. In 2005, a documentary on the AfroReggae Cultural Group (*Favela Rising*) won an award at the Tribeca Film Festival in the United States. Due to the success of the band as well as to AfroReggae as an NGO, the AfroReggae Cultural Group has set up a company that generates resources with shows and presentations and employs young people in the various careers related to artistic production. This production company, with the support of international funding (Ford Foundation, Kellogg Foundation, HP Foundation, Avina, and others), national agreements (with the Rio de Janeiro city government, the Ministry of Culture, the Globo TV network, and others), and business companies (Petrobras, Banco Real, Natura), finances the activities of the NGO. Besides the AfroReggae Band, the NGO's cultural workshops and activities have led to the creation of twelve musical groups that are also part of the project.[13] As stated on the group's MySpace page, "In 2006 AfroReggae runs 61 social projects in Rio de Janeiro. It has founded permanent cultural bases in four different favelas. It now multiplies its workshop programs across Brazil and in other countries."[14] Although the AfroReggae Band is largely what gives the group audiovisual and stage presence, it is impossible to separate an understanding of the band and its music from the different activities and subgroups of the AfroReggae Cultural Group.

The group has always refused to get involved in political parties and electoral campaigns. It maintains a solid neutrality with respect to the various drug-dealing gangs, which has allowed for the band to enter and play in communities that are dominated by different criminal gangs. The AfroReggae Cultural Group uses the dimensions of the private, corporate, commercial market and the social activist community, concentrates its efforts on racial and territorial affirmation, and produces a first-person discourse on behalf of the young and socially excluded who live in the slums and urban periphery. The AfroReggae Cultural Group seems to understand the numerous risks that such endeavors entail, including the risk of seeing its projects "co-opted" by the state or private companies, the danger of exploiting "culture at the service of the social," and the tendency to create "new stereotypes" by presenting well-behaved young black people playing percussion instruments.[15] One of the signs that the group is aware of these risks is its refusal to expand and multiply its nuclei indefinitely, the understanding being that it should not substitute for the state in generating alternatives for young people from the poorer classes, preferring to operate in the symbolic field by showing the potential of these actions through strong and original examples.[16] But undoubtedly, one of the most controversial issues of the group, among certain sectors, is precisely this association between spectacle, entrepreneurship, and social activism, an issue we will return to later. For now, we want to briefly explore the role of the band's musical style in the construction of its ideal of social activism.

As stated before, the AfroReggae Band was made up of youngsters who participated in the first workshops organized by the AfroReggae Cultural Group in the favela of Vigário Geral. Some of their initial stylistic elements come directly from these workshops, such as the use of capoeira moves in their shows, circus-style dramatizations and movements, and, notably, the central stage presence given to the drums called *tambor de Minas,* especially the *caixas de folia,* which hang from the waist of three of the musicians who move around with them in the central part of their stage performances. During the period of the AfroReggae Band's consolidation, Olodum became one of the bands that inspired its members, especially in terms of "its fantastic percussive force, its politicized lyrics and the process of conquest of self-esteem and citizenship that the band put forth."[17] But crucial to them was the creation of a sound that would be characteristic of a Rio de Janeiro favela (in contrast to Olodum, for example); thus, they took elements from such genres as funk, *pagode, forro,* hip hop, and *ragga* as well as elements from music genres such as *jongo, maractu,* and *congada,* among others. Anthropologist Hermano Vianna defined the music of the AfroReggae Band as a

> multi-style that is the product of the coming together of some of the most vital manifestations that have recently arisen in Brazilian music: mangue beat; São Paulo rap; Bahia samba-reggae; Rio de Janeiro funk. Here and there you catch echoes of Jamaican reggae translated by the Rappa group, of hip-hop-hardcore transformed by the Planet Hemp band, of Northeastern xaxado rhythms and techno beats, or else touches of capoeira dancing and candomblé rituals. It is not fusion. But it is more than juxtaposition. "Shack Musica": put together with a variety of elements joined according to a method, a plan and transformed into households (sonorous or not), with all the households forming a community.[18]

As asserted by Vianna, the issue here is not generic fusion but rather a sonic usage for which genre is not the primary binding or defining category. In Latin America, the process of mixtures across different genres (and not just in Afro-based groups or musics) has been a crucial aesthetic practice of musical creativity. To reiterate that this is the case with AfroReggae is simply to locate AfroReggae in a long historical lineage of Pan-African mixing, which in the case of Brazil actually became the standard definition of vanguard aesthetics in musical manifestos or movements such as *antropofagia* in the early twentieth century or *tropicalismo* in the 1960s. That is, in one sense, the mixing of sonic elements across genres is an assumed procedure in AfroReggae's musical aesthetics with profound Pan-African and Brazilian historical roots. Thus, when read as such, one of the characteristics we find in critical appraisals of AfroReggae is that different critics will refer to different genres as fundamental to its music—as if we each tried to find in its sound the acoustic traces of those sonic snippets with which we are more familiar. But ultimately, this music is conceptualized less in terms of generic traces and more in terms of what Anderson Sá, one of the band's lead singers, calls "information": "In a show, we have a lot of stuff, of physical presence, of scenic elements, and a lot of things happening at the same time, it is a lot of information. If someone pays attention to my choreography, that person is going to lose what another musician is doing, for example, with the drumset. It is a lot of things."[19]

"Information" is used by Sá to speak of the multiple formal elements that make up the band's compositions, rather than, for example, "mixture" or "hybridization" to signal the taking of music from several generic sources. It is also the term used by rapper MV Bill from the City of God (a famous slum in Rio de Janeiro, immortalized in the film *City of God*) to name his second CD, *Trafficking Information*. This word provides a key entry point into two features of the AfroReggae Band's music: one, the band's songs have a highly dramatic style where narration, dramatization of the story on stage, and usage of movements that are derived from carnival samba, capoeira, hip hop, theater, and circus techniques combine with elements and information taken from different musics; and two, the band includes a DJ who samples both music and sounds—notably voices of children and sounds of bullets and helicopters. "Information" here refers to the fact that the visual, the sonic, and the dramatic are profoundly united in the aesthetics of the band, and the embodiment of these sounds is crucial to its aesthetic. This is not a feature that is incorporated when the video clips are done—it is a feature of the performance of the music itself. Thus, another main feature of the music of the AfroReggae Band is the profound interrelationship between image and sound, so much so that it has been reiterated by music critics, analysts, and even the band members themselves that there is a big difference between listening to their CD and seeing them perform live or watching their video clips.

Here, the defining compositional mode of operation is not necessarily that of pushing the limits of a specific genre but rather of finding a means of organization for multiple musical, visual, and dramatic features that are being viewed as possible information. What takes center stage as a conscious aesthetic preoccupation is the relationship between image, drama, embodied sound, and lived life. The issues that mark members' crucial concern are the relationship between a daily life marked by violence, the representation of that aspect of their life in the media, and their mode of intervention in that representational space through embodied music and through highlighting elements from their Afro-Brazilian heritage. This, in turn, is related to another formal characteristic of AfroReggae's work—in its songs, video clips, and live performances, there is always a blurry boundary between reality and fiction or, if one wishes to map this on to mediated genres, between the video clip, the documentary, and the newscast or, if onto political discourse, between the semblance and the real.

This aestheticization of violence is a strategic site of political intervention. In order to understand how AfroReggae does this, we need to understand not only the organization of the band or of the AfroReggae Cultural Group but of the emergence of what Silvia Ramos has labeled a "new mediator" in the Brazilian political scene of the 1990s.[20]

Young People in the Slums and Urban Periphery: The New Mediators

AfroReggae is not alone. As stated at the beginning of this chapter, within the context of the civil responses to violence, there is an important recent process of mobilization of young people from the slums and peripheral neighborhoods. These responses are in the form of projects, programs, or local initiatives based on cultural and artistic actions that are often developed and coordinated by the young people themselves. Some examples of these initiatives are the Olodum group in Salvador; AfroReggae, Nós do Morro, Cia. Étnica de Dança, and the Central Única das Favelas in Rio de Janeiro; and hundreds of local groups, mobilized around the hip-hop culture, on the periphery of São Paulo, in the poor *vilas* of Porto Alegre, among the population of Belo Horizonte, and in the poor neighborhoods of Recife, Brasília, and São Luís. There emerged in Brazil in the 1990s a new political figure: the youth from the periphery or the youth from the favela (*jovem de periferia, jovem de favela*).

The groups that speak in the name of this new political subject express through different languages—such as music, theater, dance, and cinema—ideas and perspectives of the young people from the favelas. At the same time, they seek to produce alternative images to the stereotypes of criminality associated with that sector of society and engage in a symbolic dispute with drug traffickers for the identification of the young who live in those areas. They do so by constructing an attractiveness and seduction process linked to artistic glamour, visibility, and success.

These groups are committed to constructing peace strategies in tune with contemporary spirit and interests: in addition to culture and art, they value the Internet, computers, fashionable clothes and shoes, travel, and regional and international exchange. In general, the projects are characterized by four innovative objectives found in the repertoire of principles of human rights entities of the 1980s and of the NGOs of the 1990s: 1) to lend incentive to generating income and employment in the short term, seeking success for their members by placing them in the market and training them in some profession; 2) to emphasize individual affirmation, including the training of artists and leaders involved in cultural and artistic activities, whose fame attracts and serves as an example for other young people; 3) to emphasize territorial affirmation, often by showing the names of the communities and groups and the words of the songs on T-shirts and clothes (Vigário Geral, Cidade de Deus, and the like, which appear everywhere, including outside Brazil, as a sign of commitment to change in the community); 4) to denounce racism and affirm the black race, whether in the lyrics and music of the songs, in attire (Afro hairdos and clothes), or in the names of the projects (Black Brazilian Music, AfroReggae, Ethnic Company, Black Awareness Unity). With regard to violence and criminality, most of these initiatives range from denouncing police violence and corruption on the one hand to the ever-difficult quest for autonomy and independence in relation to the armed drug trafficking groups on the other hand, always in a very fragile balance.

Thus, one of the main forms of creativity in many of these groups is to take the stereotypical images of discrimination—the flashiness and fame of the drug trafficking symbolism of their black heritage and their aggressive bodily presence—and, through a process of aestheticization, turn them into sites of political intervention, of competition for identification processes of youth, of political activism. This is not just the symbolic corollary of other political activities—it is the very locus where political activities coalesce. Thus, the image of well-behaved black youth that the AfroReggae Cultural Group projects is based on the resignification of the very elements that symbolically characterize drug traffickers. José Junior states: "Our language and other methodological instruments were similar to those of narcoculture that has reigned in Rio for thirty years. We speak of power and hierarchy. We use clothes with logos because we like it and because it is a way of attracting youth. Our major objective is that the youths of the favelas do not take the narcotraffickers as their idols any longer. Instead of guns, we offered musical instruments. Our power is not that of death, but that of life."[21] There is a performativity of power that resides not in the possession of guns but in the embodiment of a strong and hierarchical masculinity framed in terms not of a dead body but of a live body that is able to dance and fight; capoeira is one of the crucial elements of this body. This spectacularization of masculinity as a space made performatively attractive through music becomes the opposite of the male body as the privileged locus for the space of violent death. The excess of information that characterizes AfroReggae's presentations undoubtedly has to do with a celebration of the masculine body as a carrier of life and not only as the embodiment of that which needs to be killed or disposed of.

These projects and initiatives gained importance during the 1990s as bridges between the youth of the slums on the one hand and the governments, media, researchers, and often international actors such as foundations and cooperation agencies on the other hand. These new mediators offer to the field of the NGOs, the Left, and the traditional Brazilian social movements, trade-unions, and the like such novelties as interest in the market and "lucrative ends" combined with a commitment to the community; the affirmation of territorial and racial identity combined with identification with universal signs; and emphasis on the subjective, individual trajectories, and success and fame, which are associated with the world of culture and art.

Various crucial questions emerge here: What forms of political intervention have these groups created through the use of art as a locus for political activism and struggle? How are these either different from or similar to previous histories of the relationship between art and political intervention in Brazil, such as *música engajada* (politically committed song of the 1960s) or Tropicália? Moreover, what do these groups that use art as a primary mediator have to offer to the field of NGOS, the Left, and the traditional Brazilian social movements, trade-unions, and the like?

Regarding violence and criminality, the majority of these initiatives search for an equilibrium between denouncing police violence and autonomy regarding the despotism of armed groups of drug traffickers. Some of these artistic groups try to take on the role of mediators of the "armed conflict" between different factions of drug traffickers and openly assume a mission of "making youth leave narcotrafficking," but this is not necessarily a rule common to all groups.[22] For example, the group Nós do Morro from Rio de Janeiro refuses to participate in the discussion about drug trafficking, and band members do not make reference to it when they state their mission.[23] Other initiatives, in turn, even assume ambiguous positions in relation to "the world of crime." Such is the case of some of the hip-hop groups that identify with "their brothers in prison" and concentrate their denunciations on the fact that criminality is stereotypically associated with the black youth from the periphery. Thus, in contrast to the political activism of committed song of the 1960s, for example, the activities of these groups emerge from within the aesthetics, contradictions, and complex patterns of simultaneous identification and rejection of a world of crime and its symbolism.

Moreover, these initiatives, which in this chapter are identified as new modes of mediation and responses to violence, are neither the only ones nor necessarily the most effective to take youth away from narcotrafficking. Numerous religious groups, especially Pentecostal ones, are dedicated today to the religious conversion of youth involved with criminal activity. Besides this, soccer schools and sports programs meant to combat the lack of opportunities, discover talents, and create professional opportunities flourish in favelas and poor neighborhoods. In the field of art, we find innumerable dance, circus, theater, and music projects that are both private and promoted by the government and do not necessarily emerge as initiatives of the favela youth themselves. It is in the midst of all these complex networks of interaction that the "new mediators" develop their activities.

Despite all these initiatives and their difficulties and shortcomings, it is possible to distinguish the main characteristics of these new mediators. First, the leadership of the groups is in the hands of youths from the favelas themselves. This leadership role is accompanied by the production of a discourse in the first person singular that underlines their own processes of constituting alternative subjectivities. The music, as well, emerges from all sorts of discursive practices that are listened to in the favelas and by these musicians. Second, such mediators have the capacity to construct and express signs with which the youth from the favelas can identify while rejecting the traditional and stereotypical images associated with favela youth. Third, they have the capacity to move simultaneously within the community and in the mainstream mass media, between different social classes, and between different factions and governments. In terms of music, this means a simultaneity of practices considered either countercultural with those that, until a few years ago, were considered prohibited, such as funk, along with artistic practices that have historically been accepted into the mainstream, such as samba and capoeira. As stated before, this is not just the Tropicália style of mixing but rather an eclecticism that juxtaposes sonic activism, entrepreneurship, and spectacle into one. That is, these groups have a tremendous capacity to move back and forth between the local and the universal. Finally, these young mediators cannot be confused with the idea of liberators put forth by the Enlightenment and that, since the eighteenth century, has come to often stand as a (tragic) model of an enlightened modern citizen who struggles for ideals of freedom.[24] These are rather heterogeneous groups constituted by very different types of subjects and which are predominantly male. Evident traces of misogyny and homophobia can be seen in the different discursive constructions and practices of these groups.[25]

If, according to Yúdice, culture has come to occupy the space of politics, this does not mean that politics may be conceptualized in terms of the ideal citizen of the liberal state. Despite all the discourse of citizenship, what this new type of mediator puts forth is a specific kind of questioning of the locus of music in terms of political participation. Rather than an idealized version of music as resistance or music as spiritual transcendence of material conditions, which is a liberal musical ideology that frequently accompanies practices of music as response to violence, what we have here is a complex musical activism, one that is ambiguously located at the fracture between racial identificatory practices and the construction of a discourse that emerges from the *favelados* (favela dwellers) themselves.[26] This activism is also related, though in an ambiguous way, to crime, machismo, misogyny, and other types of (often impossible) transactions stemming from mediators' daily lives. While these groups indeed endorse a turn to culture as a strategy of political expediency, they simultaneously show culture's fracture at the site of dealing with the presence of violence in a rapidly changing globalized society.

We would like to suggest, following Elizabeth Povinelli, that the fact that late liberalism is still thought of as rational and regulatory places incongruent demands on people who have to participate in one or more of these incommensurable worlds. These demands often generate deep inner ruptures and require of people that they get involved with different agendas that are often contradictory with each other. Such contradictions become impossible to resolve.[27] As such, the music generated by these groups cannot be simply interpreted as an emancipatory cultural response at the sight of the failure of politics or as a new form of bricolage à la Tropicália from the subaltern classes. Rather, it should be seen as an activity that puts forth the difficulties of simultaneous participation in incongruous worlds and desires: that of artistic activism, that of drug trafficking and police brutality, that of spectacle and its modes of production, that of the right to dignity and respect, among others.

Despite this complex context and some of the problems mentioned above, the youth from the favelas are, today, the main source of denunciation, reflection, and discussion in the national Brazilian context about the relationships between youth and police, racism among the police, and the discrimination that the youth from the periphery suffer everyday, not only in their relation with the police but also with their employers, in the media, and among all those who continue to associate a stereotypical image of the youth from the peripheries with that of someone who is basically dishonest and a criminal. The Youth and the Police project, developed by AfroReggae in Minas Gerais along with CESeC, is a good example of the possibilities open to social movements that are directly intervening in the adoption of public security policies that are democratic, contemporary, and based on reforms of the police.[28]

A Last Reference: The Youth and the Police Project

In 2002, the AfroReggae Band produced a clip for the song "Tô Bolado," which included a succession of powerful images of police violence, thereby configuring the AfroReggae Cultural Group's strong opposition to the police. In the same year, one of the members of the band, Paulo Negueba, was shot in the foot during a police operation inside Vigário Geral. Almost all the young people associated with AfroReggae have experienced situations of violence, corruption, and humiliation at the hands of policemen, making for a vast repertoire of hatred and resentment that constituted a natural "anti-police culture" among the group. Surprisingly, in late 2002, José Junior, coordinator of the AfroReggae Cultural Group, visited CESeC at Candido Mendes University and said that he would like to consider a project with the police (rather than against the police, as would be expected). A project of cultural invasions of the police barracks was presented to the Ford Foundation, which gave its immediate approval. But the negotiations with the military police of Rio de Janeiro were thwarted, and the original project presented by the AfroReggae Cultural Group could not be developed. In June 2004, the Secretariat for Security and the military police of the state of Minas Gerais invited the AfroReggae Cultural Group and CESeC to develop the project in the police barracks of Belo Horizonte.

It turned out to be a four-stage pilot project aimed at establishing a dialogue between police culture and youth culture, reducing the huge gap between these two groups through music and art: percussion workshops, theater, graffiti, circus, dance, and shows. The surprising results of the four weeks of activities confirm the success of an innovative, creative, and radical proposal for integration between the police and society, unprecedented in Brazil. In addition, the project proved that it is possible to value and highlight the human, playful, and artistic side of the police while decreasing prejudice toward young residents of slums and housing projects. Among the distinctive aspects of the experience, in contrast to traditional ways of working with police forces (courses, meetings, and lectures on human rights), the following key elements are worth emphasizing.

First, the experience involved not only reasoning, which would typically be included in teaching human rights to police officers, but hearts, minds, and especially bodies through the workshops of music, theatre, graffiti and others.

Second, the essence of the intervention was not merely to "change the police," intellectually teaching them something that they appeared not to want to understand or that they resisted assimilating, but rather to propose new and unique experiences for both the police and the young people who were entering a military police barracks for the first time. The young instructors dressed, spoke, and had the "attitude" of slum kids, changing their stereotypes about the police and challenging the police with their sense of rhythm and music and the plasticity of theater, dance, and graffiti. What was essential was the exchange, and it took place primarily in the sphere of aesthetics, the music, the body, and the experience of creating a new "image and attitude" in the police. The police and the youth—constructed as opposing groups—were then both protagonists in a new moment.

Third, sound and image were central to this project. The idea was to challenge the image that society and youth have of the police and the image that the police and society have of youth, especially young black slum dwellers. Stereotypes are archaic, frozen images, even if they are not true. In particular, the police are "all about image": the uniforms, the weapons, the military aesthetic, and the patrol cars. AfroReggae, in turn, "is image" as mentioned above: the performers, the shows, a new projection of the slum and of the youth. All the stages in the project were filmed, photographed, and tape-recorded. During the project, two experiences proved to be important: the video workshops and the photo sessions. During the video workshops, the police discussed images of the force; during the photo sessions, they were exposed to a selection of images taken by themselves in the previous weeks. It was amazing to see the police looking at the beautiful pictures they had taken during the workshops, shows, and closing meetings. On these occasions, the police saw themselves just as they had been seen through the photographer's lens and discussed the "effects" that the images would produce in the photo exhibit held in 2005. Equally essential was the media coverage. The numerous stories in newspapers and radio and TV programs invariably led to debate, laughter, and emotion the next day. Several times, the instructors would sit with the police in a circle after the activities to discuss one of these media stories. It was also moving to watch the journalists get emotional watching scenes of uniformed police playing tambourines, snare drums, and bass drums, dancing and painting graffiti. As a result of this "pedagogy of the drums," new sounds and new images of the police were created. As one police officer said in an interview, "The time must come for the curse to be broken," referring to the gap between the police and society. Or, as a musician from the AfroReggae Band said: "The suffering we had with the police, those bad memories, all of this was a big barrier. I confess that, in the beginning, I had to overcome this anti-police feeling which was very strong among us. Afterwards, when I saw the percussion instruments, these drums that had saved our lives, in the hands of the policemen, when I saw them playing with joy and happiness, very motivated, dancing, working their self-esteem that really moved me."

After four years of work, as requested by the military police in the state of Minas Gerais, the project continues to go on.[29] Its political impact extends far beyond the expectations of a pilot project such as this one. Of course, there are enormous barriers to be overcome, considering the police on the national level. But initiatives where young people, through music and art, come into direct contact with policemen are powerful instruments to transform police officers and the police organization itself. What is most important in this experience is the role played by the young people from the slums who are involved in the tragedy of violence as its main victims and protagonists. In this case, they are "new mediators" who use music to show that it is possible to offer creative answers to the problem of violence in Brazil.

Notes

1. The statistics used in this chapter express the data available when the essay was submitted for editorial review.

2. George Yúdice, *The Expediency of Culture: Uses of Culture in the Global Era* (Durham, N.C.: Duke University Press, 2003).

3. Willem Assies, Gemma van der Haar, and André Hoekema, "La diversidad como desafío: una nota sobre los dilemas de la diversidad," in *El reto de la diversidad. Pueblos indígenas y reforma de estado en América Latina,* ed. Willem Assies, Gemma van der Haar, and André Hoekema (México: El Colegio de Michoacán, 1999), 356–94; Elizabeth Povinelli, *The Cunning of Recognition: Indigenous Alterities and the Making of Australian Multiculturalism* (Durham, N.C.: Duke University Press, 2002); Yúdice, *Expediency of Culture.*

4. Silvia Ramos and Leonarda Musumeci, *Elemento suspeito: abordagem policial e discriminação na cidade do Rio de Janeiro* (Rio de Janeiro: Civilização Brasileira, 2005).

5. Julio Jacobo Waiselfisz, *Mapa da Violência* (Brasília: Rede de Informação Tecnológica Latino Americana, 2008).

6. Elizabeth Leeds, "Rio de Janeiro," in *Fractured Cities: Social Exclusion, Urban Violence and Contested Spaces in Latin America,* ed. K. Koonings and D. Kruijt (London: Zed Books, 2007), 22–35.

7. Luiz Eduardo Soares, *Meu casaco de general: quinhentos dias no front da segurança pública do Rio de Janeiro* (São Paulo: Companhia das Letras, 2000).

8. Julita Lemgruber, Leonarda Musumeci, and Ignacio Cano, *Quem vigia os vigias?* (Rio de Janeiro: Record, 2003).

9. Ignacio Cano, *Letalidade da ação policial no Rio de Janeiro* (Rio de Janeiro: ISER, 1997).

10. For a detailed description of the emergence of the AfroReggae Cultural Group, see Yúdice, *Expediency of Culture.*

11. Grupo Cultural AfroReggae, www.afroreggae.org.br (accessed January 20, 2008).

12. José Junior, *Da favela para o mundo: a história do Grupo Cultural AfroReggae* (Rio de Janeiro: Aeroplano Editora, 2003), 124.

13. These are Afro Circo, Afro Lata, Afro Mangue, Afro Samba, Akoní, Bloco Afro Reggae, Kitoto, Levantando a Lona, Makala Música e Dança, Párvati, Tribo Negra, and Trupe Teatro AfroReggae.

14. "AfroReggae," www.myspace.com/afroreggae (accessed January 20, 2008).

15. Yúdice, *Expediency of Culture.*

16. Junior, *Da favela para o mundo.*

17. The Olodum Cultural Group is an organization created in 1979 and dedicated to music and social activism that reaffirms Afro-Brazilian music and culture and struggles against discrimination. It is centered in Salvador, Bahia. See also the Grupo Cultural AfroReggae Web site.

18. Hermano Vianna, *Nova Cara,* CD, AfroReggae Release, 2001.

19. Santuza Cambraia Naves, Frederico Oliveira Coelho, and Tatiana Bacal, *A MPB em discussão: Entrevistas* (Belo Horizonte: Editora UFMG, 2006), 315.

20. Silvia Ramos, "Jovens de favelas na produção cultural brasileira dos anos 90," in *Por que não? Rupturas e continuidades da contracultura,* ed. Maria Isabel Mendes de Almeida and Santuza Cambraia Neves (Rio de Janeiro: 7 Letras, 2007), 239–56.

21. Junior, *Da favela para o mundo,* 96.

22. Patrick Neat and Damian Platt, *Culture Is Our Weapon: AfroReggae in the Favelas of Rio* (London: Latin America Bureau, 2006); Luiz Eduardo Soares, MV Bill, and Celso Athayde, *Cabeça de Porco* (Rio de Janeiro: Objetiva, 2005); MV Bill and Celso Athayde, *Falcão: Meninos do Tráfico* (Rio de Janeiro: Objetiva, 2006).

23. Nós do Morro, www.nosdomorro.com.br (accessed January 20, 2008).

24. David Scott, *Conscripts of Modernity: The Tragedy of Colonial Enlightenment* (Durham, N.C.: Duke University Press, 2004).

25. Junior, *Da favela para o mundo;* Soares, Bill, and Athayde, *Cabeça de Porco.*

26. Ana María Ochoa, "Introducción: la materialidad de lo musical y su relación con la violencia," *TRANS, Revista Transcultural de Música* [Transcultural Music Review], 10 (2006), http://www.sibetrans.com/trans/trans10/ochoa.htm (accessed June 20, 2008).

27. Povinelli, *Cunning of Recognition.*

28. See Silvia Ramos, *Youth and the Police,* Boletim Segurança e Cidadania (Rio de Janeiro: CESeC, 2006), http://www.ucamcesec.com.br/arquivos/publicacoes/boletim12web_eng.pdf (accessed January 20, 2008).

29. For an evaluation of its results, see ibid.

9 In Search of a Cross-Cultural Legal Framework

Indigenous Musics as a Worldwide Commodity

FELICIA SANDLER

In the liner notes of his 1973 recording *African Sanctus,* David Fanshawe writes, "The raw material for this section [the Credo] I discovered quite by accident one moonlit night when I was riding my camel across the Marra mountains in West Sudan. I left the camel and climbed a steep mountainside drawn by strange utterances which excited me beyond words. On top of the mountain under a full moon I saw four men on a prayer mat. They were in a trance swaying backwards and forwards reciting the Koran in a strange mixture of local dialects and Arabic. I recorded them for half an hour and they never knew I had been there."[1]

For many people in Fanshawe's audience, there is nothing in his account that would appear unusual or extraordinary except, perhaps, the adventure he describes. Fanshawe's rhetoric, the way he depicts people and places, and his explanation of the manner in which he engages (or does not engage) people and their music would not be considered rare or unacceptable by most of his listeners, thirty years ago or today. There are, however, some very serious issues embedded in this text—issues perhaps more obvious to his African subjects and troubling for many sensitive to relationships between music, the expression of culture, and both individual and cultural rights.

The manner in which musics from indigenous societies are engaged and used in the global marketplace by people outside of those communities raises legal, ethical, and emotional issues for musicians, the music industry, curators, and consumers.[2] Using the Fanshawe account as one possible scenario, I wish to explore some of these issues and then examine them in a couple of different cultural contexts. The thrust of this chapter involves a consideration of cultural frameworks and, in particular, the manner in which behaviors regarded as normal within one framework can be viewed as a curiosity, at times unacceptable, and sometimes even illegal in another.

Individual and Cultural Rights—What Are They?

Before looking more closely at issues raised in the Fanshawe quotation, let us take a moment to consider what is meant by "individual" and "cultural" rights.

Individual Rights

Cross-cultural conceptions of "rights" of individual persons received global acceptance in the United Nations Universal Declaration of Human Rights of 1948.[3] Entitlements such as those to life, dignity, and the security of person are said therein to be inalienable rights—something that is due to a person by virtue of his or her birth. These rights are noted to be the foundation of freedom, justice, and peace in the world. They, and others recorded in the declaration, should be protected, it is agreed by all signatories, as a rule of law. Individual rights, then, as defined in the declaration, are upheld through consensus in the document as well as legally in national legislations and international treaties. In fact, it is in such legal documents that individual rights are often further delineated and described.

In the musical arts, for roughly 190 governments around the world, the individual rights of authors are upheld in national copyright laws.[4] Copyright is the domain of intellectual property (IP) that deals with expressive creativity. The other domain is industrial property, which includes inventions (patents), trademarks, industrial designs, and geographic indications of source. There are also rights related to copyright, which protect the rights of performers, producers, and broadcasters. Rights protected in IP laws are primarily economic and in this regard relate to entitlements of livelihood. "Moral rights" are not defended in all national copyright laws but are broadly upheld in European copyright legislation and address entitlements of a more personal nature related to one's reputation.[5]

Copyright grants to authors, or to those to whom copyright has been transferred from an author, limited rights to permit or prevent certain actions, including reproductions, public performances, broadcasting, translations, arrangements, adaptations, and, through moral rights, mutilations and modifications of any kind. The reason these protections are given is that it is believed that exclusive rights bolster creativity. That is, by prohibiting other musicians from using one's music without authorization, composers find freedom economically to create and build upon their ideas. This creativity is deemed to be ultimately for the common good. As the World Intellectual Property Organization (WIPO) contends:

> Copyright protection is above all one of the means of promoting, enriching and disseminating the national cultural heritage. A country's development depends to a very great extent on the creativity of its people, and encouragement of national creativity is a *sine qua non* for progress. Copyright constitutes an essential element in the development process. Experience has shown that the enrichment of the national cultural heritage depends directly on the level of protection afforded to literary and artistic works. The higher the level, the greater the encouragement for authors to create; the greater the number of a country's intellectual creations, the higher its renown; the greater the number of productions in literature and the arts, the more numerous their auxiliaries in the book, record and entertainment industries; and indeed, in the final analysis, encouragement of intellectual creation is one of the basic prerequisites of all social, economic and cultural development.[6]

There are limitations to copyright protections. First, a work will be deemed eligible for protection only if it meets specific criteria. It must be a production in the literary, scientific, or artistic domain, and it must be an original creation of an author. In the vast majority of national laws, these original creations of the author must also be fixed in material form in order to be protected.[7] Once a work is deemed eligible for protection based on the fulfillment of said criteria, limitations to coverage include limits on the duration of copyright, geographical limitations, and limits on the author's rights to prevent others from utilizing his or her creation if the proposed application fits into "fair use" categories. These limits on authors' rights are administered for the public good, providing the greatest amount of access at the soonest time possible.

Authors' rights are protected across borders through treaty. Copyright entered the international arena in 1886 with the Berne Convention for the Protection of Literary and Artistic Works.[8] Signatories in 1886 numbered sixteen. In 2009, that number stands at 164, roughly 84 percent of the world's countries.[9] Other musically creative persons, namely performers, broadcasters, and producers of phonograms, are protected in laws neighboring on copyright, such as the Rome Convention of 1961, or the WIPO Performances and Phonograms Treaty of 1994 (WPPT), or in industrial property laws dealing with trademarks.[10] IP was first recognized as a trade commodity in 1994 at the Uruguay Round of trade negotiations under the auspices of the General Agreement on Tariffs and Trade (GATT) system. There are two important outcomes resulting from these negotiations: the World Trade Organization (WTO) was formed and superceded the GATT, and the TRIPS accord came into being. TRIPS is the agreement on Trade Related Aspects of Intellectual Property Rights and is administered by the WTO in cooperation with WIPO.[11] In the realm of copyright, TRIPS absorbs the Berne Convention in its entirety for the purposes of trade, minus the section on moral rights. Although the effects of the TRIPS accord are most pronounced for developing countries in the realms of biodiversity and pharmaceuticals, the impact in regard to cultural expressions is quite profound, particularly in the ways in which TRIPS has shaped copyright laws and reinforced views of arts as singularly "products," as will be discussed later in this chapter.

Cultural Rights

The concept of "cultural" rights is also mentioned in the Universal Declaration of Human Rights of 1948. Article 22 states: "Everyone, as a member of society, has the right to social security and is entitled to realization, through national effort and international co-operation and in accordance with the organization and resources of each State, of the economic, social and cultural rights indispensable for his dignity and the free development of his personality." What makes up these cultural rights is unstated.

The International Covenant on Economic, Social, and Cultural Rights of 1966 is the document that serves as the primary source for a consideration of cultural rights as international rights.[12] Subsequent interpretive documents provide their guidance for international consideration of cultural rights based on this covenant. Though cultural rights are not explicitly defined in this covenant, they are clearly tied to conservation and development. Culture is taken up in four articles in the covenant.

> Article 1.1:
> All peoples have the right to self-determination. By virtue of that right, they freely determine their political status, and freely pursue their economic, social and cultural development.
>
> Article 3:
> The States [*sic*] Parties to the present Covenant undertake to ensure the equal right of men and women to the enjoyment of all economic social and cultural rights set forth in the present Covenant.
>
> Article 6.2:
> The steps to be taken by a State Party to the present Covenant to achieve the full realization of this right [the right to work] shall include technical and vocational

guidance and training programmes, policies and techniques to achieve steady economic, social and cultural development and full and productive employment under conditions safeguarding fundamental political and economic freedoms to the individual.

Article 15:

1. The States Parties to the present Covenant recognize the right of everyone:
   (a) To take part in cultural life;
   (b) To enjoy the benefits of scientific progress and its applications;
   (c) To benefit from the protection of the moral and the material interests resulting from any scientific, literary, or artistic production of which he is the author.
2. The steps to be taken by the States Parties to the present Covenant to achieve the full realization of this right shall include those necessary for the conservation, the development and the diffusion of science and culture.
3. The States Parties to the present Covenant undertake to respect the freedom indispensable for scientific research and creative activity.
4. The States Parties to the present Covenant recognize the benefits to be derived from the encouragement and development of international contacts and co-operation in the scientific and cultural fields.

Cultural rights are referred to as well, though again are not defined, in the International Covenant on Civil and Political Rights of 1966 and in the more recent United Nations Educational, Scientific, and Cultural Organization (UNESCO) Convention for the Safeguarding of the Intangible Cultural Heritage of 2003.

The fact that cultural rights are underarticulated in these legal documents is not surprising. Understandings of culture vary in and between arenas of discourse, whether those forums be social, academic, political, legal, or otherwise. In her article on cultural rights and world trade agreements, Shalini Venturelli recognizes that "cultural concepts, either in intellectual history or in social discourse, are always ambiguous and contradictory, with the lines between conceptualizations very thinly drawn, allowing for considerable overlap and transitional processes."[13] Further, a definition of cultural rights is contingent on understandings of what culture is and to whom it belongs. Though cultural rights are perhaps not the most plentifully studied of human rights, there is literature in which important movements toward clarification of understanding is taking place.[14]

Let us turn our attention now to the recently approved United Nations Declaration on the Rights of Indigenous Peoples.[15] In this document, the drafters are more specific about what they mean by cultural rights as they seek to confer noted individual rights to groups in relation to their culture. The following articles taken from that declaration illustrate:

Article 11

1. Indigenous peoples have the right to practise and revitalize their cultural traditions and customs. This includes the right to maintain, protect and develop the past, present and future manifestations of their cultures, such as archaeological and historical sites, artefacts, designs, ceremonies, technologies and visual and performing arts and literature.
2. States shall provide redress through effective mechanisms, which may include restitution, developed in conjunction with indigenous peoples, with respect to their cultural, intellectual, religious and spiritual property taken without their free, prior and informed consent or in violation of their laws, traditions and customs.

Article 31

1. Indigenous peoples have the right to maintain, control, protect and develop their cultural heritage, traditional knowledge and traditional cultural expressions, as well as the manifestations of their sciences, technologies and cultures, including human and genetic resources, seeds, medicines, knowledge of the properties of fauna and flora, oral traditions, literatures, designs, sports and traditional games and visual and performing arts. They also have the right to maintain, control, protect and develop their intellectual property over such cultural heritage, traditional knowledge, and traditional cultural expressions.
2. In conjunction with indigenous peoples, States shall take effective measures to recognize and protect the exercise of these rights.

The inclusion of rights related to intellectual property signals that the drafters of the document were abreast of copyright and industrial property laws. It also points to an attempt to gain the rights conferred to individuals in such laws for indigenous peoples as a group.

There are three rights being asserted in these articles. The first is articulated in the beginning part of Article 11: "Indigenous peoples have the right to practise and revitalize their cultural traditions and customs." This right is echoed in the Universal Declaration of Human Rights, but for all persons, not indigenous peoples in particular. The second cultural right that the declaration seeks to confer has to do with restitution, as noted in point 2 of Article 11.[16] The third cultural right relates to ownership and control and is articulated in Article 31. Where an author or inventor through protections delineated in IP laws is entitled to the recognition and full ownership, control, and protection of his or her intellectual property, here these rights are sought for groups toward their "cultural" and intellectual property. The cultural property is noted to include an array of disciplines, resources, knowledge, and practices, from sciences and technologies to genetic resources and know-how and the visual and performing arts.

A number of gatherings regionally, nationally, and internationally made up substantially of delegates from indigenous communities have been convened since the early 1980s through the present.[17] Reports emerging from such meetings have similar goals as the 2007 declaration—to assist indigenous peoples in their attempts to gain political sovereignty as well as control over the interpretation and disposition of their cultural heritage.

There is a precedent in the history of revisions to the Berne Convention for us to allow such a backdrop to serve as a legally binding understanding of cultural rights as intellectual property rights. Strides have been made at various times to address the needs and expectations of indigenous peoples in the treaty. An important revision came in 1967 with the Stockholm Act. Article 15(4) was added, granting governments the right to appoint a competent authority to stand for the author in the event that the author is unknown but deemed to be a citizen of the country. Authorial rights could then be conferred and enforced. Efforts were then undertaken in both WIPO and UNESCO to develop sample model laws to assist developing countries in the revision of their own domestic laws in order to attend to their concerns regarding folklore. Two such documents are notable: the Tunis Model Law on Copyright for Developing Countries (1976) and the Model Provisions for National Laws on the Protection of Expressions of Folklore against Illicit Exploitation and Other Prejudicial Actions (1982). Inquiries have been made into the effective use of these models by the committee attending to global issues at WIPO. Results from the questionnaire show that the Model Provisions are underutilized.[18]

Although cultural rights are taken up for the most part in conventions that are not legally binding, the impact of UN conventions and declarations as well as other regional and national declarations cannot be underestimated. States' practices have been shaped by values held therein, and, combined with judicial interpretations of stated provisions in practice, a significant impact on international customary law can be noted.[19] The development of a Permanent Forum on Indigenous Issues, likewise, bears witness to significant shifts in thinking and attitude related to the needs and expectations of indigenous peoples.[20]

Individual Rights and *African Sanctus*

Regarding individual rights violations in the *African Sanctus* project, perhaps most conspicuous in Fanshawe's account are issues related to the recording and commercial release of a private moment. As Fanshawe remembers, "I recorded them for half an hour and they never knew I had been there." The singers had gone to a remote place to pray. They were not performing, and certainly not for an audience. Yet, through Fanshawe's recording, their voices were incorporated into an electro-acoustic work that is performed regularly in concerts and has been released on compact disc—at least two different versions of the complete work and an accompanying source-material recording.[21] The first issue concerns a right to privacy. This entitlement is asserted in the Universal Declaration of Human Rights. Consider Article 12: "No one shall be subjected to arbitrary interference with his privacy, family, home or correspondence, nor to attacks upon his honour and reputation. Everyone has the right to the protection of the law against such interference or attacks." The Rome Convention, the international treaty related to the rights of performers, broadcasters, and producers of phonograms, recognizes three specific ways in which this violation of privacy is to be prevented for performers in Article 7: "1) The protection provided for performers by this convention shall include the possibility of preventing: a) the broadcasting and the communication to the public, without their consent, of their performance except where the performance used in the broadcasting or the public communication is itself already a broadcast performance or is made from a fixation; b) the fixation, without their consent, of their unfixed performance; c) the reproduction, without their consent, of a fixation of their performance."

Another concern that surfaces in *African Sanctus,* specific to artistic expression, is that of a lack of proper attribution on the recordings.[22] Royalties, likewise, will not be forthcoming for the performers' contribution. The practice of leaving performers of traditional musics out of the monetary loop has been an unfortunate aspect of much of the recording industry's history.[23]

But missing royalties are just one aspect of financial loss in mainstream projects where traditional musics feature prominently. In 1996, Ralph Oman, former registrar of the United States Copyright Office (September 1985–January 1994), addressed the issue of commercial gain involving music from indigenous communities from his perspective in an article he wrote for the *Intellectual Property Law Newsletter:* "They [representatives of developing countries] watched with a growing sense of frustration as foreign composers visited, carefully studied, and in some cases recorded the country's rich folkloric music, and then rushed back home to use these rhythms and harmonies to write hit songs or symphonies which enjoyed full copyright protection. Meanwhile, the interpretive performers, the village bards, the travelling troubadours, and the wandering minstrels, who have created these original variations of works derived from traditions with deep roots in the culture, get neither credit, nor money, nor protection for their creative expression."[24]

It is heartening to read in the liner notes to the 1994 recording of *African Sanctus* that "a proportion of royalties from the sale of this is to be given to

International Aid Organisations for the benefit of Africa." This is a positive gesture, especially insofar as the performers cannot be located. Fanshawe attests to his attempts in this regard in program notes to the Vancouver Symphony Orchestra performance in 2001 benefiting South Africa and the AIDS epidemic there: "Out of respect for the African musicians represented in African Sanctus, David Fanshawe gives four per cent of his personal royalties from CD sales to African AIDS organisations. Sadly, this is the only way he can acknowledge and share with the people he recorded in African Sanctus. Many of the musicians have now died, either from AIDS, natural causes or, in many cases, from the civil wars that have wracked the continent. 'I know that,' he said, 'I've gone back and tried to find them.' In a sense, African Sanctus has become an unintentional requiem."[25]

There is a need for us to put this discussion in historical context. We are exploring notions regarding rights delineated in modern legal documents. Did the protections for performers in place today exist in 1973 when Fanshawe released his recording? Certainly, the Rome Convention was in place, having entered into force in 1961, and Fanshawe's native England was one of the first to ratify it. The dilemma with Fanshawe's recording appears clear-cut upon reading Article 7 from the Rome Convention above, until it is understood that performers were protected by the law only if the music they performed was protected. The music these singers sang was not considered a "literary or artistic work" eligible for protection in the Rome Convention. Since the music was not protected, neither were the performers.[26] This circumstance has been remedied in the 1994 WPPT, which allows performers of folklore to enjoy the same rights as performers of copyrighted works.[27]

In this regard, Fanshawe did not conduct himself dishonorably according to his own cultural norms, apart from the privacy issue. However, the fact that he was within the law does not mitigate the emotional responses that surface for many when considering the project. The Rome Convention, for instance, does not distinguish between types of performers but rather does not recognize rights for any performer when that performer renders non-copyrighted works. Would Fanshawe have as readily dismissed Plácido Domingo's performer's rights had he secretly recorded him singing folklore? Instinctively, I suggest he probably would not. I have not posed this question to Fanshawe yet, but I have discussed it with a number of composer colleagues here in the United States. The discussions are always emotional and bring up important ethical concerns regarding personal and professional entitlements. If time is taken to sift and sort through the various emotions that surface, the possibility arises for a reconsideration of professional standards and conduct in our present age, as well as of the legal systems themselves that help shape conduct.

Concerning individual rights in *African Sanctus*, the primary issues are those of an invasion of privacy and a disregard for the performers' rights, even though a strict reading of the prevailing convention disregards these particular performers.

Cultural Rights and *African Sanctus*

Cultural rights, by the manner in which they are used in the various conventions mentioned, are understood to pertain to inalienable rights that a cultural group has to express and develop their culture. There is also the more controversial but significant aspect that relates to the entitlements that a cultural group has to claim ownership and control the disposition of their cultural heritage. If moral rights are included, cultural groups would also have some control over interpretation.

When adapting the rights afforded individuals regarding their creations to the cultural group regarding their cultural heritage, concerns that surfaced for individuals are now present for the cultural group at large. For instance, the issue of permission acquisition, or a lack thereof, from the singers in the Credo reemerges now, but with more layers. Did Fanshawe, for instance, play this recording for the broader community and seek their permission for its use? I do not have the answer to this question to date. We do know that Fanshawe at least sought permission from the government of Sudan for his use of the recordings made in that country. We also know that he did not acquire permission from the performers—certainly in the Credo, and perhaps in other recordings made for the project as well.

The permission he sought from the government may not have been a satisfactory solution, for those recorded contentious relationships between governments and indigenous nationals are common across the globe. Certainly, such relationships have been present throughout Sudan's history, from the Islamic invasion in the Middle Ages through to the present day. Erica-Irene Daes speaks to the phenomenon for indigenous peoples in general in her report on the discrimination of indigenous peoples. She notes that members of indigenous communities are "usually viewed as 'backward' by Governments," and as such, "they have been the targets of aggressive policies of cultural assimilation."[28] Cultural rights would lie with those whose culture one is seeking to use. Likewise, all economic rights for the use of a cultural expression would lie with the cultural group.

When the moral rights conferred on individuals in the Berne Convention (Article 6) are attributed to cultural groups, these groups enjoy rights to "claim authorship; [and] to object to certain modifications and other derogatory actions." Questions related to interpretation would then come into play.

One aspect in *African Sanctus* related to interpretation that causes me pause is the absorption of this recitation from the Koran into a work modeled on the Latin Mass. This Koranic recitation is "strange" and unfamiliar to Fanshawe. The mixture of local dialects and Arabic is described by him also as "strange." He is not from West Sudan, where certainly the language and, depending on local custodial roles, the music and song texts, too, perhaps, would be familiar. The Sudanese singers cannot speak to any of this, however, as they are not engaged in any direct way. As Fanshawe creates his own context for the music and then recontextualizes the moment by incorporating it into a Credo of the Latin Eucharistic Liturgy, he ascribes to the performers what Rosemary Coombe would call a "mythical and inarticulate status in the writer's imagination."[29] Certainly, his expression is an authentic expression for him. How closely it mirrors, or not, the experience of the Sudanese holy men is another question. As Fanshawe recounts, "The driving force of [*African Sanctus*] is one of 'Praise' and a firm belief in 'One God.'"[30] Islam and the Judeo-Christian tradition share much in common. At the same time, conflicts between people of these different faiths are well known, with battles at times fueled on religious grounds. Nowhere, perhaps, is this truer than in Sudan, where civil unrest was raging at the time of Fanshawe's travels, and along both ethnic and religious lines. The sentiments expressed in Fanshawe's goal attest to a strong ecumenical spirit and desire for global harmony. The appeal of such a goal is affirmed in review after review of the project.[31] Yet, the politics between peoples renders the absorption of an Islamic recitation into the framework of this Western Christian form troubling for me. Unfortunately, the singers in the Credo, at this point, cannot speak to their approval or disapproval of the use of their Koranic recitation in this context.

Concerning cultural rights, then, in *African Sanctus,* the primary issues are: 1) disregard for the rights of those in the cultural group to determine how their cultural heritage will be used; 2) absence of a means to repatriation of recordings of their performance in the event that those in the cultural group do not agree with its use; and 3) inattention to the obligation, insofar as a cultural group has economic and moral entitlements, to provide benefits to the group directly from sales.

An Exploration of Contexts

At this point, we have teased out a few of the more salient issues embedded in the short quotation Fanshawe provides regarding the Credo of his *African Sanctus.* The issues have legal and ethical components and bring a few questions to the surface. I present the questions first through one lens that clearly finds Fanshawe's posture problematic: 1) What is it that allows for a distancing of a musical expression from those who make and use it? 2) How are outsiders able to engage the music of a people without engaging the people? 3) What is it that prompts a composer who uses music from a foreign land to present the music in a brand-new context, dismissing or ignoring the social, religious, and cultural requirements regarding its use in that land? I suggest that answers to these questions can be found embedded in Western views regarding private property and the public domain, commodification, and the place of image—especially the exotic image—in the marketplace.

Now let me reframe my three questions, here peering through a different lens: 1) What is it that makes the distancing of a musical expression from those who make and use it unacceptable to someone? 2) What is it that makes the engagement of people, or people and their music, preferable to an engagement of the music alone? 3) Why is it problematic to use sounds that one encounters in the world—especially those considered to be in the public domain—outside of their cultural contexts? Why, especially, would it be considered problematic if the composer isn't claiming to reflect traditional authenticities? Possible answers to these questions can be found in worldviews in which a holistic approach to life is practiced, where public enterprise and human relationships are valued more highly than private enterprise and the market, and where the arts are sometimes recognized as agents in their own right and hence require special care and regulation. I do not wish to set up binary oppositions by asking the questions in this way. I do not think such an approach is helpful. Rather, I am seeking to turn each question in upon itself in order to explore the possibilities of multiple frameworks simultaneously.

No system is airtight or static. Any framework is, at the same time, a container and a crucible. It seems to me that, while allowing for diversity, a new, wider, and all-inclusive container is necessary in a global environment.

Framework No. 1—The Market Paradigm

The first framework I will discuss is one in which it is normal to engage music one encounters without necessarily engaging those who make it. We can get an idea of how interpersonal engagement is understood and practiced in the Western context by looking at artistic codes of conduct, legal norms, and market practice.

ARTISTIC CODES OF CONDUCT As a composer in twentieth-century England, Fanshawe inherited professional standards—that is, standards within his musical profession—in which certain kinds of musical borrowings were deemed to be appropriate and others not, and he operated within these guidelines. Using preexisting materials in new works is a practice evident in every era of Western musical history and has served a number of different musical and social purposes. These might include modeling for purposes of learning or honoring the work of another, parody, homage, referencing musical ideas or trends or meanings, quotation, postmodern recontextualizations, and pastiche—all are examples of appropriate borrowings in the Western context.[32] Artistically, Fanshawe's behavior was consistent with his tradition.

LEGAL NORMS Legally, the incorporation of a musical sample of traditional African culture in a new work by David Fanshawe was sanctioned by the Berne Convention.[33] As noted above, literary and artistic works that have no named author, are not fixed in material form, exceed term limits for protections, and/or are not sufficiently "original" are considered to be ineligible for copyright protections and, in common parlance, are said to reside in the public domain. These musics are available for use in new works and adaptations or arrangements. In the international arena, the fact that traditional musics are not eligible for protections—insofar as there is often no identifiable author, they are often passed on from generation to generation orally and hence have exceeded all term limits, and often are not deemed novel due to their prized adherence to a tradition—means that they are available for use, at least in the eyes and ears of those who appeal to the Berne Convention.

As it stands, the music David Fanshawe encountered in West Sudan fit none of the necessary criteria for copyright protection. Fanshawe did not need to seek authorization for using music considered to be in the public domain. There were no specifications, then, in Fanshawe's professional or legislative worlds suggesting that he should have engaged with the musicians who made the music he wanted to use.

MARKET PRACTICES: LICENSING The Western market practices of publishing, transfer of copyright, and licensing can provide further occasions for the disengagement of artists. For instance, I am a composer. Many of my compositions are published by publishing firms that I do not own or run. Copyright rests with them for my works. This is standard practice except for those who publish their own works or who negotiate a different relationship with their publisher, usually with the assistance of a lawyer. A publisher as copyright holder can grant a license to a third party who seeks to do a new arrangement, record the composition, recontextualize the work, and so forth. I need not be contacted for such permissions to be made, and usually am not. Others can engage my work and never engage me. It is interesting to consider that, because Fanshawe retains copyright for *African Sanctus*, others must get permission from him to license a recontextualization of the African recordings he made.

MARKET PRACTICES: IMAGE-MAKING David Fanshawe placed the music of the Sudanese singers in a new context by embedding their voices via his recording in a Latin Mass. Others can, with license (or not, though unauthorized use would be illegal), recontextualize his *African Sanctus,* or the recordings themselves. In this sense, recontextualization is linked to the legal apparatus. Artistically, however, recontextualization involves the pursuit of a fresh presentation. In the Western market, especially in the pop music world and entertainment industry, this is often framed as "image." Here, artists accept, and often invent, fictions about themselves and their art in order to create an image that will more effectively market their product by appealing to the tastes of their public. Within this market-driven framework, titillating, bizarre, mysterious fabrications make perfect sense. Exotic fictions are part and parcel of the practice of image-making and, quite frankly, can be fun. Many industry agents would contend that if a particular packaging of indigenous culture appeals to the consumer, even if it does not resonate with any meanings for those who create and sustain it, that's acceptable and actually preferable if it sells products.

These new products—sounds one would not encounter in the local context—are often the ones circulating in the marketplace. They not only define nonlocal impressions of a culture but, through transnational exchange, can even redefine local practices and, in turn, local identities.

We have here, then, a framework in which it is common practice to engage music and not necessarily those who make it through use of musics in the public domain, through market practices such as licensing, and through participation in an industry that operates according to agreed-upon artistic codes of conduct.

Framework No. 2—A Paradigm Featuring the Primacy of Relationships

The second framework is one in which it is often objectionable to engage music one encounters without engaging those who make it.

CUSTOMARY LAWS Much of what Fanshawe deemed available for his use may not have been deemed so by community members whose music he recorded. Customary laws in traditional societies around the world often impose stringent restrictions on composition, performance, use, and reception of cultural materials. These restrictions, of course, vary from region to region and community to community. In his article regarding African customary law and the protection of folklore, Paul Kuruk addresses the nature of African customary law: "Customary law consists of the indigenous customs of traditional communities. Every ethnic group in Africa has evolved its own discrete customary legal system of rules that are binding on its members. Unlike ordinary social habits and observances, the rules carry along with them local sanctions for their breach. For the most part, the rules are unwritten, though efforts are now being made to compile them in written form."[34] Kuruk also addresses the reality that customary laws are not static. Rather, they are marked by a dynamic flexibility in which rules change to adapt to changing social and economic conditions.

Regarding music, he states:

> Generally, rights to folklore are vested in particular segments of African communities and exercised under carefully circumscribed conditions. For instance, with regard to song, the recitation of *oriki,* a praise singing poetry among the Yoruba in Nigeria, is restricted to certain families. Among the Lozi in Zimbabwe, each traditional leader has his own praise songs containing both historical lore and proverbial wisdom that are recited on important occasions by a select group of bandsmen. In some communities, precise rules govern who can make, or play certain musical instruments, at what time and for what reasons they are played. Thus, the great national drums of the Lozi which are beaten only for war, or in national emergencies, are kept under watchful eyes of a special council of elders. Each Baganda king in Uganda has a select group of drummers who play special drums to ensure the permanency of his office. Among the Bahima of Uganda, only women keep harps while the Banyankole authorize only women to make harps which they use at home. Among the Baganda, fifes are owned and played mainly by herd boys. In Nigeria, certain musical instruments are dedicated to the use of particular cults.[35]

J. H. Kwabena Nketia speaks to the importance of context in African ceremonial and festival music:

> Implied in the internal organization of musical items and musical types is the exercise of some measure of social control. The music for a rite, a ceremony, or festival may not normally be performed in another context unless there is some special reason for doing so. On the same basis, the choice of musical resources—for example, the use of musical instruments—may be regulated; special drums not used elsewhere may be set aside for the worship of the divinities, while musical instruments dedicated to kings may not be played for individuals. Where the same instruments are used, the repertoire may be different. Furthermore, the type of performance allowed for different occasions or situations may be controlled. . . . Sometimes the schedule of musical activities is related to the

> beliefs of a community—to the wishes of the gods they worship or to the reactions evoked from the spirits and forces that are believed to play a vital role in the drama of human existence. Among the Lele of Kasai, for example, rules about drums are enforced by religious sanctions. Drumming is a legitimate nighttime activity, and may occur in full daylight only on days of rest; during periods of mourning that may last up to three months, dance drums may not be beaten in this particular village.[36] Similarly, in Ga society, drumming is banned for three weeks before the annual harvest festival begins.[37]

Of course, more examples are available from all around the globe, with specific examples from each community possible.

Because Fanshawe's *African Sanctus* journey spanned from the Mediterranean to Lake Victoria and from the mountains of West Sudan to the Red Sea, his recordings archive the musics of numerous tribes, each with their own customary laws. To be certain that he respects those laws, more than government approval is necessary.

In at least one important way, customary laws and national copyright laws are alike. Through prescriptions of conditions and formalities, each sets up a framework within which people can (or cannot) engage musics in their culture. Through compliance with standards and protocols for engagement, behaviors are defined and shaped and become normative. Laws reflect shared values.

THE INTERRELATIONSHIPS WITHIN THE NATURAL/SUPERNATURAL WORLDS

One characteristic value for many traditional societies is that of the interrelationships within the natural world of all living things, the spirit realm, and the land. Creations that emerge from these relationships are held in high esteem. The Working Group on Indigenous Peoples from the Office for the High Commissioner of Human Rights (OHCHR) at the United Nations describes it succinctly:

> Indigenous peoples regard all products of the human mind and heart as interrelated, and as flowing from the same source: the relationships between the people and their land, their kinship with other living creatures that share the land, and with the spirit world.[38]
>
> Possessing a song, story or medicinal knowledge carries with it certain responsibilities to show respect to, and maintain a reciprocal relationship with, the human beings, animals, plants and places with which the song, story or medicine is connected. For indigenous peoples, heritage is a bundle of relationships, rather than a bundle of economic rights.[39]

In this context, the focus is not on the individual but on the group. Permission for use is not conferred according to individual rights but according to an individual's role within and for the community. Permissions for use come with responsibilities. The "rights language" of copyright law is not adequate to capture these realities.

I have a personal example from another region on the African continent: Ghana. In the summer of 1997, while learning songs from Zablong Zakania Abdallah, master drummer of the Dagomba tribe of northern Ghana, I asked to learn the verses of one of the traditional songs. He told me that these songs are not for public consumption. I explained that my interest was educational—that I had no intentions of sharing it commercially. He thought carefully for a few moments, then suggested that there was perhaps a way I could learn the songs: I could move to Ghana, to his village, and live there with his family for a number of years—roughly twelve. At the point I was accepted and incorporated into the family of drummers, I could learn these verses, songs sung only for the Yanna, the chief leader of the tribe.[40] Abdallah is a custodian. Clearly he takes his position seriously, realizing his role is essential to the well-being of his tribe.

Of course, not all traditional musics are ceremonial, though even non-ceremonial musics—as noted above—can have regulations regarding their creation, performance, and reception. What became evident in that moment with Zablong Zakania Abdallah for me is that musics can be intimately tied to people and to a group's cultural identity. Restrictions placed on these musics help shape roles and social structure for those who recognize them. When these musics are sounded outside of an intended context without permission, and hence with a disregard for the music's cultural significance for those who created and sustain it, relationships are affected. And as noted by Daes above, not only human relationships are affected but also relationships with any animals, plants, and places with which the music is connected.

Sherylle Mills provides another layer to this notion of relationship by speaking to music's power for many native peoples: "Traditional communities . . . frequently ascribe vast powers to their music: the power to heal sickness, create bountiful game, cause lightning to strike, kill, and, in one case, free a man from prison. With such immense powers, it is logical to carefully restrict and regulate the use, rather than financial profits, of music."[41]

The music Mills describes goes beyond "product." When this music is separated from the people who use it, from those who are to be affected by it, and from the spirits that attach to it through ritual or ceremony, then the society suffers. Does anyone else have "rights" to such cultural materials? Where governments might grant permission for their taking and copyright treaties may give access through designations of these musics as being unauthored, "unoriginal," and unfixed, customary laws restrict access. Though it is highly probable that a number of the recordings Fanshawe made were not of musics that carried ritual "powers," his status as an outsider without the ability to communicate with the musicians places him in a vulnerable position of not knowing.

This second framework, then, is one in which music is an integral part in a network of relationships. Here, it is important—sometimes crucial—to engage directly with those who create and sustain music one wishes to use.

Framework No. 3—Toward a New Global Paradigm

The third framework is one that I envision will be a structure in which cross-cultural appropriation respectfully works.

INTERNATIONAL LAW—ON WHOSE TERMS? Currently, rights that are honored through international law—rights of authors in particular, for our purposes—are disregarded in the indigenous context because authors often cannot be named and/or the music is deemed to be ineligible for protections based on criteria developed in the Western context. In fact, though customary law might restrict use, our international copyright treaty sanctions it, and our treaty promoting trade liberalization champions it. It is for these reasons that I consider the Berne Convention and the TRIPS agreement as instruments that not only allow but in some measure actually facilitate—at least as they are currently employed—appropriation of indigenous musics, however unwittingly. What is missing are nonproprietary emphases. As Rosemary Coombe expresses it, "Too much of the world's creativity is unrecognized, and when it is recognized, our global intellectual property regimes provide rights without recognizing the responsibilities that many peoples in the world hold—responsibilities to others, to their ancestors, to future generations, and to the plants, animals, and spirits that occupy and animate the worlds they inhabit."[42]

The TRIPS accord has come under attack in recent years by advocates for developing nations due to its emphasis on proprietary rights over and above rights to cultural development. Willem Pretorius notes the power imbalance in the passing of TRIPS: "TRIPS was a triumph for the pharmaceutical community in particular, and for the intellectual property exporting countries generally. The developing countries, on the other hand, were clearly outgunned by the army of experts advising the negotiators of then developed countries and the end result for these countries was unsatisfactory, to say the least. First and foremost it removed the ability of these countries to balance their particular developmental need with the need for the protection of intellectual property rights."[43] Pretorius is quite compelling in this article, recounting the skewed negotiations at the Uruguay Round where TRIPS was passed and the failed attempts of developing countries to keep intellectual property out of the GATT. Now, as developing countries scramble to make their national copyright laws TRIPS-compliant, they find themselves obliged to adjust their laws or develop new ones to fit a legal apparatus that does not uphold values reflected in their culture. Nowhere, perhaps, has this problem been more pointed than in the Novartis-India patent lawsuit.[44] As I mentioned above, although the greatest impact to date of the TRIPS accord has in fact been in the realm of biodiversity and pharmaceuticals, the impact in regard to cultural expressions is profound. This is true particularly in the ways in which TRIPS has shaped copyright laws and reinforced views of literary and artistic expressions as singularly "products," dismissing through neglect various other aspects of music's value and import for so many.[45]

For roughly the past four decades, native activists in nearly every geopolitical arena have been seeking access to copyright protections. The hope is to gain some control over the disposition and interpretation of their cultural heritage. In many ways, this is a logical step, at least in the realm of artistic works, where like items are protected in the first world. Yet, whether or not copyright protections make sense in the realm of traditional musics is a big question.[46] In fact, there are many examining the ways that copyright is being exercised in general in the arts, principally in the United States. These advocates for creative artists are seeking to cleanse an overlitigated culture of corporate greed while simultaneously attempting to reclaim a vital and burgeoning public domain from which artists can draw for new creations. I am sympathetic to these views.[47] If and how IP laws, then, should or even could be applied to traditional expressions and enforced are central queries present on agendas of all forums addressing this issue.[48]

My interest in looking at the law and at the efforts of WIPO now is not to discuss the merits of such a direction or the inherent possibilities or impossibilities held out there. Rather, I am attracted to the notion that laws in general reflect values of those who create them as well as shape behaviors and worldviews. In this sense, law is ritual. It expresses a value held in common and, through compliance, forms us. I am also interested in observing how, when views and values foreign to those who shaped the laws are brought to the table, these instruments change or do not change. In this regard, the law becomes a symbol of successful or failed negotiations.

People who structure their lives in vastly different ways are being brought together over the desire to use and/or protect traditional culture. Those who live according to the law of copyright, to date, have been able to glean the benefits of the copyright system—their system—without responsibilities to other systems. What will it take to create a larger container—a larger framework—where diverse values can coexist and be respectfully acknowledged? I sense that a possible answer may come in view by exploring the process underway in the Intergovernmental Committee (IGC) on Intellectual Property and Genetic Resources, Traditional Knowledge and Folklore of WIPO.

WIPO AND THE IGC WIPO is the specialized agency of the United Nations that administers the international treaty related to copyright. An intergovernmental committee, the IGC, was established by the WIPO General Assembly in October 2000 as a forum for dialogue regarding the intersection between IP and genetic resources, traditional knowledge, and traditional cultural expressions. Their renewed mandate calls for the IGC to add to its agenda consideration of the international dimension of its work, not excluding the possibility of the development of an international instrument, or instruments.[49] What I find heartening in recent pursuits of the organization is the manner in which different principles and objectives for protections have been delineated. These principles and objectives reflect values other than those that prop up the current copyright system.

In the seventh season of the IGC (November 1–5, 2004), the committee began discussion of a document prepared by the secretariat of WIPO at the request of the members entitled Protection of Traditional Cultural Expressions/Expressions of Folklore: Overview of Policy Objectives and Core Principles, and discussion continued in the following five sessions.[50] Many of the values reflected in the document are different from those that underlie the international copyright treaty. To entertain objectives and principles so blatantly out of step with those propping up the current system begs for a deep kind of listening and for ample doses of human imagination. Whether or not consensus will be achieved remains to be seen. The process itself attracts me. That these different values can be presented and discussed in an international forum dedicated to the prospect of developing legal mechanisms that address the needs and expectations of current copyright holders and traditional practitioners alike is encouraging. It holds out promise for the development of new instruments that may actually provide a fresh and more respectful cross-cultural paradigm for the use of and protections for cultural materials.

Let me give a brief example of what I mean regarding values reflected in standing international law and how they contrast with values reflected in the IGC documents. When reading the Berne Convention, I note that Article 2 of the 1886 treaty reads: “The country of origin of the work shall be considered to be that in which the work is first published, or if such publication takes place simultaneously in several countries of the Union, that one of them the laws of which grant the shortest term of protection." One possible understanding of the consensus of this working group is that a robust public domain is valuable.

"Terms of protection" are taken up in Article 6 of the Annex to the IGC's revised document on the policy objectives and core principles for the protection of folklore.[51] In the commentary on Article 6, it reads:

> Many indigenous peoples and traditional communities desire indefinite protection for at least some aspects of expressions of their traditional cultures. Calls for indefinite protection are closely linked to calls for retroactive protection. . . . On the other hand, it is generally seen as integral to the balance within the IP system that the term of protection not be indefinite, so that works ultimately enter the public domain. The suggested provision embodies a trademark-like emphasis on current use, so that once the community that the TCE [traditional cultural expression] is characteristic of no longer uses the TCE or no longer exists as a distinct entity (analogous to abandonment of a trademark, or a trademark becoming generic), protection for the TCE would lapse. Such an approach draws upon the very essence of the subject matter of protection, it being recalled that at the heart of TCEs/EoF [expressions of folklore] is that they are characteristic of and identify a community. . . . When a TCE ceases to do so, it ceases by definition to be a TCE and it follows that protection should lapse. In addition to this general principle, specific provision is made for the term of protection of two categories, namely those TCEs/EoF which are registered or notified and those that are secret, undisclosed or confidential.

The subject matter of protection referred to in this commentary relates to those items noted in Article 1 in the Annex to the document. They are significantly different from items recognized in the Berne Convention and are worth noting in their entirety here:

> (a) "Traditional cultural expressions" or "expressions of folklore" are any forms, whether tangible and intangible, in which traditional culture and knowledge are expressed, appear or are manifested, and comprise the following forms of expressions or combinations thereof:
> (i) verbal expressions, such as stories, epics, legends, poetry, riddles and other narratives; words, signs, names, and symbols;
> (ii) musical expressions, such as songs and instrumental music;
> (iii) expressions by action, such as dances, plays, ceremonies, rituals and other performances, whether or not reduced to a material form; and
> (iv) tangible expressions such as productions of art, in particular drawings, designs, paintings (including body-painting), carvings, sculptures, pottery, terracotta, mosaic, woodwork, metalware, jewelry, baskets, needlework, textiles,

> glassware, carpets, costumes; handicrafts; musical instruments; and architectural forms;
> which are:
> — (aa) the products of creative intellectual activity, including individual and communal activity;
> — (bb) characteristic of a community's cultural and social identity and cultural heritage; and
> — (cc) maintained, used or developed by such community, or by individuals having the right or responsibility to do so in accordance with the customary law and practices of that community.
>
> (b) The specific choice of terms to denote the protected subject matter should be determined at the national and regional levels.[52]

This is vastly different from Berne. First, the creators may be individual or communal; the artistic expressions may be tangible or intangible and may or may not be reduced to a material form; and, most significant, these expressions are considered subject matter for protection if they are characteristic of a community's cultural and social identity and heritage—maintained, used, and developed by that community or the custodians for that community.[53] Second, the terms for protection, keeping in mind the desire for a strong public domain, shall reflect a prioritization of a community's right to retain control over those cultural expressions that characterize the community and sustain members' sense of identity.

To itemize each principle and objective in the WIPO document here would add fifty pages to this chapter. I mention these two principles—of subject matter and term limits—to illustrate new ideas that are being brought to the table as the IGC seeks to address the needs and expectations of indigenous peoples while attempting to adapt the IP apparatus to their lives. These principles reflect the values laid out in the policy objectives on the first page of the Annex. There are thirteen objectives. According to the document, the protection of traditional cultural expressions, or expressions of culture, should, in part, aim to

> meet the actual needs of community. [It should aim to] be guided by the aspirations and expectations expressed directly by indigenous peoples and by traditional and other cultural communities, respect their rights under national and international law, and contribute to the welfare and sustainable economic, cultural, environmental and social development of such peoples and communities. . . . [The protection of TCEs/EoF should aim to] prevent the misappropriation of traditional cultural expressions/expressions of folklore. . . . [It should aim to] provide indigenous peoples and traditional and other cultural communities with the legal and practical means, including effective enforce-

> ment measures, to prevent the misappropriation of their cultural expressions and derivatives therefrom, control ways in which they are used beyond the customary and traditional context and promote the equitable sharing of benefits arising from their use.[54]

What would be an appropriate legal mechanism to reflect this value? This is what the IGC is setting out to determine, and the principles and objectives are providing a template of values upon which a new legal apparatus might be based. A document that includes such items as these principles and objectives presents in no uncertain terms a new backdrop for the development of a very different code reflecting values underrepresented in current binding instruments. For a document like this to emerge from the institution that currently administers the international copyright convention is significant. Those who have enjoyed the benefits of use sanctioned by the Berne Convention in conjunction with national laws are no longer able to operate in isolation, ignorant of different systems or values. Insofar as the "other" is now certainly known, those who support the current protections as they stand must choose to allow for revisions or for an overhaul of the conventions or must dismiss the other point of view, overtly.

As of late, I am conscious of a dangerous transformation point at which the protective fence erected to safeguard something precious within its boundaries becomes a border checkpoint through which one must successfully pass in order to be deemed worthy of acknowledgment. When we realize that we have moved from the point of safeguarding rights to the point of requiring assimilation in return for the reward of those rights, it is time to review the values we espouse in the binding frameworks we uphold and, if necessary, to entertain radical change.

Notes

I am grateful to Andrew Weintraub and Bell Yung for their insightful comments on the first draft of this paper.

1. David Fanshawe, liner notes to *African Sanctus, Salaams* CD, Philips D—105578, 1973, 7.

2. The definition of "indigenous" is not unanimously agreed upon. In January 2004, the secretariat of the UN Permanent Forum on Indigenous Issues (UNPFII) prepared a background paper for the department of Economic and Social Affairs of the United Nations for a workshop on Data Collection and Disaggregation for Indigenous Peoples:

> After long consideration of the issues involved, the Special Rapporteur who prepared the above-mentioned study [the 1989 Convention concerning Indigenous and Tribal Peoples in Independent Countries, No. 169, adopted by the International Labour Orga-

nization (ILO)] offered a working definition of "indigenous communities, peoples and nations." In doing so he expressed a number of basic ideas to provide the intellectual framework for this effort, which included the right of indigenous peoples themselves to define what and who is indigenous. The working definition reads as follows: "Indigenous communities, peoples and nations are those which, having a historical continuity with pre-invasion and pre-colonial societies that developed on their territories, consider themselves distinct from other sectors of the societies now prevailing on those territories, or parts of them. They form at present non-dominant sectors of society and are determined to preserve, develop and transmit to future generations their ancestral territories, and their ethnic identity, as the basis of their continued existence as peoples, in accordance with their own cultural patterns, social institutions and legal system. This historical continuity may consist of the continuation, for an extended period reaching into the present of one or more of the following factors:

a) Occupation of ancestral lands, or at least of part of them;
b) Common ancestry with the original occupants of these lands;
c) Culture in general, or in specific manifestations (such as religion, living under a tribal system, membership of an indigenous community, dress, means of livelihood, lifestyle, etc.);
d) Language (whether used as the only language, as mother-tongue, as the habitual means of communication at home or in the family, or as the main, preferred, habitual, general or normal language);
e) Residence on certain parts of the country, or in certain regions of the world;
f) Other relevant factors.

"On an individual basis, an indigenous person is one who belongs to these indigenous populations through self-identification as indigenous (group consciousness) and is recognized and accepted by these populations as one of its members (acceptance by the group). This preserves for these communities the sovereign right and power to decide who belongs to them, without external interference." (UN Permanent Forum on Indigenous Issues, 2004/WS.1/3)

The World Intellectual Property Organization (WIPO) is grappling with terminology as well. In its documents regarding intellectual property as it relates to genetic resources, traditional knowledge, and folklore, WIPO uses a number of terms for groups who create and sustain cultural expressions, including "indigenous peoples," "traditional communities," "local communities," "cultural communities," and even "'other' communities." In the document WIPO/GRTKF/IC/8/4: Intergovernmental Committee on Intellectual Property and Genetic Resources, Traditional Knowledge and Folklore from the eighth session dated April 8, 2005, footnote 38 reads: "The broad and inclusive term 'indigenous peoples and traditional and other cultural communities,' or simply 'communities' in short, is used at this stage in these draft provisions. The use of these terms is not intended to suggest any consensus among Committee participants on the validity or appropriateness of these or other terms, and does not affect or limit the use of other terms in national or regional laws." The full text can be found on the WIPO Web site, http://www.wipo.int/meetings/en/details.jsp?meeting_id=7130 (accessed January 11, 2008). I realize that any term I might choose to identify the music I wish to consider will be problematic. Insofar as the musics

I wish to explore are those created and sustained by groups that most closely match the UNPFII definition, "indigenous" is the term I adopt.

3. The full text can be found on the Web site of the Office for the High Commissioner of Human Rights (OHCHR), http://www.un.org/Overview/rights.html (accessed January 11, 2008). Further quotes in this chapter from the declaration are from this site.

4. Many of these national laws are available electronically in the "Collection of Laws for Electronic Access" on the WIPO Web site, http://www.wipo.int/clea/en/clea_tree1 .jsp (accessed January 10, 2008).

5. Moral rights protect the personal rights of the author and his or her reputation. The full range of moral rights is not altogether clear and differs from country to country but often include rights such as the right to claim authorship of one's work or to prevent the use of one's name with a work one did not create; the right to prevent distortion, mutilation, or modifications that would be prejudicial to one's honor or reputation; the right to prevent the destruction of one's work; and the right to determine whether or not and how one's work is presented to the public.

6. WIPO, *Introduction to IP Theory and Practice* (Geneva: WIPO, 1997), 151. This view, suggesting that cultural development is directly dependent upon copyright protections, is not substantiated when considering thriving artistic activity in some traditional societies where copyright is not operative. The poor economic life of indigenous peoples often contrasts with a very rich and burgeoning cultural life marked by artistic expressions of great power and beauty that have been created and continue to come forth without IP protections.

7. The Berne Convention leaves this decision to the member states, almost all of which require it.

8. The full text can be found on the WIPO Web site, http://www.wipo.int/treaties/en/ip/berne/index.html (accessed January 11, 2008). Further quotes in this chapter from the convention are from this site.

9. Contracting parties are listed on the WIPO Web site, http://www.wipo.int/treaties/en/ShowResults.jsp?lang=en&treaty_id=15 (accessed January 22, 2009).

10. The title of the "Rome convention" is the International Convention for the Protection of Performers, Producers of Phonograms, and Broadcasting Organizations—Done at Rome on October 26, 1961. The full text can be found on the WIPO Web site, http://www.wipo.int/treaties/en/ip/rome/pdf/trtdocs_wo024.pdf (accessed January 11, 2008). Further quotes in this chapter from this convention are from this site. The full text of the WPPT is available on the WIPO Web site, http://www.wipo.int/treaties/en/ip/wppt/pdf/trtdocs_wo034.pdf (accessed January 11, 2008). Further quotes in this chapter from this treaty are from this site.

11. The full text can be found at the WTO Web site, http://www.wto.org/english/docs_e/legal_e/legal_e.htm#TRIPs (accessed January 10, 2008).

12. The full text can be found at the OHCHR Web site, http://www2.ohchr.org/english/law/cescr.htm (accessed January 10, 2008).

13. Shalini Venturelli, "Cultural Rights and World Trade Agreements in the Information Society," *International Communication Gazette* 60 (1998): 49.

14. See, for instance Jane K. Cowan, Marie-Bénédicte Dembour, and Richard A. Wilson, eds., *Culture and Rights: Anthropological Perspectives* (New York: Cambridge University

Press, 2001); Asbjørn Eide, "Cultural Rights as Individual Human Rights," in *Economic, Social and Cultural Rights: A Textbook,* ed. Asbjørn Eide, Catarina Krause, and Alaan Rosas (Dordrecht: Martinus Nijhoff, 1995), 229–40; Isfahan Merali and Valerie Oosterveld, eds., *Giving Meaning to Economic, Social, and Cultural Rights* (Philadelphia: University of Pennsylvania Press, 2001); David P. Forsythe and Patrice C. McMahon, eds., *Human Rights and Diversity: Area Studies Revisited* (Lincoln: University of Nebraska Press, 2003); Ian Shapiro and Will Kymlicka, eds., *Ethnicity and Group Rights* (New York: Kluwer Law International, 2001); and Amnesty International, *Human Rights for Human Dignity: A Primer on Economic, Social and Cultural Rights* (London: Amnesty International, 2005). The twelfth session of the Intergovernmental Committee was convened in February 2008. Discussion related to ten issues that were identified after the tenth session pointed to the importance of gaining specificity regarding definition in the artistic realm. The first issue was stated thus: "[What is the] definition of traditional cultural expressions (TCEs)/expressions of folklore (EoF) that should be protected?" The second issue relates to notions of ownership in regard to culture: "Who should benefit from any such protection or who hold the rights to protectable TCEs/EoF?" For a listing of the complete set of issues, consult the IGC Web site, http://www.wipo.int/tk/en/igc/issues.html (accessed January 10, 2008).

15. The declaration has had a difficult coming to term, having been in draft form for more than two decades. Approval came at the General Assembly on September 13, 2007. The full text can be found on the UNPFII Web site, http://www.un.org/esa/socdev/unpfii/en/declaration.html (accessed January 10, 2008).

16. The Native American Graves Protection and Repatriation Act (NAGPRA) of 1990 was instituted to do just this regarding remains and artifacts removed from burial sites in the United States. The full text can be found at http://www.cr.nps.gov/nagpra/MANDATES/INDEX.HTM (accessed January 10, 2008).

17. Some important reports and declarations from such gatherings include: the Mataatuua Declaration on Cultural and Intellectual Property Rights of Indigenous Peoples (New Zealand, 1983); Charter of the Indigenous-Tribal Peoples of the Tropical Forests (Malaysia, 1992); Kari-Oca Declaration and the Indigenous Peoples' Charter (Brazil, 1992); *Discrimination against Indigenous Peoples: Study on the Protection of the Cultural and Intellectual Property of Indigenous Peoples* (OHCHR, 1993); Recommendations from the Voices of the Earth Congress (Amsterdam, 1993); COICA/UNDP Regional Meeting on Intellectual Property and Bio-Diversity (Bolivia, 1994); UNDP Consultation on Indigenous Peoples' Knowledge and Intellectual Property Rights (Fiji, 1995); *Our Culture, Our Future: Report on Australian Indigenous Cultural and Intellectual Property* (Surry Hills: Michael Frankel and Company, 1998); *Protecting Indigenous Intellectual Property* (Redfern, N.S.W.: Australian Copyright Council, 1998); and *Principles and Guidelines for the Protection of the Heritage of Indigenous People* (OHCHR, 2000).

18. There are many reasons for this, some logistical and some due to weak agency infrastructures; see note 33 below. I reason, as well, that the provisions have been underutilized due in part to the fact that redress is afforded through national treatment. This means, essentially, "as to our own, so then to you." In other words, if a national of the United States appropriates traditional music from Senegal, where folklore is protected in the domestic law, the case would be tried in U.S. courts according to U.S. law in the event that charges are claimed and where folklore is not protected.

19. For judicial opinions acknowledging local practice, see, for instance, Nancy Guy's article on the favoring of aboriginal singers as plaintiffs in a case involving the band Enigma ("Trafficking in Taiwan Aboriginal Voices," in *Handle with Care: Ownership and Control of Ethnographic Materials,* ed. Sjoerd R. Jaarsma [Pittsburgh: University of Pittsburgh Press, 2002]); the breach-of-confidence case involving publication by anthropologist Charles Mountford of information about the Pitjantjatjara people in *Foster v. Mountford* (Australian Copyright Council, 1998); and the historic land rights case in the Belize Supreme Court affirming the rights of indigenous Mayan communities in Belize. The legal decision in the Belize court case is the first to cite the newly passed UN Declaration on the Rights of Indigenous Peoples. See http://www.rainforestfoundation.org/?q=en/node/108 (accessed January 11, 2008).

20. The UNPFII is an advisory body to the Economic and Social Council at the United Nations. The mandate of the UNPFII is to advise on indigenous issues related to economic and social development, culture, the environment, education, health, and human rights. The formation of the forum was an idea of indigenous peoples. Prior to its formation in 2002, indigenous issues were championed by the Working Group on Indigenous Populations of the Sub-commission on the Prevention of Discrimination and Protection of Minorities, established by the UN Economic and Social Council in 1982. See the UNPFII Web site at http://www.un.org/esa/socdev/unpfii (accessed January 11, 2008).

21. For a listing of upcoming performances, see Fanshawe's Web site, www.africansanctus.com (accessed January 11, 2008). A UK-based group called Phuture Assassins has created two new remixes in the "hardcore" genre in which sections of *African Sanctus* have been embedded. Recordings by Phuture Assassins are sold on the Energy Flash Records' Web site, http://www.energyflashrecords.co.uk/search.phtml?fuzzy=1&format_id=0&genre_id=0&showStock=0&searchBy=0&searchWord=african+sanctus (accessed January 11, 2008). I did not hear the singers of the Credo in this work, but in a climate of sampling and the "Free Culture" movement prominent in the United States at the moment, such new collage-type projects are possible with any tracks from Fanshawe's work, whether legal or not.

22. WPPT chapter 2, article 5.

23. Anthony Seeger speaks to his experience with the Smithsonian Folkways Recordings ("Ethnomusicologists, Archives, Professional Organizations, and the Shifting Ethics of Intellectual Property," *Yearbook for Traditional Music* 28 [1996]: 87–105). Terri Janke notes that in Australia, "record companies continue to sell and distribute copies of 'traditional' music recordings, but allege they do not have to pay royalties because the music reproduced is not a copyright work" (*Our Culture, Our Future,* 34). See also the case of Kuo Ying-nan (Guy, "Trafficking in Taiwan Aboriginal Voices").

24. Ralph Oman, "Folkloric Treasures: The Next Copyright Frontier?" in *Intellectual Property Law Newsletter* (publication of the American Bar Association Section of Intellectual Property Law) 15, no. 4 (1996): 3–4.

25. David Fanshawe, "Program Notes," in VSO Program of *African Sanctus,* October 13, 2001, The Usher Hall, Edinburgh, Scotland, 22.

26. Even if the performers had been protected—for instance, if they were singing copyrighted works—Sudan had not ratified the convention yet. Only two African countries were signatories to the Rome Convention at this time: the Congo and Niger. The govern-

ment of Sudan would need to be a signatory in order for Fanshawe to be bound by the Rome Convention regarding these Sudanese singers.

27. Some lawyers sympathetic to the desires of indigenous peoples seeking to prevent misappropriations of their cultural heritage have pointed to the WPPT as a possible means of gaining some control. The control, however, would be over a "version" and not the material itself. There is a legal case in which a singer did receive author's rights for a rendition of folklore (Kuo Yang-lin of the Amis tribe in Taiwan; see Guy, "Trafficking in Taiwan Aboriginal Voices"). This was possible because the performance practices of the Amis rely heavily on creativity—much of the individual composition happens at the actual moment of performance. This was a rare example, and it was settled out of court, so there is no legal precedent on which future prosecutors might rely.

28. Erica-Irene Daes, *Protection of the Heritage of Indigenous People,* Publication E.97. XIV.3. (New York: UNOHCHR, 1997), 21. In the press release applauding the approval of the Declaration on the Rights of Indigenous Peoples, the commissioner called the moment a triumph for justice and human dignity, noting that the declaration "outlaws discrimination against indigenous peoples" and "explicitly encourages harmonious and cooperative relations between States and Indigenous Peoples." Sheer mention of the point indicates that the need persists. The press release can be found at http://www.unhchr.ch/huricane/huricane.nsf/view01/B8C805CF07C5ED86C125735500612DEA?opendocument (accessed January 10, 2008).

29. Rosemary Coombe, *The Cultural Life of Intellectual Properties* (Durham, N.C.: Duke University Press, 1998), 213.

30. Fanshawe, liner notes to *African Sanctus, Salaams* CD, 4.

31. One can read some of these reviews at http://www.africansanctus.com/ (accessed January 11, 2008).

32. Examples of such borrowings can be found in works of the following composers, among many others: modeling—Mozart's Haydn quartets, Beethoven's First Symphony for Haydn; parody—Dufay, Palestrina, Bach in many parody masses; homage—Schoenberg's Opus 25 (Bach motif), Ravel's *La Valse* homage to Strauss; referencing ideas—Sofia Gubaidulina's orchestration of the Bach motif in *Offertorium* with references to Webern's arrangement of the same; referencing trends—Satie's *Le Feu d'artifice* as a blasting of Debussy and impressionism represented in Debussy's work *Feux d'artifice,* Michael Daugherty's referencing of the 1960s American genre the spaghetti western in his orchestral work by the same name; referencing meanings—Ives's reference to Americana in his use of "The Star-Spangled Banner" in *Flanders Fields,* Crumb's reference to childhood in his use of a work from the Anna Magdalena Bach piano book in the *Ancient Voices of Children* on a toy piano (both of these final works are also examples of quotation). John Cage's *Europas* is a good example of pastiche and could be considered postmodern recontextualization, though Pauline Oliveros's *Bye Bye Butterfly* is an undeniable example of the latter.

33. The recitation Fanshawe encountered in West Sudan may have been on the African continent, but it reflected some traditions not indigenous to Africa. Hybrid forms, that is, genres reflecting the blending of cultural traditions, are one of the most significant impediments to a successful categorization of cultural heritage. Regarding the Sudanese recitation, Kwabena Nketia provides some background: "The general tendency [of Africans in cross-cultural musical encounters] was to integrate wherever possible by making it a functional part of an area of musical activity which formed an integral part

of the musical life of the society. The elements that were accepted from Arabic musical culture by African societies that came into contact with it in the Islamic period appear to have been integrated in this manner into the general culture. That is why those who practice them regard them as their varieties of traditional African music no matter how 'Arab-influenced' they may appear to the observer" (J. H. Kwabena Nketia, "Tradition and Innovation in African Music," *Jamaica Journal* 11, no. 3 [1989]: 3–9).

34. Paul Kuruk, "African Customary Law and the Protection of Folklore," *Copyright Bulletin* 36, no. 2 (2002): 6. Available at http://portal.unesco.org/culture/en/ev.php-URL_ID=6259&URL_DO=DO_TOPIC&URL_SECTION=201.html (accessed January 11, 2008).

35. Ibid., 7–8.

36. See Mary Douglas, *African Worlds: Studies in the Cosmological Ideas and Social Values of African Peoples,* ed. Daryll Forde (London: Oxford University Press, 1954), 1–26.

37. J. H. Kwabena Nketia, *The Music of Africa* (New York: W. W. Norton, 1974), 26–27. This description of the importance of customary law in African societies does not necessarily translate into prohibitions for cross-cultural appropriation in all cases. In fact, quite the opposite is true, and Nketia in particular clearly values explorations and appropriations that cross borders, as can be noted in some of his other writings. See, for instance, "Universal Perspectives in Ethnomusicology," *World of Music* 26, no. 2 (1984): 3–21.

38. Erica-Irene Daes, *Discrimination against Indigenous Peoples: Final Report of the Special Rapporteur, Mrs. Erica-Irene Daes in Conformity with Subcommission Resolution 1993/44 and Decision 194/105 of the Commission on Human Rights,* Document no. E/CN.4/Sub.2/1995/26, June 21, 1995 (Geneva: UNOHCHR, 1995), 7. It seems important to note that throughout the UN reports, indigenous peoples are represented—or represent themselves—in a singular fashion, asserting a cohesive "indigenous" position. This is a conscious decision on the part of the indigenous delegates who attend these meetings. An allied position, acquired through negotiation and consensus, provides the delegates with bargaining power. There is a focus on commonalities rooted in concrete life experiences that unite indigenous peoples all over the world: common experiences of exploitation and common desires to resist globalization efforts by engaging in activities that promote indigenous values and lifestyles. So, the consensus of the writers in the group drafting *Discrimination against Indigenous Peoples* is clearly that the interrelation of products of the mind and heart is a common experience of all indigenous peoples. This can allow the non-indigenous reader to speak at least provisionally of "the" indigenous point of view.

39. Daes, *Protection of the Heritage of Indigenous People,* 3.

40. In 1997, when I was studying with Zablong Zakania Abdallah, he was a member of the Ghana Dance Ensemble in residence at the International Center for African Music and Dance, University of Ghana in Legon, Accra, Ghana, West Africa. To my knowledge, he still holds this post. This report recounts my recollection of our discussion during my training.

41. Sherylle Mills, "Indigenous Music and the Law: An Analysis of National and International Legislation," *Yearbook for Traditional Music* 28 (1996): 57. See John Von Sturmer, "Aboriginal Singing and Notions of Power," in *Songs of Aboriginal Australia,* ed. M. Clunies Ross, T. Donaldson, and S. Wild (Sydney: University of Sydney, 1987), 63–76.

42. Rosemary Coombe, "Fear, Hope and Longing for the Future of Authorship and a Revitalized Public Domain in Global Regimes of Intellectual Property," *DePaul Law Review* 52, no. 4 (2003): 1173.

43. Willem Pretorius, "TRIPS and Developing Countries: How Level Is the Playing Field?," in *Global Intellectual Property Rights: Knowledge, Access and Development,* ed. Peter Drahos and Ruth Mayne (New York: Palgrave Macmillan, 2002), 185.

44. In this case, Novartis brought a lawsuit against the government of India to overturn key points in its patent law of 2005. The Washington College of Law at American University encapsulates the proceedings thus: "In 2006, an Indian court ruled that imatinib mesylate, sold by Novartis as Glivec in India, is not patentable under India's patent law, because it is a new form of a known substance. Novartis responded by taking the nation of India to court, charging that its revised patent law violates its international commitments under the WTO TRIPS Agreement, as well as the Indian Constitution. Health advocates fear that a success for Novartis will limit the availability of future generic medicines from India—which is currently a major supplier of generic drugs for the world's poor. On August 6, 2007, the Madras High Court rejected Novartis' challenge of the Indian patent law. The company announced that it is unlikely to appeal the ruling." India's desire was to make necessary medicines accessible for the poor in their borders and beyond. This "accessibility" value is not provided for in TRIPS. Supporting documents are available at the college's Web site, http://www.wcl.american.edu/pijip/novartis_india.cfm (accessed January 11, 2008).

45. In 2001, the International Federation of Library Associations and Institutions, for instance, came forward to address concern regarding the ways that TRIPS shapes national copyright policy and law. "In one instance to date, a WTO dispute panel has found a permitted use in a national copyright law in violation of international trade treaty commitments. Ranging from fair use and similar fair practices to preservation copying by libraries, permitted uses lay out the rights of users of copyrighted content. There is little assurance that the balance between the public interest and rights of content owners sought in national copyright policy debate will be considered by the WTO in any intellectual property disputes which come before it. WTO dispute panels are *'likely to resolve competing claims to intellectual property with little regard for the non-commercial values upon which a reasonable balance of private rights and public interest depends.'*" See the International Federation of Library Associations Web site at http://www.ifla.org/III/clm/p1/wto-ifla.htm (accessed January 11, 2008).

46. The reasons for this are many and quite complex. Consideration of the IGC's ten issues for the twelfth session bring it into focus. See the WIPO Web site, http://www.wipo.int/tk/en/igc/issues.html (accessed January 11, 2008). One concern regarding the logic of applying IP protections to folklore has to do with the mismatch of copyright protections with the needs and expectations of traditional practitioners. Take, for instance, the Suya Indians of Brazil, for whom the naming of an author is quite problematic. The "compositional" process for the Suya involves the teaching of songs to a member of the community by one in the spirit world. Further, this learner does not present the song to the community, but another is afforded that task. See Anthony Seeger, *Why Suyá Sing: A Musical Anthropology of an Amazonian People* (Cambridge: Cambridge University Press, 1987). There are the problems of extending the privatization that comes with copyright law to items in the first world that currently reside in the public domain, namely, folklore. Depleting the public domain is a serious concern for those in the free culture movement

(Lawrence Lessig, *Free Culture: The Nature and Future of Creativity* [New York: Penguin Books, 2004]), those who value a robust public domain (Coombe, *Cultural Life of Intellectual Properties*), and those who support transformative appropriation as a creative process (Joanna Demers, *Steal This Music: How Intellectual Property Law Affects Musical Creativity* [Athens: University of Georgia Press, 2006]). There are also the concerns of providing support for practices that, though customary in some cultures, are viewed as rights violations in others—for instance, the denial of access to particular professions or instruments or information. See in particular two works by Michael F. Brown, "Can Culture Be Copyrighted?" *Current Anthropology* 39, no. 2 (1998): 193–222, and *Who Owns Native Culture?* (Cambridge, Mass.: Harvard University Press, 2003); and also Henrietta Fourmile, "Aboriginal Arts in Relation to Multiculturalism," in *Culture, Difference and the Arts,* ed. Sneja Gunew and Fazal Rizvi (Australia: Allen and Unwin, 1994), 69–85.

47. Many interesting authors are addressing how corporations in the West are exercising control over culture with the help of law in attempts to retain social and economic positions of power. Copyright laws are being expanded to cover more materials and to be in effect for longer terms than ever before in its history. The effects on creativity are staggering. See, for instance, Coombe, *Cultural Life of Intellectual Properties;* Demers, *Steal This Music;* Lessig, *Free Culture;* and Siva Vaidhyanathan, *Copyrights and Copywrongs: The Rise of Intellectual Property and How It Threatens Creativity* (New York: New York University Press, 2001).

48. There are many issues here. For example, some cultural materials are considered to be indigenous to multiple countries. Consider the cultural forms of the Ewe people, whose tribes were divided arbitrarily by European powers into present-day Ghana and Togo. (Betty Mould-Iddrisu addresses this issue in "Preservation and Conservation of Expressions of Folklore: The Experience of Africa," in *UNESCO-WIPO World Forum on the Protection of Folklore—Phuket, Thailand, April 8 to 10, 1997* [Geneva: WIPO, 1998].) Related to this issue is one of categorization of folklore. Who can speak as a competent authority for a group, and who decides? There are strained relationships between indigenous peoples and national administrations, and in such circumstances, a "protection" of traditional music in a national copyright law may not be protection at all. See, for instance, Mills, "Indigenous Music and the Law"; Theodore Levin, "A Tale of Tuva," paper presented at the fortieth annual meeting of the Society for Ethnomusicology, UCLA, October 19–22, 1995; Janke, *Our Culture, Our Future.* Even where a relationship might be strong between a government and the indigenous peoples inside borders, there is the problem of a lack of infrastructure for administration and enforcement of rights (see again Mould-Iddrisu, "Preservation and Conservation.")

49. Information on the IGC is available on the WIPO Web site, http://www.wipo.int/tk/en/igc (accessed January 23, 2009).

50. This is document WIPO/GRTKF/IC/7/3.

51. This document, WIPO/GRTKF/IC/9/4, can be accessed on the WIPO Web site, http://www.wipo.int/edocs/mdocs/tk/en/wipo_grtkf_ic_9/wipo_grtkf_ic_9_4.pdf (accessed January 23, 2009).

52. Ibid.

53. In copyright law, there is a provision for the author to be individual or corporate, but where the author is corporate, individual authors are still named in the group.

54. See note 51.

Glossary of Chinese Characters

A jie gu	阿姐鼓
Alai	阿来
Ba gua	八卦
baohu	保护
Basang	巴桑
Beijing chenbao	北京晨報
Beijing de jin shan shang	北京的金山上
Beijing guqin yanjiuhui	北京古琴研究會
Beijing qinxun	北京琴訊
bentuhua	本土化
bu kexue	不科学
Caidanzhuoma	才旦卓玛
Changshu	長熟
Chen'ai luo ding	尘埃落定
Cheung Sai-bung	張世彬
chuancheng yu kaituo	傳承與開拓
chuantong wenhua baohu qu	传统文化保护区
Chuncheng wanbao	春城晚报
Chunjie lianhuan wanhui	春节联欢晚会

chunzheng	纯正
Cui Zundu	崔遵度
Da tian zaiyang yang lian yang	大田栽秧秧连秧
dage	大歌
dande qinzhongqu, helao xianshangsheng	但得琴中趣，何勞絃上聲
Dayan guyuehui	大研古乐会
Dazhen	达珍
Debai	德白
Deqianwangmu	德乾旺姆
Dongba gong	东巴宫
Dongjing	洞经
Du Yaxiong	杜亚雄
Fanshen nongnu ba ge chang	翻身农奴把歌唱
fengge	风格
gaibian	改变
Gao Liang	高粱
Gechang	歌唱
Gesangzhuoma	格桑卓玛
Gong Yi	龔一
Guo Song	郭颂
Guqin buzai chenmo	古琴不再沉默
Han Hong	韩红
Hanhua	汉化
He Jiaxiu	和家修
Huang Hong	黄虹
Huang Shuzhi	黃樹志
Huangshan	黃山
Hui dao Lasa	回到拉萨
Jiangnan sizhu	江南丝竹
Jiaxiang	家乡
jing yuan	靜遠

Jinyu qinshe	今虞琴社
Juyong	居庸
Kunqu	昆曲
Langlashan qing	浪拉山情
langma	朗玛
Lau Chor Wah	劉楚華
Li Na	李娜
Li Xiangting	李祥霆
Liang Mingyue	梁銘越
Lijiang Xuan Ke Naxi guyue wenhua youxian gongsi	丽江宣科纳西古乐文化有限公司
Lin Zhiyin	林之音
Lishan	梨山
Liu Minglan	劉明瀾
Liu Tieshan	刘铁山
Liu Yong	刘勇
liuxing	流行
luohou	落后
Ma Tieying	马铁英
Ma Zheng	马征
Mei'an qinshe	梅庵琴社
meiyou wenhua	没有文化
Meizhuo	梅桌
Miao Jianhua	苗健華
min'ge re	民歌热
minjian	民间
minjian yinyue	民间音乐
minzu	民族
minzu minjian yishu chuancheng ren	民族民间艺术传承人
minzu yinyue	民族音乐
Nanjia Cairang	南加才让

Nanyin	南音
Naxi guyue	纳西古乐
Qiao Jianzhong	乔建中
qin	琴
qing wei dan yuan	清微澹遠
Qingren	情人
Qingzang gaoyuan	青藏高原
Qinshi chubian	琴史初編
Qiongxuezhuoma	琼雪卓玛
quyi	曲艺
Renmin yinyue	人民音乐
Riga	日嘎
Rikaze	日喀则
ronghe	融合
Rongzhongerjia	容中尔甲
Shan ying	山鹰
Shanghai Yinyue Xueyuan	上海音樂學院
shaoshu minzu	少数民族
shehuihua	社會化
shengcun	生存
Shoudu tiyuguan	首都体育馆
shouji zhengli	收集整理
Siqin'gerile	斯琴格日乐
sizhu	丝竹
T'ao Ch'ien	陶潛
Tao Qian	陶潛
Teng Ge'er	腾格尔
Tian Liantao	田联韬
Tian lu	天路
Tianliang le	天亮了
Tianya	天涯

Wang Luobin	王洛宾
Wei Se	唯色
wenhua li xian	文化立县
wenhua lüyou	文化旅游
wenhuaquan	文化权
wenren qinjia	文人琴家
wenrenqin	文人琴
Wu Xueyuan	吴学源
Wu Zhao	吳釗
Wusuli chuan'ge	乌苏里船歌
Xiao Mei	萧梅
Xiaohe tang shui	小河淌水
xiexin	寫心
Ximalaya	喜马拉雅
Xin yinyue	新音乐
Xizang biji	西藏笔记
Xizang re	西藏热
Xu Jian	許健
Xuan Ke	宣科
Xue yu guangmang	雪域光芒
Yadong	亚东
Yan Cheng	嚴澂
Yang Mu	杨沐
Ye Xiaogang	叶小刚
yi	意
yijing	意境
Yimannali	依曼那利
Yin Yigong	尹宜公
Yinyue yanjiusuo	音樂研究所
yirenqin	藝人琴
Yishu pinglun	艺术评论

yishuqin	藝術琴
Yongxi	雍西
yuan shengtai	原生态
yuan shengtai min'ge	原生态民歌
yuansheng	原生
yuji	娱己
yuren	娱人
Yushan	虞山
Zangzu	藏族
Zangzu geshou	藏族歌手
Zhang Jian	张建
Zhang Qingshan	张庆善
Zhaxi Dawa	扎西达娃
Zheng Jun	郑钧
Zhong Wenxin	鍾文心
zhong zheng ping he	中正平和
Zhongguo guqin dasai	中國古琴大賽
Zhongguo guqin xinwenwang	中國古琴新聞網
Zhongguo minzu guanxianyue xuehui guqin zhuanye weiyuanhui	中國民族管絃樂學會古琴專業委員會
Zhongguo qinhui	中國琴會
Zhongguo yinyue	中国音乐
Zhonghua minzu	中华民族
Zhongyang Yinyue Xueyuan	中央音樂學院
Zhu Zheqin	朱哲琴
Zhuang Zi	莊子
zhuanye qinshi	專業琴師

Bibliography

Adam, Aladar, Evheniia Navrotska, and Yulia Zeikan. *Bilyi Kamin z Chornoi Kativni* [White Rock from the Black Prison]. Uzhhorod, Ukraine: Uzhhorod City Press, 2006.

Adams, Vincanne. "Karaoke as Modern Lhasa, Tibet: Western Encounters with Cultural Politics." *Cultural Anthropology* 11, no. 4 (1996): 510–46.

Albro, Robert, and Joanne Bauer. "Introduction." In "Cultural Rights." Special issue, *Human Rights Dialogue,* ser. 2, no. 12 (Spring 2005), Carnegie Council. http://www.cceia.org/resources/publications/dialogue/index.html (accessed February 26, 2007).

Alfaro Rotondo, Santiago. "Estado del arte del patrimonio inmaterial en el Perú." Lo Centro Regional para la Salvaguardia del Patrimonio Cultural Inmaterial de América Latina (CRESPIAL). 2005. http://www.crespial.org/web/peru.php (accessed January 23, 2008).

———. "El lugar de las industrias culturales en las políticas públicas." In *Políticas culturales: Ensayos críticos,* edited by Guillermo Cortés and Víctor Vich. Lima: Instituto de Estudios Peruanos, 2006. 137–75.

Amnesty International. *Human Rights for Human Dignity: A Primer on Economic, Social and Cultural Rights.* London: Amnesty International, 2005.

Anand, Dibyesh. "(Re)imagining Nationalism: Identity and Representation in the Tibetan Diaspora of South Asia." *Contemporary South Asia* 9, no. 3 (2000): 271–87.

Arce, Moisés. "The Sustainability of Economic Reform in a Most Likely Case: Peru." *Comparative Politics* 35, no. 3 (2003): 335–54.

Assies, Willem, Gemma van der Haar, and André Hoekema. "La diversidad como desafío: una nota sobre los dilemas de la diversidad." In *El reto de la diversidad. Pueblos indígenas y reforma de estado en América Latina,* edited by Willem Assies, Gemma van der Haar, and André Hoekema. México: El Colegio de Michoacán, 1999. 356–94.

Bambula, Volodymyr. *Tsyhanska Dolia—Yak Viter u Poli* [Gypsy Fate—Like Wind in the Steppe]. Pereiaslav-Khmelnytsk, Ukraine: Karpuk Press, 2002.

Baranovitch, Nimrod. "Between Alterity and Identity: New Voices of Minority People in China." *Modern China* 27, no. 3 (2001): 359–401.

———. *China's New Voices: Popular Music, Ethnicity, Gender, and Politics, 1978–1997.* Berkeley: University of California Press, 2003.

———. "Compliance, Autonomy, and Resistance of a 'State Artist': The Case of Chinese-Mongolian Musician Teng Ge'er." In *Lives in Chinese Music,* edited by Helen Rees. Urbana: University of Illinois Press, 2009. 173–212.

———. "From Resistance to Adaptation: Uyghur Popular Music and Changing Attitudes among Uyghur Youth." *China Journal* 58 (2007): 59–82.

———. "From the Margins to the Centre: The Uyghur Challenge in Beijing." *China Quarterly* 175 (2003): 736–38.

———. "Inverted Exile: Uyghur Writers and Artists in Beijing and the Political Implications of Their Work." *Modern China* 33, no. 4 (2007): 469–84.

Barclay, Barry. *Mana Tuturu: Maori Treasures and Intellectual Property Rights.* Honolulu: University of Hawai'i Press, 2005.

Barker, Nicholas. "Revival of Religious Self-flagellation in Lowland Christian Philippines." In *Religious Revival in Contemporary Southeast Asia,* edited by Naimah Talib and Bernhard Dahm. Singapore: Institute of Southeast Asian Studies, 1997. 13–26.

Barnett, Robert. "Symbols and Protest: The Iconography of Demonstrations in Tibet, 1987–1990." In *Resistance and Reform in Tibet,* edited by Robert Barnett and Shirin Akiner. Bloomington: Indiana University Press, 1994. 238–58.

Barr, Robert R. "The Persistence of Neopopulism in Peru? From Fujimori to Toledo." *Third World Quarterly* 24, no. 6 (2003): 1161–78.

Bartók, Béla. "Hungarian Folk Music." In *Béla Bartók Essays,* edited by Benjamin Suchoff. Lincoln: University of Nebraska Press, 1976. 3–4.

Barwick, Linda, Allan Marret, and Guy Tunstill. *The Essence of Singing and the Substance of Song: Recent Responses to the Aboriginal Performing Arts and Other Essays in Honour of Catherine Ellis.* Sydney N.S.W.: University of Sydney, 1995.

Batt, Herbert J., ed. and trans. *Tales of Tibet: Sky Burials, Prayer Wheels, and Wind Horses.* Lanham, Md.: Rowman and Littlefield, 2001.

Bauman, Richard. *Reflections on the Folklife Festival: An Ethnography of Participant Experience.* Bloomington: Folklore Institute, Indiana University, 1992.

Bell, Lynda S., Andrew J. Nathan, and Ilan Peleg. "Introduction: Culture and Human Rights." In *Negotiating Culture and Human Rights,* edited by Lynda S. Bell, Andrew J. Nathan, and Ilan Peleg. New York: Columbia University Press, 2001. 3–20.

Bengwayan, Michael A. *Intellectual and Cultural Property Rights of Indigenous and Tribal Peoples in Asia.* London: Minority Rights Group International, 2003.

Bill, MV, and Celso Athayde. *Falcão: Meninos do Tráfico.* Rio de Janeiro: Objetiva, 2006.

Bishop, Peter. *Dreams of Power: Tibetan Buddhism and the Western Imagination.* London: Athlone Press, 1993.

———. *The Myth of Shangri-La: Tibet, Travel Writing, and the Western Creation of a Sacred Landscape.* Berkeley: University of California Press, 1989.

Bloch, Anne-Christine. "Minorities and Indigenous Peoples." In *Economic, Social and Cultural Rights: A Textbook,* edited by Asbjørn Eide, Catarina Krause, and Alaan Rosas. Dordrecht: Martinus Nijhoff, 1995. 309–21.

Body, Jack. "'One of Yunnan's Most Unique Features Is Its Music': Zhang Xingrong on His Fieldwork among Minorities in Southern China." *Chime* 8 (1995): 59–66.

Bohlman, Philip V. *The Study of Folk Music in the Modern World.* Bloomington: Indiana University Press, 1988.

———. *World Music: A Very Short Introduction.* New York: Oxford University Press, 2002.

Bourdieu, Pierre. "The Field of Cultural Production, or: The Economic World Reversed." In *The Field of Cultural Production,* edited by Randal Johnson. New York: Columbia University Press, 1993. 29–73.

Brady, Erika. *A Spiral Way: How the Phonograph Changed Ethnography.* Jackson: University of Mississippi Press, 1999.

Brown, Michael F. "Can Culture Be Copyrighted?" *Current Anthropology* 39, no. 2 (1998): 193–222.

———. *Who Owns Native Culture?* Cambridge, Mass.: Harvard University Press, 2003.

Buchanan, Donna A. *Performing Democracy: Bulgarian Music and Musicians in Transition.* Chicago: University of Chicago Press, 2006.

Bulag, Uradyn E. "Ethnic Resistance with Socialist Characteristics." In *Chinese Society: Change, Conflict and Resistance,* edited by Elizabeth J. Perry and Mark Selden. London: Routledge, 2000. 178–97.

Cadena, Marisol de la. *Indigenous Mestizos: The Politics of Race and Culture in Cuzco, Peru, 1919–1991.* Durham, N.C.: Duke University Press, 2000.

Calkowski, Marcia S. "The Tibetan Diaspora and the Politics of Performance." In *Proceedings of the 7th Seminar of the International Association for Tibetan Studies: Graz 1995.* Vol. 4, *Tibetan Culture in the Diaspora,* edited by Frank J. Korom. Wien: Österreichischen Akademie Der Wissenschaften, 1997. 51–57.

Cano, Ignacio. *Letalidade da ação policial no Rio de Janeiro.* Rio de Janeiro: ISER, 1997.

Ceribašić, Naila. "Musical Faces of Croatian Multiculturality." *Yearbook for Traditional Music* 39 (2007): 1–26.

Chan Hing-yan. "Syncretic Traditions and Western Idioms: Composers and Works." In *Garland Encyclopedia of World Music,* vol. 7, edited by Robert C. Provine, Yosihiko Tokumaru, and J. Lawrence Witzleben. New York: Routledge, 2002. 345–51.

Chapin, Helen G. *Guide to Newspapers of Hawai'i 1834–2000.* Honolulu: Hawaiian Historical Society, 2000.

———. *Shaping History: The Role of Newspapers in Hawai'i.* Honolulu: University of Hawai'i Press, 1996.

Chaudhuri, Shubha. "Preservation of the World's Music." In *Introduction to Ethnomusicology,* edited by Helen Myers. London: Macmillan, 1992. 365–74.

Cheng, David. "The New Development of Intellectual Property Protection for Traditional Music in China." In *Preservation of Traditional Music: Report of the Asia-Europe Training Programme,* edited by Xiao Mei, Zhang Gang, and Delfin Colomé. Beijing: Chinese Academy of Arts/Asia-Europe Foundation, 2003. 215–20.

Cheng, Vincent J. *Inauthentic: The Anxiety over Culture and Identity.* New Brunswick, N.J.: Rutgers University Press, 2004.

Cheng Yu. "The Precarious State of the Qin in Contemporary China." *Chime* 10/11 (1997): 50–61.

Cheung Sai-bung. *Zhongguo yinyueshi lunshugao* [Historical studies of Chinese music]. Hong Kong: Union Press, 1975.

Chin Ming. "How the Peacock Dance Reached the Stage." *China Reconstructs* 12, no. 3 (1963): 10–11.

Clark, Paul. *Chinese Cinema: Culture and Politics since 1949*. Cambridge: Cambridge University Press, 1987.

———. "Ethnic Minorities in Chinese Films: Cinema and the Exotic." *East-West Film Journal* 1, no. 2 (1987): 15–31.

Collins, John. "Copyright, Folklore, and Music Piracy in Ghana." *Critical Arts* 20, no. 1 (2006): 158–70.

The Common Program and Other Documents of the First Plenary Session of the Chinese People's Political Consultative Conference. Peking: Foreign Languages Press, 1950.

Connerton, Paul. *How Societies Remember*. Cambridge: Cambridge University Press, 1989.

Cooley, Timothy. *Making Music in the Polish Tatras: Tourists, Ethnographers, and Mountain Musicians*. Bloomington: Indiana University Press, 2005.

Coombe, Rosemary. *The Cultural Life of Intellectual Properties*. Durham, N.C.: Duke University Press, 1998.

———. "Fear, Hope and Longing for the Future of Authorship and a Revitalized Public Domain in Global Regimes of Intellectual Property." *DePaul Law Review* 52, no. 4 (2003): 1171–91.

Cortés, Guillermo, and Víctor Vich. *Políticas culturales: Ensayos críticos*. Lima: Instituto de Estudios Peruanos, 2006.

Cowan, Jane K., Marie-Bénédicte Dembour, and Richard A. Wilson, eds. *Culture and Rights: Anthropological Perspectives*. Cambridge: Cambridge University Press, 2001.

Crawford Seeger, Ruth. "Music Preface." In *Our Singing Country: A Second Volume of American Ballads and Folk Songs*, compiled by John A. Lomax and Alan Lomax, edited by Ruth Crawford Seeger. New York: Macmillan, 1941. xvii–xxiv.

Cultural Center of the Philippines. *Pahiyas sa Mundo*. VHS. Directed by Clodualdo del Mondo Jr. Manila: Cultural Center of the Philippines, 1999.

Daes, Erica-Irene. *Discrimination against Indigenous Peoples: Final Report of the Special Rapporteur, Mrs. Erica-Irene Daes in Conformity with Subcommission Resolution 1993/44 and Decision 194/105 of the Commission on Human Rights*. Document no. E/CN.4/Sub.2/1995/26, June 21, 1995. Geneva: UNOHCHR, 1995.

———. *Protection of the Heritage of Indigenous People*. Publication E.97.XIV.3. New York: UNOHCHR, 1997.

Dai Xiaolian. "Jinyuqinshe sheming de laili" [The origin of the name Jinyu Qin Society]. In *Jinyu qinkan xu: Jinian Jinyu qinshe chengli liushinian* [Jinyu qin journal, supplement: In memory of the 60th anniversary of the establishment of Jinyu Qin Society]. Shanghai: Jinyu qinshe, 1996. 9.

Daughtry, J. Martin. "Russia's New Anthem and the Negotiation of National Identity." *Ethnomusicology* 47, no. 1 (2003): 42–67.

Davis, Sara L. M. *Song and Silence: Ethnic Revival on China's Southwest Borders*. New York: Columbia University Press, 2005.

Dayan guyuehui. "Baogao" [Report]. Manuscript, kept by Dayan Ancient Music Association, Dayan Town, Lijiang County, Yunnan, 1992.

Demers, Joanna. *Steal This Music: How Intellectual Property Law Affects Musical Creativity*. Athens: University of Georgia Press, 2006.

Deng Jun. "'Wenhua li xian' yu minjian yinyue de baohu yu kaifa—Yu dongnan Youyang xian minjian yinyue wenhua ziyuan kaocha shulüe" ["Building a county on culture" and the protection and development of folk music—report on an investigation into the folk music culture resources of Youyang County in southeast Chongqing]. *Renmin yinyue* [People's music] 445 (2003): 26–28.

Dening, Greg. *Islands and Beaches: Discourse on a Silent Land, Marquesas 1774–1880.* Honolulu: University Press of Hawai'i, 1980.

"Di yi pi guojia fei wuzhi wenhua yichan minglu yinyue lei tuijian xiangmu mingdan" [List of recommended musical items in the first national intangible cultural heritage registry]. *Renmin yinyue* [People's music] 483 (2006): 53–54.

Diehl, Kiela. *Echoes from Dharamsala: Music in the Life of a Tibetan Refugee Community.* Berkeley: University of California Press, 2002.

———. "Tibetan Diaspora." In *Continuum Encyclopedia of Popular Music of the World.* Vol. 5, *Asia and Oceania,* edited by John Shepherd, David Horn, and Dave Laing. London: Continuum, 2005. 24–27.

Dodin, Thierry, and Heinz Räther, eds. *Imagining Tibet: Perception, Projections, and Fantasies.* Boston: Wisdom Publications, 2001.

Dongo, María del Carmen. *El cajón es del Perú.* Lima: Dongo Producciones, 2003. CD-ROM Multimedia.

Douglas, Mary. *African Worlds: Studies in the Cosmological Ideas and Social Values of African Peoples.* Edited by Daryll Forde. London: Oxford University Press, 1954.

Dreyer, June Teufel. *China's Forty Millions: Minority Nationalities and National Integration in the People's Republic of China.* Harvard East Asian Series No. 87. Cambridge, Mass.: Harvard University Press, 1976.

Du Yaxiong. "Recent Issues in Music Research in the People's Republic of China." *Association for Chinese Music Research Newsletter* 5, no. 1 (1992): 9–12.

Eide, Asbjørn. "Cultural Rights as Individual Human Rights." In *Economic, Social and Cultural Rights: A Textbook,* edited by Asbjørn Eide, Catarina Krause, and Alaan Rosas. Dordrecht: Martinus Nijhoff, 1995. 229–40.

Fanshawe, David. Liner notes to *African Sanctus, Salaams* CD. Philips D—105578. 1973.

———. "Program Notes." In VSO Program of *African Sanctus.* October 13, 2001. The Usher Hall, Edinburgh, Scotland.

Fei Denghong. "Dui guqin yishu zhenxing qianjing de chuangxin gouxiang" [A creative envisioning of the future of the revival of qin musical art]. *Zhongguo yinyue* [Chinese music] 95 (2004): 21–27.

Feigon, Lee. *Demystifying Tibet: Unlocking the Secrets of the Land of the Snows.* Chicago: Ivan R. Dee, 1998.

Feldman, Heidi Carolyn. *Black Rhythms of Peru: Reviving African Musical Heritage in the Black Pacific.* Middletown, Conn.: Wesleyan University Press, 2006.

Fentress, James, and Chris Wickham. *Social Memory: New Perspectives on the Past.* Oxford: Blackwell, 1992.

Folktales of Hawai'i. Collected and translated by Mary Kawena Pukui and Laura C. S. Green. Honolulu: Bishop Museum Press, 1995.

Forsythe, David P., and Patrice C. McMahon, eds. *Human Rights and Diversity: Area Studies Revisited.* Lincoln: University of Nebraska Press, 2003.

Fourmile, Henrietta. "Aboriginal Arts in Relation to Multiculturalism." In *Culture, Difference and the Arts,* edited by Sneja Gunew and Fazal Rizvi. Australia: Allen and Unwin, 1994. 69–85.

Gellner, David N. "From Group Rights to Individual Rights and Back: Nepalese Struggles over Culture and Equality." In *Culture and Rights: Anthropological Perspectives,* edited by Jane K. Cowan, Marie-Bénédicte Dembour, and Richard A. Wilson. Cambridge: Cambridge University Press, 2001. 177–200.

Ginsberg, Faye. "Indigenous Media: Faustian Contract or Global Village?" *Cultural Anthropology* 6, no. 1 (1991): 92–112.

Gladney, Dru C. "Representing Nationality in China: Refiguring Majority/Minority Identities." *Journal of Asian Studies* 53, no. 1 (1994): 92–123.

———. "Tian Zhuangzhuang, the Fifth Generation, and Minorities Film in China." *Public Culture* 8, no. 1 (1995): 161–75.

Gong Yi. "Guqin bisai jiqi shehuihua fazhan" [Qin competition and the development of the qin tradition as an integral part of society]. *Renmin yinyue* [People's music] 470 (2005): 25–27.

Goodale, Mark. "Introduction to Anthropology and Human Rights in a New Key." *American Anthropologist* 108, no. 1 (2006): 1–8.

Gray, Judith. "Returning Music to the Makers: The Library of Congress, American Indians, and the Federal Cylinder Project." *Cultural Survival Quarterly* 20, no. 4 (1997): 42.

Greene, Shane. "Entre lo indio, lo negro, y lo incaico: The Spatial Hierarchies of Difference in Multicultural Peru." *Journal of Latin American and Caribbean Anthropology* 12, no. 2 (2007): 441–74.

Gulik, Robert van. *The Lore of the Chinese Lute: An Essay on Qin Ideology.* Monumenta Nipponica, no. 3. 1940. Reprint, Tokyo: Sophia University Press/Charles E. Tuttle Company, 1969.

Guy, Nancy. "Trafficking in Taiwan Aboriginal Voices." In *Handle with Care: Ownership and Control of Ethnographic Materials,* edited by Sjoerd R. Jaarsma. Pittsburgh: University of Pittsburgh Press, 2002. 195–209.

Hagedorn, Katherine J. *Divine Utterances: The Performance of Afro-Cuban Santeria.* Washington, D.C.: Smithsonian Institution Press, 2001.

Hale, Charles R. "Neoliberal Multiculturalism: The Remaking of Cultural Rights and Racial Dominance in Central America." *Political and Legal Anthropology Review* 28, no. 1 (2005): 10–28.

Hansen, Mette Halskov. *Lessons in Being Chinese: Minority Education and Ethnic Identity in Southwest China.* Seattle: University of Washington Press, 1999.

Harrell, Stevan, ed. *Cultural Encounters on China's Ethnic Frontiers.* Seattle: University of Washington Press, 1995.

———. "Introduction: Civilizing Projects and the Reaction to Them." In *Cultural Encounters on China's Ethnic Frontiers,* edited by Stevan Harrell. Seattle: University of Washington Press, 1995. 3–36.

Harris, Clare. "Struggling with Shangri-La: A Tibetan Artist in Exile." In *Constructing Tibetan Culture: Contemporary Perspectives,* edited by Frank J. Korom. Quebec: World Heritage Press, 1997. 160–77.

Harris, Rachel. "Cassettes, Bazaars, and Saving the Nation: The Uyghur Music Industry in Xinjiang, China." In *Global Goes Local: Popular Culture in Asia,* edited by Timothy J. Craig and Richard King. Honolulu: University of Hawaii Press, 2002. 265–83.

———. "From Shamanic Ritual to Karaoke: The (Trans)migrations of a Chinese Folksong." *Chime* 14–15 (1999–2000): 48–60.

———. "Wang Luobin: Folk Song King of the Northwest or Song Thief? Copyright, Representation, and Chinese Folk Songs." *Modern China* 31, no. 3 (2005): 381–408.

He Jiaxiu. "Naxi guyue de jin yi bu baohu he kaifa" [Further protection and development of Naxi Ancient Music]. *Yulong shan* [Jade dragon mountain] 74 (1996): 43–45.

———. "Naxi guyue zhenhan Ying Lun" [Naxi Ancient Music rocks London, England]. *Yulong shan* [Jade dragon mountain] 74 (1996): 101–13, 99.

Heberer, Thomas. "Old Tibet a Hell on Earth? The Myth of Tibet and Tibetans in Chinese Art and Propaganda." In *Imagining Tibet: Perceptions, Projections, and Fantasies,* edited by Thierry Dodin and Heinz Räther. Boston: Wisdom Publications, 2001. 111–50.

Helbig, Adriana. "The Cyberpolitics of Music in Ukraine's 2004 Orange Revolution." *Current Musicology* 82 (2006): 81–101.

———. "Ethnomusicology and Advocacy Research: Theory and Action among Romani NGOs in Ukraine." *Anthropology for East Europe Review: Special Issue on Roma and Gadje* 25, no. 2 (2007): 78–83.

Hemetek, Ursula. "Applied Ethnomusicology in the Process of the Political Recognition of a Minority: A Case Study of the Austrian Roma." *Yearbook for Traditional Music* 38 (2006): 35–57.

Hemment, Julie. *Empowering Women in Russia: Activism, Aid, and NGOs.* Bloomington: Indiana University Press, 2007.

Henrion-Dourcy, Isabelle. "Women in the Performing Arts: Portraits of Six Contemporary Singers." In *Women in Tibet,* edited by Janet Gyatso and Hanna Havnevik. New York: Columbia University Press, 2005. 195–258.

Hickerson, Joseph C., and Katherine W. Johnston. "Copyright and Folksong." Typescript. Washington, D.C.: Archive of Folk Song, Library of Congress, 1978.

Horkheimer, Max, and Theodor W. Adorno. *Dialectic of Enlightenment.* Edited by Gunzelin Schmid Noerr, translated by Edmund Jephcott. Stanford, Calif.: Stanford University Press, 2002.

Hunt, Paul. "Reflections on International Human Rights Law and Cultural Rights." In *Culture, Rights, and Cultural Rights: Perspectives from the South Pacific,* edited by Margaret Wilson and Paul Hunt. Wellington, New Zealand: Huia, 2000. 25–46.

Iemets, Hryhorii. *Tsyhany Zakarpattia* [The Gypsies of Transcarpathia]. Uzhhorod: Karpaty Press, 1993.

Impey, Angela. "Culture, Conservation and Community Reconstruction: Explorations in Advocacy Ethnomusicology and Participatory Action Research in Northern KwaZulu Natal." *Yearbook for Traditional Music* 34 (2002): 9–24.

Instituto Nacional de Cultural (INC). *Directorio de la cultura y las artes en el Perú.* Lima: Instituto Nacional de Cultura, 2006.

International Folk Music Council. *Statement on Copyright in Folk Music Adopted by the General Assembly of the International Folk Music Council, August 26, 1957.* London: International Folk Music Council, 1957.

IP Protection in China: The Law. 2nd ed. Hong Kong: Asia Law and Practice Publishing, 1998.

Jabbour, Alan. "Folklore Protection and National Patrimony: Developments and Dilemmas in the Legal Protection of Folklore." *Copyright Bulletin* 17, no. 1 (1983): 10–14.

Janke, Terri. *Our Culture, Our Future: Report on Australian Indigenous Cultural and Intellectual Property.* Surry Hills: Michael Frankel and Company, 1998.

Jiang Mingdun. *Hanzu min'ge gailun* [Overview of folksongs of the Han]. Shanghai: Shanghai wenyi chubanshe, 1982.

Jones, Stephen. *Folk Music of China: Living Instrumental Traditions.* Oxford: Clarendon Press, 1995.

———. *Plucking the Winds: Lives of Village Musicians in Old and New China.* Leiden, Netherlands: CHIME Foundation, 2004.

———. "Suzhou Daoists in Europe." *Chime* 7 (1993): 130–31.

———. Liner notes to *Walking Shrill: The Hua Family Shawm Band* CD. 2109. Leiden, Netherlands: Pan Records, 2004.

Ju Qihong. "Minjian yinyue de xiandai chuancheng ji qi zhuzuoquan guishu" [Modern transmission of folk music and copyright ownership]. *Renmin yinyue* [People's music] 348 (1994): 13–16.

Junior, José. *Da favela para o mundo: a história do Grupo Cultural AfroReggae.* Rio de Janeiro: Aeroplano Editora, 2003.

Kim Il Sung. "On Creating Revolutionary Literature and Art." In *Selected Works,* vol. 4. Pyongyang: Foreign Languages Publishing House, 1971. 149–64.

Kim Jong Il. "Let Us Compose More Music Which Will Contribute to Education in the Party's Monolithic Ideology." In *Selected Works,* vol. 1. Pyongyang: Foreign Languages Publishing House, 1992. 195–207.

———. "On the Direction Which Musical Creation Should Take." In *Selected Works,* vol. 1. 1967. Reprint, Pyongyang: Foreign Languages Publishing House, 1992. 390–97.

Klieger, Christiaan P. "Shangri-La and Hyperreality: A Collision in Tibetan Refugee Expression." In *Proceedings of the 7th Seminar of the International Association for Tibetan Studies: Graz 1995.* Vol. 4, *Tibetan Culture in the Diaspora,* edited by Frank J. Korom. Wien: Österreichischen Akademie Der Wissenschaften, 1997. 59–68.

Koch, Gisela Cánepa. "La ciudadanía en escena: fiesta andina, patrimonio y agencia cultural." In *Mirando la esfera pública desde la cultura en el Perú,* edited by Gisela Cánepa Koch and María Eugenia Ulfe Young. Lima: Consejo Nacional de Ciencia, Tecnología e Innovación Tecnológica, 2006. 221–42.

Koch, Grace. "Songs, Land Rights, and Archives in Australia." *Cultural Survival Quarterly* 20, no. 4 (1997): 38–41.

Kouwenhoven, Frank. "The Tianjin Buddhist Music Ensemble's European Tour: Group Takes European Audiences by Surprise." *Chime* 7 (1993): 104–12.

Kouwenhoven, Frank, and Antoinet Schimmelpenninck. *Chinese Shadows: The Amazing World of Shadow Puppetry in Rural Northwest China.* DVD. 9607. Leiden, Netherlands: Pan Records, 2007.

Krupnik, Igor, and Lars Krutak. *Akuzilleput Igaqullghet: Our Words Put to Paper.* Washington, D.C.: Arctic Studies Center, National Museum of Natural History, Smithsonian Institution, 2002.

Kurin, Richard. *Reflections of a Culture Broker: A View from the Smithsonian.* Washington, D.C.: Smithsonian Institution Press, 1997.

Kuruk, Paul. "African Customary Law and the Protection of Folklore." *Copyright Bulletin* 36, no. 2 (2002): 4–32.

Lau, Frederick. "Forever Red: The Invention of Solo *Dizi* Music in Post-1949 China." *British Journal of Ethnomusicology* 5 (1996): 113–31.

———. "'Packaging Identity through Sound': Tourist Performances in Contemporary China." *Journal of Musicological Research* 17, no. 2 (1998): 113–34.

Leeds, Elizabeth. "Rio de Janeiro." In *Fractured Cities: Social Exclusion, Urban Violence and Contested Spaces in Latin America,* edited by K. Koonings and D. Kruijt. London: Zed Books, 2007. 22–35.

Lemgruber, Julita, Leonarda Musumeci, and Ignacio Cano. *Quem vigia os vigias?* Rio de Janeiro: Record, 2003.

Lemon, Alaina. *Between Two Fires: Gypsy Performance and Romani Memory from Pushkin to Post-Socialism.* Durham: Duke University Press, 2000.

León, Javier F. "The 'Danza de las Cañas': Music, Theatre and Afroperuvian Modernity." *Ethnomusicology Forum* 16, no. 1 (2007): 127–55.

———. "Mass Culture, Commodification, and the Consolidation of the Afro-Peruvian Festejo." *Black Music Research Journal* 26, no. 2 (2006): 213–47.

———. "El que no tiene de inga, tiene de mandinga: Negotiating Tradition and Ethnicity in Peruvian Criollo Popular Music." Master's thesis, University of Texas at Austin, 1997.

Lessig, Lawrence. *Free Culture: The Nature and Future of Creativity.* New York: Penguin Books, 2004.

Levin, Theodore. "A Tale of Tuva." Paper presented at the fortieth annual meeting of the Society for Ethnomusicology, UCLA, October 19–22, 1995.

Li Xiangting. "Guqin yishu yinggai chengwei meige zhongguoren de jichu zhishi zhiyi" [The art of qin should be among the fundamental knowledge of every Chinese]. *Renmin yinyue* [People's music] 456 (2004): 36–37.

———. *Tangdai guqin yanzou meixue ji yinyue sixiang yanjiu* [Study of the aesthetics of qin performance and musical ideology in the Tang dynasty]. Taipei: Wenhua jianshe weiyuanhui, 2003.

Liang, David Ming-yüeh. *Music of the Billion: An Introduction to Chinese Musical Culture.* New York: Heinrichshofen Edition, 1985.

Lieberman, Fredric. *A Chinese Zither Tutor: The Mei-an Ch'in-p'u.* Seattle: University of Washington Press, 1977.

Lipsitz, George. *Time Passages: Collective Memory and American Popular Culture.* Minneapolis: University of Minnesota Press, 1990.

Liu Chenghua. "Wenrenqin yu yirenqin guanxi de lishi yanbian" [Historical changes of the relationship between the literati's qin and the artists' qin]. *Zhongguo yinyue* [Chinese music] 98 (2005): 9–19.

Liu Hongqing. "Xuan Ke shenhua" [The myth of Xuan Ke]. *Yishu pinglun* [Arts criticism] 1 (2003): 27–36.

Liu Minglan. "Kongzi de wenrou dunhou dui guqin yinyue de yingxiang" [The influence of Confucius ideal of *wenrou dunhou* on the music of qin]. In *Jinyu qinkan xu: Jinian Jinyu qinshe chengli liushinian* [Jinyu qin journal, supplement: In memory of the 60th anniversary of the establishment of Jinyu Qin Society]. Shanghai: Jinyu Qinshe, 1996. 32–35.

Liu Yong. "Wenhua lüyou yu chuantong yinyue de chuancheng" [Cultural tourism and the transmission of traditional music]. *Zhongguo yinyue* [Chinese music] 97 (2005): 109–10.

Liu Zhao, Li Shuji, and Liu Shu. "Yi minjian yinyue cujin Shanxi lüyouye fazhan de shexiang" [Thoughts on promoting the development of the tourism industry in Shanxi through folk music]. *Renmin yinyue* [People's music] 468 (2005): 30–31.

Lomax, Alan. "Appeal for Cultural Equity." *World of Music* 14, no. 2 (1972): 3–17.

———. *Folk Song Style and Culture.* Publication No. 88. Washington, D.C.: American Association for the Advancement of Science, 1968.

Lopez, Donald S., Jr. "New Age Orientalism: The Case of Tibet." *Tricycle: The Buddhist Review* 3, no. 3 (1994): 37–43.

———. *Prisoners of Shangri-La: Tibetan Buddhism and the West.* Chicago: University of Chicago Press, 1998.

Lü Ji. "Lüelun qixianqin yinyue yichan" [Brief discussion of the legacy of qin music]. In *Qinqu jicheng* [Compendium of qin compositions], edited by Zhongyang yinyue xueyuan Zhongguo yinyue yanjiusuo [Chinese Music Research Institute, Central Conservatory of Music] and Beijing guqin yanjiuhui [Beijing Society of Qin Research]. Beijing: Zhonghua shuju, 1962. 1–18.

Lui, Tsun-yuan. "A Short Guide to Ch'in." *Selected Reports of the UCLA Institute of Ethnomusicology* 1, no. 2 (1968): 179–204.

Lumbreras, Luis Guillermo. "El papel del Estado en el campo de la cultura." In *Políticas culturales: Ensayos críticos,* edited by Guillermo Cortés and Víctor Vich. Lima: Instituto de Estudios Peruanos, 2006. 71–111.

Lundberg, Dan, Krister Malm, and Owe Ronström. *Music—Media—Multiculture: Changing Musicscapes.* Stockholm: Svenskt visarkiv, 2003.

Luo Haolin. "Guqin yinyue CD changpian mulu huibian" [A list of CD recordings of qin music]. In *Jinyu qinkan xu: Jinian Jinyu qinshe chengli liushinian* [Jinyu qin journal, supplement: In memory of the 60th anniversary of the establishment of Jinyu Qin Society]. Shanghai: Jinyu qinshe, 1996. 120–21.

Lynch, Frank S. J. *Four Readings on Philippine Values.* Quezon City: Institute of Philippine Culture, Ateneo de Manila, 1968.

Mackerras, Colin. "Folksongs and Dances of China's Minority Nationalities: Policy, Tradition, and Professionalization." *Modern China* 10, no. 2 (1984): 187–226.

Malm, Krister. "Music in the Field of Tension between Human Rights and Cultural Rights." In *Music and Minorities: Proceedings of the 1st International Meeting of the International Council for Traditional Music (ICTM) Study Group on Music and Minorities.* Ljubljana: ICTM, 2001. 31–36.

Malvinni, David. *The Gypsy Caravan: From Real Roma to Imaginary Gypsies in Western Music and Film.* New York: Routledge, 2004.

Malyk, L. P., M. I. Pitiulych, O. S. Peredrij, and B. A. Shynkar. *Tsyhany Zakarpattia: Problemy, Shliakhy Vyrishennia* [Gypsies of Transcarpathia: Problems, Ways to Solutions]. Uzhhorod: Carpathian Division of the International Institute of Management, Uzhhorod National University, 1991.

Mao Tse-tung [Mao Zedong]. *Talks at the Yenan Forum on Literature and Art.* 1942. Reprint, Peking: Foreign Languages Press, 1967.

Mao Zedong. "A Talk to Music Workers (August 24, 1956)." *Beijing Review* 22, no. 37 (1979 [1956]): 9–15.

Masterpieces of the Oral and Intangible Heritage of Humanity: Proclamations 2001, 2003 and 2005. Paris: Intangible Heritage Section, Division of Cultural Heritage, UNESCO, 2006.

McCann, Anthony. "All That Is Not Given Is Lost: Irish Traditional Music, Copyright, and Common Property." *Ethnomusicology* 45, no. 1 (2001): 89–106.

McDougall, Bonnie S. *Mao Zedong's "Talks at the Yan'an Conference on Literature and Art": A Translation of the 1943 Text with Commentary.* Michigan Monographs in Chinese Studies No. 39. Ann Arbor: Center for Chinese Studies, University of Michigan, 1980.

———. *Popular Chinese Literature and Performing Arts in the People's Republic of China, 1949–1979*. Berkeley: University of California Press, 1984.

Merali, Isfahan, and Valerie Oosterveld, eds. *Giving Meaning to Economic, Social, and Cultural Rights.* Philadelphia: University of Pennsylvania Press, 2001.

Messer, Ellen. "Anthropology and Human Rights." *Annual Review of Anthropology* 22 (1993): 221–49.

Miao Jianhua. "Guqin meixuezhong de ru dao fuo sixiang" [The Confucian, Daoist, and Buddhist philosophies in the aesthetics of qin]. *Yinyue yanjiu* [Music research] 105 (2002): 7–13.

Miao Tianrui, Ji Liankang, and Guo Nai'an, eds. *Zhongguo yinyue cidian* [Dictionary of Chinese music]. Beijing: Renmin yinyue chubanshe, 1985.

Mills, Sherylle. "Indigenous Music and the Law: An Analysis of National and International Legislation." *Yearbook for Traditional Music* 28 (1996): 57–86.

[Mirano, Elena R.]. *Subli: One Dance in Four Voices.* Manila: Cultural Center of the Philippines, 1989.

Mookini, Esther K. *The Hawaiian Newspapers.* Honolulu: Topgallant, 1974.

Mooney, Paul. "Digital Music Project Race to Save Tibetan Folk Songs." *National Geographic News,* June 29, 2007. http://news.nationalgeographic.com/news/2007/06/070629-tibet-music.html (accessed March 13, 2008).

Moore, Charles. *Daniel H. Burnham Architect: Planner of Cities.* Boston: Houghton Mifflin, 1921.

Mould-Iddrisu, Betty. "Preservation and Conservation of Expressions of Folklore: The Experience of Africa." In *UNESCO-WIPO World Forum on the Protection of Folklore—Phuket, Thailand, April 8 to 10, 1997.* Geneva: WIPO, 1998.

Muhambetova, Asiya Ibadullaevna. "The Traditional Musical Culture of Kazakhs in the Social Context of the Twentieth Century." *World of Music* 37, no. 3 (1995): 66–83.

Naves, Santuza Cambraia, Frederico Oliveira Coelho, and Tatiana Bacal. *A MPB em discussão: Entrevistas.* Belo Horizonte: Editora UFMG, 2006.

Neat, Patrick, and Damian Platt. *Culture Is Our Weapon: AfroReggae in the Favelas of Rio.* London: Latin America Bureau, 2006.

Nettl, Bruno. *The Study of Ethnomusicology: Twenty-nine Issues and Concepts.* Urbana: University of Illinois Press, 1983.

Nketia, J. H. Kwabena. *The Music of Africa.* New York: W. W. Norton, 1974.

———. "Tradition and Innovation in African Music." *Jamaica Journal* 11, no. 3 (1989): 3–9.

———. “Universal Perspectives in Ethnomusicology.” *World of Music* 26, no. 2 (1984): 3–21.

Norbu, Jamyang. “Dances with Yaks: Tibet in Film, Fiction and Fantasy of the West.” *Tibetan Review*, January 1998, 18–23.

Ochoa, Ana María. *Entre los deseos y los derechos, Un ensayo crítico sobre políticas culturales.* Bogotá: Instituto Colombiano de Antropología e Historia, 2003.

———. “Introducción: la materialidad de lo musical y su relación con la violencia.” *TRANS, Revista Transcultural de Música* [Transcultural Music Review] 10 (2006). http://www.sibetrans.com/trans/trans10/ochoa.htm (accessed June 20, 2008).

Oles, Brian P. “Dangerous Data from Mokil Atoll.” In *Handle with Care: Ownership and Control of Ethnographic Materials,* edited by Sjoerd R. Jaarsma. Pittsburgh: University of Pittsburgh Press, 2002. 174–94.

Olson, Laura. *Performing Russia: Folk Revival and Russian Identity.* London: Routledge-Curzon, 2004.

Oman, Ralph. “Folkloric Treasures: The Next Copyright Frontier?” *Intellectual Property Law Newsletter* (publication of the American Bar Association Section of Intellectual Property Law) 15, no. 4 (1996): 3–4.

Osorio, Jonathan K. “‘What Kine Hawaiian Are You?’ A *Moʻolelo* about Nationhood, Race, History, and the Contemporary Sovereignty Movement in Hawaiʻi.” *Contemporary Pacific* 13, no. 2 (Fall 2001): 359–79.

Park, Yun-Joo, and Patricia Richards. “Negotiating Neoliberal Multiculturalism: Mapuche Workers in the Chilean State.” *Social Forces* 85, no. 3 (2007): 1319–39.

Peng Shanshan. “Renlei caifu, huaxia guibao—shou jie ‘Zhongguo fei wuzhi wenhua yichan baohu chengguo zhan’ ji zhuanchang biaoyan guanhou” [One of the riches of humanity, and a treasure of China—the first “Exhibition of the results of protecting China’s intangible cultural heritage” and special performances]. *Renmin yinyue* [People’s music] 483 (2006): 55–58.

Pettan, Svanibor. *Roma muszikusok koszovóban: Kölcsönhatás és kreativitás/Rom Musicians in Kosovo: Interaction and Creativity.* Budapest: Magyar Tudományos Akadémia Zenetudományi Intézet, 2002.

Pian, Rulan Chao. *Sonq Dynasty Musical Sources and Their Interpretation.* Cambridge, Mass.: Harvard University Press, 1967.

Polu, Lance. “Cultural Rights and the Individual in the Samoan Context.” In *Culture, Rights, and Cultural Rights: Perspectives from the South Pacific,* edited by Margaret Wilson and Paul Hunt. Wellington, New Zealand: Huia, 2000. 57–68.

Porter, James. “Documentary Recordings in Ethnomusicology: Theoretical and Methodological Problems.” *Association for Recorded Sound Collections Journal* 6, no. 2 (1974): 3–16.

Povinelli, Elizabeth. *The Cunning of Recognition: Indigenous Alterities and the Making of Australian Multiculturalism.* Durham, N.C.: Duke University Press, 2002.

Pretorius, Willem. “TRIPS and Developing Countries: How Level Is the Playing Field?” In *Global Intellectual Property Rights: Knowledge, Access and Development,* edited by Peter Drahos and Ruth Mayne. New York: Palgrove Macmillan, 2002.

Price, Richard. *On the Mall: Presenting Maroon Tradition-Bearers at the 1992 FAF.* Bloomington: Folklore Institute, Indiana University, 1994.

Prott, Lyndel V. "Some Consideration on the Protection of the Intangible Heritage: Claims and Remedies." In *Safeguarding Traditional Cultures: A Global Assessment,* edited by Peter Seitel. Washington, D.C.: Center for Folklife and Cultural Heritage, Smithsonian Institution, 2001. 104–8.

Qiao Jianzhong. "Ecology and Transmission of Chinese Folk Songs Today—Concurrent Discussion on the Oral Version and Written Version of Folk Music." In *Preservation of Traditional Music: Report of the Asia-Europe Training Programme,* edited by Xiao Mei, Zhang Gang, and Delfin Colomé. Beijing: Chinese Academy of Arts/Asia-Europe Foundation, 2003. 33–36.

———. "Hanzu chuantong yinyue yanjiu sishi nian" [Forty years of research on traditional music of the Han]. In *Tudi yu ge—chuantong yinyue wenhua ji qi dili lishi beijing yanjiu* [Land and song: research on traditional music and its geographical and historical background]. Ji'nan: Shandong wenyi chubanshe, 1998. 322–48.

———. "Xiandai qinxue lungang" [Outline of contemporary qin research]. *Tianjin yinyue xueyuan xuebao* [Journal of the Tianjin Conservatory of Music] 2 (2000): 4–9. Reprinted in Qiao Jianzhong, *Yongtan bainian: Qiao Jianzhong yinyuexue yanjiu wenji* [Collected articles in musicology by Qiao Jianzhong]. Ji'nan: Shandong wenyi chubanshe, 2002. 202–13.

———. "'Yuan shengtai min'ge' suoyi" [Incidental views on "original ecology folksongs"]. *Renmin yinyue* [People's music] 477 (2006): 26–27.

Qin Xu. "Qinyue shiyige buduan biange fazhan de duoyuan kaifang xitong" [The qin tradition is an open system that is ever changing and developing]. *Zhongguo yinyuexue* [Chinese musicology] 72 (2003): 5–20.

Qu Sanqiang. *Copyright in China.* Beijing: Foreign Languages Press, 2002.

Quiroz, Teresa. "Políticas e industrias culturales en las políticas públicas." In *Políticas culturales: Ensayos críticos,* edited by Guillermo Cortés and Víctor Vich. Lima: Instituto de Estudios Peruanos, 2006. 113–35.

Ramos, Silvia. "Jovens de favelas na produção cultural brasileira dos anos 90." In *Por que não? Rupturas e continuidades da contracultura,* edited by Maria Isabel Mendes de Almeida and Santuza Cambraia Neves. Rio de Janeiro: 7 Letras, 2007. 239–56.

———. *Youth and the Police.* Boletim Segurança e Cidadania. Rio de Janeiro: CESeC, 2006. http://www.ucamcesec.com.br/arquivos/publicacoes/boletim12web_eng.pdf (accessed January 20, 2008).

Ramos, Silvia, and Leonarda Musumeci. *Elemento suspeito: abordagem policial e discriminação na cidade do Rio de Janeiro.* Rio de Janeiro: Civilização Brasileira, 2005.

Rees, Helen. "The Age of Consent: Traditional Music, Intellectual Property and Changing Attitudes in the People's Republic of China." *British Journal of Ethnomusicology* 12, no. 1 (2003): 137–71.

———. "'Authenticity' and the Foreign Audience for Traditional Music in Southwest China." *Journal of Musicological Research* 17, no. 2 (1998): 135–61.

———. *Echoes of History: Naxi Music in Modern China.* New York: Oxford University Press, 2000.

———. "'Naxi Ancient Music Rocks London': Validation, Presentation, and Observation in the First International Naxi Music Tour." *Ethnomusicology* 46, no. 3 (2002): 432–55.

Rice, Timothy. *May It Fill Your Soul: Experiencing Bulgarian Music.* Chicago: University of Chicago Press, 1994.

Ricoeur, Paul. *Memory, History, Forgetting.* Translated by Kathleen Blamey and David Pellauer. Chicago: University of Chicago Press, 2004.

Rivkin-Fish, Michele. *Women's Health in Post-Soviet Russia: The Politics of Intervention.* Bloomington: Indiana University Press, 2005.

Roberts, Helen H. *Ancient Hawaiian Music.* Honolulu: Bishop Museum, 1926.

Romero, Raúl R. "Black Music and Identity in Peru: Reconstruction and Revival of Afro-Peruvian Musical Traditions." In *Music and Black Ethnicity in the Caribbean and Latin America,* edited by Gerard H. Béhague. Miami: University of Miami North-South Center, 1994.

———. *Debating the Past: Music, Memory and Identity in the Andes.* New York: Oxford University Press, 2001.

Salazar, Milagros. Liner notes to *Cajón peruano: A golpe de tierra,* CD by María del Carmen Dongo y Manomadera. Lima: Play Music & Video, 2006.

Santa Cruz Castillo, Rafael. *El cajón afro peruano.* 2nd ed. Lima: RSANTACRUZ Ediciones, 2006.

Schell, Orville. *Virtual Tibet: Searching for Shangri-La from the Himalayas to Hollywood.* New York: Henry Holt, 2001.

Schiaffini, Patricia. "Book Review: *Tales of Tibet: Sky Burials, Prayer Wheels, and Wind Horses.*" *Persimmon: Asian Literature, Arts, and Culture* 4, no. 2 (2003). http://www.persimmon-mag.com/summer2003/Bookreview10.htm (accessed January 3, 2005).

Schimmelpenninck, Antoinet. *Chinese Folk Songs and Folk Singers: Shan'ge Traditions in Southern Jiangsu.* Leiden, Netherlands: CHIME Foundation, 1997.

Scott, David. *Conscripts of Modernity: The Tragedy of Colonial Enlightenment.* Durham, N.C.: Duke University Press, 2004.

Scottish Museums Council. "Cultural Rights and Entitlements in the Scottish Museums Context." 2004: 7–13. http://www.scottishmuseums.org.uk/pdfs/Cultural_Rights_and_Entitlements.pdf (accessed September 1, 2004).

Scruggs, T. M. "Cultural Capital, Appropriate Transformations, and Transfer by Appropriation in Western Nicaragua: 'El baile de marimba.'" *Latin American Music Review* 19, no. 1 (1998): 1–30.

Seeger, Anthony. "Ethnomusicologists, Archives, Professional Organizations, and the Shifting Ethics of Intellectual Property." *Yearbook for Traditional Music* 28 (1996): 87–105.

———. "The Role of Sound Archives in Ethnomusicology Today." *Ethnomusicology* 30, no. 2 (1986): 261–76.

———. *Why Suyá Sing: A Musical Anthropology of an Amazonian People.* Cambridge: Cambridge University Press, 1987.

Seeger, Charles. "Contrapuntal Style in the Three-Voice Shape-Note Hymns." *Musical Quarterly* 26, no. 4 (1940): 483–93.

———. "Music and Musicology in the New World 1946." In *Studies in Musicology 1935–1975,* by Charles Seeger. Berkeley: University of California Press, 1977. 211–22. Originally published as "Music and Musicology in the New World." *Proceedings of the Music Teachers National Association,* ser. 40 (1946): 35–47.

———. "Who Owns Folklore?—A Rejoinder." *Western Folklore* 21, no. 2 (1962): 93–101.

Shakya, Tsering. "Foreword: Language, Literature, and Representation in Tibet." In *Tales of Tibet: Sky Burials, Prayer Wheels, and Wind Horses,* edited and translated by Herbert J. Batt. Lanham, Md.: Rowman and Littlefield, 2001. xi–xxiii.

Shapiro, Ian, and Will Kymlicka, eds. *Ethnicity and Group Rights.* New York: Kluwer Law International, 2001.

Shay, Anthony. *Choreographic Politics: State Folk Dance Companies, Representation, and Power.* Middletown, Conn.: Wesleyan University Press, 2002.

Sheehy, Daniel. "A Few Notions about Philosophy and Strategy in Applied Ethnomusicology." *Ethnomusicology* 36, no. 3 (1992): 323–36.

Shelemay, Kay Kaufman. *Let Jasmine Rain Down: Song and Remembrance among Syrian Jews.* Chicago: University of Chicago Press, 1998.

Shen Qia. "Ethnomusicology in China." Translated by Jonathan P. J. Stock. *Journal of Music in China* 1 (1999): 7–38.

Soares, Luiz Eduardo. *Meu casaco de general: quinhentos dias no front da segurança pública do Rio de Janeiro.* São Paulo: Companhia das Letras, 2000.

Soares, Luiz Eduardo, MV Bill, and Celso Athayde. *Cabeça de Porco.* Rio de Janeiro: Objetiva, 2005.

Solís, Ted. *Performing Ethnomusicology: Teaching and Representation in World Music Ensembles.* Berkeley: University of California Press, 2004.

Sperling, Valerie. *Organizing Women in Contemporary Russia: Engendering Transition.* Cambridge: Cambridge University Press, 1999.

Spivak, Gayathri. "Can the Subaltern Speak? Speculations on Widow Sacrifice." *Wedge* 7/8 (Winter/Spring 1985): 120–30.

Stavenhagen, Rodolfo. "Cultural Rights and Universal Human Rights." In *Economic, Social and Cultural Rights: A Textbook,* edited by Asbjørn Eide, Catarina Krause, and Alaan Rosas. Dordrecht: Martinus Nijhoff, 1995. 63–77.

Stillman, Amy Ku'uleialoha. "Of the People Who Love the Land: Vernacular History in the Poetry of Modern Hawaiian Hula." *Amerasia* 28, no. 3 (2002): 85–108.

———. "Resurrecting Archival Poetic Repertoire for Hawaiian Hula." In *Handle with Care: Ownership and Control of Ethnographic Materials,* edited by Sjoerd R. Jaarsma. Pittsburgh: University of Pittsburgh Press, 2002. 130–47.

Stock, Jonathan P. J. *Huju: Traditional Opera in Modern Shanghai.* Oxford: Oxford University Press, 2003.

———. *Musical Creativity in Twentieth-Century China: Abing, His Music, and Its Changing Meanings.* Rochester, N.Y.: University of Rochester Press, 1996.

Sturmer, John Von. "Aboriginal Singing and Notions of Power." In *Songs of Aboriginal Australia,* edited by M. Clunies Ross, T. Donaldson, and S. Wild. Sydney: University of Sydney, 1987. 63–76.

Thornbury, Barbara E. *The Folk Performing Arts: Traditional Culture in Contemporary Japan.* Albany: State University of New York Press, 1997.

Thurner, Mark. *From Two Republics to One Divided: Contradictions of Postcolonial Nationmaking in Andean Peru.* Durham, N.C.: Duke University Press, 1997.

Tian Liantao. "Ping 'Wusuli chuan'ge' yu Hezhezu min'ge de zhuzuoquan susong" [Assessing "Wusuli Boat Song" and the copyright lawsuit over folksongs of the Hezhe ethnic group]. *Renmin yinyue* [People's music] 443 (2003): 15–20.

———. "Suben qiuyuan 'Xiaohe tang shui'—jian ping gequ 'Xiaohe tang shui' de zuopin shuxing yu zhuzuoquan guishu" [Tracing the source of "The Babbling Brook"—evaluating the attribution and copyright ownership of the song "The Babbling Brook"]. *Renmin yinyue* [People's music] 463 (2004): 28–33.

———. "Yong falü gainian shenshi Wang Luobin xibu min'ge de zhuzuoquan" [Using legal concepts to examine the copyright in Wang Luobin's western folksongs]. *Renmin yinyue* [People's music] 354 (1995): 18–19.

Tibet Information Network (TIN). *Unity and Discord: Music and Politics in Contemporary Tibet.* London: Tibet Information Network, 2004.

[Tolentino] Aquino, Francisca Reyes. *Philippine Folk Dances,* vol. 2. Manila: Francisca Reyes Aquino, 1953.

Tolentino [Aquino], Francisca Reyes. *Philippine National Dances.* New York: Silver Burdett, 1946.

Tompkins, William David. "The Musical Traditions of the Blacks of Coastal Peru." Ph.D. diss., University of California, Los Angeles, 1981.

Trimillos, Ricardo D. "More Than Art: The Politics of Performance." In *Looking Out,* edited by David Gere. New York: Schirmer, 1994. 23–39.

———. "Vocal Music among the Tausug of Sulu, Philippines." In *Traditional Drama and Music of Southeast Asia,* edited by Mohd. Taib Osman. Kuala Lumpur: Kementerian Pelajaran Malaysia, 1974. 274–89.

Tsitsishvili, Nino. "Social and Political Constructions of Nation-Making in Relation to the Musical Styles and Discourses of Georgian Duduki Ensembles." *Journal of Musicological Research* 26, nos. 2–3 (2007): 241–80.

Tsui Yingfai. "Ensembles: The Modern Chinese Orchestra." In *Garland Encyclopedia of World Music,* vol. 7, edited by Robert C. Provine, Yosihiko Tokumaru, and J. Lawrence Witzleben. New York: Routledge, 2002. 227–32.

Upton, Janet. "The Poetics and Politics of *Sister Drum:* 'Tibetan' Music in the Global Marketplace." In *Global Goes Local: Popular Culture in Asia,* edited by Timothy J. Craig and Richard King. Honolulu: Association for Asian Studies and University of Hawai'i Press, 2002. 99–119.

Vaidhyanathan, Siva. *Copyrights and Copywrongs: The Rise of Intellectual Property and How It Threatens Creativity.* New York: New York University Press, 2001.

Venturelli, Shalini. "Cultural Rights and World Trade Agreements in the Information Society." *International Communication Gazette* 60 (1998): 47–76.

Venturino, Steven J. "Where Is Tibet in World Literature?" *World Literature Today* 78 (2004): 51–56.

Vich, Víctor. "Gestionar riesgos: Agencia y maniobra en la política cultural." In *Políticas culturales: Ensayos críticos,* edited by Guillermo Cortés and Víctor Vich. Lima: Instituto de Estudios Peruanos, 2006. 45–70.

Waiselfisz, Julio Jacobo. *Mapa da Violência.* Brasília: Rede de Informação Tecnológica Latino Americana, 2008.

Wang Yuhe. "New Music of China: Its Development under the Blending of Chinese and Western Cultures through the First Half of the Twentieth Century (Part 2)." Translated by Liu Hongzhu. *Journal of Music in China* 3, no. 2 (2002): 187–228.

Watt, James. "The Qin and the Chinese Literati." *Orientation* 12 (1981): 38–49.

Weintraub, Andrew. *Power Plays: Wayang Golek Puppet Theater of West Java.* Athens: Ohio University, Center for International Studies, 2004.

Wenhuabu wenxue yishu yanjiuyuan yinyue yanjiusuo, ed. *Minzu yinyue gailun* [Overview of Chinese music]. Beijing: Renmin yinyue chubanshe, 1980.

Whisnant, David. *All That Is Native and Fine.* Chapel Hill, N.C.: University of North Carolina Press, 1983.

WIPO. *Introduction to IP Theory and Practice.* Geneva: WIPO, 1997.

Witzleben, J. Lawrence. "*Jiangnan Sizhu* Music Clubs in Shanghai: Context, Concept and Identity." *Ethnomusicology* 31, no. 2 (1987): 240–60.

Wong, Chuen-Fung. "Peripheral Sentiments: Encountering Uyghur Music in Urumchi." Ph.D. diss., University of California, Los Angeles, 2006.

Wong, Isabel K. F. "*Geming Gequ:* Songs for the Education of the Masses." In *Popular Chinese Literature and Performing Arts in the People's Republic of China 1949–1979,* edited by Bonnie S. McDougall. Berkeley: University of California Press, 1984. 112–43.

Wong, Victor. "Deep in the Jungle; Taiwan Aboriginal Singers Settle Copyright Lawsuit." *Billboard Magazine,* July 31, 1999, p. 14. Also appears at http://www.deepforestmusic.com/dfpress_99-31-07difanglawsuit.htm (accessed September 12, 2005).

Wu Xueyuan, "'Naxi guyue' shi shenme dongxi?" [What is "Naxi Archaic Music"?]. *Yishu pinglun* [Arts criticism] 1 (2003): 21–26.

Wu Zhao. "Chuantong yu xiandai: Zhongguo guqin yishu mianlin de tiaozhan" [Tradition and modernity: the challenges to the art of guqin]. *Renmin yinyue* [People's music] 470 (2005): 22–24.

Xiamili Xiake'er [Xamil Xakir]. "Guanyu Wang Luobin yu xibu min'ge de lai xin" [Letter concerning Wang Luobin and western folksongs]. *Renmin yinyue* [People's music] 352 (1995): 19–22.

Xiao Mei. "Foreword." In *Preservation of Traditional Music: Report of the Asia-Europe Training Programme,* edited by Xiao Mei, Zhang Gang, and Delfin Colomé. Beijing: Chinese Academy of Arts/Asia-Europe Foundation, 2003. 13–15.

Xizang zizhiqu dangwei xuanchuanbu wenyichu and Xizang zizhiqu yinyuejia xiehui [The Art and Literature Office of the Propaganda Department of the Tibet Autonomous Region's Party Committee and the Musicians' Association of the Tibet Autonomous Region], eds. *Chang gei taiyang de ge* [Songs sung for the sun]. Lhasa: Xizang renmin chubanshe, 2003.

Xu Facang. "Yunnan minzu minjian wenhua baohu de lifa yu shijian yanjiu" [Research on the legislation and practice of preservation of ethnic folk culture in Yunnan]. *Minzu yishu yanjiu* [Studies in national art] 84 (2001): 19–23.

Xu Jian. *Qinshi chubian* [First study of qin history]. Beijing: Renmin yinyue chubanshe, 1982.

Yang Jongsung. "Folklore and Cultural Politics in Korea: Intangible Cultural Properties and Living National Treasures." Ph.D. diss., Indiana University, 1994.

Yang Mu. "Academic Ignorance or Political Taboo? Some Issues in China's Study of Its Folksong Culture." *Ethnomusicology* 38, no. 2 (1994): 303–20.

Yang Yinliu. *Zhongguo gudai yinyue shigao* [Draft history of ancient Chinese music]. 2 vols. Beijing: Renmin yinyue chubanshe, 1981.

Yaremenko, O. O., and O. H. Levtsun. *Osoblyvosti Sposobu Zhyttia ta Problem Sotsialnoii Intehratsiii Romiv v Ukraiini: Analitychnyi Zvit za Rezultatamy Sotsiolohichnoho Doslidzhennia* [Lifestyle Characteristics and Problems of Romani Social Integration in Ukraine: An Analytical Report Based on the Results of Sociological Surveys]. Kyiv:

Ukrainian Institute of Sociological Studies, International Renaissance Foundation, 2003.

Yúdice, George. *The Expediency of Culture: Uses of Culture in the Global Era.* Durham, N.C.: Duke University Press, 2003.

Yung, Bell. "Choreographic and Kinesthetic Elements in Performance on the Chinese Seven-String Zither." *Ethnomusicology* 28, no. 3 (1984): 505–17.

———. "Music of Qin: From the Scholar's Study to the Concert Stage." *ACMR Reports* (Journal of the Association for Chinese Music Research) 11 (1998): 1–14. Originally published as "La musique du guqin: du cabinet du lettré à la scéne de concert." In *Cahiers de musiques tranditionnelles 2: Instrumental* (1989): 31–62.

Yunnan nianjian 2002 [Yunnan yearbook for 2002]. Kunming: Yunnan nianjian zazhishe, 2002.

Yunnan yishu xueyuan yinyue xueyuan. "Yunnan yishu xueyuan yinyue xueyuan tuixing 'minzu yinyue bentuhua jiaoyu' de tese ji youshi" [The Music College of Yunnan Art Institute implements the special characteristics and preference for "nativized education in ethnic music"]. *Yunling gesheng* [Voice of the cloud mountains] 186 (2005): 28–30.

Zemp, Hugo. "The/An Ethnomusicologist and the Recording Business." *Yearbook for Traditional Music* 28 (1996): 36–56.

Zhang Guangrui. "China's Tourist Development since 1978: Policies, Experiences, and Lessons Learned." In *Tourism in China: Geographical, Political, and Economic Perspectives,* edited by Alan A. Lew and Lawrence Yu. Boulder, Colo.: Westview Press, 1995. 3–18.

Zheng Peikai, ed. *Kouchuan xinshou yu wenhua chuancheng* [Oral transmission and cultural continuity]. Guilin: Guangxi Normal University Press, 2006.

Zheng, Su de San. "From Toisan to New York: Muk'yu Songs in Folk Tradition." *Chinoperl Papers* 16 (1992–93): 165–205.

Zhong Wenxin. "Chuancheng yu kaituo" [To inherit and to develop]. *Mingpao Monthly* (Dec. 2006): 119–20.

Zhongguo min'ge [Chinese folksongs], edited by Yinyue yanjiusuo [Music research institute], vol. 2. Shanghai: Shanghai wenyi chubanshe, 1982.

Zhongguo shaoshu minzu yishu yichan baohu ji dangdai yishu fazhan gouji xueshu yantaohui [Preservation of the arts heritage of Chinese ethnic groups and development of the contemporary arts]. Beijing: Zhongguo yishu yanjiuyuan, 2003.

Zhongguo yishu yanjiuyuan yinyue yanjiu ziliao shi, ed. *Zhongguo yishu yanjiuyuan yinyue yanjiusuo suo cang Zhongguo yinyue yinxiang mulu (luyin cidai bufen)* [Catalog of Chinese music recordings (recorded tape portion) housed in the Music Research Institute of the Chinese Academy of Arts]. Ji'nan: Shandong youyi chubanshe, 1994.

Contributors

NIMROD BARANOVITCH is a lecturer in the Department of Asian Studies at the University of Haifa, Israel. His publications include *China's New Voices: Popular Music, Ethnicity, Gender, and Politics, 1978–1997;* contributions to the edited volumes *Lives in Chinese Music* and *Understanding Charles Seeger, Pioneer in American Musicology;* and articles in *China Quarterly, Modern China,* and *China Journal.*

ADRIANA HELBIG is an assistant professor of music at the University of Pittsburgh, where she teaches courses in ethnomusicology and popular music and directs a Carpathian music ensemble. Her research addresses the relationship between music and politics, post-socialist cultural policy in particular, and post-socialist music industries in Ukraine and Russia. She has coauthored *Culture and Customs of Ukraine* and has published articles in edited volumes, *Current Musicology* and *Anthropology of East Europe Review.* Her most recent project, funded by American Councils for International Education, IREX, and the National Endowment for the Humanities, focuses on the relationship between hip hop, African migration, and racialized class identities in Ukraine.

JAVIER F. LEÓN is an assistant professor of ethnomusicology in the Department of Folklore and Ethnomusicology at Indiana University. His research has focused on nationalism and Peruvian criollo popular music and Afroperuvian music and modernity. His work has been published in *Latin American Music Review, Selected Reports in Ethnomusicology, Ethnomusicology Forum,* and *Black Music Research Journal.* He is currently working on a book on the impact of neoliberalism, cultural policy, and multiculturalism in contemporary Afroperuvian music-making.

ANA MARÍA OCHOA is an associate professor in the music department at Columbia University. Her topics of research include the relationship between music and violence, the politics of musical globalization in Latin America, the emergence of digital technologies and informal musical economies, and the history of listening in Colombia. Her published books include *Músicas Locales en Tiempos de Globalización* and *Entre los Deseos y los Derechos, Un Ensayo Crítico sobre Políticas Culturales.*

SILVIA RAMOS is a social scientist and coordinates the area for minorities, social movements, and citizenship at the Candido Mendes University Center for Studies on Public Security and Citizenship in Rio de Janeiro, Brazil. She has developed studies and research projects on youth, violence, and police as well as on media and violence. Since 2004, she has coordinated the Youth and the Police project in partnership with young men and women from the AfroReggae Cultural Group. Ramos has coauthored *Elemento Suspeito: Abordagem policial e discriminação na cidade do Rio de Janeiro* (with Leonarda Musumeci) and *Media and Violence* (with Anabela Paiva).

HELEN REES is a professor of ethnomusicology at the University of California, Los Angeles. She is the author of *Echoes of History: Naxi Music in Modern China* and editor of *Lives in Chinese Music.* She has also collaborated with Chinese musicians and scholars on numerous CD and video projects and has interpreted and presented for Chinese musicians at venues including the Amsterdam China Festival (2005) and the Smithsonian Folklife Festival (2007).

FELICIA SANDLER, composer and theorist, is on the faculty at the New England Conservatory. Her recent commissions include *Pulling Radishes* for the NEC percussion ensemble directed by Frank Epstein, which will be included on a forthcoming CD featuring works composed for the ensemble; *Hysteria in Salem Village* for the Big East Conference Band Director's Association; *Frozen Shadow–Quiet Light* for saxophone and percussion, commissioned by Eliot Gattegno; and *The Waking,* for SATB split chorus, for the Dale Warland Singers. As a scholar, Sandler continues to explore the use of musics from indigenous societies by Western composers. Her writings include a number of papers given at numerous regional, national, and international conferences. Her research has included a month-long stay in Geneva at the World Intellectual Property Organization; participation in the United Nations Office for the High Commissioner of Human Rights redrafting session of *Principles and Guidelines for the Protection of the Heritage of Indigenous People;* and a research trip to Ghana, West Africa. Sandler has received awards from Meet the Composer, the Presser Foundation, the Jerome Foundation, and the American Composers Orchestra, among others.

AMY KU'ULEIALOHA STILLMAN is an associate professor of American culture and music at the University of Michigan. An authority on Polynesian music and dance traditions (Hawai'ian and Tahitian in particular), Stillman is the author of *Sacred Hula: The Historical Hula 'Āla'apapa* and more than twenty articles appearing in such publications as *Ethnomusicology, Hawaiian Journal of History, Journal of American Folklore,* and *Music Library Association Notes.* She is also coproducer of two CDs, *Kalākaua* and *Kapi'olani,* with Kūlia i ka Pūnāwai (Kumu Hula Association of Southern California) and Grammy Award–winning Daniel Ho Creations.

RICARDO D. TRIMILLOS is the chair of Asian studies and a professor of ethnomusicology at the University of Hawai'i. His research and teaching specializes in music related to folk Catholicism in the Philippines, the arts, gender, and public policy. Trimillos has published articles in numerous books and journals; his most recent contribution appears in *Performing Ethnomusicology: Teaching and Representation in World Music Ensembles.*

ANDREW N. WEINTRAUB, an ethnomusicologist specializing in the music of Indonesia, particularly Sundanese music, dance, and theater of West Java, is an associate professor of music at the University of Pittsburgh, where he teaches graduate and undergraduate courses in ethnomusicology and popular music and directs the University of Pittsburgh gamelan program. He is the author of *Power Plays: Wayang Golek Puppet Theater of West Java,* and his articles have appeared in edited books and journals, including *Ethnomusicology, Asian Music, Asian Theatre Journal, Perfect Beat,* and *Popular Music.* Publications include a complete English translation and text transcription of an all-night Sundanese puppet theater performance and articles on music of ethnic communities in Hawai'i.

BELL YUNG is professor of music and former director of the Asian Studies Center at the University of Pittsburgh. He has also taught at the University of Hong Kong, the Chinese University of Hong Kong, the University of California at Davis, and Cornell University. A recipient of numerous fellowships and grants, including Ford, Guggenheim, Mellon, Fulbright, and the National Endowment for the Humanities, his most recent publication is *The Last of China's Literati: The Music, Poetry, and Life of Tsar Teh-yun.*

Index

Page numbers in italics refer to illustrations.

The University of Illinois Press
is a founding member of the
Association of American University Presses.

Composed in 10.5/13 Adobe Minion Pro
by Jim Proefrock
at the University of Illinois Press
Manufactured by Sheridan Books, Inc.

University of Illinois Press
1325 South Oak Street
Champaign, IL 61820-6903
www.press.uillinois.edu

CPSIA information can be obtained
at www.ICGtesting.com
Printed in the USA
BVHW032149170321
602869BV00008B/85